THE INSIDERS' ®
GUIDE
TO

Florida's
GREAT NORTHWEST

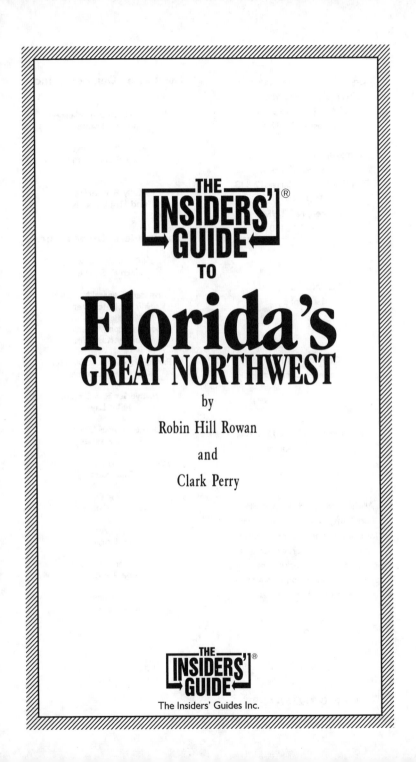

THE INSIDERS' GUIDE ®
TO
Florida's
GREAT NORTHWEST

by

Robin Hill Rowan

and

Clark Perry

THE INSIDERS' GUIDE ®

The Insiders' Guides Inc.

Co-published and marketed by:
Tallahassee Democrat, Inc.
227 N. Magnolia Drive
Tallahassee, FL 32302

Co-published and distributed by:
The Insiders' Guides Inc.
The Waterfront • Suites 12 &13
P.O. 2057
Manteo, NC 27954
(919) 473-6100

•

SECOND EDITION
1st printing

•

Copyright ©1995
by *Tallahassee Democrat, Inc.*

•

Printed in the United States
of America

•

Tallahassee Democrat, Inc.

Sales and Marketing Manager
Thomas Tomasi

Account Executive
Sally Richardson

Artists
Kelly Broderick
and Lisa Lazarus

The Insiders' Guides® Inc.

Publisher/Editor-in-Chief
Beth P. Storie

President/General Manager
Michael McOwen

Vice President/Advertising
Murray Kasmenn

Partnership Services Director
Giles Bissonnette

Creative Services Director
Mike Lay

Online Services Director
David Haynes

Sales and Marketing Director
Julie Ross

Managing Editor
Theresa Chavez

Project Artist
Mel Dorsey

Fulfillment Director
Gina Twiford

Controller
Claudette Forney

ISBN 0-912367-70-9

Preface

Pull up a chair, and let us tell you a little about this place, in our estimation, one of the most beautiful in America. Biased? Perhaps. Even though we weren't born and raised here, we've lived here long enough to feel like we're "dug in," giving us a unique perspective on the area as we've moved from being "outsiders" to "Insiders."

We remember fondly when our friends from "up north" would call and say, "We're coming to Florida to visit Disney World next month; any chance you can meet us halfway for lunch?" Sure, we'll just hop the next *plane*. If you look at a map of the United States, Northwest Florida is closer to New Orleans, Atlanta, Memphis and Nashville than it is to Miami. From Pensacola, Key West and Chicago are about equidistant.

Yet, the farther north you travel in Florida, the more Southern it gets. You hear more Southern accents here. See more grits served as a side dish in place of hash browns or baked potatoes. But it's not *all* slow drawls and porch-settin'. An influx of military families and "transplants" from other places gives a cosmopolitan feel to most larger resort areas. It's a good blend of past and present, the old ways and the new ways, tradition and progress.

Here, too, is so much more of Florida the way it "used" to be — verdant, expansive woodlands of slash pine, live oak and magnolia; preserved coastal wetlands that make better homes for herons and alligators than for people.

But above everything else, surpassing Southern charm, down-home cooking and even a rich and colorful past, there's the main attraction that visitors can't quite seem to get enough of: endless expanses of snow-white beaches and dunes framing glittering gulf waters in hues of emerald and aquamarine. More miles of beachfront are preserved here than any other place in Florida. And when you roll up your pants legs and wade into still-warm gulf water in mid-October, look behind you at white, rolling dunes and ahead at a school of playful dolphin . . . well, that, my friend, is why we stay.

How To Use This Guide

Florida's Great Northwest stretches from Pensacola to Tallahassee, and there's a lot of diversity between the two cities. In fact, you're likely to see a wider range of people and places along this stretch than you will anywhere else in the state.

We've tried to reflect this diversity in the book by geographically dividing the northwest into five large areas that include surrounding communities and points of interest. These are:

Pensacola area — Pensacola, Pensacola Beach, Gulf Breeze, Navarre Beach, Milton, Perdido Key;

Fort Walton Beach/Destin/Beaches of South Walton — Fort Walton Beach (Niceville, Valparaiso, Shalimar), Destin,

Beaches of South Walton (Sandestin, Seaside, Grayton Beach, Point Washington);

Panama City area — Panama City, Panama City Beach;

Florida's Forgotten Coast — Mexico Beach, Port St. Joe, Cape San Blas, St. Vincent Island, Apalachicola, Eastpoint, St. George Island and Carrabelle.

Tallahassee area — Tallahassee, Wakulla, St. Marks, plus inland areas of Chipley, Marianna and the Dead Lakes region.

We also include Daytrips chapters for Pensacola and Tallahassee. Mobile, Alabama, and Thomasville, Georgia, invite residents and visitors to sample these area's annual events, shopping districts and fine restaurants.

Our experience tells us that vacationers move freely throughout one area, but there isn't a great amount of crossover from one area to the next. Although it only takes around 3½ hours to drive from Pensacola to Tallahassee, there's such an incredible array of things to see and do in between that most visitors may find it simply too exhausting and demanding to explore all five areas at once.

You should note that street numbering is not used consistently except within city limits, so directions such as "along the beach road" or "near the intersection of . . ." may be more helpful than street addresses.

Keeping all this in mind, we must say that the best way to use this guide is just to read it. Then pick a place and go. No matter where it is, we've been there, too, and we can help you find the magic.

About the Authors

Robin Hill Rowan chose speaking over writing at first; she cut her career teeth as a disc jockey while majoring in speech at the University of Wisconsin. While "marking time" in between radio jobs, she landed a position with a Chicago-based incentives company, writing about places she'd never been. Rio de Janeiro, Cozumel, the Swiss Alps, South Africa — the pieces she produced were meant to inspire salespeople to win fabulous trips to exotic destinations.

But the urge to play DJ was still stronger than the one to write, and in 1982, Rowan headed to Pensacola, sight unseen, where she'd been hired as an all-night country DJ. Simultaneously, she voiced commercials for an ad agency's production studio and, before long, was both running the studio and writing commercials. Working two full-time jobs left little time for sleep, so Rowan dropped the radio life to go full-time at that agency, then another, and she finally took on a full-time writing career in 1988.

Rowan's credits include state vacation guides for Florida and Alabama and travel videos for numerous Southeastern markets. She continues to voice commercials and videos while writing advertising, public relations and travel pieces. Rowan makes her permanent home in Pensacola with her husband, Michael, and daughter Rachel, 5.

Clark Perry was born in the hills of Alabama but has called Florida his home for nearly a decade now. He has worked as a soda jerk, photographer, dishwasher and obituary clerk, all with varying degrees of success. He attended the University of North Alabama and Michigan State University and graduated from the University of Tampa in 1988 with a bachelor's degree in writing.

Since that time, he's worked mainly as a freelance writer, with work appearing in magazines and newspapers such as *Creative Loafing*, *Tampa Tribune*, *Science Fiction Age*, *The Silver Web* and *Starlog*. As a technical writer, he's also produced user manuals for several software companies.

His hobbies include technology and the arts, especially those areas where the two converge. Although he's basically a happy and upbeat fellow who enjoys sunshine and the beach, Clark has been known to acknowledge his dark side through his writing. His sometimes horrific short stories can be found in several anthologies, including *Young Blood* (Zebra, 1994), edited by Mike Baker, and *Ghosts* (Pocket, 1995), a Horror Writers Association anthology edited by Peter Straub.

He lives in Tallahassee with his wife, Donna Long, and their four cats.

Acknowledgments

Robin...

Special thanks to the following people who helped make this book possible:

Andy Witt, executive director, and The Arts Council of Northwest Florida, for permission to use listings from the *Northwest Florida Cultural Directory* — the information provided in the directory was accurate, complete and saved me a month of research!

The Pensacola Historical Society receives special accolades for providing me with a wealth of material and photographs for the book.

To the late Norm Simons for his brilliance and vast stores of knowledge about Pensacola — it was his inspiration that caused me to continue my research into Pensacola history long after my first projects were completed.

Jerry Eubanks, Superintendent of Gulf Islands National Seashore and his staff (and especially Mary Jones) for providing missing pieces of the puzzle throughout the Gulf Islands National Seashore chapter.

Karen Lee Tucker of the Florida Park Service for providing information and photos for Northwest Florida's scenic state parks; Geiger & Associates, Tallahassee, for sending zillions of photos and assisting with information on the Beaches of South Walton; John Daniels and Tom Muir of the Historic Pensacola Preservation Board for giving me access to information and exhibits for the Pensacola Colonial Archaeological Trail; the staff at the Emerald Coast Tourist Development Council for information, photos, and their opinions (and comments) about this book; and, most of all, to my husband Michael, fellow adventurer, writing critic ("That metaphor doesn't really work for me"), patient listener and steadfast supporter.

Clark...

My sincerest thanks go to the following for their invaluable assistance and advice in the preparation of this book: Coleen David, Director of Programs and Services for the Tallahassee Area Convention and Visitors Bureau; Helen E. Rouse of the Monticello Opera House; Eleanor B. Hawkins, Jefferson County Clerk of Circuit Court; Nan L. Baughman, executive vice-president of the Monticello-Jefferson County Chamber of Commerce; Phyllis C. McVoy, Education Specialist with the Knott House Museum; Kathy Anderson, Festival Director for Springtime Tallahassee; Shari Hubbard, Senior Account Supervisor with Geiger & Associates Public Relations; Trey Morgan, P.E., President of Sterling & Greene, Inc., of Havana; Clifton L. Maxwell of the Florida Department of Environmental Protection; the staff of the Destination Thomasville Tourism Authority; Catherine Cameron of the Wakulla County Chamber of Commerce; Sally Richardson of Pensacola;

Hollis Wade of the ARTemis Gallery in Apalachicola; Marilyn and Charles Schubert of the Coombs House Inn in Apalachicola; Cindy Clark of Bay Media Services in Apalachicola; Chuck and Virginia Spicer, publishers of the *Coast Line* in Apalachicola; Deborah Heath, manager of Melissa's in Thomasville, Georgia; the staff of the Panama City Beach Chamber of Commerce; Marcia Bush, Marketing Manager for the Bay County Tourist Development Council and the Panama City Beach Convention & Visitors Bureau; Candi Antonetti of the Tallahassee Area Convention & Visitors Bureau; Liisa Syvaniemi-Laami, media relations coordinator of the Panama Beach Convention & Visitors Bureau; Catherine Koran of St. Andrews State Recreation Area; the Tallahassee Historical Society, whose voluminous writings and accounts were invaluable during the preparation of this book; Dr. James W. Covington, professor emeritus of the University of Tampa, whose wonderful book *The Seminoles of Florida* and stimulating conversation shed much light on Tallahassee's turbulent, controversial and always fascinating history; the helpful gang at The Insiders' Guides, Inc.; and last but not least my wife Donna, whose love and encouragement proved to be the most valuable resource of them all.

Photo: Destin/Fort Walton Beach TDC

A pat on the head will win you a new friend at the Gulfarium, one of North Florida's first attractions.

Table of Contents

Photo: Apalachicola Bay Chamber of Commerce

*You'll find plenty of beachcombers along beautiful beaches of
Florida's Great Northwest*

Beach Areas
Getting Around

Getting here is almost as important as getting around, and we'd like to assist you in doing so without eating up days (and dollars) from your vacation. If you're coming in from more than 400 miles away, the quickest trip is by air, with the greatest number of flights coming into Pensacola. But, be warned that there's no such thing as a nonstop flight from that distance. You'll have to make connections in Atlanta, Charlotte, Memphis or Nashville. If time isn't a problem, the Amtrak is comfortable and ambles its way right through Northwest Florida. Buses seem to stop at every place that has a pay phone, and a 400-mile trip could seem like days. If you can wait until you get to Florida to rent a car, it's the best way to get around. Weekly rates are still some of the best in the country, and the rental agencies have gotten away from plastering their cars with rental bumper stickers that scream "Tourist!" from 100 paces away.

For a complete guide to getting around in the capital city see the Getting Around chapter in the Tallahassee section of this book.

By Car

Florida, geographically, is somewhat isolated from the rest of the United States, surrounded almost completely by water. Northwest Florida got the recognition it deserved from the state with the slogan "See Florida Coast to Coast to Coast,"

meaning the Atlantic Coast and the Western and Northern Gulf coasts.

There are only two ways in by car; from the west and from the north. Pensacola is the first city of any size from the west on Interstate 10. Northern entryways offer several options. Highway 29 from Flomaton, Alabama, will put you directly into Pensacola. Take Highway 331 from Florala, Alabama, through DeFuniak Springs, which eventually hooks up with the Beaches of South Walton. U.S. 231 from Alabama is the quickest route to the coast at Panama City Beach; and U.S. 319 from Thomasville, Georgia, is just a short hop from Tallahassee.

From I-10, the main east-west route ending in Jacksonville, you won't notice much difference in the scenery, but the landscape along the Alabama-to-Florida beaches on Fla. 292 changes dramatically. For some reason, the sand changes from light brown to brilliant white, and if it weren't for the 2 miles of Perdido Key that Florida gave away over a monetary dispute some years ago, you'd know immediately you were in Florida by that color alone.

Welcome Centers greet Florida visitors from three entry points: from the west on I-10 near Pensacola, from the north on U.S. 231 near Campbellton and inside the Capitol building in Tallahassee. This might be a good place to start your trip through Florida's Great Northwest (and have a complimentary glass of Florida orange or grapefruit juice).

The most direct route from Pensacola to Tallahassee is on I-10, but it's also one of the most boring drives in the state. Infinitely more scenic, but also much longer (but you're not in a hurry, are you?) is the beach route, which mostly follows U.S. 98 except on Perdido Key, Pensacola Beach and Navarre Beach.

If you're coming into Florida on I-65, there's no good way to get into Pensacola right now. You can get here from there, but you'll have to veer off the interstate way before you reach Florida, where it's small towns and mostly two-lane highways for the remainder of the trip. After you pass Evergreen, Alabama, on I-65, look for the Pensacola/Flomaton Exit (113). This two-lane country road dead ends after a few miles; turn right and follow the signs for U.S. 29 S. Make a quick left at the Hardee's and you'll be on the right road. Follow U.S. 29 into Century, Florida, then continue through several rural communities until you reach Pensacola (it's about an hour's drive from the turnoff at U.S. 29). A few miles into Pensacola, there's an I-10 interchange going east (to the beaches, the I-110 spur, the University of West Florida and Tallahassee), and west (to Naval Air Station Pensacola and Mobile). There's been much talk about connecting I-10 with I-65 via the I-110 spur, which would make everybody's life easier, but this is still years away. Sigh.

Now a few words about traffic: To say that drivers in Northwest Florida are a little ... casual ... about the rules of the road is an understatement. Only Boston drivers can relate. Since it goes on all year long we can't blame the tourists. Just be extra careful at stoplights and stop signs.

For some reason, drivers here refuse to pull into the intersection when turning left, causing cars behind them to wait through another light, and most are completely unfamiliar with turn indicators! Most locals will show a bit of added courtesy to cars with out-of-state license plates (we call them "tags" here).

There's a bit of the Old South left in us, too. In Pensacola and a few other scattered communities, all traffic stops to allow funeral processions to pass.

If you've had any experience with the Beltway near Washington, D.C., you will certainly scoff when we talk about traffic jams, but folks here aren't used to waiting long for *anything*. Serious backups can occur on the Three Mile Bay Bridge from Gulf Breeze into Pensacola from about 3 until 7 PM every day in the summer months. Accidents and stalled vehicles can make it an even longer wait. The stretch of U.S. 98 between Fort Walton Beach and Destin is slow going from about 3 until 6 PM all year long, although the new Mid-Bay Bridge over Choctawhatchee Bay has alleviated that somewhat. The gulf-front route through Panama City Beach is fun, with lots to see, but you'll creep through snail-like in all but the winter months. Back Beach Road is a better option.

By Air

PENSACOLA REGIONAL AIRPORT
Airport Blvd. at 12th Ave.   435-1745

Northwest Florida's largest airport is in Pensacola, with 45 daily departures spread over eight carriers, more than any of the other regional airports. Delta, USAir, USAir Express, Continental, American Eagle, ComAir and Atlantic Southeast (Delta's commuter carrier), serve Pensacola Regional. The new terminal, opened in 1990, now has several jetways, allowing passengers to board and deplane without walking outside, as was previously the case. From Pensacola, non-stop flights go to Atlanta, Charlotte, Dallas, Houston, Memphis, Mobile, Nashville, New Orleans, Orlando, Tallahassee and Tampa. If you need to go any farther than that, you'll have to change planes, most likely in Atlanta.

You may save yourself some headaches if you can make a connecting flight from either Charlotte or Memphis, which are much smaller airports than Atlanta and not as spread out, avoiding that last-minute dash through three terminal sections to make a flight.

Pensacola Regional Airport is located smack in the middle of town at Airport Boulevard and 12th Avenue near Cordova Mall and Pensacola Junior College.

Shuttle service is provided to the Pensacola Grand Hotel downtown and the Holiday Inn University Mall on the north end of town; call individual hotels to inquire about other shuttles to and from the airport. There are always several taxis lined up in front of the terminal waiting for fares; this may be the simplest way to get to your hotel in town. Taxi fares to the beach are steep; it may be in your best interest to find other travelers going that way and double up, or rent a car yourself. Right across from baggage claim are the following rental agencies.

Avis	433-5614, (800) 331-1212
Hertz	432-2345, (800) 654-3131
Dollar	474-9000, (800) 800-4000
National	432-8338, (800) 227-7368

OKALOOSA COUNTY AIR TERMINAL
Hwy. 85 between Niceville and
Fort Walton Beach   *651-7160*

Okaloosa is serviced by Atlantic Southeast (Delta connection), American Eagle, USAir Express and Northwest Air-

lines. National, Hertz, Budget and Avis rental car agencies are located right in the terminal. Budget's toll-free number is (800) 527-0700. For other toll free numbers, see our preceding entry.

PANAMA CITY-BAY COUNTY INTERNATIONAL AIRPORT
Lisenby Ave.   *763-6751*

Panama City is also equipped with a small airport, recently designated an international airport, with 27 daily incoming flights. Delta, ASA, Northwest Airlink, USAir Express and ComAir all service the airport. Cross the Hathaway Bridge as you come into town, go about 2 miles to Lisenby Avenue and turn left. Lisenby dead-ends at the airport. Car rental agencies in the airport terminal are Avis, 769-1411, Budget, 769-8733, and Hertz, 763-6673. Toll free numbers are listed under the Pensacola Regional Airport.

TALLAHASSEE REGIONAL AIRPORT
Capital Cir.   *891-7800*

The Tallahassee Regional Airport currently offers air service through four national and regional carriers: Atlantic Southeast, 282-3424; ComAir (800) 354-9822; Delta (800) 221-1212; and USAir (800) 428-4322. The airport is located just 6 miles south of the city on Capital Circle and also hosts several car rental agencies. Need a taxi or limo instead? Just check the listings for Avis, Budget, Dollar, Hertz and National under the Pensacola Regional Airport. Alamo's toll-free number is (800) 327-9633; call (800) 527-0700 for rental car rates from Budget.

Private Charters

Pensacola Aviation at Pensacola Regional Airport, 434-0636; **Bob Sikes Air-**

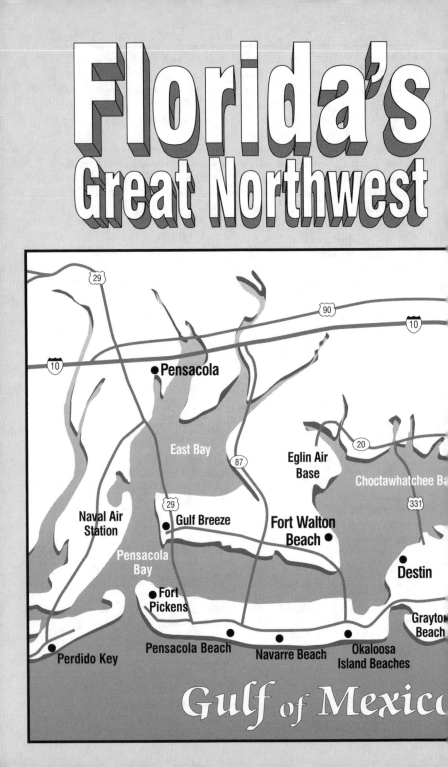

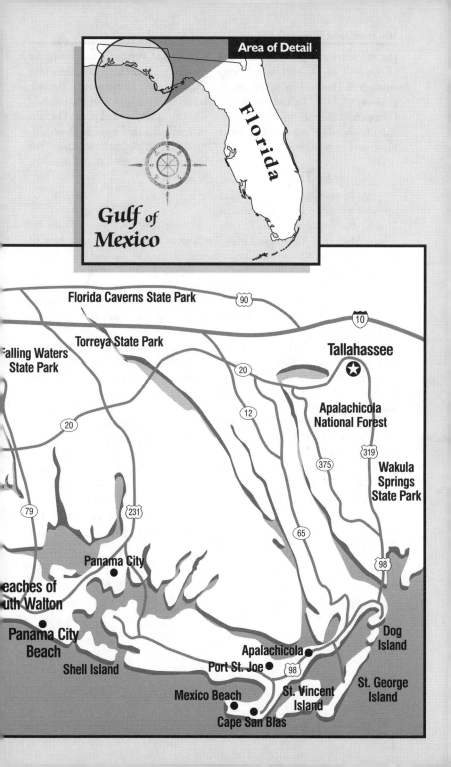

port in Crestview on John Gibbons Road off Airport Road, 682-6395; **Miracle Strip Aviation** in Destin, Airport Road off of Highway 98, 837-6135; and **Tallahassee Commercial Airport** on Highway 27, 562-1945, handle charter service, private planes and corporate jets.

By Train

After 20 years, Amtrak started back up passenger service through Northwest Florida, closing the last gap on a Los Angeles to Miami run. The Sunset Limited offers weekly service. If you never understood why people would pay almost as much as an airplane ticket to ride something almost as slow as a bus, you may just have to see for yourself. The seats are gigantic and terribly comfortable with plenty of leg room, you can get up and stretch at anytime, visit the dining car, the lounge/observation car and the smoking lounge, or just take a walk through the entire train, upstairs and downstairs.

The trip from Pensacola to Tallahassee on the *Sunset Limited* takes about an hour longer than driving it yourself (about 4½ hours), and remember, you'll lose an hour traveling east. Don't expect to see some of Florida's most beautiful scenery, however; this is the CSX railroad line, made for freight trains. The *Sunset Limited* passes through mostly rural sections of inland Florida where the major attractions are swamps, rivers and small-town communities. The prettiest section of the entire trip is in Pensacola: The train crosses over Bayou Texar, then winds its way around Pensacola Bay along the wooded red-dirt Bay Bluffs, then over Escambia Bay. Unfortunately, the ride occurs at about 5 or 6 in the morning when it's usually too dark to see. The *Sunset Limited* makes stops in Pensacola, Crestview, Chipley and Tallahassee. For information and reservations, call (800) 872-7245.

By Sea

Major waterways, especially the Intracoastal Waterway, stay fairly busy all year, packed with pleasure boats, barges, foreign cargo ships, shrimpers, trawlers, fishing charters and sailboats. Short jaunts, say from Pensacola to Destin, offer spectacular scenery and relative safety within the confines of the shipping channel. Just be sure you're comfortable with the navigation of your watercraft, weather conditions and regulations before shipping out.

By Bus

The **Escambia County Transit System**, 436-9383, runs a fleet of 27 buses to get you around the Pensacola area. Intercity service is provided by **Greyhound-Trailways**, 222-4240. You can arrange Greyhound-Trailways service at the following stations.

505 W. Burgess Rd. off Hwy. 29	
Pensacola	*476-4800*
Chestnut Ave. and Hwy. 98	
Fort Walton Beach	*243-1940*
917 Harrison Ave.	
Panama City	*785-7861*

Inside
General Beach Information

Miles and miles and miles of white-sand beaches and dunes . . . crystalline gulf waters . . . gentle breezes and a sun that shines 340 days a year. Kind of makes you want to jump into the gulf the minute you first lay eyes on it. And do so, by all means, but please take a few moments to read over this section first. Information contained here pertains mostly to Gulf of Mexico beaches, but some is pure common sense to use *wherever* you swim. We're not trying to scare you or dissuade you from enjoying our beautiful beaches. But it is absolutely essential that newcomers and vacationers know what to expect in unfamiliar waters. And this information really could save your life.

Tides: Two a day, low and high, about 12 hours apart. Check the local papers' front section back page; times should be listed. At low tide the current is going out to sea; high tide means the water is coming into shore. If you're out swimming, floating or snorkeling in the gulf, pay particular attention to tides. You could be carried far from shore in a matter of minutes.

Undertows: Sometimes a clue that an undertow's not far from shore is a bowl-shaped indentation in the shoreline (many people are more familiar with the term "riptide"). The surf may also appear flatter here. If you do get caught in an undertow, don't panic. Drownings oc-

Source: Robin Rowan

A sunset stroll along the shore is relaxing and scenic, but remember to stay alert for quickly changing water conditions, even at waterline.

cur when people try to swim against them, with unfortunate results. An undertow will only carry you about 30 yards out — *out* but not *under*. Your best bet is to swim parallel to the shoreline until you feel you are past the pull of the water. Can't swim? Just turn on your back, close your mouth and float.

Lifeguards: Many of the public beaches are protected by lifeguards for a good part of the day during peak months. If you're visiting the beach with small children, an extra pair of eyes and ears is always a good idea. In some areas, swim flags are posted in lieu of lifeguards, advising of current water conditions. Since the beaches are so vast, lifeguards and park rangers cannot hope to patrol the entire area. *Never* swim, surf, snorkel or dive by yourself. Period.

Keep an eye on the kids: Perhaps the best tip here is to only swim where and when lifeguards are on watch. If children get a little too adventuresome, they're called back into an area where a lifeguard can reach them quickly. Good places for young children are Quietwater Beach on Santa Rosa Sound (Pensacola Beach), Big Lagoon State Park near Perdido Key, Okaloosa Island at the Gulf Islands National Seashore (on Choctawhatchee Bay), and the kiddie pools at the jetties in St. Andrews State Recreation Area (Panama City Beach).

Marine life: Jellyfish make their annual appearance around July every year and stay for about a month. There are many, many different kinds, from flat bluish disks to the long-tentacled Portuguese man-of-war. Not all will sting, but moving to a less infested area of the beach or switching from the gulf to the sound side may save you from painful stings. If you do encounter a jellyfish sting, neutralize it with ammonia, then sprinkle on some Adolph's Meat Tenderizer (regular or seasoned) or make a paste of baking soda and water. If none of these remedies is immediately handy, put some beach sand on the sting until you can get first aid. Sometimes very hot water works well too. With all the aforesaid, only sprinkle the remedy on; don't rub it onto the skin. Rubbing will make the sting worse.

Other than jellyfish, there's not too much to be concerned about in the gulf. The abundant marine life is mostly harmless and much more terrified of you than you are of them. Still, a good rule to follow is: If you don't know what it is, don't pick it up!

What to leave at home: Glass containers and pets. Neither is permitted on the beaches at any time, and fines are imposed on offenders.

We don't want it either: When the signs say, "Take only pictures. Leave only footprints," they mean it. Please clean up after yourself; it would be nice if you would pick up an extra piece of litter on your way out.

Swimming and alcohol: A bad mix anytime but especially in the ever-changing conditions of the Gulf of Mexico. High summer temperatures and equally high humidity can dehydrate a sober person quickly; alcohol will intensify the effect. Jumping into the bathwater-warm gulf will not sober a person up, it will only make them tired.

Tanning tips (if you must): Florida sun is hotter and much more intense than just about any other place in the United States. Add to that reflection off the gulf and the white sand and you could be headed for trouble. Take note of these precautionary measures.

• Start out with small amounts of sun instead of one long stretch. Just an hour of sun during peak periods can burn you enough to ruin an entire week's vacation.

• Use sunscreen, no matter if you were "born to tan" or not. Lather up on hot spots — nose, lips, tops of the ears, shoulders, hair part and any place that hasn't seen the sun for awhile.

• Peak sun hours are 10 AM until 2 PM. Use at least a 15 SPF sunblock or stay out of the sun altogether during these hours.

• If you see any red or pink on your skin at all, it's time to get out of the sun. You're burned.

• Post-sun skin care: After a warm, soapy shower, apply an aloe-based lotion. If you do burn, take the heat off with a cloth soaked in vinegar. You'll smell like a salad, but you'll feel much better!

What to wear: Casual and comfortable is the rule of the day at all but the fanciest restaurants and resorts. Shirts and shoes are required in just about every establishment, although you can get away with only swimsuits and flip-flops in some beach bars. From May through October, shorts and short-sleeved shirts are the accepted mode of dress. You may want to pack a light jacket or sweater for occasional cold snaps or for restaurants that keep the temperature on deep freeze. The rest of the year, and especially for windy beach walks in January, you'll need warmer attire, with temperatures dipping sometimes into the 40s. We call it fireplace weather, and northern vacationers still think it a far cry from snow, sleet and gray skies.

Always wear shoes or sandals unless you're actually on the beach. Trying to cross the dunes in bare feet is a bad idea, since sand spurs will always find the most tender flesh to stick. The South is also blessed with the dreaded fire ants that build mounds in front yards, public parks and on beaches. They look harmless enough, but their bite is painful and leaves a nasty-looking blister. Shoes and socks won't prevent fire ants from attacking, but will offer better protection than bare feet.

Seasons: Unlike our neighbors to the south, Northwest Florida has four distinct seasons. Although snow is nearly unheard of, we get a flurry or two every few years. Our rainiest months are January and July, but don't let it change your vacation plans; showers along the Gulf Coast rarely last more than 20 minutes at a time. Camellias and Japanese magnolia make their showing in December and January, and most everything stays green all year, so although it might be cold, it doesn't really *seem* like winter.

Azaleas herald the spring's return, beginning as early as late February. The dogwoods' showy blossoms follow close behind, and even the humblest of homes appears grander when framed by mounds of bright flowers. The temperature cranks up in earnest by May, although flocks of spring breakers and surfers have been lining the beaches since March.

We won't try to gloss over summer: it's *hot, hot, hot*. On some days you'll feel like you were sealed in Tupperware. Take

Ever notice the squeaking sound the sand makes as you cross the dunes? We call it barking sand.

Insiders' Tips

The Experts Concur: Our Beaches Really Are The Best

Visitors are finally discovering what locals have known all along: Northwest Florida has some of the best beaches in the United States. Early in 1994, a Maryland researcher surveyed top geographers and coastal experts to compile a list of the top-20 beaches based on 50 environmental criteria. Not surprisingly, five of the top 12 were in Northwest Florida.

- St. Andrews State Recreation Area, Panama City Beach, No. 4
- St. Joseph Peninsula State Park, near Port St. Joe, No. 5
- St. George Island State Park, St. George Island, No. 9
- Perdido Key State Recreation Area, near Perdido Key, No. 12

And the **No. 1** beach in the United States? Grayton Beach State Recreation Area in South Walton County.

Photo: Division of Tourism

Grayton Beach, hailed as the No. 1 beach in the continental United States.

a 95 degree day, throw in a brief afternoon rainshower for added humidity, and you'll probably want to relax in your air-conditioned condo. There is, however, one saving grace if you're on the beach — an almost constant ocean breeze that can make the heat a little easier to take. June 1 through November 30 is also hurricane season, but not to worry; if a storm is headed our way (the last big hit was in 1926), you'll have at least 24 hours' warning, and hurricane evacuation routes are well marked.

Summer stays with us right through September, but by early October, we can look forward to highs *only* in the 80s — no frost on the pumpkin here. Fall is, weather-wise, the very best time of the year in Northwest Florida. Gulf waters are still quite warm, the huge crowds have thinned and fishing and arts festivals abound.

Time Zones: Northwest Florida covers two time zones: Central and Eastern. From its western entry point in Pensacola and for about two hours into Florida, you're on Central Time. The jump ahead to Eastern Time occurs around Marianna (just before Apalachicola on the beach road); there are highway markers notifying you of the exact moment to set your watch ahead an hour.

Area Codes: Every phone number in Northwest Florida is in the 904 area code. When calling from Pensacola to Fort Walton Beach or from Panama City to Tallahassee, you must first dial the area code before the number, even though you are in the same area code. The phone number, preceded only by a 1 (for toll calls) is no longer in operation.

Boating Safety

Whether chartering a boat for deep-sea fishing, tooling around the bay in a pontoon boat or feeling the wind in your face at the helm of your own sailboat, getting out on the water offers a delightfully different perspective on the area and its many surrounding waterways. Water in Northwest Florida is so popular, in fact, that a quick lesson in boating safety is essential for both captain and crew.

Leave a list of all members of your party with someone back on land, plus your intended destination, route and expected time of return. Even if you're renting a boat from a reputable concessionaire, take a few minutes to inspect safety equipment before leaving the dock. One Coast Guard-approved life vest is required for each person on board. Many marinas have special child-size vests for children less than 50 pounds. Make sure that children wear their safety vests at all times, as well as all those adults who can't swim. A life preserver ring is also a good backup.

For motor or sailboats less than 20 meters in length, a ship's bell or whistle, audible up to a quarter-mile, is required. If you plan to be out on the water between sundown and sunrise, your boat will also need navigation lights. The last piece of equipment is a good, strong anchor, capable of staying the boat in severe weather.

Pontoon boats probably require the least amount of nautical know-how, with motor boats and sailboats next. If you're a first-time captain, however, be sure to ask for a demonstration of boat operation and safety features. Since many accidents are caused by improper boat handling, take a few moments to review the following safety precautions.

• Do not attempt to outrun another boat. Sailboats are at the mercy of the wind and always have the right of way. It is sometimes impossible to tell how fast a distant boat is going, and you may not be able to get out of the way in time.

• Pick up a *Florida Boater's Guide* at any Marine Patrol Office. Knowing speed limits, identifying buoy markers and learning on-the-water courtesy will help prevent accidents!

• Stay in the shipping channel to avoid running aground. Water close to shore can change suddenly and dramatically.

• Never drink while operating any boat. The Coast Guard reports that 60 percent of all boating accidents involve alcohol or drugs.

• Keep passengers off of elevated surfaces, especially the bow or casting platforms. Sunbathers could easily roll off should you hit a wake or sudden high seas.

• And, finally, respect your fellow boaters and the environment. Please don't throw *anything* overboard! Save your trash to dispose of back on shore.

Now go out there and enjoy yourself, relax and stay safe!

Pensacola
History

Pensacola ought to be pretty good at hosting visitors by now. They've been doing it for more than 400 years, longer than almost anyone in America. This scenic area, with its wide, sugar-white beaches, abundant marine life and natural deep-water port, became a brass ring for countries vying for their stake in the New World. Seventeen times Pensacola would change flags, batted about like a volleyball among French, Spanish, British, Confederate and finally U.S. forces.

Although Native Americans had occupied Northwest Florida for more than 10,000 years, no written account exists of their lifestyle, only the numerous artifacts now on display in local museums. So it was the Spanish who "officially" laid claim to La Florida, or "Land of the Flowers." It was they, too, who gave names to the early tribes: Apalachee, Choctaw, Coosa, Chickasaw, Creek, Mobile, Pensacola (or Panzacola, meaning "long-haired people").

We Were First

Early in the 16th century, a few Spanish explorers sailed to Pensacola (which was called "Ochuse" until the 18th century) remarking on her beauty, natural harbor and their desire to establish a fortress here. But it wasn't until August 14, 1559, that Spaniard Don Tristan de Luna made landfall along the red bluffs of Pensacola (the exact spot is widely disputed) with an entourage of 1,400 colo-

Photo: Pensacola Historical Society

Mining Northwest Florida's "yellow gold." Between 1870 and 1930, virtually all large stands of yellow pine were clear cut.

nists, among them women, children, blacks and Indians. Their mission: to beat out the French in establishing the first crown-sponsored settlement in the land explored earlier by Hernando de Soto, to build a defensible fortress and to bring Christianity to the Indians.

Not much was accomplished in the first days after the landing; the new settlers enjoyed some leisure time, swimming and fishing and racing boats. But before any building was begun in earnest, a massive hurricane ripped through Pensacola, sinking or destroying seven of the 13 ships, many with cargo and livestock still aboard. The expedition was a disaster, leaving the colonists shipwrecked in a strange land.

For about 18 months the discouraged Spanish colonists wandered inland in search of food. Luna was finally fired, and in the spring of 1561, a new team sailed in with fresh supplies and an energetic crew of officers and Catholic friars. Since the colonists didn't care to plant and harvest the land, choosing instead to trade with Indian tribes and exploit existing resources, the settlement was doomed to fail. By summer of that year, the entire colony was abandoned. And so it is that St. Augustine, established six years later in 1565, holds the title of "America's oldest city." What they certainly have over Pensacola is permanence, since another attempt at settlement wasn't made in Pensacola for 139 years.

Today's Governing Country Is...

By the time another Spanish expedition set out to colonize Pensacola in 1698, the French had made some attempt to settle West Florida, which at that time included lands clear over to the Mississippi River. The two countries became uneasy neighbors, the Spanish in Pensacola, the French in Mobile. They did a bit of trading but mostly stayed out of each other's way.

The Spanish started with a fort settlement at the present-day Naval Air Station. By 1719, a second Spanish fort went up near present-day Fort Pickens on Santa Rosa Island. This crucial year saw Pensacola change flags four times in six months between French and Spanish forces. Finally, the French lost Pensacola to the Spanish in a 1722 treaty.

Spain lost no time in establishing yet another settlement on Santa Rosa Island, which ended 30 years later (1722-52) when nature's hand again intervened: A powerful hurricane sent them scurrying back to the mainland. In 1757, the King of Spain officially named the town Panzacola. England was next in line to claim the prize from Spain in the Treaty of Paris. During this British period, 1763-1783, Englishman Elias Durnford surveyed the city, drawing up a grid plan that is today's Seville Historic District. Homeowners each received a corresponding garden plot at the northern edge of town for planting flowers and vegetables (today's Garden Street).

Expansion of British West Florida brought more immigrants, many families, even a few educated people into the area, but it also brought problems with fresh drinking water, garbage and illness. But, those everyday annoyances seemed insignificant once Gen. Bernardo de Galvez marched into Pensacola with 4,000 soldiers in March of 1781. The siege of Pensacola lasted about 60 days, with the Spanish emerging victorious.

The new Spanish government saw to it that most vestiges of British rule were eliminated. Although the street grid re-

The First Tourist Attraction

A train arriving at the Louisville and Nashville depot on October 25, 1886, was causing quite a stir. A huge crowd had gathered downtown to catch a glimpse of the train's cargo: 17 Apache men, among them the famed medicine man Geronimo. The group was to be incarcerated at Fort Pickens for their crimes, skirmishes with the U.S. Army in the Southwest.

Even before the new prisoners had settled in, Geronimo gained instant celebrity stature. Boatloads of spectators sailed over from the mainland just to get a distant look at the fierce Apache; others came by rail from New Orleans. Once the wives and children joined their men at the fort, a condition of the Apache surrender, more of the curious followed.

For the next year and a half, Geronimo's presence at the fort was fodder for newspaper gossip columns. Geronimo began selling buttons off his shirt to willing takers for $1 apiece. When the boatload ferried back to the mainland for more passengers, he'd sew on a few more buttons in preparation for the next wave. He also learned to write his name at the fort, and made a tidy profit selling signed flat stones or shells.

Apache medicine man Geronimo, incarcerated at Fort Pickens for 18 months.

But without any warning, Geronimo, along with the other Apaches, were moved out under cover of darkness to Mobile, and then to Mount Vernon, Alabama. The people stopped coming.

mained intact, street names were one significant change; Prince, Granby, Charlotte and George streets became Romana, Intendencia, Alcaniz and Palafox.

Soon the War of 1812 fell upon the country, with Spain and Britain aligning themselves against the United States. After Andrew Jackson's victory over the Creeks in the Battle of Horseshoe Bend two years later, the United States controlled all land in present-day West Florida, save for Pensacola and St. Marks.

Let Me Do My Job and Let Me Leave...

Perhaps feeling the flush of newly found power, Jackson was outraged that the Spanish had allowed the British to use their forts and harbor to train the Creeks for battle, and he quickly moved in. He drove the British out, leaving the Spanish disgraced, then departed as quickly as he had come. However, Jackson's attacks had no authorization from President James Monroe, so to placate the Spanish, Pensacola was returned to them. But it no longer played the vital role of military stronghold it once had. A treaty signed by both Spain and the United States handed the remaining land over to the United States. The transfer was officially completed in a somber ceremony in Plaza Ferdinand on July 17, 1821. Andrew Jackson was sanctioned to accept the territory from Spain and become its first provisional governor.

Jackson performed his duties with remarkable precision and leadership. Within a week, he'd appointed a local governing body and organized Escambia County. But both he and his wife Rachel were less than happy during their stay in Pensacola. They disliked the heat, disliked the squalor and lack of morality of the residents and disliked the cabinet President Monroe had chosen to help govern. Rachel spoke of the filthy streets and the disorderly and unholy residents. By October of that same year, the Jacksons packed their belongings and headed off to Jackson's native Tennessee, never to return.

Pensacola Gets a Leg Up

Despite the Jacksons' feelings about the area, the city's groundwork had been well laid. Pensacola's future as a thriving city with strong military backing and a busy port was virtually assured. President John Quincy Adams authorized federal monies for development of a Navy yard in 1825. A location was chosen about 7 miles southwest of the city. Through local petitioners, Adams also became convinced that this city on the Gulf of Mexico was easily defensible, warranting a major military presence. Money poured in to begin construction of three military fortifications, completing a triangle guarding the entrance to Pensacola Bay.

Capt. William H. Chase of the U.S. Army Corps of Engineers was assigned to oversee the fort-building concern. A well-respected leader, the veteran military engineer and entrepreneur helped turn brickmaking into Pensacola's first industry. Forty million bricks were needed to construct Fort Pickens at the tip of Santa Rosa Island, Fort McRee on Foster's Island (now Perdido Key) and the expansion of Fort San Carlos de Barrancas.

The real problems with building the massive forts were not in brickmaking. Scarce free labor forced Chase to contract for supply slaves through local owners, in essence expanding slavery where there had previously been very little. Although built during the 1820s and 1830s, the forts saw negligible action until the Civil War.

> **Insiders' Tips**
>
> South of Main Street in downtown Pensacola are 60 acres of "made" land jutting out into Pensacola Bay, created from the ballast of steamboats and square-riggers from ports all over the world. The shoreline in this part of town is partially made up of red granite from Sweden, blue stone from Italy, broken tile from France and dredging material from the River Thames and the Scheldes of The Netherlands.

Photo: Pensacola Historical Society

*Giant red snapper like these earned Pensacola the title
"the red snapper capital of the world."*

Secession

In 1861, Florida was the third state to secede from the Union. And Pensacola, having a major strategic impact because of its supply base and shipyard, became a volatile place. Shots were fired at Fort Barrancas four months before the war-opening shots at Fort Sumter. The exchange took place when Federal guards at Fort Barrancas fired on Confederate soldiers on a reconnaissance mission.

Deciding that perhaps Fort Barrancas might be a weak link, Federal troops instead occupied Fort Pickens, leaving Barrancas and the Navy Yard to the Confederacy. After a lengthy standoff, where the Union refused to surrender to Confederate forces, a truce was reached; no additional Union forces would be sent to Fort Pickens if the Confederacy agreed not to attack.

This arrangement was short-lived, however, when Gen. Winfield Scott ordered reinforcements at Fort Pickens. The war droned on for soldiers on both sides, who might have preferred a gun battle to months of suffocating heat, mosquitoes and dysentery.

A "grand and sublime" artillery exchange shook Pensacola to its rafters on November 22, 1861. The three forts, plus two Union vessels in the bay, fired upon one another for the better part of two days. Only the thick smoke, darkness and a drenching rain silenced the guns, but even as dawn crept over the horizon, shelling began anew. The Union ships, the *Niagara* and the *Richmond*, both concentrated their fire on Fort McRee, reducing it to ruins in a matter of hours and sufficiently crippling its capacity to return fire.

Even though the fort was destroyed, most cannon fire missed its mark. Either the ships couldn't get close enough to their targets, Forts McRee and Barrancas, and kept running aground at low tide, or the cannon were not large or powerful enough to hurl the balls the 2 miles across the bay. Small numbers on both sides were killed and wounded. But no one bothered to count the greatest number of casualties — the thousands of mullet floating belly-up in the bay!

Weeds and Charred Remains

Prior to the North-South conflict, Pensacola was the largest city in Florida, with nearly 3,000 residents. By the time the Confederate troops moved out in May of 1862, most residents had already left. Weeds grew in the streets, buildings and homes were abandoned and Southern troops saw to it that what was left was of no use to the North; sawmills, brickyards and ships were torched. Most of the city lay in ruins. It wasn't until war's end that families, merchants and soldiers quietly moved back, looking for anything salvageable and beginning the painstaking process of rebuilding.

Surprisingly, free blacks fared better in Pensacola than in many other Southern cities, and for the most part were treated fairly in the county courts. Much of the attitude that prevailed may have been attributed to former U.S. Senator Stephen Mallory, a highly respected leader whose opinions about the treatment of former slaves were echoed by many. Several hundred blacks were employed at the Navy Yard, which had been left in ruins by fleeing Confederates.

So the citizens turned their attention away from the military and ahead to more profitable ventures — lumber and shipping. Harvesting the vast tracts of yellow pine had already proved lucrative in the decades before the war. There certainly seemed to be enough to go around, and the demand for it in Europe and South America was tremendous. Great ships were built to carry it off; wharves sprang up at the foot of Palafox, Commandancia and Tarragona streets. There was work for every able-bodied person aboard the ships, in the sawmills or among the pines. Money, Northern investors and new residents came streaming in. What had been a virtual ghost town at the close of the war was now a bustling city of 8,000. But again the population waned as the Yellow Fever epidemic of 1873-74 sent the unacclimated scurrying for northern climates, quarantined every boat coming into port and caused a general panic in the streets. More than 80 people succumbed to the disease; hundreds more were afflicted.

The Naples of America

Almost nothing, not war, disease nor dissension, could stop this city. Why, it was paradise on earth with its mild winters, bustling downtown and prosperous lumber and shipping trades. And there was no better person to promote the advantages of Pensacola than W.D. Chipley. The Civil War veteran turned railroad magnate sought to expand the Pensacola and Louisville Railroad line to Northern markets and the Atlantic Coast. He got his reward in 1881, when the Florida Legislature incorporated the Pensacola and Atlantic Railroad Company, handing over millions of acres of land. Chipley became the railroad's vice president and general manager.

To build up the passenger railroad business, Chipley published a booklet on the benefits of the area called *Pensacola: The Naples of America*:

". . . Pensacola offers more stir, variety, and reality of life than any city in Florida . . . The resident of a colder and less congenial clime will enjoy the most perfect transformation . . . Winter and summer its healthfulness is marvelous, except during epidemics. . . ."

Lumber was Pensacola's yellow gold. Lumber, shipping and railroad families amassed obscene wealth and loved to show it off. Architectural styles, mostly from Europe, were incorporated into homes owned by the "new rich." The North Hill Preservation District, a 60-block neighborhood north of downtown, sprang up around 1870 with giant estate homes touting their one-upmanship with their neighbors. With homes looking like Swiss chalets, English manor homes and antebellum mansions, North Hill remains one of the most eclectic mixtures of architectural styles in the country.

Most of the lumber passed through the Port of Pensacola. At times, ships from such exotic ports of call as Denmark, Norway, Italy and Australia were lined up three deep waiting to dump their ballast and take on timber.

It was during the last part of the century, too, when two Northern entrepreneurs realized that the possibilities for even greater wealth lay right at their feet

Photo: Pensacola Historical Society

An early Marine Corps avaitor takes off in a Curtiss AH-3 (1915).

in offshore waters. The Gulf of Mexico harbored a vast assortment of tasty delicacies, the most abundant and prized among them the red snapper. So many snapper could be caught at one time that ever larger ships were needed to carry them back to Pensacola. One-hundred-foot, 100-ton schooners sometimes spent weeks in the gulf, packing their catches in the tons of ice they'd brought along.

Two huge fishing fleets, belonging to the Warren Fish Company and E.E. Saunders and Company, prospered with little or no competition for nearly 80 years until overfishing made this commercial venture unprofitable. At its peak, between 1900 and 1920, 10 million pounds of snapper per year were caught and shipped fresh by rail to markets all over the United States.

Flying High

You might guess that it was rather a fine time to live in Pensacola. The city was a cultural gumbo of lifestyles, languages and religions, and because of it, people here seemed to have quite a tolerance for diversity.

Despite all the affluence, Pensacola was dealt a major blow when the U.S. Navy ordered the closing of the Navy Yard in 1911. In ruins since the Civil War, the Navy had never made any attempt to restore buildings or send troops to be stationed here. But just three years later, the surprised residents of Pensacola learned that their fair city was to become the new

home of the fledgling Naval Aeronautic Service.

Within a very short time, the aviation unit transferred from Annapolis and began training in Pensacola. The move was to have a significant impact on the city for decades, as Naval Air Station Pensacola became the largest flight training center in the country. Since its inception in 1914, Pensacola NAS and the city have worked hand-in-hand creating thousands of jobs, constructing housing for the influx of personnel and their families and bringing prosperity to many of its citizens.

End of the Trail

The Depression years hit Pensacola hard, but three major hurricanes in 1906, 1916 and 1926 did their best to wipe her out even before economics became a factor. By the late 1920s, nearly all of the usable pine had been clear cut, with very little reforestation left in its wake. Many families followed the last of the lumber out of town, presumably to start over somewhere else. The fishing industry hit rock bottom as well, causing more people to flee.

For the next few decades, Pensacola was a desolate place. There was virtually no industry; abandoned buildings were left to decay; families left the city for modern subdivisions in outlying areas.

But it wasn't all bad news for those who chose to wait out the hard times. A couple of bright spots in development

Sure It's A Neon Nightmare, But You Gotta Love It

It's tacky. It's kitschy. It's out of style and out of date. But the 40-foot-high neon monstrosity near the foot of the bridge crossing onto Pensacola Beach is a slice of Pensacola history and dear to the hearts of both visitors and locals.

Photo: Robin Rowan

Built by Lamar Advertising's neon shop in the 1950s, the sign was commissioned by the Santa Rosa Island Authority to direct downtown tourists to the beaches. The gigantic billfish originally towered over most downtown buildings atop Escambia Motors at Gregory and Palafox streets, now the Civic Inn parking lot.

Once the Bob Sikes Bridge opened up traffic to the beach from Gulf Breeze in 1960, the fish sign was relocated. Residents whose families vacationed here in the 1960s remember the sign as a beacon, welcoming them to the beach after a long trip in the car.

The neon billfish — a Pensacola landmark

"That sign breaks every code in the book," says Lamar representative Bobby Switzer. "You couldn't build a sign like that today."

And, after dark, as you make the wide swing to the right, ready to cross the beach bridge, there it is, like a beacon, its orange and yellow neon stripes lighting up "Turn Right — Pensacola Beach" in marquee fashion, the fish's skinny proboscis pointing the way. No . . . no, you really couldn't build a sign like that today . . .

gave locals and visitors easy access to tourist areas. The 1920s saw the construction of Gulf Beach Highway joining Pensacola and Perdido Key. In the decade that followed, a 3-mile-long bridge spanning Pensacola Bay brought the communities of Pensacola and Gulf Breeze together for the first time.

A New and Thriving Industry

The outbreak of World War II turned things around for Pensacola, at least temporarily. Pilots streamed into the Navy base for flight training. The demand for talented pilots was so great that the program was shortened from 14 to just seven months. Foreign trainees were welcomed to the air station as well, among them 3,000 British and a smaller entourage of French pilots.

The Navy newspaper, *The Gosport*, sent out the call for hundreds of civilian personnel to work as engineers, riggers, electricians and others. Many positions were filled by area women until after the war, the Navy even establishing ferry service to help them get to and from work.

Expansion plans were quickly initiated for auxiliary bases at Corry Station and Saufley Field. Realignment of the command created the Naval Air Training Center at Pensacola. With the vast amount of personnel either in training or employed as support workers, the bases enjoyed regular visits by entertainers and other notables including Jack Dempsey, Helen Keller, Mary Pickford, Tyrone Power and Bob Hope.

Being far from home during the war, many local blacks became increasingly irritated at continued segregation in the South. Blacks were allowed, however, to serve as jurors in Escambia County, and the local Tolerance Club pushed hard for full citizenship for its black residents, including the right to vote.

The Push for Pensacola

By the 1950s, so many "outsiders" from all over the world had visited Pensacola that word of her friendly residents and sparkling beaches became widespread. The time was ripe for promotional efforts to begin in earnest.

One of the city's first endeavors was to commission a sign pointing the way to the "World's Whitest Beaches." The neon fish sign has become an area landmark (see sidebar). Both locals and out-of-towners carved out their little piece of paradise on the beach. Very quickly, dozens of cinder block homes rose from the dunes to be used by families as summer cottages. The homes were built as cheaply as possible, since no hurricane or flood insurance existed. To have their home swept away in a storm would be no great loss to the owners.

Through the 1950s and '60s, the downtown area stagnated as subdivisions spread northward and malls sprang up to service them.

Local history buffs seemed undaunted by what was happening around them. They persuaded the Chamber of Commerce to put a challenge to Pensacola residents: It's history we've got, and it's history that will bring people here. Let's give them something to come for.

The movement to preserve the city's heritage, though, was a long and arduous process. Residents had yet to see any value in the dilapidated homes in the Seville area and would have just as soon seen them replaced.

One of the first hopeful signs of the preservation effort came in the 1960s, when The Pensacola Historical Society moved into Old Christ Church on Seville Square, transforming it into a history museum. Following that, the Pensacola Heritage Foundation sought to preserve the Seville District, the oldest section of Pensacola, with the help of local businesses and residents. The Historic Pensacola Preservation Board served as liaison between business and community groups for restoration efforts.

In 1972, the North Hill Preservation District got a listing in the National Register of Historic Places, spurring renovations of grand homes north of downtown. By 1980, a third area downtown, the Palafox Place Historic and Business District, was created for restoration of commercial establishments.

For the Enjoyment of Future Generations

Santa Rosa Island had become popular for beachgoers and campers, but haphazard development, heavy public use and a lack of cohesive efforts to preserve and maintain the pristine shoreline stepped up the push for the creation of the Gulf Islands National Seashore in 1972. In Northwest Florida the move successfully protected much of Santa Rosa Island, including Fort Pickens, portions of the Navy base on the mainland, the Naval Live Oaks Preserve in Gulf Breeze and Perdido Key to the west.

In the '90s, the downtown sector is again filled with activity. Visitors stroll Palafox Street, North Hill and the Seville District with self-guiding tour books in hand, marveling at the beautifully restored buildings and stories and legends of ghosts, pirates, soldiers and privateers. Picnics in Plaza Ferdinand featuring live entertainment bring downtown workers outside for lunch, and the public turns out for numerous festivals, theatrical performances, concerts and fishing tournaments in record numbers. The establishment of the Pensacola Colonial Archaeological Trail further enhances tourism by bringing our long-buried past back to life.

Those who've chosen Pensacola as their home push hard for change in the schools, government, and whatever they find that needs fixing, preserving the best of what we already have and making the community the best place it can be for all its citizens.

Photo: Robin Kowan

A colonial soldier awaits ceremonies opening the Pensacola Colonial Archaeological Trail in November 1994. The Trail showcases artifacts found at the site of a British fort and a Spanish shipwreck, both found in Pensacola.

Inside
The Pensacola Area

Pensacola, Pensacola Beach, Gulf Breeze, Navarre Beach, Perdido Key and Milton

The Pensacola metro area is easily the largest in Northwest Florida, covering 50 miles and two counties from east to west with something like 300,000 year-round residents. Beginning with Perdido Key at the state's western entrance and moving east, it includes Pensacola, Gulf Breeze, Pensacola Beach and Navarre Beach. Milton is a town about 15 miles north of Pensacola but is of interest because of its proximity to the area's many scenic rivers.

From white-sand beaches and dunes to bayfront mossy oaks and bustling downtowns brimming with history, this geographically diverse portion of Northwest Florida is grouped together around its anchor city, Pensacola. The city of 65,000 is a major transportation hub and is the largest Florida city for 200 miles.

. . . we say put your money in your pockets and come see us. . . . To the invalids, we offer our sea breezes and the gushing spring water, to the sportsman, a bay crowded with fish, and a forest crowded with game, to the pleasures of man our billiard rooms, to the athlete our nine pin alleys & to all, the safest blandest air that ever breathed upon the cheek of beauty.

— Pensacola newspaper promoting tourism, 1850s

The words may be written differently today, but the message is the same. We are fortunate enough to live in a place that gets better with time; a place where the beaches are so dazzling, the gulf waters so clear, the fish so abundant, the climate so mild and the people so friendly that we're spreading the word: We'd like to share it.

And share it we have. There is no definitive method for counting the number of tourists visiting the Pensacola area, but we do know that more than 3.5 million cars drove over the Bob Sikes Bridge onto Pensacola Beach in 1994. But we're not Ocean City or Coney Island. You needn't fight for a spot of sand on the beach. Even at the height of the season you can find a secluded spot along the miles of open shoreline.

Pensacola is a really big small town. For the most part, locals are friendly and accommodating and are fiercely proud of the few who have achieved celebrity status. Middleweight boxing champion Roy Jones Jr. and Dallas Cowboys running back Emmit Smith are both nationally known but still find time to do some community service work or just hang out with friends and family in Pensacola.

But all the scenic beauty and neighborliness aside, Pensacola seems to have more than its share of — well, weirdness. Like a

Visitor Information

**PENSACOLA CONVENTION &
VISITOR INFORMATION CENTER**
*1401 E. Gregory St.434-1234, (800) 874-1234
Pensacola in Florida (800) 343-4321*

PENSACOLA BEACH CHAMBER OF COMMERCE/VISITORS INFORMATION CENTER
*735 Pensacola Beach Blvd.
Pensacola Beach   932-1500, (800) 635-4803*

**SANTA ROSA COUNTY
TOURIST DEVELOPMENT COUNCIL**
*P.O. Box 5337
Navarre 32566 (800) 480-SAND*

**PERDIDO KEY AREA
CHAMBER OF COMMERCE**
*15500 Perdido Key Dr.
Perdido Key 492-4660*

**NAVARRE BEACH AREA
CHAMBER OF COMMERCE**
*8543 Navarre Pkwy.939-3267
Navarre Beach (800) 480-7263*

SOUTH SANTA ROSA WELCOME CENTER
*8543 Navarre Pkwy.
Navarre 939-2691*

**GULF BREEZE AREA
CHAMBER OF COMMERCE**
*1170 Gulf Breeze Pkwy.
Gulf Breeze 932-7888*

**PENSACOLA AREA
CHAMBER OF COMMERCE**
*117 W. Garden St.
Pensacola 438-4081*

**SANTA ROSA
COUNTY CHAMBER OF COMMERCE**
*501 Stewart St., S.W.
Milton 623-2339*

drive-up funeral parlor. A train that travels up the middle of a downtown street with traffic rolling along on either side. A 22-minute church service for people in a hurry. And enough sightings of strange shapes and beams of light in the night sky for 27 Arthur C. Clarke novels.

Over the past few decades, Pensacolians have come to realize that what they have here is unique. Battles of wits and words were waged at the local, state and national levels to protect huge tracts of our pristine shoreline from development and to save 18th- and 19th-century homes and commercial buildings from the wrecking ball. All the words and fund-drives and bonds and bake sales couldn't save the old San Carlos Hotel, however. The once glorious downtown landmark, which stood at the corner of Palafox and Garden streets since 1912, was laid to rest by a wrecking crew in 1993.

But there are plenty of success stories too, chief among them the emergence of urban and underwater archaeology. It's exciting to Pensacolians to think that they may be standing on the very spot where Andrew Jackson accepted West Florida from Spain in 1821 or where a British soldier slept in a cramped and uncomfortable wooden fortress more than 200 years ago.

What's good for tourism is usually good for business. The main downtown core, once blighted and nearly dead, is seeing new life in renovated warehouses and in stores vacant for decades. A group out of Washington state is buying up vacant waterfront property and proposing a downtown bayfront development. Water ferries may soon begin shuttling visitors to Fort Pickens and the Naval Air Station from downtown. And out on Pensacola Beach, major construction will reroute traffic and put up boardwalks, new landscaping and an outdoor amphitheater. This year, two hotels have opened in place of a failed condo complex and a water slide park. It's amazing to think that only a dozen or so years ago, attracting tourists to "L.A.," or "Lower Alabama," as we were called, was about the last thing on anybody's mind.

Pensacola is a little offbeat, sometimes tacky, often surprisingly sophisticated. It's the combination of those things that makes it such an extraordinary place to live.

Photo: Zwing Advertising

Enjoy fine dining all along the Gulf Coast.

Pensacola Area
Restaurants and Nightlife

Although there may be one or two exceptions, we're skipping the chains, since you can find those nearly anywhere. We prefer instead to concentrate on those dining establishments that are one-of-a-kind — the best of local cuisine. Unfortunately, a few of our favorites have passed into history — Strega Nona's went belly up in 1994, and the owner of The Bay Window Deli decided to pack it in after 12 years. Other landmarks, such as Hopkins House, Jerry's Drive-In and the Coffee Cup, continue in fine tradition decade after decade.

Our pricing code is set up to offer you a *general* idea of what a dinner for two will cost, including appetizer, entree, beverage and dessert. What's *not* included are cocktails, 7-percent sales tax (higher on the beach) and gratuity. As a general rule, dinner at an in-town restaurant will cost less than one on the beach with a view of the water.

One especially nice aspect of dining out in the Pensacola area is that there is literally no place requiring ties or even coats. It's a beach resort area, for heaven's sake, where the only dress code is — be comfortable! If anybody tells you differently, you tell them to come talk to us! Again, take your cues from the write-ups; while bikinis and bare feet may be acceptable at a beach bar, they're definitely taboo for most sit-down restaurants.

And speaking of comfort, here's a good tip: You don't have to wait into next week for a table just to get a good meal. Please use this chapter as your guide; if one restaurant is too crowded, there's another just as good or better just a short drive or walk away.

Most of the restaurants listed accept major credit cards; exceptions are noted.

Price codes for the Pensacola area are as follows:

Less than $20	$
$21 to $40	$$
$41 to $60	$$$
More than $60	$$$$

Perdido Key

THE OYSTER BAR
Under the Perdido Key Bridge   492-3162
$$$

An all-around wonderful place for lunch or dinner, The Oyster Bar does a good job of everything, from drinks to food to service. The view of the marina and the Intracoastal Waterway is nice anytime, but you may be lucky enough to have a flock of pelicans or dolphins grace your path during lunch; the procession of pleasure boats makes you feel like you're in some sort of magical place. And you are, right down to the sea-inspired artwork and the peach and green tablecloths and napkins. Seafood is tops on the menu, as you might expect, and comes broiled, chargrilled, Cajun blackened or fried. Families aren't left out — prices are reasonable, and the children's menu offers several big favorites. The open-air Oyster Bar downstairs (hours are seasonal) is more casual, serving oysters, sandwiches and cold libations. It's open for lunch and dinner every day; it's closed Monday.

FLORA-BAMA LOUNGE
At the Florida-
Alabama line   *492-0611, (334) 981-8555*
$

Another local flavor hangout, the Flora-Bama looks as bad on the outside as it does on the inside. But go in anyway, and you'll probably really enjoy yourself. This fairly famous honky-tonk is home of the annual Interstate Mullet Toss in April and one site of November's International Songwriters' Festival. Stop in any day of the week and there'll be some performer or band cranked up beginning about 5 PM (they start at 12:30 PM on the weekends). The regular musicians do their own brand of beach music with plenty of requests thrown in, and you can't help singing along. Occasionally some notable celeb stops in. Yep, Jimmy Buffett has graced the stage there as has Cajun blues singer and keyboardist Marcia Ball, who haunts the seedier clubs of New Orleans. One of the Oak Ridge Boys keeps a house on nearby Ono Island and may pop in for a beer and a tune. But the place will be jumpin' any time you care to go, and we recommend that you do.

Pensacola

HOPKINS HOUSE
900 N. Spring St.   *438-3979*
$

In the lovely old North Hill Preservation District, eating at Hopkins House is a local tradition. More than likely you'll have to wait out on the huge wrapped veranda for a table (they don't take reservations), but there are lots of porch swings and rockers to make the wait more pleasant.

Once inside, your party will be seated at a table with people you don't know,

The Yacht Restaurant offers fine dining on a 153-foot luxury yacht once owned by Carl Fisher.

but they won't remain strangers for long. Since 1949, Hopkins has been known for its family-style, pass-me-the-grits meals, which consist of black-eyed peas, squash, sweet potato pie, greens, corn bread muffins, roast beef and gravy and some of the best fried chicken you ever put a lip-lock on. It's also an undisputed Hopkins House rule that diners take their dishes to the kitchen when they're done!

Menus change daily, but the most popular nights are Tuesdays and Fridays, when that famous fried chicken is served. Beverage and dessert are included in the paltry $6.95 price tag. No alcohol is served. It's open for breakfast, lunch and dinner and closed Saturday and Sunday night and all day Monday. Hopkins takes cash and local checks only.

SKOPELOS ON THE BAY

670 Scenic Hwy.   432-6565
$$$$

Skopelos has been here for years, although a move from W. Cervantes Street to the current location on Pensacola Bay some years ago has doubled its space and its clientele. This is a favorite special-occasion place for lots of Insiders; the decor is a little eccentric with its mirrors and twinkling lights, the dining is first-class in every respect. Specializing in both steaks and seafood, Skopelos is also famous for nightly seafood specials and Greek-inspired dishes.

The restaurant is built atop the bluffs overlooking Pensacola Bay, and the view is every bit as nice as at the beach. After lunch or dinner, walk around the nicely landscaped grounds to the edge of the bluffs. As you might expect, the lawn is a perfect setting for outdoor weddings and receptions. Reservations are recommended. It's open for dinner Tuesday through Saturday and for lunch on Friday only.

NEW WORLD LANDING

600 S. Palafox St.   434-7736
$$$

New World Landing made a most successful transformation from 19th-century warehouse to elegant restaurant, inn and meeting hall. Oversized bay windows in the restaurant overlook a flowering courtyard with fountains and brick walkways; inside, peach and white linens and sparkling crystal grace the tables. Other dining and meeting areas reflect Pensacola's rich history through old photographs, enlarged to cover half the wall.

New World Restaurant serves gourmet continental cuisine, so your favorite steaks and seafood are there, but also dishes with some new twists. Chicken Escambia is a boneless breast of chicken stuffed with veal and basil then wrapped in a pastry and baked. Try your steak blackened with Cajun spices or a delicate filet mignon. Pensacola's favorite red snapper can be made your way, or for a meatier white fish, try grouper topped with crab, mushrooms, shrimp and artichoke hearts. It's open for lunch Tuesday through Friday with a daily buffet. Dinner is served Tuesday through Saturday.

SCOTTO'S RISTORANTE ITALIAN

300 S. Alcaniz St.   434-1932
$$

Scotto's is simply the finest Italian restaurant Pensacola has to offer. The atmosphere is quiet and intimate for a business lunch or a romantic evening out for two.

All your favorite Italian dishes are here, such as Chicken Parmesan, lasagna, antipasto and spaghetti. A sampling of appetizers will get you in the mood for spaghetti marinara, ravioli, fettuccine Alfredo and oysters Florentine. Scotto's makes all its own pasta; combine that with fresh seafood catches and you've got something really special. Stuffed snapper combines the delicate, slightly sweet taste of fresh red snapper with seasoned crabmeat dressing, then adds a side of pasta. Fettucine Scotto is sauteed crabmeat and shrimp in butter covered with a light cream and Parmesean cheese sauce over homemade fettucine. Try a bottle of wine with your meal in the historic surroundings of Seville Square. It's open for lunch Monday through Friday; dinner is served Monday through Saturday.

BODENHEIMER'S

304 S. Alcaniz St.   *434-5588*
$$

You'll find this charming spot right on Seville Square next to Scotto's in the heart of the historic district. This German-inspired restaurant takes you to another place and time with its dark polished wood, lace curtains and a wall of cubbyholes under the stairs displaying beers, wines, mugs and other German memorabilia.

The dining room is big enough for only about 10 tables; its centerpiece is a pre-20th-century double hearth fireplace, which is kept stoked up during the cooler winter months.

German mugs hang from long pegs overhead, and at Christmas are replaced with hand-dipped candlesticks. German background music does more for overall ambiance than for constant listening but helps to carry off the Old World feel. Your luncheon menu is posted on a sign and brought to your table, since it tends to change daily. Soups are robust and homemade; sandwiches such as sausage and sauerkraut or corned beef are ample. Do try the ginger vinaigrette salad dressing. Dinners range from sauerbraten and wiener schnitzel to fish and pasta specialties. For a tourist area, prices are pretty good — dinners start at $5 and run up to $13. Bodenheimer's is open Tuesday through Saturday for lunch and dinner and accepts cash and checks only.

COCONUTS COMEDY CLUB

7200 Plantation Rd.   *484-NUTS*

Pensacola's *only* comedy club features nationally touring comedians every Thursday, Friday and Saturday. Many of the performers have appeared on Showtime's *Comedy Club Network* and other national venues. Thursday shows are $4; shows on the weekends are $6, and reservations are recommended. Look for Coconuts Comedy Club adjacent to the Holiday Inn - University Mall.

UDORA'S

608 E. Wright St.   *469-1589*
$

For breakfast, a mid-morning or afternoon coffee break, or a late-night "after the theater" place, Udora's special blends, specialty coffees and fresh muffins and baked goods seem to make the day a little brighter. The coffeeshop is in one of the older homes in the West East

Insiders' Tips

Watching the sun sink into the bay at Chris' Seafood Grille is a favorite local activity; it's the best seat in the house for the nightly show.

Kathryn's
RESTAURANT

Utmost in Elegant Dining
Specializing in Seafood and Southern Cooking

Jazz Entertainment Thursday, Friday and Saturday
Open for Lunch & Dinner

Corner of 9th & LaRua Street • Pensacola, Florida
438-4525

Hill neighborhood, right behind the Pensacola Grand Hotel and just a block from the Pensacola Civic Center. Local artwork and sculptures hang on the walls and decorate the fireplace mantles to provide lots to look at if you come in alone. You could also take a table out on the wrapped porch, although it tends to be a bit noisy when a train goes by! Poetry readings are held here every Thursday night. Udora's could be just what Pensacola has been missing!

JAMIE'S FRENCH RESTAURANT
424 E. Zaragoza St.   *434-2911*
$$$$

Jamie's may be the only restaurant in Pensacola serving authentically prepared French cuisine. The intimate restaurant is in one of the renovated Seville Historic District homes. Inside, the decor is tasteful: muted peaches, burgundies and ivories mesh with dark wood antiques and fireplaces in each of the dining rooms.

Seafood selections change daily; the preparation and presentation remain the restaurant's hallmark. Breast of chicken, chargrilled filets, veal medallions, pork tenderloin, French-cut lamb chops and

Norwegian salmon dishes are expertly prepared with different sauces by chefs Mike Liebeno and owner Gary Serafin. Wines are recommended with each dish. It's open for lunch Tuesday through Saturday and for dinner Monday through Saturday.

SEVILLE QUARTER
130 E. Government St.   *434-6211*
$$

This dining and entertainment complex was one of the first to open in the wake of the downtown restoration movement. Bob Snow, who also owns Church Street Station in Orlando, has long since sold the place, but its reputation is so well established that it's still one of *the best* places to go for dancing and mingling in Pensacola. The **Palace Oyster Bar** has a full menu of appetizers, dinners such as fresh seafood, barbecued shrimp, fried oysters, Chicken Parmesan and New York strip steak in a turn-of-the-century setting. A Good Eats menu is available in other parts of the complex as well, which is mainly sandwiches, burgers and appetizers. Of course, *all* the lounges and restaurants serve every drink imaginable.

Enjoy the foot-stompin' show at **Rosie O'Grady's** featuring a Dixieland band, acoustic music at the **End O' the Alley** outdoor courtyard, jazz in **Apple Annie's**, or high-energy dance music in **Phineas Phoggs**. A $2 cover is charged after 8 PM. Membership cards are available. It's open for lunch, dinner and late-night dining and dancing.

TRADER JON'S

511 S. Palafox St.   433-7113
$

The world-famous bar has been a favorite of naval aviators since World War II. Order up a bottled beer and take a tour of the inside — you've never seen so much Navy memorabilia that wasn't in a museum. Photographs of Trader Jon with Blue Angels pilots, astronauts and other rich and famous visitors crowd the walls, while miniature planes, flags and garage sale finds hang from the ceiling. Prince Andrew, Bob Hope and Brooke Shields have all stopped by to pay their respects. It's a local landmark, as is Trader Jon himself with his ball cap and mismatched socks.

Trader's hosts bands of all sorts on the weekends. But leave the kids at home; it can get pretty raunchy at times. It's open from 12 PM until 3 AM every day.

DAINTY DEL
STEAK AND SEAFOOD RESTAURANT

286 N. Palafox St.   438-1241
$$

The Dainty Del began life as a fruit stand on the street with a deli and an oyster bar inside more than 90 years ago. It's changed hands only a couple of times since then, but the owners have always been Greek families. They obviously found the good life here in Pensacola and have a fiercely loyal clientele! Locals swear by the Oysters Rockefeller, the sauteed

snapper with artichokes and George's Special Snapper, a succulent filet of broiled snapper ladled with sauteed mushrooms, peppers, fresh tomatoes and onions. The inside of the restaurant is nothing fancy, but it's certainly nice enough to make a pleasant evening out — and a nice walk to the theater afterwards! It's open for breakfast, lunch and dinner seven days.

TOKYO CHAYA

53 E. Chase St.   433-6905
$$

Tokyo Chaya looks like it might be abandoned, sitting there so forlornly on the corner of Chase Street and Tarragona. But don't be fooled, it's one of the most popular lunchtime places in all of downtown. Inside it's *tiny* — only nine tightly packed tables and room at the sushi bar for six. Try some authentic Japanese cooking and you'll see what we mean. Katsu don is a pork cutlet simmered with vegetable and egg served over a large bowl of rice. Yakitori is three skewered chicken pieces broiled with Tokyo Chaya's special sauce, and gyoza are grilled dumplings filled with pork and beef with vegetables. The restaurant serves seafood prepared in the Japanese tradition (tempura, teriyaki), steaks, pork and chicken, all with the Tokyo Chaya touch, so know you're in for some wonderful eating! We would encourage you to try a delicious bean sprout salad with your meal, simply because Tokyo Chaya's homemade ginger salad dressing can't be missed (you can also take home a pint for $3.95). Stop in for lunch Monday through Friday or dinner Tuesday through Saturday.

KATHRYN'S RESTAURANT

901 E. LaRua St.   438-4525
$$$

This new kid on the block is causing

quite a sensation in its short lifetime. We're not sure why it is, but many of Pensacola's favorite local restaurants have absolutely zero appeal from the outside; we think maybe they spend their time on the stuff that really matters — making your meal the best it can be. So look hard on the right side of the street if you're driving north on Ninth Avenue. You'll see Kathryn's painted pink cinder block building a few blocks before you reach Cervantes Street.

Inside, things are cozy and comfortable, the service staff is friendly, and the food is irresistible. Begin your culinary adventure with an appetizer of oysters remique, baked with a tangy horseradish sauce and topped with Swiss cheese. Seafood can be prepared just the way you like it, or sample a Kathryn's signature item such as coconut shrimp — jumbo gulf shrimp rolled in sweet coconut, deep fried and served with orange sauce. Desserts seem steep, but these are big enough for two, served with a flourish and a flambè right at your table: Cherries Jubilee, Bananas Foster, Strawberries Romanoff or Praline Jessica. Kathryn's is open for lunch Monday through Friday and again on Sundays. Dinner is served Tuesday through Saturday.

THE ALE HOUSE
Harbour Village at Pitt Slip Marina 435-9719
$$

This is a favorite lunchtime spot and after-hours social gathering place for lo-cal business people, so expect to see a lot of suits as you settle in at your inside or outside table. The Ale House serves up homemade soups, sandwiches (these are *big*), steamed veggies and seafood, burgers, steaks, hot dogs, salads and more than a dozen appetizers. There's a children's menu too.

The Mighty Mudsharks are the house band, playing jazz, blues and popular favorites several nights a week. It's open every day for lunch and dinner.

LANDRY'S SEAFOOD HOUSE
905 E. Gregory St.   *434-3600*
$$$

Landry's replaced longtime landmark Cap'n Jim's, another seafood place; the new restaurant attempts to be more upscale than its predecessor. It's fairly touristy, from the garish neon marquis visible almost all the way to Gulf Breeze to the tacky cartoon beach scenes painted on the walls to the prices. But the food is very good, although an intimate restaurant it's not. Tables are crammed together and large, open rooms take advantage of the beautiful bay views. Sit out on the open-air deck for an early dinner; later in the evening enjoy the band (also set up on the deck).

Nearly every type of seafood is first-class in every respect (the crawfish bisque is outstanding), service is good, and presentation is obviously important to Landry's, as they do a good job of it. Landry's does not take reservations, and

Several of our favorite places look fairly rough from the outside, but the locals have kept many of them in business for decades. In all sincerity, however, if we're going to recommend them, we won't steer you wrong. Go in, have a seat and order up some fine eating. You'll thank us for it.

Insiders' Tips

at times the wait can be painfully long. It's open for lunch and dinner seven days a week.

PICADILLY DELI

102 Palafox Pl.   438-DELI
$

You really couldn't ask for a better downtown lunch place than this — good, hearty, inexpensive food you order the way you like it. Order at the counter for eat-in or take-out; they'll bring it to your table or package it to go. Sandwiches all have names such as the Stuffed Knight (a pita pocket stuffed with ham, pastrami, corned beef, Swiss and American cheese with lettuce, tomato and mayo), the Merry Minstrel (a bagel with cream cheese and Nova Lox) and the Robin Hood (hot corned beef, sauerkraut and Swiss with Reuben dressing and pumpernickel bread). Or pick your own bread, meat, cheese and condiments and get it your way. Soups, vegetarian sandwiches, salads, kosher foods and fresh (and sinful) desserts have made Picadilly a lunchtime favorite since 1981. It's open for lunch only Monday through Saturday.

JERRY'S DRIVE-IN

2815 E. Cervantes St.   433-9910
$

This ancient greasy spoon is a place the locals can't get enough of. Jerry's has been in Pensacola longer than Baptists have been in the South. You want local color? Jerry's provides every hue imaginable with its roadhouse atmosphere — pennants, posters, old snapshots and framed witticisms cover the walls; the rigid bright orange booths, stained ceiling tiles and ragged curtains may have never been updated, at least, not in our lifetime.

But what's important to know about Jerry's is this: cheeseburgers. Huge, thick, juicy and greasy enough to soak through twelve napkins, Jerry's cheeseburgers are cholesterol-packed diet-busters. There's not one menu item that would qualify as remotely "light," so don't even ask. The menu is down and dirty — chili dogs, grilled cheese, Dixie Dog on a Stick, barbecue, boiled shrimp, fried chicken gizzards, milk shakes and beer. Try it once; you'll be hooked. The grill starts cranking up for breakfast at 8:30 AM and doesn't cool down until late every day but Sunday. Bring a little bit of cash — it's all you'll need and all they take.

MARINA OYSTER BARN

505 Bayou Blvd.   433-0511
$

Not too far from Jerry's is another local hangout, and by locals we mean people and pelicans. The Marina Oyster Barn can be spotted from the Cervantes Street bridge across Bayou Texar (Ta-HAR), but to get there, go to the first light (Perry Street), turn left, then veer off to the water. It's easier by boat — just tie up at the dock.

The decor is spare, with all-around windows for that unparalleled view. Seafood dominates the menu selections; get it baked, fried, broiled or gumboed. Fish chowder and chicken dumplings are specialties of the house. If the weather's fine, take your meal out on the deck, where flocks of sea gulls and pelicans create a pleasant diversion. Beer and wine are available. It's open for lunch and dinner every day but Sunday.

THE YACHT RESTAURANT

Harbor Village at Pitt Slip   432-3707
$$$$

How about dining on a yacht tonight? This 153-foot grand lady, once owned by Carl Fisher (of "Body by Fisher" fame) has been converted into a floating restaurant. The Yacht's floating billboard in Pensacola Bay is a sore spot to locals, and we really wish they'd remove it and buy some *real* advertising. The Yacht doesn't go anywhere, but it doesn't need to with Seville Square, Pensacola Bay and the Pitt Slip Marina providing the scenery.

Impeccable service is the hallmark of the glass-enclosed dining room. Tuxedoed waiters make sure your water (and wine) glasses are constantly filled, and in every way, make you feel like a VIP. Chicken, steaks and seafood are prepared in traditional and gourmet dishes. Most seafood is local, but for visitors who long for a taste of home, try the Atlantic Salmon dusted in Caribbean spices, seared, then placed on a painted plate of raspberry Bordelaise and spiked with Hollandaise sauce or grilled and served in a pool of champagne cream.

After dinner, take in a breathtaking sunset in the Topside Lounge, where bay breezes stir the imagination. Alternate menu items are available from 4:30 PM until midnight Tuesday through Saturday and from noon to sundown on Sunday. A special Sunday brunch, offering Eggs Florentine, Hunard and Benedict, roast beef, ham, Seafood Newberg and a variety of desserts, soups, salads and side dishes begins at 11:30 AM and lasts until 2:30 PM. It's open for dinner every day but Monday.

FOUNARIS BROS. GREEK RESTAURANT
1015 N. Ninth Ave.   432-0629, 432-0639
$

This is one of those restaurants you probably wouldn't give a second thought to unless someone told you to go there. So we're telling you to go there! Short on atmosphere, long on good eating, Founaris Bros. makes a mean Greek pizza (Feta cheese, Greek olives, peppers,

gyro meat — you pick the ingredients) and an even meaner Greek salad. Sure, you'll smell like Feta cheese for three days, but it'll be worth it! Ever try Greek lasagna? There's quite an assortment of house specialties. Founaris Bros. is a local favorite. It's been here for years, and in a seasonal resort town, you need local business in the off-season, so you'd better be good. And they are. It's open Monday through Saturday for lunch and dinner.

COFFEE CUP
520 E. Cervantes St.   432-7060
$

The Coffee Cup serves old-fashioned fast food in a 1940s diner. Cooks sling eggs, pancakes, sandwiches, grits and burgers behind the counter while waitresses, many who've been here for 30 years, sing out orders. It's noisy with all that chatter, clanging pots and dishes and the ringing cash register, but it's cheap, good and the coffee is exceptional. It's open for breakfast and lunch every day. Cash only, please.

MESQUITE CHARLIE'S
5901 N. "W" St., Pensacola   434-0498
$$

You almost *have* to love steak if you come to Mesquite Charlie's. They're hanging-off-the-plate huge; the smallest one is 8 ounces (filet mignon); the largest is 32 ounces. (porterhouse). Steaks, chicken and ribs are all cooked over an open mesquite grill and seasoned with Charlie's natural spices.

The exterior is built like an old Western town, but it's all one huge restaurant inside with high ceilings, balconies and a huge stuffed moose in the corner. There's a little cowpokes menu available and a big bowl of barbecued beans to go with your steak. Make reservations for this popular restaurant. It's open every day for dinner.

JERRY'S CAJUN CAFE & MARKET
Ninth at Creighton in the
K&B Shopping Center   484-6962
$$

The word is spreading of the best Cajun food anywhere in the area. Pensacolians like to travel to New Orleans for good Cajun cooking (which is actually closer to here than Tallahassee!), so imagine their delight at finding the real thing so close to home! Gobble down a plateful of Boudin, red beans and rice, Crawfish Etouffé or a giant oyster po-boy. Nobody does a Muffuletta like Jerry's — ham, Genoa salami, mortadella and provolone cheese are drenched in the authentic New Orleans' Central Grocery Olive Salad, then slapped on what looks like an overgrown English muffin. A whole one feeds two people easily. Take home a six-pack of Dixie Black Voodoo beer, Zapp's potato chips or one of the many deli items available. It's open for lunch and dinner and closed Sunday.

YAMATO JAPANESE RESTAURANT
131 New Warrington Rd.   453-3461
$$

Here's a fun, authentic experience for a special night out! Step over the tiny bridge through the Japanese garden to enter the restaurant. From here, you have three dining options: regular dining at tables, Japanese-style, where you slip off your shoes and sit on heavy mats on the floor and eat from low tables, or sit around the huge grilling tables where your Japanese chef entertains while he cooks. Order up authentic cuisine such as tempura, teriyaki, sakura and sushi, which all come with Yamato soup or a Sunomono (Japanese) salad and rice.

If you opt for the family dinners, the

> For Insiders only, the secret Bushwacker recipe, courtesy of the Sandshaker Lounge.
> I part Kahlua or coffee liqueur
> I part white Creme de Cocoa
> ½ part Cream of Coconut
> 2 parts whole milk
> I part rum
> blend with ice

entire meal is one price, which includes an egg roll, soup, a salad and one of six entrees cooked on the open grill. It's open for lunch Monday through Friday and dinner Sunday through Thursday.

DINNER BELL DELIVERY SERVICE
$-$$$ 453-4656

Now there's a terrific option for people who are too tired to cook or for families who can't make up their minds about where to eat. Dinner Bell Delivery Service offers menus from nearly 40 local restaurants. Call one number and have full meals delivered directly to your home or hotel! Prices are the same as if you'd ordered the meal at the restaurant with a $1 delivery charge tacked on for the first restaurant, $2 for the second restaurant and only $1 more for each additional restaurant. Unbelieveable! Choose from Greek, deli, Italian, Hunan, steaks, Chinese, seafood, Mexican, barbecue, subs, oysters, Cajun and just about anything else you can dream up!

Be sure to tip your driver just as you would your server in a restaurant — happy eating!

McGUIRE'S IRISH PUB AND BREWERY
Gregory St. (Hwy. 98)between the Bay Bridge
and the Civic Center   433-6798
$$$

Popular with the fly boys on the weekends, McGuire's is a big draw for its Irish

Photo: Robin Rowan

Jamie's French Restaurant in Pensacola's Seville Historic District offers contemporary French cuisine in an elegant setting.

entertainment and home-brewed ale. McGuire's is famous for its USDA Certified Prime steaks, burgers and Irish specialties such as steak and mushroom pie and fish 'n' chips. Incredible but true, McGuire's has more than 100,000 dollar bills signed and stapled to the walls and ceilings. It's all part of McGuire's initiation process for those who want to be officially Irish.

Come on the weekends if you like crowds and people-watching. It's open daily for lunch and dinner and doesn't close until well into the wee hours.

Gulf Breeze

CHRIS' SEAFOOD GRILLE
47 Gulf Breeze Pkwy.   934-3500
$$

Swing a right turn just as you come over the Pensacola Bay Bridge and you'll be in Chris' parking lot. This wonderful little restaurant used to be called Pier I, and since the name change, it's every bit as nice if not better. Obviously seafood is the prime catch here — shrimp, seafood gumbo, oysters, mullet, crab, amberjack or whatever the catch of the day might be. This might be a good place to experiment with some of the local seafood; the prices are reasonable, so if you don't like it, you won't be out a lot of money. (We put our money on the amberjack every time.) If you enjoy fishing while you're here, Chris' will cook your catch to your liking (just be sure it's dressed).

If you're not a seafood lover (stick around here long enough, you'll turn into one), or if you've had seafood vacation overkill, there are also fine steaks, sandwiches, pasta, veggies, even tacos. Pull up to Chris' in your boat to one of the slips out back. It's open for lunch and dinner seven days.

BON APPETIT CAFE & BAKERY
Hwy. 98 E.
Inside the Holiday Inn Gulf Breeze   932-3967
$$$

Bon Appetit is *not* your typical hotel fare, as a sign at the entrance points out. To begin with, there's a panoramic view of Pensacola Bay from every table, which is bound to put you into a good mood no matter what your day's been like. Thick, tasty soups, giant meal-size salads, outstanding gumbo, pastas and seafood sum up the unique offerings at Bon Appetit, but what we especially like is the complimentary wine with your meal. Santa Rosa County is dry, so the restaurant can't *sell* you the wine, but they can sure enough *give* it away. Both families and couples out for an intimate evening can fit in here with equal aplomb. And if the view doesn't get you, turn around — the giant glassed-in cases of freshly baked yummies certainly will. Bon Appetit is open for breakfast, lunch and dinner daily.

Pensacola Beach

BOY ON A DOLPHIN

400 Pensacola Beach Blvd.　　　932-7949
$$$

Greek legend or not, this is a strange name for a restaurant. The Greek-inspired steaks, seafood and pasta dishes are good. Boy On A Dolphin is a classy place right on the water — cloth napkins, peach and ivory decor, a little gazebo in the restaurant's center and huge windows to catch the view. Fish dishes depend on what's been caught that day, but the traditional Greek preparation comes highly recommended. Chef's recommendations are starred on the menu; if you can't decide, try one of the house specialties. It's open for dinner only every day.

SANDSHAKER LOUNGE, PACKAGE STORE & SANDWICH SHOP

731 Pensacola Beach Blvd.
Lounge　　　　　　　　　932-2211
Sandwich Shop　　　　　　932-0023
$

Serving up really tasty sandwiches with equally tasty prices, the Sandshaker Sandwich Shop is a nice complement to the Sandshaker Lounge, which has been in place at the corner of Pensacola Beach Boulevard and Fort Pickens Road for nearly two decades. Clubs, open-face, subs and many other varieties of sandwiches are offered for just $3.75 (you get a pickle with that). For the same price, pick one of the daily specials (a full meal except for beverage) such as chicken spaghetti, meat loaf or a taco salad.

Next door, the tiny Sandshaker Lounge is a beach landmark, made famous by the creation of Pensacola's own local concoction, the Bushwacker, which tastes something like a milkshake (an *adult* milkshake, that is, since the alcohol content in two of these could put you in a haze for days). The place is barely big enough to stand up and turn around in but worth a stop for this sinfully sweet and frothy treat. The sandwich shop is open daily at 11 AM and closes at 9 PM Monday through Wednesday, 10 PM the remainder of the week.

JUBILEE TOPSIDE

Quietwater Beach Boardwalk　　934-3108
$$$$

Jubilee Topside is one of the finest restaurants anywhere in the area, period.

Bring your charge card, though; since it's the beach, you'll pay tourist prices. But oh, what a meal! Start with crab claws delicately sauteed in garlic butter, oysters Rockefeller or soft-shell crab and pasta topped with honey-roasted nuts swimming in a garlic beurre blanc and sauce bearnaise.

A special treat at Jubilee is the bread and butter service, where a "baker's helper" comes around to your table two, three, maybe four times to deliver fresh-baked rolls and an array of butters — whipped, garlic and one specialty — chocolate butter . . . sounds strange, but ooooohhh, it's melt-in-your-mouth good!

Ready for the entree? It's Florida cuisine, through and through, with some Cajun twists. Blackened grouper is served over seasoned rice, topped with sauteed mushrooms then finished with a red wine sauce and lemon beurre blanc. Grouper chardonnay is pan-sauteed with vegetables in a light lobster cream sauce then finished with Parmesean cheese and broiled to a golden brown. Landlubbers might go for hand-cut Angus Filets Roland, sauteed with artichokes, lump crabmeat and white wine, topped with sauce bearnaise or Steak "Dano," a filet mignon wood-grilled over an open flame, served over fresh angel hair pasta and finished with blackened shrimp and scallops with a light beurre blanc and sauce bearnaise.

The decor is elegant with big, comfortable chairs, stained glass, an open-beam ceiling and dining on two levels with more room to come in '95. The view — and the service — are outstanding. This successful restaurant has expanded, both upstairs and downstairs with a $1.3 million two-story, open-air deck, increasing seating capacity and banquet facilities and expanding both kitchens.

Jubilee is open for lunch and dinner daily with a Sunday brunch served from 9 AM until 3 PM.

JUBILEE BEACHSIDE
Quietwater Beach Boardwalk　　934-3108
$$$

Downstairs at Jubilee, you'll find the atmosphere a little "beachier" and the prices a bit easier to handle. Hand-painted walls and tables by talented local artist Sheilagh Foster offer diners something to contemplate while they eat. Or sit in the Celebration Room and admire local ceramist Peter King's work. Some menu items ditto the ones upstairs and are every bit as scrumptious. Salads, sandwiches, burgers and deli selections are good anytime. For dinner, try shrimp scampi, blackened amberjack or chicken and broccoli fettuccine. A kid's menu is available. It's open daily for lunch and dinner. You'll enjoy the live entertainment by Clark & Co. Wednesday through Sunday and the great view everyday.

FLOUNDER'S CHOWDER & ALE HOUSE
At the traffic light on
Pensacola Beach　　932-2003
$$$

Flounder's has fun with everything from the menu to the decor and only gets serious when it comes to making good food. "Eat, drink, and Flounder" is the motto, and several other "famous" quotes appear in the menu, slightly askew, such as "Better to have Floundered and Lost, Than Never to Have Floundered at All" — Alfred, Lord Flounder.

The folks who own McGuire's Irish Pub in town run this place too, so the same fresh seafood, prime steaks and service apply.

Florida seafood is presented almost three dozen ways; steaks start at 10 ounces if you're not very hungry and grow to 16 ounces if you are! Chowders, salads, light pasta dishes, poultry, burgers and sandwiches offer everybody something they like, including Julius Flounder, who says: "I Came, I Saw, I Floundered." It's open every day for lunch and dinner with live entertainment Fridays and Saturdays.

CHAN'S GULFSIDE

2½ Via de Luna Dr.   932-3525

$

We can't believe it, either, but Chan's is the first gulf-front restaurant on the beach! Chan's opened in 1994 and seems to be doing quite a business by serving excellent food at good prices. The Chan's in town (by University Mall) is known for its imported beers; the same stock can be found at the beach. Wherever you sit inside or out, you'll have a nice view with which to enjoy your meal. Sandwiches, burgers, and po-boys are huge, and you get your choice of either fries or a pasta salad (skip the fries, the salad is *great*). There are plenty of seafood entrees and salads on the menu, including a Cajun Popcorn Caesar, Seafood Gumbo and Chan's Crawslaw (with crawfish tails, naturally!) Service is about what you might expect at a beach restaurant, probably a few surfers trying to make some money in the off-season, but overall, the atmosphere is friendly and classy. It's open for lunch and dinner seven days.

Pensacola Area
Accommodations

Step out your back door onto the Gulf of Mexico beaches . . . peer down from your window onto manicured gardens . . . spread out in a rental vacation house that sleeps 16 . . . snuggle into a sleeping bag surrounded by nothing but stars and tall pines . . . enjoy sweeping panoramas from a ninth-floor beachfront balcony. Condos, high-rise hotels and private villas on the beach offer many modern conveniences, while in-town bed and breakfasts and historic hotels slow the pace a bit, reminiscent of a time when tradition and family took center stage. If it's a back-to-nature vacation you want, commune with wildlife and rough it under the stars in a serene wooded campground.

If you've spent vacations at Disney World or anywhere in South Florida, you'll be thrilled to find that even at the peak of the season, Pensacola area rates are surprisingly low. A four-bedroom house with full kitchen, living room and three baths across the street from the gulf rents for as little as $800 a week! Similar deals can be found through area rental agencies.

Hotels and Motels

If you've absolutely, positively got to have the surf coming in your door, then the beaches are the place, and that's that. But for the rest of you, check into downtown, north or near-the-airport properties. You could be paying less and get-

Photo: Robin Rowan

The 1912 Louisville & Nashville Train Depot now serves as the lobby for the Pensacola Grand Hotel.

ting more and still end up with a nice view.

We're providing a general pricing guide to help you plan what accommodation best fits your needs. Price structure is based on double occupancy for one night and does not include tax, which can add up to 12.2 percent to the final bill.

Have a great night's rest!

$60 or less	$
$61 to 85	$$
$86 to 99	$$$
$100 or more	$$$$

Perdido Key

BEST WESTERN PERDIDO KEY

13585 Perdido Key Dr.   492-2755
$ (800) 554-8879

Not much has changed since Best Western took over from the Comfort Inn in February. The location is still near the beach, just a short drive from the Gulf Islands National Seashore, Big Lagoon State Park and the Navy base. For all guests, there's an outdoor pool, an indoor Jacuzzi, volleyball court and children's playground. Room rates include continental breakfast, and all rooms have queen beds. There's a $10 per person charge for more than two people in a room, and rates jump about $15 on the weekends. Military and AAA rates are also offered.

Pensacola

EXECUTIVE INN

6954 Pensacola Blvd. (Hwy. 29)   478-4015
$$

A favorite overnight spot for corporate travelers, the Executive Inn has 36 spacious units, some with microwaves and refrigerators; all have cable TVs with HBO and remote control. Take a refresh-

ing swim in the pool and enjoy complimentary coffee in the morning. Double rooms have two full-size or one king bed and sitting areas. Nonsmoking and handicapped-accessible rooms are available.

HOLIDAY INN UNIVERSITY MALL

7220 Plantation Rd.   474-0100
$$ (800) HOLIDAY

A truly outstanding Holiday Inn in north Pensacola features Coconuts Comedy Club, Coconut Bay Lounge and Bon Appetit Cafe & Bakery in addition to airport shuttles, in-room movies, complimentary coffee and a newspaper with your wake-up call. Believe it or not, this Holiday Inn allows small pets in the room with you — but no pets in the pool. Sorry. Nonsmoking and handicapped accessible rooms are available. The property is right across the street from University Mall.

HOSPITALITY INN

6900 Pensacola Blvd. (Hwy. 29)   477-2333
$$$ (800) 321-0052

The Hospitality Inn is a full-service hotel convenient to the airport with a spacious multistory lobby. Mini-suite kitchens have private patios. Guests may take advantage of the pool, a complimentary breakfast buffet, an exercise room, laundry, barbecue grills and handicapped facilities.

RAMADA INN NORTH

6550 Pensacola Blvd. (Hwy. 29)   477-0711
$ (800) 2-RAMADA

You're only about a 10-minute drive from the Pensacola Regional Airport (a straight shot down Airport Boulevard) at this newly renovated 106-room hotel. The lobby is especially pretty here, featuring a grand, sweeping staircase and a fountain graced by a bronze heron sculpture. Get a regular room with two queen beds, or a

FIVE FLAGS INN

Pensacola Beach, Florida

Spectacular views with all guest rooms facing the Gulf of Mexico.
Enjoy a relaxed island atmosphere and warm friendly people.
(904) 932-3586
299 Fort Pickens Road ■ Pensacola Beach, FL 32561

When making reservations reference the Insider's Guide for free gift upon arrival

suite with a whirlpool bath, mini fridge, wet bar and coffeemaker. Free local calls, complimentary coffee, and HBO come with your room. An Olympic-size pool, full-service restaurant and golf packages are also available to guests.

NEW WORLD LANDING

600 S. Palafox St.   432-4111
$$

Surprisingly affordable rooms offer lots of little extras at this motel in the heart of the downtown historic district. All 16 rooms are decorated in antique reproductions and overlook a landscaped courtyard with fountains or Palafox Street to the bay. Complimentary continental breakfast comes with your room. A full-service restaurant provides views of the lovely courtyard.

THE PENSACOLA GRAND HOTEL

200 E. Gregory St.   433-3336
$$-$$$$ (800) 348-3336

Formerly the Pensacola Hilton, this 15-story beauty is directly across the street from the Pensacola Civic Center, so naturally, many performers stay here while in town. The lobby is the old Louisville & Nashville train depot (1912), remarkably

restored into shops, restaurants and convention space. Gorgeous antiques and period fixtures grace the lobby, lounges and restaurants. A glass atrium connects the depot to the main hotel. Room rates go up incrementally — the higher the floor, the higher the rate — but remain the same year round.

RAMADA BAYVIEW

7601 Scenic Hwy.   477-7155
$$ (800) 282-1212

This gorgeous new facility has 150 rooms overlooking Escambia Bay in north Pensacola. In-room whirlpools are a favorite. All guests can enjoy the outdoor pool and a complimentary newspaper in the morning. The restaurant features live entertainment, a seafood buffet on Fridays and a jazz brunch on Sundays.

Pensacola Beach

BEACHSIDE RESORT & CONFERENCE CENTER

14 Via de Luna Dr.   932-5331
$$$$ (800) BEACH-16

Formerly the Sunset Lodge, which was formerly the Howard Johnson's (things change so fast in a resort area!), this newly expanded and renovated resort sits right on the gulf and right in the hub of beach activity. Owned now by the Innisfree Hotels, the 116 rooms are getting a facelift with casual, contemporary furnishings and bright colors. Gulf-front suites provide kitchenettes; handicapped-accessible rooms are also available. On site are a large pool, a children's pool, a beach volleyball net, a cookout area, a restaurant and meeting rooms for up to 700.

CLARION SUITES RESORT & CONVENTION CENTER

20 Via de Luna Dr.   932-4300
$$$$ *(800) 874-5303*

The Clarion all-suite resort looks more like a village of beach cottages than a hotel. The 86 luxury one-bedroom suites have living and dining areas, a master bedroom, a kitchenette with refrigerator, microwave, toaster oven and coffee maker, two TVs and complimentary continental breakfast. Families and couples will especially like the extras: a swimming pool, beach pavilion, children's play area, fitness room and location right on the gulf.

BEST WESTERN PENSACOLA BEACH

16 Via de Luna   934-3300
$$$$ *(800) 934-3301*

Right after it opened, the Best Western hosted the annual UFO conference, its marquis announcing, "Welcome Earthlings." Maybe you don't need a sense of humor to run a hotel, but we like their style. The 122 rooms come with refrigerators, coffee makers, wet bars and either one king or two queen beds. Some rooms are equipped for the disabled; all are just a few steps from the gulf. Take advantage of two gulf-front pools, one of the golf packages and your free continental breakfast.

COMFORT INN

40 Fort Pickens Rd.
Pensacola Beach   934-5400
$$-$$$

The old Mai Kai hotel was razed last year after vandalism and fires took their toll on the long-vacant property. The Comfort Inn, newly opened in May 1995, fits in splendidly with all of the renovation/construction/revamping undertaken in the beach's core. The four-story business-friendly hotel features 100 inland or soundside rooms (great sunsets), including a few handicapped accessible rooms. For the cost of your room, you'll get a coffee maker, a fridge, wet bar and microwave all to yourself, while you'll have to share the conference facilities (1,300 square feet), an exercise room, pool and business room with phones, desks, fax machines and room to work. Business, corporate and military rates are offered year-round.

THE DUNES

333 Fort Pickens Rd.   932-3536
$$$$ *(800) 83-DUNES*

The most luxurious high-rise hotel on the beach, The Dunes hosted Michael Jackson for a month while he was in town rehearsing for his "Dangerous" tour.

Insiders' Tips

Several short scenes in *Jaws II* were filmed on the white shores of Navarre Beach.

Rooms are decked in beach peach and seafoam green with tropical wallpaper, bedspreads and pictures. Double rooms offer a king-size or two queen beds; prices jump $10 on weekends and holidays. Penthouse suites are available with two rooms, a full kitchen (no stove), a four-person Jacuzzi and either a rooftop terrace or double balcony overlooking the gulf. Take a room in the older part of the hotel and save, save, save.

HOLIDAY INN PENSACOLA BEACH
165 Fort Pickens Rd.   *932-5361*
$$$-$$$$ *(800) HOLIDAY*

This Holiday Inn was the first high-rise hotel on Pensacola Beach and has been here for years. Renovations have come at regular intervals, so expect your room to be as nice as new. Rooms look either east or west along the beach or overlook the gulf; first-floor rooms are $10 extra. All have private balconies. A pool, tennis courts, gift shop, game room and the Casino Restaurant are right on the property, and the ninth-floor Penthouse Lounge offers spectacular views from every side.

FIVE FLAGS MOTEL
299 Fort Pickens Rd.   *932-3586*
$

This small mom-and-pop hotel has the best rates on the beach and *all* its rooms face the gulf. You might get a room with one king bed or two doubles; if you have more than two in the room, you need to specify your preference. Rooms are awfully tiny, but if all you're doing there is sleeping, that's all you could possibly need. You also have the added benefit of waking to the sound of surf and sea gulls. Local calls, coffee and kids are free.

Volleyball is a favorite pastime on Pensacola Beach.

Navarre Beach

HOLIDAY INN - THE TROPICS
8375 Gulf Blvd.   939-2321
$$-$$$$

Walk out your back door and onto the sugar-white sands of the gulf—that's how close you'll be in a gulf-front room. This older Holiday Inn has been revamped and is looking great. The Holidome pool is the center of activity; game rooms, guest rooms and snack bars surround it. An open staircase leads to the second floor reception area with floor-to-ceiling windows overlooking the emerald waters of the gulf on one side and the cool blue of the pool on the other. The three-story-high ceiling over the pool creates something of an echo chamber, but it isn't bothersome. Room rates re-main fairly inexpensive here since Navarre Beach is a little out of the way. Most rooms offer two double beds, but you can get king-size beds for a little extra. A lounge and a restaurant on the property take care of most of your needs; the Sunday brunch is one of the best in the area. A special "Beach Brigade" gives the kids plenty to do while you relax in the pristine surroundings of Navarre Beach.

Condos/Townhomes/ Vacation Cottages

Condominiums are, for the most part, individually owned, meaning that each will be furnished differently. Ask about specific properties when you call. Prices reflect the weekly cost of a two-bedroom/two-bath condo or house during the peak summer season. Most rental agencies want a deposit up front that can amount to up to a third of the week's rental. The rest is due upon check-in. Prices do not include tax.

$500 or less	$
$501 to 750	$$
$751 to 999	$$$
More than $1,000	$$$$

PENSACOLA BEACH PROPERTIES, INC.
1200 Fort Pickens Rd.
Pensacola Beach   932-9341
$$ (800) 826-0614

PBP manages rentals for the 15-story Tristan Towers condominiums on Santa Rosa Sound. Every room has either a view of the sound or the Gulf of Mexico, which is right across the street (the island is only a half-mile wide). Besides 24-hour security, guests have access to the Olympic-size swimming pool, lighted tennis courts, a clubhouse, gazebo and boardwalk to the beach (sound side). Be sure to ask for a corner condo, which is the same price as a regular condo, but has a wraparound balcony for panoramic views. Condos rent weekly only from mid-June to mid-August.

PENSACOLA BEACH REALTY, INC.
Pensacola Beach Blvd.   932-5337
$$-$$$ (800) 874-9243

More than 150 condominiums, townhomes and private homes are offered by Pensacola Beach Realty. Portside Vil-

las (two-story townhomes with first-story parking), Gulf Winds (gulfside condos, four stories) and Sans Souci (high-rise condos, gulfside) are a few examples on Pensacola Beach. Prices can vary by up to $200 for a two-bedroom/two-bath unit depending on location, size of the unit and amenities.

NAVARRE AGENCY, INC.
8512 Navarre Pkwy. (Hwy. 98 near the bridge)
Navarre   939-2366
$$-$$$ (800) 821-8790

All townhomes and condos are gulfside on Navarre Beach; some have pools; most have two cable TVs. Navarre Villas and San Dollar are townhomes. Emerald Surf is a mid-rise with a pool, and Sun Dunes is a high-rise. Half of the weekly rental is due within 10 days of the reservation.

PROFESSIONAL REALTY OF PENSACOLA BEACH
Quietwater Beach Boardwalk
Pensacola Beach   934-4333
$$$ (800) 239-4334

The Palm Beach Club condos are the newest on the beach with views of both the sound and the gulf. Master bedrooms and living rooms have separate private balconies overlooking the beaches, a two-person Jacuzzi in the master bath, 24-foot cathedral ceilings, fireplaces, wet bars and security. Share a pool and a 16-person hot tub with 15 of your closest friends.

Look for all kinds of new accommodations springing up throughout the beach areas — Perdido Key, Pensacola Beach and Navarre Beach. At this writing, a new Hampton Inn on Pensacola Beach, a Fairfield Inn at I-10 and Davis Highway in Pensacola and about a dozen new condominiums are all under construction.

Insiders' Tips

EDEN CONDOMINIUM

16281 Perdido Key Dr.
Perdido Key   492-3336
$$$$ (800) 523-8141

This unusual stepped condominium on Perdido Key is the epitome of a luxury vacation resort. Huge units feature private gulf-front balconies, a full kitchen, washer and dryer, whirlpool tub and wet bar. West wing units are slightly larger, and consequently more expensive, than their eastern counterparts. You could say Eden has pools, but that's like saying the Taj Mahal is a house. The 176-foot pool overlooking the gulf is surrounded by lush tropical foliage, fake rocks and waterfalls and is all lit up for late-night dips. The outdoor landscape pools are filled with Japanese Koi fish. Indoors you'll find a heated solarium pool and more tropical gardens. Add to that a fitness center, two lighted tennis courts and a private 24-slip boat dock, and you might never want to go anywhere else.

SOUNDSIDE HOLIDAY BEACH RESORT

19 Via de Luna Dr.
Pensacola Beach   433-5701
$$$ (800) 445-9931

You're right in the center of the beach action in one of these 28 waterfront condos on Santa Rosa Sound. All are two-bedroom/two-bath with kitchens, towels, linens, fireplaces, Jacuzzis and a washer and dryer. An outdoor hot tub, pool and tennis courts make this a great family retreat.

PERDIDO SUN CONDOMINIUMS

13753 Perdido Key Dr.
Perdido Key   492-2390
$$$$ (800) 227-2390

Treat yourself to luxury living on the white sands of Perdido Key with views of the gulf or the Intracoastal Waterway all around. Perdido Key is a less frenzied atmosphere, more suitable for enjoying the natural amenities the area has to offer. Man-made amenities at the Sun include a 24-hour front desk, heated indoor pool and outdoor pool, hot tub, sauna and fitness room. Big Lagoon State Park and Johnson Beach, part of the Gulf Islands National Seashore, are nearby.

Campgrounds and RV Parks

ADVENTURES UNLIMITED

Tomahawk Landing
Milton   623-6197

The place that made Northwest Florida's inland rivers famous goes one better with overnight accommodations at Tomahawk Landing, also known as canoe trip central. Spacious wooded campsites on the water with a full hookup are just $15. Rustic treehouse-style cabins on either Coldwater or Wolfe Creek have screened-in porches and porch swings outside and nothing more than a bed and a lantern inside. A campfire ring, picnic tables and grills are centrally located, with the restroom and bathhouse nearby. These are just $29 a night for two people. Slightly larger and with more amenities are the rustic camping cabins in Pine Forest. These have porches too, but inside they offer relief from summer's heat with ceiling fans and air conditioning for $39 a night. One-bedroom cabins with room for four are $59 per night, and a one-bedroom cottage (sleeps four) with a fireplace and fully equipped kitchen is $69. Granny Peaden's cabin is a relic, now completely restored to sleep four with two bedrooms, bath, kitchen and air conditioning.

Photo: The Dunes

The Dunes played host to Michael Jackson during rehearsals for his Dangerous tour.

NAVARRE BEACH
FAMILY CAMPGROUND

9201 Navarre Pkwy. (Hwy. 98)   939-2188

This older park has 91 shady and grassy sites on Santa Rosa Sound; many of those are taken up by year-round residents. The sound side offers shallow, safe swimming for young children, and the woodsy backdrop is terrific for a break from the sun. Sites have full hookups (including cable TV!) and pull-throughs. A pool, pier, boat ramp, playground, four bathhouses, a laundry and a store are right on the grounds. Overnight fees are $18 for two ($2 extra for each additional person). Weekly rates are $96 for six days, with the seventh day free.

BY THE BAY RV PARK & CAMPGROUND

5550 Michael Dr., Milton   623-0262

This campground is right on beautiful Escambia Bay about 15 miles north of Pensacola in Milton. The view is great, the price is right and your hosts the Blanchards are eager to make your stay as pleasant as they can help make it. Overnight sites are just $15 for two people ($1 more for each additional person). Both weekly and monthly rates are also available. Pets on leashes are welcome. You'll find By the Bay 3 miles south of I-10 at Exit 7.

Pensacola Area
Shopping

Two large malls, 70-plus strip shopping centers, tiny boutiques, art galleries, surf shops, antique stores, flea markets and one-of-a-kind shops in renovated historic homes highlight offerings in the Pensacola area. Spend some time downtown and on the beaches to find antiques, handmade, specialty items unique to this area and well-stocked chain bookstores such as Books-A-Million, B. Dalton and Waldenbooks.

Pensacola

UNIVERSITY MALL

Davis Hwy. at I-10   478-3600

More than 70 stores are anchored by Sears, JCPenney and McRae's department stores, plus 11 theaters and the Foodworks food court.

CORDOVA MALL

Ninth Ave. at Bayou Blvd.   477-5355

More than 140 specialty shops make Cordova one of the Southeast's largest malls, with anchors Gayfers, Dillard's, Montgomery Ward and Parisian. Four inside theaters, a food court, puppet shows and entertainment year round make this a fun place to shop.

TOWN & COUNTRY PLAZA

3300 N. Pace Blvd.   432-7766

Pensacola's original shopping center has covered walkways connecting its 27 stores. Gayfers is the main department store, but there are some wonderful specialty shops and restaurants as well (Windy City Dogs is a favorite).

J.W. RENFROE PECAN COMPANY

2400 W. Fairfield Dr.438-9405, (800) 874-1929

The Renfroe family has been around for many years selling nuts and gifts for all occasions. Jake Renfroe oversees the operation himself, allowing only top-quality pecans into his shelling factory. Pecans come shelled and unshelled. The gift shop also tempts buyers with cashews, almonds, walnuts, pistachios, peanuts, natural food mixes, pecan candy and homemade fudge. The Renfroe Pecan Shelling Plant is just a block north of the retail shop, where pecans are shelled, roasted and salted daily. Mail orders are welcome. It's open Monday through Saturday 8 AM to 5 PM.

BAYOU COUNTRY STORE

Corner of Ninth Ave.
and E. Jackson St.   432-5697

Although the Bayou Country Store sells antiques such as rockers and benches and tables, it's also a wonderful place for finding old kitchenware such as washboards, sifters, rolling pins and mixing bowls. In the West East Hill neighborhood, the store features handmade items and lots of folk art. Christmas is an especially good time to shop, when hand-carved ornaments, wreaths and mantle decorations are sold.

EVER'MAN NATURAL FOODS

1200 N. Ninth Ave. 438-0402

This is a *great* food co-op, offering organically grown produce and other natural foods, some which can't be found anyplace else. Pay one tiny membership fee and get a discount all year long. Besides sponsoring occasional seminars on health and nutrition-related topics, Ever'man's gets involved with many issues of local interest such as offshore drilling, recycling and growing your own organic herbs.

STONEHAUS

2617 N. 12th Ave. 438-3273

We're going to stick our necks out and make a prediction: 12th Avenue is going to become the new trendy shopping mecca in Pensacola in the next few years. Stonehaus, near Cross Street and 12th Avenue in the East Hill neighborhood, has established a reputation for superb ceramic works. Ceramist Peter King creates working fountains, inlaid tile floors and countertops, fireplaces, entryways and many other custom works for his clients. Stop in to see some of the smaller items for sale, or peruse Stonehaus' huge portfolio and commission your own one-of-a-kind architectural ceramic piece.

C&M CENTRAL MARKET

1010 N. 12th Ave., Ste. 130 434-9888

Just down the street from Stonehaus in the old Sacred Heart Hospital building is this delightful gourmet food store, or maybe we'll just call it a neighborhood grocery store. If you've ever been to the Central Grocery in the French Quarter of New Orleans or one of the neighborhood grocers in New York City, you know

what we mean. What you'll find here are imported cheeses and meats, pastas, fresh produce, herbs, whole bean coffee and ground chickory, ice cream, Italian pastries and much, much more. If you're missing the old Strega Nona's restaurant that used to be in this old hospital building, you'll be happy to know that Central Market's deli features fresh-baked breads just like they used to make, plus curried rice salad, homemade soups and giant sandwiches.

FARLEY'S OLD AND RARE BOOKS

5855 Tippin Ave. 477-8282

Looking for a first edition of *Gone With The Wind*? How about an original copy of a Hemingway classic? Owen and Moonean Farley will gladly assist you in finding a special book, which can include a computer search of all editions currently available. Farley's is wonderfully cluttered and great fun for browsing with a collection of vintage magazines, newspapers, postcards, even original copies of Dr. Seuss! Book cleaning, repair and restoration are also available.

LADS & LASSIES

1339 E. Creighton Rd. 477-8748

This is still a little hard to get to with all of the construction on Creighton Road, but it will all be over soon, and the newly-widened road will make accessibility a breeze. Lads & Lassies offers pre-owned clothing for infants, children and women on consignment, but the real beauty is finding designer kids' clothes that are almost new for a fraction of the new price! Used toys, books, shoes and accessories are also sold.

"T" STREET, PENSACOLA

"T" Street, off Fairfield Drive on Pensacola's west side, is an antique- and bargain-hunter's dream. Start at one end and stop anywhere along the way for everything from old hubcaps to beautifully restored antiques. There are plenty of junk shops here, but a keen eye can spot a diamond in the rough. Searching through the cluttered shelves might reveal a porcelain doll, an old railroad lantern or a vintage hand-cranked Victrola.

Downtown Pensacola

ARTESANA INC.
242 W. Garden St.   433-4001

This beautifully rendered import shop features a stunning collection of basketry, hand-painted china, specialty books and cookbooks, exotic wrapping paper, children's toys, herbs and spices, candles, housewares, linens and many gift items. At certain times during the year, Artesana offers shoppers glasses of iced tea or mulled cider; there's always a delicious aroma hanging in the air.

PAGE & PALETTE
106 S. Palafox St.   432-6656

More than 60,000 titles grace the floor-to-ceiling shelves of this downtown bookstore. And that's just the front room. The middle room is filled with wonderful cards, stationery and gift wrap for all occasions. In the back, find artist's supplies — canvas, palettes, brushes, paints and accessories. Book signings are held here regularly for local and regional authors.

MY BOOKSTORE
112 S. Palafox Pl.   436-2096

Debbie Hagler and her staff will assist you in selecting books for tots to teens. Just two doors down from Page & Palette, My Bookstore specializes in selling books that are not usually available in the chain bookstores. They are even sorted according to age for gift-giving. Special orders are welcome, and you'll especially like all the no-pressure personal attention.

IRON GATE GALLERY
114 S. Palafox Pl.   433-1838, 438-4656

Right next door to My Bookstore, Iron Gate Gallery features many unusual gift items, books, pictures and artwork that you won't find anywhere else in town. At Christmas, the store becomes a showplace for the unique. The Santas of the Sea are Santas dressed all in white adorned by nets, shells, starfish and other deep-water treasures. An entire back room is given over to wooden, glass, ceramic and porcelain figures and Christmas ornaments. Iron Gate will gift wrap your purchase free and ship it anywhere.

QUAYSIDE ART GALLERY
15-17 E. Zaragoza St.   438-2363

This gallery across from Plaza Ferdinand and the Pensacola Cultural Center is an artist's co-op, actually — the largest one in the Southeast. Take your time browsing through watercolors, acryl-

Pensacola is gaining a reputation as a mecca for talented artists, and the numerous downtown art galleries showcase the variety and quality of local works. Soho, Bayfront, Artel, Billingsley, Casa de Cosas, Gallerie E'lan, Gallery of Lovely Things, Quayside, Art Attack and Schmidt's, all downtown, offer a good selection of area and regional talent.

Insiders' Tips

Photo: Robin Rowan

As pretty outside as it is inside, Artesana's creatively designed interior is a visual feast.

ics, oils, sculptures, pottery, batik, stained glass, photography and more on three levels. The building itself is rather historic. Constructed in 1873 just north of the old wooden quays, or wharves for square rigged sailing ships, the building housed the Germania Steam Fire Engine and Hose Company, complete with a 2.5-ton horse-drawn steam pumping engine.

CLELAND ANTIQUES
412 E. Zaragoza St.   *432-9933*

Cleland's is an established and reputable antiques dealer in a renovated home in the Seville Historic District. The shop specializes in 18th-century antiques, both formal and primitive. Most furniture and furnishings are restored. Look upstairs for everything from four-posters to spinning wheels. Cook Cleland was a Thompson Trophy winner in the 1930s; the plane he flew is on display at the National Museum of Naval Aviation.

STORYBOOK GALLERY
505 S. Adams St.   *438-0075*

In the heart of the Seville Historic District just off the square is this little find, featuring children's books, original art works, prints and many other treasures, big and small. Be sure to see the unusual works by Michael Parkes, who taught at Pensacola Junior College from 1968 to 1972, and the whimsical original watercolors and pig art, titled "Out of My Mind," by owner/artist Dick Winkowski.

Insiders' Tips

Visit the seafood markets along the Pensacola waterfront where the fishing fleets dock at the markets' back doors. You won't find fresher fish anywhere!

Find the Storybook Gallery in the string of shops just across the street from Old Christ Church on Seville Square.

QUAYSIDE MARKET
712 S. Palafox St.   *433-9930*

Books, antiques, handmade linens and clothing, jewelry, candies, gourmet coffees and more are offered at this one-of-a-kind indoor marketplace in historic downtown Pensacola.

JOE PATTI'S SEAFOOD CO.
South of Main St. on "A" St.   *434-3193*

A wonderful local experience for visitors, Joe Patti's is an institution in Pensacola. Where "A" Street dead-ends, a gazebo and lively recorded music welcome you to one of the area's most popular seafood markets. When you step inside, you'll most likely be overwhelmed by the smell of fish, but not to worry; after a few minutes you'll hardly notice it. Laid out before you is a breathtaking array of fresh seafood — about six different sizes of shrimp, oysters, live crawfish, flounder, red snapper, triggerfish, amberjack, mullet, even shark! Buy them whole or filleted. The fishing fleet backs right up to Joe Patti's docks, where pelicans and sea gulls abound. It's a commercial fishing area, so you won't see many pleasure craft here; these are hard-working fleets that look like they've been around a few years.

Gulf Breeze

ALLAN DAVIS SEASHELLS & SOUVENIRS
Gulf Breeze Pkwy.   *932-2151*

Here's a little Gulf Coast history, right in the middle of Gulf Breeze. The locals pass by this place every day and never give it a second thought, but it's become a local landmark. For the area's many visitors, Allan Davis is like a sideshow of beach mania: carved shell nightlights, little figurines made of shells, T-shirts, jewelry boxes with shell motifs, inexpensive kids' toys and thousands, maybe millions, of seashells of every description offered for sale. But Allan Davis isn't like most other souvenir shops, first, because it opened here in 1950 and became more of an attraction than a place to shop, and second, because it has a fantastic collection of shells on display. These shells are definitely *not* for sale; the shells under glass throughout the store represent a lifetime of collecting from all over the world. That alone makes the shop more like a museum, but wait — there's more. Lining some of the shop's walls are specimens of the deep floating in formaldehyde — tiny squids, octopi, sea robins and creatures that were captured so long ago the name on the jar has worn off. The real Allan Davis is in his '90s but still makes an occasional appearance in the store.

THAT PHOTO PLACE
231 Gulf Breeze Pkwy.   *932-8832*

The reason we're telling you about this photo processing spot is that it's good, cheap, and *fast!* Get your slides processed in two hours, your photos in 1. They'll make reprints in one day, enlargements in about the same amount of time, and it's all because they do everything right there. You'll find That Photo Place at one end of a tiny strip shopping center in the heart of Gulf Breeze. Look for the Blockbuster Video store and the Big "B" Drug store as landmarks.

AWAKENINGS
19 Harbourtown Shopping Village   *932-1779*

This was formerly the New Age shop, but this name seems to fit what you'll find within much better. Crystals, new age CDs, self-improvement books and posters, incense and exotic wind chimes might all be expected, but Awakenings has some of the best greeting cards and unusual gifts of any place in the area. Browsing is encouraged, and you may even sit on the comfortable padded bench in the middle of the store and preview any of the CDs for sale on personal headsets.

THE FLEA MARKET
5760 Gulf Breeze Pkwy.   934-1971

This new flea market across from The ZOO is one of the largest in the area with more than 400 exhibit spaces. Scout for bargains on clothing, plants, jewelry, artwork, antiques, CDs and garage sale finds in the gigantic outdoor marketplace. It's open weekends only from 9 AM to 5 PM.

HURRICANE BOOKS
Delchamp's Shopping Center
366 Gulf Breeze Pkwy.   932-6254

Hurricane Books just blew across the street from its former location on Hoffman Drive and is now more accessible than ever. Try it out for all your favorite light reading on a variety of topics, especially fiction. Also look for blank books, bookends, bookmarks, cards, stationery and more. Owner Kris Lalumiere and her competent staff provide personal service and can special-order any title in print.

Pensacola Beach

ALVIN'S ISLAND
TROPICAL DEPARTMENT STORE
400 Quietwater Beach Rd. at
Quietwater Beach Boardwalk   934-3711

Two stories of fun and tackiness for the beach are featured at Alvin's, including beachwear, swimwear, sportswear, gifts, souvenirs and airbrush art.

Outside the Pensacola Area

RIVIERA CENTRE FACTORY STORES
Hwy. 59 S.   (334) 943-8888
Foley, Ala.   (800) 5-CENTRE

Let's hit those cheaper-than-retail outlets! This is one of our favorites, with more than 110 factory-direct outlet stores and more going up every week! Riviera Centre is about an hour's drive from Pensacola and a short trip if you're staying on Perdido Key. Savings up to 75 percent off retail make it possible to buy twice as much as you came there for. Make a day of it! It's just 10 minutes north of Gulf Shores and Orange Beach, Alabama.

Pensacola Area
Historic Sites and Attractions

Beaches, beaches, beaches. State beaches, national seashore beaches, nude beaches, gulf beaches, gay beaches, sound beaches, bay beaches, crowded beaches, secluded beaches. They're the No. 1 attraction throughout Northwest Florida and almost always the reason given by first-time visitors for why they come.

But next to those, most of the best sightseeing and family fun is on the mainland in the Pensacola area. And you don't want to spend all your vacation getting a sunburn . . . do you?

Here's a quick rundown on how to get to the areas described in this chapter:

Perdido Key — The barrier island is 15 miles west of Pensacola. From downtown, follow Garden Street W. (Highway 98), which turns into Navy Boule-

vard. Turning right from Navy Boulevard onto Gulf Beach Highway will get you there, but you'll travel through some fairly shabby areas. You can also take Highway 98 W. straight on through to Blue Angel Parkway (Highway 173). Turn south (left) on Blue Angel to Highway 292. Turn right (west) and follow the signs to Perdido Key.

Pensacola — The city and surrounding communities are built around the water — Pensacola Bay and Escambia Bay, Bayou Texar and Bayou Chico, Grand Lagoon and the Intracoastal Waterway. I-10 spur is a quick north-south route; however, there's no easy (or fast) way to get from east to west. Your best bet to the west (toward Perdido Key and the Naval Air Station) is to follow the

Photo: Curt Shields Photography

"Lap dogs" at the Pensacola Greyhound Track.

water as closely as possible from downtown.

Milton — This area is easily accessed from Pensacola via Highway 90 (also Scenic Highway) or on I-10 going east. From I-10, cross the bridge over Escambia Bay, then take the first exit (Avalon Boulevard), turn left, and travel north to the intersection of U.S. 90. Downtown Milton is to your right.

Gulf Breeze — Jump on the Pensacola Bay Bridge from downtown, (17th Avenue and Bayfront Parkway at the Visitor Information Center), and 3 miles later you're there. Keep traveling east on Highway 98, Gulf Breeze Parkway, for Navarre Beach and The ZOO.

Pensacola Beach — From Gulf Breeze, turn right at the neon fish sign and continue over the Bob Sikes Bridge ($1 toll).

Attractions that are fun for families with kids will be denoted by an asterisk (*). Before you tackle one of the area's varied attractions, you may want to stop at the Pensacola Tourism and Convention Center at the foot of the Three Mile Bridge for information on prices, times and special programs.

1914, and up through World War II, every Navy pilot got his training here. The 250,000 square feet of museum space packs in more than 100 Navy, Marine Corps and Coast Guard aircraft and traces the history of naval aviation from biplanes to the space age. There's a gigantic NC-4, the first aircraft to cross the Atlantic, the first F-14 Tomcat (flown in the movie *Top Gun*) and a Navy F-18 fighter jet.

The seven-story Blue Angel Atrium, used for social events and military ceremonies, features four Blue Angels' Skyhawks suspended in diamond formation from the ceiling. In the works are an IMAX theater, with an over-your-head multiple-story screen and about 70 speakers. If you've ever seen a short film in one of these theaters, you know what a boost it will be to the museum and the entire area.

This is one terrific museum whether you're in the military or even know anything about the military, and kids really like the hands-on aircraft cockpits and other "touchables." The museum is open daily from 9 AM to 5 PM except Thanksgiving, Christmas and New Year's Day. Admission is free.

*NATIONAL MUSEUM OF NAVAL AVIATION

Pensacola Naval Air Station   452-3604

It's not only one-of-a-kind, it's one of the three largest air and space museums in the world. Pensacola became the country's first Naval Air Station back in

*PERDIDO KEY STATE RECREATION AREA

Off State Rd. 292, Perdido Key   492-1595

This small beach area (1.5 miles of gulf-front), smack in the middle of the Key off State Road 292, is part of a 247-acre preserve spanning both sides of the

---

Photo: E. H. Albrecht

The old Water Battery is part of Fort Barrancas at Pensacola Naval Air Station.

two-lane highway. There are picnic shelters between the gulf and Old River on the north. If you're coming for the beach, there's a parking lot on the gulf side with shelters and boardwalks for public beach access. If you plan to walk through the preserve, however, you'll find it rough going. There aren't any trails, boardwalks or roads. Remember, too, that in Florida nobody owns the beach, so feel free to walk the shoreline past the fancy condos and private residences lining the key. It's open 8 AM to sunset all year. There is a $2 honor fee per vehicle.

*BIG LAGOON STATE RECREATION AREA

12301 Gulf Beach Hwy.
Pensacola   *492-1595*

Big Lagoon is a personal favorite spot, since it combines many different landscapes and habitats, from marshlands to grassy beds to white sand beaches and pine forests, all centered around Big Lagoon, what they call the Intracoastal Waterway here. The park is beautifully maintained, very clean and nicely laid out. Two

highlights are the natural wood outdoor amphitheater and the 40-foot observation tower at East Beach.

From the top of the tower, you'll get a feel for the diversity of the park — herons bob for fish along the sandy shore, while brown thrashers, red-winged blackbirds and towhees hide among the marsh grasses. Look out across Big Lagoon to the beach area at Gulf Islands National Seashore. From this perspective, too, you'll see how fast the area is developing; homes now hug the outer boundaries of the park, sharing the area's wetlands.

For the most part, Big Lagoon is buffered by the barrier island Perdido Key but is still subject to harsh coastal conditions. Vegetation looks twisted and stubby; yellow pine swales, long troughs parallel to the dune line, thrive in waterlogged soil, with surrounding scrub buffeted and shaped into an impenetrable thicket of vines and gnarled branches.

Boardwalks lead to picnic shelters, the amphitheater, the observation tower and right down to the beach. The Long Pine,

Yaupon and Grand Lagoon hiking trails offer an opportunity for a close-up nature study of surrounding vegetation, wetlands and wildlife. Gray foxes, raccoons, skunks and opossums have been known to cross paths with patient observers. More than 75 campsites, both for RV and primitive camping, are located right in the center of the park on a sand pine ridge. Seasonal programs, guided nature walks and interpretive exhibits add an even richer dimension to your visit.

A boat ramp right along the main loop road provides easy access to Big Lagoon. Picnic areas and a swimming beach are nearby. Other picnic and designated swimming areas (no lifeguard provided) are near the amphitheater and west of the observation tower. You can fish here too; anglers catch redfish, bluefish, flounder and mullet as well as crabs.

Please remember that all plant and animal life is protected. You may take seashells, but first be sure there's nobody "home." Dogs are prohibited almost everywhere, and so is alcohol.

The park is open year round from 8 AM until sunset. Entrance fee for cars (up to eight people in one vehicle) is $3.25 (good for one day); bike and foot traffic is $1 per person. Big Lagoon State Recreation Area is on County Road 292A, about 10 miles southwest of Pensacola.

U.S.S. MASSACHUSETTS
UNDERWATER ARCHAEOLOGICAL PRESERVE
Pensacola Bay

For snorkelers and divers only, the remains of the oldest existing American battleship can be found in 26 feet of water in the Fort Pickens State Aquatic Preserve. You can spot it by boat, since the ship's gun turrets stick above the surface most of the time. If the turrets are covered up, there's a red buoy marking the spot, plus you'll find it on every nautical chart of the area. This unusual underwater preserve was dedicated in 1993, on the 100th anniversary of the ship's launching. The *Massachusetts* saw action in the Spanish American War, then became a gunnery practice ship before WWI. After decommissioning in 1919, it was towed to Pensacola in 1921 for battle practice and scuttled just outside the entrance to Pensacola Bay. Now the 350-foot hulk

Photo: Carter Photography

Clear, cool, rivers, white sand banks and lush woodlands make Northwest Florida's inland rivers delightful for canoeing, tubing, camping or sunbathing.

serves as a giant artificial reef, attracting an abundance of sealife such as flounder, sea anemones and urchins, waving purple seafans, white sponges, peaceful angelfish and blue tangs. Call any one of the area dive shops for snorkeling and diving trips to the preserve.

PENSACOLA GREYHOUND TRACK
Hwy. 98 at Dog Track Rd.
Pensacola   455-8595

"Here . . . comes . . . Swifty!" Greyhound racing seems to have taken off as fast as these dogs burst out of the starting gate, providing an enjoyable afternoon or evening's entertainment, whether you wager on your favorite hound or not. Dine in the Kennel Club, sip a cocktail in the lounge or sit in the grandstand outdoors for a close-up view of the action! Live and instant replay televisions are provided throughout the complex. When no races are scheduled, you may still enjoy simulcast thoroughbred racing. Children younger than 12 are admitted to the races, but they have to be 12 or older to have dinner in the restaurant. Rain or shine, greyhound races take place Tuesday through Sunday during the season at 7 PM, with matinee races on weekends at 1 PM. Call for post times. General admission is $1; Kennel Club and Restaurant $2.50; seniors get in free to matinees on weekends. Visitors are admitted free with a hotel or motel key (up to four people).

FIVE FLAGS SPEEDWAY
7450 Pine Forest Rd.
Pensacola   944-0466

This half-mile track has attracted racing greats such as Darrell Waltrip and Rusty Wallace as hundreds of fans turn out to cheer on their favorite drivers. Annual events such as the Snow Ball Derby and Winston Cup All-Pro races draw record crowds. The regular season runs March to September; Friday night races are $8 for adults, $3 for children 6 to 12. Admission prices vary at other times. Call for race dates and times.

*WILDLIFE RESCUE AND SANCTUARY
105 N. "S" St., Pensacola   433-9453

Foxes, raccoons, deer, eagles, owls, armadillos, alligators, herons, pelicans, snakes and many other species have put in a stay at the sanctuary. It's a unique place in the middle of the city where abandoned, sick and injured wildlife are brought for treatment. Some of the residents may have been exotic pets that got too large or may have ended up here because they were simply unwanted. Other birds and animals were accidentally shot by hunters, hit by cars or, in the case of several pelicans, got such a bad case of frostbite one year that many had to have beaks, wings or legs amputated.

Not all the wildlife can be released into the wild; the pelicans can't survive on their own, so they have become per-

While you're visiting Pensacola Beach, take a walk out onto the Pensacola Beach Fishing Pier on Casino Beach, which juts more than 1,000 feet into the Gulf of Mexico. Anglers can hook some mammoth catches from the pier's southernmost point, and the sheer abundance and variety of fish caught on the pier is interesting, educational and fun to watch!

Insiders' Tips

manent residents of the sanctuary. The Wildlife Rescue and Sanctuary relies almost solely on donations; park volunteers do a terrific job of caring for the animals and love to talk about "their" animals to everyone who comes by. Early in 1994, a fire destroyed the main house along with many of the indoor animals and birds. Money poured in from residents, businesses and the local electric company that had donated the first house to the park to rebuild. The Sanctuary is off the beaten path a couple blocks behind the Gulf Power Company building at Pace and Garden streets on "S" Street. No admission is charged, but donations are welcome.

THE WALL SOUTH AND VETERAN'S MEMORIAL PARK

Bayfront Pkwy., Pensacola   433-8200

A one-third scale traveling version of the Vietnam Veterans Memorial in Washington, D.C., came through Pensacola several years ago, making such an impact that the Vietnam Veterans of Northwest Florida started a push to build a permanent half-scale replica of The Wall here in Pensacola. With community support and an awful lot of fish fries, The Wall South and the Veteran's Memorial Park opened with great fanfare in 1992; the ceremony included several letters written by soldiers and a Blue Angels fly-over in missing-man formation. Eventually, the park will include a memorial for every war from WWI to the present. The wall is downtown Pensacola along Bayfront Parkway. No admission is charged.

SEVILLE HISTORIC DISTRICT

Downtown Pensacola   444-8905

Here is a rare neighborhood, fairly intact, dating from the early 19th century. Most of the homes, simply constructed and well adapted to the climate, now house tiny boutiques, law offices and restaurants. The Frame Vernacular, Folk Victorian and Creole homes are some of the oldest in Florida and are listed on the National Register of Historic Places. There's an excellent self-guided tour brochure of the three historic districts available at the Visitor Information Center. The district is between the bayfront and north to Wright Street and Tarragona Street east to Florida Blanca Street.

While you're in this area, stop by **St. Michael's Cemetery** on Alcaniz Street. Graves date back 200 years; 3,000 people are buried there, from slaves to nobility. Land for the cemetery was deeded by King Philip of Spain in the early 18th century. There is no admission. Look for a new self-guided tour brochure due out this year.

*HISTORIC PENSACOLA VILLAGE

Zaragoza St. at Tarragona in the Seville Historic District, Pensacola   444-8905

Several homes and commercial buildings within the Seville Historic District have been carefully restored to reflect West Florida's coastal history. The **Museum of Industry** features machinery from the Piney Woods Sawmill used during Pensacola's lumber boom. The **Museum of Commerce** recreates a streetscape of the late 19th century. The **Lavalle House, Julee Cottage, Dorr House, Quina House, Lear House** and **Weaver's Cottage** depict early life in West Florida through their architecture and period furnishings, while the grand dame of the Seville district, the **Barkley House**, serves as the official residence of Pensacola. The last museum is the **T.T. Wentworth Jr. Florida State Museum** (Pensacola's Old City Hall), an eclectic mix of artifacts collected over a lifetime by local resident T.T.

Wentworth. Other exhibits trace Pensacola's maritime history and feature artifacts found in a British fort and a Spanish shipwreck in Pensacola (see the Pensacola Colonial Archaeological Trail). On the third floor you'll enjoy the hands-on Discovery Museum made just for kids.

Tickets for Historic Pensacola Village are $5.50 for adults, $4.50 for seniors and children 4 to 16. The sheer number of museums might seem overwhelming, but please take your time. Tickets are good for two days. Museums and historic homes are open Monday through Saturday from 10 AM to 4:30 PM and Sundays from 1 to 4:30 PM between Easter and Labor Day. Tickets may be purchased at the Wentworth Museum or in the central ticket office (The Tivoli High House) on Zaragoza Street in Historic Pensacola Village.

THE PENSACOLA COLONIAL ARCHAEOLOGICAL TRAIL

Inside the T.T. Wentworth Museum and scattered locations around downtown Pensacola
444-8905

The trail showcases two of Pensacola's most remarkable archaeological finds: The British fort of Pensacola (1778) and a 16th-century Spanish shipwreck. Under the city streets for four blocks in the heart of downtown are the remnants of a British fort which once covered most of the area. In 1990, a British howitzer was unearthed under Jefferson Street and led to the discovery of the fort's foundation. A recreation of this scene as well as a scale model of the British fort and an introduction to the Trail's outdoor exhibits are all located inside the **T.T. Wentworth Jr. Florida State Museum**. Artifacts from a 16th century Spanish galleon, discovered just a half-mile from the bayshore at the Visitor Information Center, also are in-

cluded in the museum. Outdoor exhibits are free, but you'll get a much better feel for the significance of Pensacola's urban archaeology once you've visited the museum. For ticket information, please see the previous Historic Pensacola Village listing.

PALAFOX HISTORIC DISTRICT

Palafox St. Area, Pensacola   *434-5371*

The downtown business district was the very heart of this thriving port city. Several old wooden hotels, the Pensacola Opera House, and the San Carlos Hotel have been lost to hurricanes, fires and demolition, but the downtown area retains a large number of its historic commercial buildings. As you drive through this area, notice the intricate ironwork balconies, reminiscent of New Orleans architecture. This locally ordinanced historic district begins at Palafox Pier and continues up Palafox Street to Wright Street; on the west, Reus Street is the boundary, and Tarragona Street divides the Palafox district from the Seville district.

THE CIVIL WAR SOLDIERS MUSEUM

108 S. Palafox Pl.
Pensacola   *469-1900*

This museum provides an absolutely fascinating encounter with the names and faces of soldiers, generals, doctors, photographers and just plain folk. From John Brown and Frederick Douglass to the last Civil War veteran to die in 1959, The Civil War Soldiers Museum chronicles every facet of the war and is absolutely top-notch in every respect. Recorded remembrances and letters bring these long-forgotten soldiers to life again. The Pensacola Room records the significant people and events during the war in Pensacola, including a 23-minute video presentation, *Pensacola and the Civil War*, which may be more than you ever wanted to know, but certainly history buffs and locals will get a lot out of it.

One wall is devoted entirely to the more grisly side of the war — primitive surgical procedures and equipment, early anesthesia (such as a musket ball with teeth marks!), amputations and some rather disturbing photographs. The man responsible for the museum, Norman Haines, is a local doctor, so naturally he devoted a good bit of space to his particular area of interest.

In all, though, the museum is spacious, well documented, nicely laid out and worth a few hours of your time. The museum bookstore offers 500 titles on the Civil War, from fiction to biographies, histories and letters. Admission is $4 for adults; $2 for children 6 to 12; family memberships are available for $35. The Civil War Soldiers Museum is open Monday through Saturday from 10 AM until 4:30 PM.

PENSACOLA HISTORICAL MUSEUM
405 S. Adams St., Pensacola   433-1559

The oldest church building in Florida (1832) houses a history of the City of Pensacola in artifacts and a research library. The church itself, built in the romantic Norman Gothic Revival style, features huge hand-hewn heart pine beams in the ceiling and beautifully carved and highly decorated botonee crosses over the arched side doors. Federal forces used the church during the Civil War as a bar-

racks, a prison, a hospital and a military chapel. Beginning with ancient fossils, the history of the area is traced through Indian pottery, maps, Civil War exhibits, materials used during the lumber and snapper fishing periods and household items. Walk through the museum yourself or take one of the guided tours. Admission is $2 for adults, $1 for children. It's open Monday through Saturday, 9 AM to 4:30 PM and is closed Sundays and holidays. There's no charge to Historical Society members.

PENSACOLA MUSEUM OF ART
407 S. Jefferson St., Pensacola   432-6247

Here is a showcase of both local and traveling art exhibits in the old City Jail (1906). Some of the old cell blocks are still intact, with barred doors and windows, but it lends an atmosphere of history to the visual pieces. Photography, old Dutch masters, Chinese porcelain, contemporary arts and many other fascinating shows are presented each year. The Museum Store offers many art prints, unusual toys and other works of art. Donations are accepted.

NORTH HILL
PRESERVATION DISTRICT
1.5 miles north of downtown, north of Wright St. and west of Palafox St.   444-8905

Maybe it doesn't have the impact of Charleston, South Carolina, or New Orleans' Garden District, or even some ar-

The Wildlife Rescue and Sanctuary in Pensacola, a home for injured and abandoned wildlife, is like a free zoo right in your own backyard. Stop by to see hawks, eagles, baby raccoons and squirrels, snakes, alligators and pelicans. The residents of the sanctuary change frequently; no trip there is ever the same!

Insiders' Tips

eas of Mobile, Alabama, but the North Hill district is still a visual treat. The upper-middle class neighborhood developed between 1870 and 1930 with the rise, and eventual bust, of lumber. Of the 50 blocks and 500 homes, some 400 of the homes contribute to the character of the district.

Several architectural styles are represented as wealthy families all tried to outdo each other. You'll find turreted and gingerbreaded Queen Annes, as well as Craftsman bungalows, Neoclassical, Tudor Revival, Art Moderne and Mediterranean Revival. Nearly all of the homes are private residences and may only be enjoyed from the sidewalk unless a friendly resident is willing to give you a tour, which happens on occasion. Pick up a copy of the brochure *A Historical Tour of Pensacola* at the Visitor Center for walking tour highlights.

WEST EAST HILL PRESERVATION DISTRICT

Cervantes St. to Wright St. and
Ninth Ave. to Hayne St.   *433-1559*

Protected under a Pensacola city ordinance enacted in December of 1993, the neighborhood west of another called East Hill began around 1870 as a community of middle- and upper-class railroad workers. The Pensacola & Atlantic Railroad came through the city, connecting it with the rest of the state for the first time. Before the railroad, Pensacola was not easily accessible because of its many rivers and no bridges.

Many of the lovely Victorian homes, subdivided into apartments when the neighborhood began to decline in the 1930s, are being restored to their original splendor. A few old brick streets still remain. There is much work to do in the area, but a drive through will provide you with an overall feeling for what

the neighborhood once was and, with diligence, will be again.

SCENIC HIGHWAY HISTORIC TRAIL

Scenic Hwy. (Hwy. 90)
Pensacola   *477-7155*

1993 marked the 20th anniversary of Scenic Highway's designation as a state scenic parkway. First opened in 1929, the original route may have been an Indian trail, then part of the Spanish Trail trade route between El Paso, Texas, and Jacksonville, Florida. This beautiful 10-mile drive along the scenic bluffs and bayfront will one day acquire historic site markers.

Beginning at the point where Cervantes Street becomes Scenic Highway is **Emanuel** or **English Point**. Not far from the shoreline here are the remains of a 16th-century Spanish ship. About a quarter-mile down the shore is **Magnolia Bluff and Beach**, one of the first city beach areas, now developed as East Pensacola Heights. **Bay Bluffs Park**, which is marked with signs, provides a scenic overlook and wooden stairways down to the foot of the bay.

Gaberonne Point is found directly across from the Gaberonne neighborhood. It was once the site of one of the many brickmaking companies along the bluffs. Bricks made here were shipped to construct Fort Jefferson in the Dry Tortugas and Fort Taylor in Key West before the Civil War. The 30-foot-high brick chimney is all that's left of an 1854 steam-powered sawmill at **Bohemia**. The sawmill was torched by Confederate soldiers as they evacuated Pensacola in 1862.

Gull or **Diablo Point** isn't readily seen from the highway, but several homes were constructed on this 732 acres jutting out into the bay. **Stony** or **Rock Point** marks the spot where the Escambia River Bridge opened in 1926. The British operated the

These exotic white tigers have found a new home at The ZOO in Gulf Breeze.

first brickyard below the point as far back as the 1770s.

Lora or **Laura's Point**, across from the Lora's Point subdivision, marks the opening of the first bridge across Escambia Bay in 1882. And the last marker is at **River Gardens** or **Campbell Town**, which was first settled in 1766 by French Protestants. It later became another brickyard.

*EDWARD BALL NATURE PRESERVE AT THE UNIVERSITY OF WEST FLORIDA
University Pkwy., Pensacola   474-3000

The entire UWF campus sits on a 1,000-acre nature preserve on the Escambia River north of town, providing a scenic wooded landscape for university buildings. The nature preserve takes up a good portion of wetlands on the university's property. A ³/₄-mile wooden boardwalk meanders through prime hardwood swamp and over a small fork of the Escambia River (Thompson's Bayou), where turtles and alligators are spotted regularly. Visitors to the preserve often stop along the way to feed bread to the turtles and fish, who seem to congregate in areas where they know food is plentiful. Picnic areas are provided in a clearing shaded by old mossy oaks. No admission is charged. The preserve is

Insiders' Tips

The entire North Hill Preservation District sits atop a vast battlefield where Spaniard Don Bernardo de Galvez and 4,000 troops snatched Pensacola from the British in a bloody two-month-long siege in 1781. North Hill residents still find cannon balls, coat buttons and other artifacts while digging in their gardens or installing sprinkler systems! Historical markers on Spring, Palafox and Barcelona streets fill you in on Fort San Bernardo, Fort George and the battlefield site.

down the hill behind Building 13 off Blue Parking Lot 20.

*THE ZOO

5701 Gulf Breeze Pkwy.
Gulf Breeze   932-2229

It claims to be "The World's Friendliest," and after a trip, you might agree. This small zoo, 10 miles east of Gulf Breeze, packs in an impressive collection of animals, including the white Bengal tiger, but it's the layout and atmosphere here that will win you over. Impeccable landscaping, a botanical garden filled with exotic species, a farm where children may pet and feed the animals, and a nursery and incubator room for zoo babies are just a few highlights.

The **Safari Line Train** ($1.25 admission) chugs through 30 acres of free-roaming animals in re-created habitats. Look for pygmy hippos, Florida alligators and an amazing assortment of birds and horned creatures from all corners of the world. Want to see a giraffe up close? Climb to the top of the **Giraffe Feeding Tower** and get a slimy lick from a 12-inch black tongue! Yecch! Ellie the African elephant takes visitors on rides, and wildlife demonstrations are staged daily at the outdoor amphitheater.

The ZOO's star attraction, Colossus, the largest gorilla in captivity, is now on loan to the Cincinnati Zoo for breeding purposes. The ZOO tried playing matchmaker, but Colossus never hit it off with his chosen mate, Muke (MOO-key). She stayed; he's been temporarily replaced with a couple of other gorillas who are still plenty of fun to watch.

The ZOO is open daily, weather permitting, from 9 AM to 5 PM; the park closes an hour earlier during the winter months. Admission is $8.75 plus tax for adults, $5.25 for children 3 to 11 and $7.50 for seniors. The entire park is also handicapped-accessible. You may also purchase a yearly membership for $50 (individual) or $95 (family).

MILTON HISTORIC DISTRICT

Hwy. 90, Downtown Milton   626-9830

Milton was once a thriving lumber town with a port of entry on the Blackwater River. The many lovely historic homes date mostly to the late 19th century, and downtown commercial buildings have some real history packed into their walls.

The **1913 Exchange Hotel** on Elmira Street was intended for use as a telephone exchange, but when the phone office moved next door, the building became a hotel. Accurately restored in the 1980s, it spent time as a bed and breakfast but now sits vacant.

Gulf Breeze, Florida, has been called the "UFO Capital of America" for the unusually high number of unexplained sightings there. Two of the best spots for UFO watching are the foot of the Pensacola Bay Bridge (Gulf Breeze end) and at Shoreline Park, where locals gather regularly to gaze skyward. If you're lucky enough to spot one yourself, get out the video camera, then report it to MUFON's (Mutual UFO Network) hotline number, (904) 438-3313.

Insiders' Tips

The **Imogene Theatre and Milton Opera House** (1912) is the only three-story building in the city. The second floor has a tiered balcony on three sides. Occasionally used as a theater, it's the full-time Santa Rosa Historical Society headquarters and a museum of local history.

The **Milton Depot** (1909) has always been a favorite. Its architecture is reminiscent of a quaint, small town, and even though trains haven't run through here since the 1960s, if you stand on the platform, you can imagine what a busy place it once was. The inside has been converted into the **West Florida Railroad Museum** with plenty of model train displays to make a child's, and an adult's, eyes shine.

Though not part of the historic district, there's an effort afoot to preserve the Old Brick Road in Santa Rosa County, known as old Highway 90. It's the earliest (1919) and the only brick highway in Northwest Florida. Preservationists hope to incorporate the road into the county's historic and recreational trails program.

BAGDAD HISTORIC DISTRICT
C-191 and Bagdad Hwy.
Bagdad 623-8493

Very old, very rural, very Southern, the tiny village of Bagdad is a charmer. Glorious antebellum mansions sit near trailer homes with chickens in the front yards. The trees make this a sight in itself — live oaks eerily decked out in Spanish moss supply the old homes, and even the newer ones, with their "down-home" character.

Many of the most striking homes line Forsyth Street. Owners restoring the 1847 Thompson House found graffiti made by a burnt stick on an interior wall — left there by a Union soldier in 1864.

Where Forsyth Street dead-ends, a panoramic view unfolds of the Oakland Basin and Blackwater Bay. The only structure here is a derelict abandoned home. You might wonder why no one has snatched this land up to build on. It once was a park where residents went "courtin'," and perhaps the locals aren't ready yet for the change that comes with tourism. A self-guided tour brochure is in the works; check at the museum in the Imogene Theatre in Milton or with the Santa Rosa County Chamber of Commerce on Highway 87.

*ADVENTURES UNLIMITED
Tomahawk Landing, Hwy. 87
Milton 623-6197

Talk about fun! If you've never canoed one of inland Florida's scenic rivers, you're missing out on another aspect of this area's beauty. Adventures Unlimited provides canoes, giant inner tubes (for a more leisurely float) and cooler tubes (to drag your cooler along behind you!), camping supplies, cabins, you name it, to make your trip as safe and comfortable as possible.

Each of the four rivers offers its own

Photo: Robin Rowan

These grand turn-of-the-century homes sprang up as a result of Pensacola's lumber boom. The North Hill Preservation District is on the National Register.

scenic diversions, and three are relatively shallow for first-time canoe enthusiasts. Take a short trip, daytrip, or one- or two-day trip down the Coldwater, Blackwater, Perdido or Sweetwater-Juniper. The Sweetwater-Juniper offers the most stunning scenery (although it is also the shortest river); the Perdido offers the most challenging ride. The Perdido is wide and deep, and is probably best left to veteran canoe handlers, since amateurs tend to tip over a lot.

One word of caution: the Coldwater and Blackwater are the most popular rivers, and therefore the most crowded. On a Saturday in early summer, you won't feel much seclusion as one group after another passes you on the river. It might be prudent to ask the folks at Adventures Unlimited, if you truly desire a calm and quiet trip, what days of the week or months of the year are not quite so popular.

Overnight camping on the rivers opens a whole new world to the first-time visitor. Paddle gently through the tea-colored water, stopping often for a dip in the river, a walk through the woods or a picnic lunch. About two hours before dark, scope out one of the many white sandbars (yes, the sandy bottom is white), pull your canoe out and make camp. You may build a fire in the sand, just be sure you're far enough away from the woods so errant sparks from your campfire don't burn

The old Pensacola Bay Bridge, which runs parallel to the new bridge connecting Pensacola with Gulf Breeze, is one of the world's longest fishing piers. Day and night, rain or shine, the bridge is filled with rod-and-reel-wielding locals hoping to get lucky. And they usually do. The problem is keeping watchful herons and pelicans from stealing the catch!

Insiders' Tips

Gulf Islands National Seashore

Please see our separate chapter for complete information on the Gulf Islands National Seashore, GINS, the 150-mile stretch of barrier islands and keys from Mississippi to Florida. You may contact GINS by calling 934-2600.

FORT PICKENS AREA

Fort Pickens Rd., Santa Rosa Island

The pre-Civil War-era fort is the highlight of this part of the GINS. Guided tours are available, as well as park programs in the Fort Pickens Museum. Some of the area's most exquisite beaches await your discovery along this 7-mile strip (the western tip) of Santa Rosa Island. Camping, picnic shelters, concessions, a campground store and hiking and biking trails provide enough diversions to keep the family busy for a week!

SANTA ROSA DAY-USE AREA

Between Pensacola Beach and Navarre Beach

Picnic pavilions, concessions, showers and indoor exhibits take up a small part of this seemingly endless stretch of white dunes, beaches, scrub and freshwater ponds spanning both sides of the highway.

NAVAL LIVE OAKS AREA

East of Gulf Breeze

These few miles of dense oak forest were set aside by President John Quincy Adams in 1828 for the sole purpose of shipbuilding. Trails lead you through the moss-draped woods along the bay where Native American encampments thrived thousands of years ago. Exhibits and a slide show on how the wood was used in shipbuilding are provided at the Visitor Center, which also serves as the Seashore Headquarters.

FORT BARRANCAS
AND THE ADVANCED REDOUBT

Naval Air Station Pensacola

Two fortifications built for coastal defense are open for exploration and guided tours. Hike through the surrounding woodlands or enjoy the area's quiet beauty in the small picnic area. While you're here, you might also enjoy a trip to the historic lighthouse on the NAS property.

anything else! During dry periods, campfires may be prohibited, so be sure to bring a campstove (or lots of bologna sandwiches!). Each of the rivers is spring-fed, ensuring their purity (feel free to brush your teeth with the water) and constant cool temperature.

Another option for roughing it, if you don't care so much for really wide open spaces, is rental cabins. You'll find just about all the comforts of home here — showers, refrigerators, air conditioning, fireplaces — all strewn along Wolfe Creek (an offshoot of the Coldwater), or scattered deeper in the woods. Tent and hookup sites are also available at Tomahawk Landing.

Tubing or canoeing these wild rivers really is an adventure not to be missed! More detailed information on campsites and cabins is included in the chapter on Pensacola Accommodations.

*BLACKWATER RIVER STATE PARK
Off U.S. 90, Holt   *623-2363*

The Blackwater River is still considered one of the purest sand-bottom rivers in the world, mostly preserved in its natural state. The shallow river is terrific for canoeing, tubing and swimming (see Adventures Unlimited above or the chapter on Pensacola Recreation). Almost 200,000 acres are teeming with wildlife in this under-utilized state park. Camping, nature and horse trails, boating, picnicking and hunting are all offered, though some activities are seasonal. The park is open from 8 AM until sunset year round. There's a $2 entrance fee for cars. No pets are allowed. Blackwater is 15 miles northeast of Milton off U.S. 90 in Holt.

Pensacola Area
Annual Events and Festivals

You pick the time of year to be here, and the Pensacola area will do its best to provide a full plate of activities. When we talk about Pensacola area festivals and events, sometimes we just can't help but include a few events happening on the other side of the state line. Mobile is only as far to the west of Pensacola as Destin is to the east. Besides, we don't want you to miss out on anything!

Listed here are events that occur annually. Seasonal festivities, concerts, poetry readings, special museum exhibits or anything we've left out can be tapped into by contacting the Pensacola Convention & Visitor Information Center, 434-1234, or by checking the local paper. One more note: The names Pensacola Beach and Santa Rosa Island are used interchange-

ably at times. Pensacola Beach is part of Santa Rosa Island, and Quietwater Beach and Casino Beach are also part of Pensacola Beach. Confused? Sometimes, we are too. But, it's a small area out there, so if you drive around a bit, you're sure to find what you came for. Also remember that you'll pay a $1 toll to drive onto the beach from Gulf Breeze; coming onto the island from Navarre, the toll is a quarter.

January

POLAR BEAR DIP
Flora-Bama Lounge at the Florida-Alabama line
Perdido Key   492-0611

OK, so it isn't Minnesota, but the folks who participate are still crazy for donning swimsuits and splashing around in

This strolling New Orleans street band is a highlight of the Pensacola Jazzfest.

Photo: Arts Council of NW Florida

the Gulf of Mexico on New Years' Day — what a way to start the year! After the dip, the participants run into the Flora-Bama and start drinking heavily — supposedly to warm up. You can watch or participate for free.

WINTER BIRD COUNT
Big Lagoon and Perdido Key State Recreation Areas
Perdido Key 492-1595

After a big party on New Year's Eve, many Insiders can't think of anything they'd rather do than be at one of the parks at 6 AM to watch for the annual winter migration of birds — hey, some people think this is big fun. You'll be in good company with members of the Audubon Society, and you'll actually be part of a scientific study. Avid birders will want to bring binoculars, and everybody needs to dress for the weather.

SNOW FEST
Quietwater Beach Boardwalk
Pensacola Beach 932-2259

Some local kids have never seen snow, so here's their opportunity to see (and feel) what it's like. The Santa Rosa Island Authority sponsors the two-day fest, with lots of artificial snow, food vendors, crafts and ice and sand sculpture contests.

MARTIN LUTHER KING JR. PARADE
Downtown Pensacola 434-2431

This annual parade begins at Government and Spring streets at 11 AM and winds its way around downtown, ending at the Martin Luther King Jr. Memorial Plaza on Palafox Street. The parade is a tribute to the civil rights leader and to all African Americans.

February

BRIDGE TO THE BEACH RUN
At the foot of the Bob Sikes Bridge
Gulf Breeze 434-2800

It's a quickie . . . from the foot of the bridge up and over to Pensacola Beach, where runners are met with food, refreshments and live entertainment. The run is sponsored by the Pensacola Sports Association with help from the Santa Rosa Island Authority.

BLUE ANGEL MARATHON
Naval Air Station Pensacola 452-2843

This grueling 26.2 mile run is a qualifier for the big one in Boston. Skaters, bikers and walkers also join in the fun through the most scenic places on the Navy base starting in front of Building 632, out onto Barrancas Avenue, then into downtown and back again. Whew! There's a smaller 5K run in the morning, and together, about 1,700 runners take the challenge.

MARDI GRAS
Pensacola Beach 932-2259

A champagne breakfast and street dance, a street parade and a huge pot of red beans and rice for all are just a few of

Saturday and Sunday at the Great Gulfcoast Arts Festival are so crowded that it's hard to get a look at everything. If possible, try to make it over on Friday afternoon for a few hours. That's when the serious buyers make their rounds, plus you'll have the best selection to choose from if *you're* buying.

Insiders' Tips

the annual events sponsored by the Krewe of Wrecks of Pensacola Beach.

MARDI GRAS CELEBRATION
Downtown Pensacola   934-0337

The Krewe of Lafitte Parade, the Grand Mardi Gras Parade and the Fat Tuesday celebration all take place downtown. Mardi Gras Balls for the most part are by invitation only, but everyone can participate in the costume contests and the Priscus Procession, a costumed drink-'til-you-drop bar hop.

March

SPRING BREAK
Beaches at Pensacola,
Navarre and Perdido Key   932-2259

When some Florida cities that traditionally hosted the annual migration of college students turned their attention elsewhere, Northwest Florida beaches welcomed them heartily. In past years, free concerts by Bruce Hornsby, Starship and Toto brought 100,000 people to Pensacola Beach. Overstressed residents nixed the concert idea, but spring breakers can still fill their days and nights with activities and entertainment of all sorts.

MOBILE HISTORIC HOMES TOUR
Mobile, Ala.   (334) 438-6936

Each March, when the city is decked out in azaleas and dogwoods for spring, the doors to some of Mobile's finest homes open to welcome visitors. The two-day event features more than 20 homes representing architectural styles from Creole cottages and Federal-style townhomes to Greek Revival mansions and turn-of-the-century Victorian and Neoclassical homes. Day and evening candlelight tours offer varying perspectives on the homes; homeowners are your tour guides. Tour

prices vary from $10 to $40; some include progressive dinners, with one course per house that includes a tour.

GALLERY NIGHTS
Downtown Pensacola   432-9906

The Arts Council of Northwest Florida sponsors this thrice-yearly celebration of the arts in Pensacola. Downtown art galleries, frame shops, bookstores, art supply stores, dance troupes, poets, literary groups and even a few advertising people put on the dog for locals and visitors. DADA Express buses take gallery-goers to each of the 16 or so stops along the tour route; you may park your car and walk with a self-guided tour map. Most businesses serve refreshments and offer some type of entertainment, from string quartets to poetry readings. Merchants pick up the tab for the whole thing. All you have to do is show up!

ELBERTA SAUSAGE FESTIVAL
Elberta City Park
Elberta, Ala.   (334) 986-5987

For some reason Elberta has attracted a large contingent of German residents; parts of this tiny downtown look like something out of an Old World picture book. But this twice-yearly festival attracts people from all over, and they come for one thing — German sausage. Not just any German sausage, this foot-long, locally made variety could just be the best you've ever eaten.

Giant outdoor grills are set up in the park near downtown, and the lines for sausages never seem to get any shorter — maybe because people return three and four times! And while you're standing in line, or while you're trying your best to eat this monstrosity without getting too much mustard on your chin, there are cloggers, jug bands, clowns, arts and crafts and other silly and fun entertainment. It's more a celebration of sausage than German heritage, but nobody seems to mind.

Elberta is about an hour's drive from Pensacola — a straight shot along Highway 98 W. Cross over the Lillian Bridge (Lillian, Alabama) and Elberta is another 15 to 20 minutes.

St. Patrick's Day Celebration and Kite Contest
Pensacola Beach   932-2259

The beach bars, of course, have their annual Pub Crawl, complete with green beer. A kite decorating contest is now incorporated into the walking parade and other various celebratory functions.

Scratch Ankle Festival
Riverwalk, Downtown Milton   623-9418

OK, so the name's a little funny. This is an annual spring celebration of Milton's heritage that goes back to a time when Milton was called "Scratch Ankle" for the numerous stickers and sand spurs that infested the area. Food vendors, arts and crafts and live entertainment along the scenic Blackwater River are part of what is probably Milton's largest annual festival.

Pre-Easter Egg Hunt
Casino Beach
Pensacola Beach   932-2259

Here's one for the kiddies, sponsored by the beach merchants and the Island Authority. The hunt is held to the right of the Casino Beach bathhouse.

Do It In The Sand Volleyball
Pensacola Beach   944-4091

One volleyball tournament a month is held at Casino Beach from March through September. This is a chance to see some great playing while the sand flies.

April

British Car Show
Casino Parking Lot
Pensacola Beach   478-3171

A group of British car enthusiasts loves to show off its classic British motor cars at shows and in parades; this particular show may become an annual event.

Photo: Robin Rowan

A woodwind trio entertains at Bayfront Gallery during Gallery Night in downtown Pensacola.

SATURDAY IN THE
PARK CONCERT SERIES

Big Lagoon State Recreation Area
Near Perdido Key   492-1595

The first of four concerts in April features jazz bands, symphonies and local choirs in the scenic splendor of the Big Lagoon amphitheater. Call the park's main number for more information on performers and tickets.

PICNICS IN THE PLAZA

Plaza Ferdinand
Downtown Pensacola   434-5371

The Picnics in the Plaza series got its start as a way to lure downtown workers out into the sunshine during lunchtime to enjoy the beautiful weather and free live entertainment. A different local band or entertainer is featured every Friday through mid-May.

JAZZ JAM

Quietwater Beach Boardwalk
Pensacola Beach   932-2259

Jazz Jam offers a two-day festival at "the shell," the amphitheater on the boardwalk, featuring the best in local and regional live jazz and blues bands.

PENSACOLA JAZZFEST

Seville Square
Downtown Pensacola   474-2327

Sponsored by the local public radio station, WUWF-FM and other corporate sponsors, the three-day festival brings in the best of local and regional jazz and blues acts. This is an intimate, top-quality production for all ages. Seating is limited, so you may want to bring your own lawn chairs. The kickoff is Friday evening, where sponsors are recognized, and a party atmosphere prevails. Tickets for Friday only are $3. Cost is $5 for either Saturday or Sunday, and if you want to attend both Saturday and Sunday, tickets are $9.

EARTH DAY CELEBRATION

Quietwater Beach Boardwalk and
Island-wide, Pensacola Beach   932-2259

If you're concerned for Mother Earth, this free celebration provides you with a chance to help. Listen to live music, visit environmental displays, eat health food, sign petitions against oil drilling in the Gulf or get involved with causes like preserving the last tract of county-owned public beach acreage. Betcha if you spend 30 minutes here, you'll find out something you didn't know. You'll also see lots of long hair and tie-dyes, but it's the beach, man!

EARTH DAY CELEBRATION

Big Lagoon State Recreation Area
Near Perdido Key   492-1595

Guided tours by park rangers, environmental exhibits, nature walks and more will teach you about this delicate coastal environment and about one of Florida's most scenically diverse parks. Admission to the park is $3.25 per vehicle.

Insiders' Tips

If you particularly enjoy one of the area's festivals, contact the sponsors and the organizers and tell them so. Most organizers welcome input from the public and strive to make each festival better every year.

Photo: Arts Council of NW Florida

Warming up before a performance by The Airmen of Note at the Pensacola Jazzfest.

MULLET TOSS

Flora-Bama Lounge
Perdido Key at the State Line   492-0611

The wacky locals are at it again, trying to make the *Guinness Book of World Records* by tossing mullet across the state line from Florida to Alabama. Unfortunately, Guinness refuses to recognize mullet tossing as a viable record for the book, so the pure enjoyment of the sport will have to suffice for the Flora-Bama crowd. As you might expect, these antics are free to the public.

May

SPRINGFEST

Downtown Pensacola   477-8998

The warm weather's arrived for good, the flowers are blooming, the sun is shining and the streets of downtown Pensacola are alive with music, dancing and people! SpringFest marks its fifth year in 1995, billed as a musical and cultural celebration, and each year seems to get better. The first year showcased the performances of local jazz, blues, rock and

acoustic performers, and the response was so positive that SpringFest sponsors brought in some heavy-hitters: The Fabulous Thunderbirds, Roger McGuinn (former lead singer of The Byrds), Bo Diddley, Joan Baez, Clarence "Gatemouth" Brown, the Neville Brothers and Maria Muldaur in addition to the local groups. A Fine Arts & Masters Show adds another facet to this weekend-long event. More than 70,000 are expected to attend SpringFest, which closes off all major thoroughfares in downtown to set up huge sound stages. SpringFest may turn out to be one of Northwest Florida's very best offerings.

ASSOCIATION OF VOLLEYBALL PROFESSIONALS MILLER LITE PRO-BEACH VOLLEYBALL TOURNAMENT

Casino Beach
Pensacola Beach   932-2259

These are the real pros, who provide plenty of action for spectators. The event is also nationally televised. Hi, Mom! It's also free.

CINCO DE MAYO

Quietwater Beach Boardwalk and
Island-wide, Pensacola Beach   932-2259

This Spanish-influenced festival features Latin performers, arts and crafts and, of course, *food*! Admission is free.

SATURDAY IN THE
PARK CONCERT SERIES

Big Lagoon State Recreation Area   492-1595

A variety of entertainers perform at the park's open amphitheater. Call for featured entertainers and tickets.

FIREMATICS COMPETITION

Casino Parking Lot
Pensacola Beach   932-2259

This frenetic competition pits fire department teams against each other in a series of timed events. In the fire brigade competition, teams must try to put out a simulated burning building — by handing buckets of water down a line and throwing them on the fire! The busted hose competition means that the hose springs a leak; each team must find, clamp and replace the hose, get the water back on and hit a target before time runs out! Aside from being good for a few laughs, the competition helps to train both paid and volunteer fire departments. Trophies are awarded. Come and watch — it's all free.

BRITISH FESTIVAL

Seville Square
Downtown Pensacola   456-5474

The British Festival is a celebration of Pensacola's British heritage (loosely interpreted, that means all of Great Britain) with strolling costumed actors, native foods (yes, there will be tea and crumpets), crafts and music.

CAMPFIRE PROGRAM

Big Lagoon State Recreation Area
Near Perdido Key   492-1595

After the Saturday in the Park performances, right around sunset, park rangers put on their own shows covering a variety of topics on natural Florida. Programs are held after the concerts May through June. Admission charge to the park is $3.25 per vehicle.

JUBILEE'S LOBSTER FEST

Quietwater Beach Boardwalk
Pensacola Beach   934-3108

How do I love thee, lobster? Jubilee Restaurant sponsors the annual event, believes there are enough serious lovers of the popular crustacean that they go to a great deal of trouble for this event. Live Maine lobsters are shipped here on a special flight. A refrigerated truck meets it on the runway in Pensacola, where the lobsters are taken to the restaurant and kept very cold until cooking time. The live lobsters (about 1.5 pounds each) are stuffed into net bags along with baby new potatoes, corn-on-the-cob, fresh clams and Andouille Cajun sausage and tossed into a Cajun boil. To complement your meal, there's live entertainment and children's activities. Proceeds go to a local children's charity.

Insiders' Tips

Look in the *Weekender* magazine, appearing in the *Pensacola News Journal* every Friday, for listings of special events, concerts, festivals and attractions for the upcoming week.

June

DE LUNA LANDING,
FIESTA OF FIVE FLAGS

Quietwater Beach
Santa Rosa Island   433-6512

Don Tristan de Luna, a Spaniard, and a contingent of 1,400 colonists disembarked at Pensacola in August 1559, hoping to build the first settlement in the New World. After just a few weeks, a hurricane tore through Pensacola, destroying most of the ships and the provisions. However, the fate of the mission isn't important. What is important is that we were first, a fact of which Pensacolians are fiercely proud. The loosely historical re-enactment of the landing is fun (and free) for both the actors and onlookers.

FIESTA OF FIVE FLAGS

Various locations throughout
the Pensacola area   433-6512

Pensacola's own celebration of a rich heritage under five flags (Spanish, French, British, Confederate and United States) might be more fun for locals than visitors, but there are plenty of parades, contests and balls to go around. A British Street Party, fishing tournaments, the Fiesta Mass, a yacht parade, a Confederate Encampment, outdoor concerts and treasure hunts highlight the 10-day festival. And all the while, a tacky 10-foot statue of Don Tristan de Luna, held to the ground with painfully visible buckets of concrete and ropes, peers out at festival-goers from a downtown median. Most events are free. A treasure hunt nets the finder $5,000 in cash and prizes. Wow, that's worth practicing for!

CHILDREN'S TREASURE HUNT
AND SANDCASTLE CONTEST

Quietwater Beach
Santa Rosa Island   433-6512

What fun for the kids! Building sand castles and finding treasures on the beach could win them prizes. The contests are part of the Fiesta of Five Flags celebrations.

PENSACOLA INTERNATIONAL
BILLFISH TOURNAMENT

Bayfront Auditorium
Downtown Pensacola   453-4638

The Pensacola Big Game Fishing Club sponsors this tournament, held over the July 4th weekend. Prizes are awarded to the largest catch in several divisions: Billfish (blue marlin, white marlin, sailfish); Tuna, Wahoo and Dolphin; Ladies; and Junior Anglers. Although participating in the tournament must be great fun, the weigh-ins at the auditorium are the real crowd-pleasers. Spectators gather around sunset to watch the huge charter boats dock and unload the day's catches, which are hoisted up on the scales for everyone to ogle.

EVENINGS IN OLDE SEVILLE SQUARE

Seville Square, Pensacola   438-6505

Come enjoy a superb series of outdoor concerts under the oaks in historic Seville Square. Jazz, country, bluegrass,

New to the community? Area special events are some of the best ways to get a feel for the atmosphere of a city, meet new people and enjoy yourself at the same time!

Insiders' Tips

blues and many other types of music are presented every Thursday throughout the summer months. Many concert-goers come early, bring a picnic and make a night of it. The concerts are well attended, so bring your blankets and lawn chairs and arrive early. Concerts are simulcast on the local public radio station, WUWF-FM. This is a wonderful family evening of entertainment that's absolutely free.

BATTLE OF MOBILE BAY RE-ENACTMENT
Fort Gaines Historic Site
Dauphin Island, Ala.   *(334) 861-6992*

"Damn the torpedoes! Full speed ahead!" commanded Admiral David Farragut during the daring 1864 battle. See it recreated before your eyes and enjoy a special candlelight tour of the fort while you're there. Admission to Fort Gaines is $2 for adults, $1 for children 7 to 12, and free for kids younger than 7.

NAVARRE CHAMBER OF COMMERCE FUN FEST
Navarre Beach 939-2691, (800) 480-SAND

This is two full days of bands, eats, arts, crafts, fireworks and even more ways to play. The Fest starts getting festive just as soon as you cross the Navarre Beach Bridge (and pay your 25¢ toll).

July

JULY 4TH FIREWORKS
Casino Beach, Santa Rosa Island   932-2259

Come early and bring lawn chairs and a cooler. Better yet, bring your boat and watch the fireworks from the water. Also bring a boom box, if you have one, since one of the radio stations plays patriotic music, which is supposed to be synchronized with the fireworks. It only sort of works, but it's nice to have the musical accompaniment anyway. There's no admission fee.

SERTOMA'S JULY 4TH
Seville Square
Downtown Pensacola   476-0042

Local Sertoma Clubs put together this two-day family celebration, culminating with the fireworks show on the 4th. One spectacular show is held at the beach and the other in the historic district downtown for folks who don't want to travel all the way to the beach. The two fireworks shows are staggered; when the show on the beach ends, the show in town begins. The in-town show (along the bayfront) is also accompanied by patriotic music on one of the local radio stations. All this sparkling entertainment is free.

RIVERFEST
The Riverwalk and Willing St.
Milton   623-2339

Milton's historic downtown along the beautiful Blackwater River is the setting for free water skiing shows, a children's festival, a boat parade, arts and crafts and plenty of food. The Riverwalk is a fairly recent addition to downtown. Now visitors can stroll along wooden boardwalks to a covered gazebo right on the water. All this family fun is free.

PENSACOLA BEACH AIR SHOW WITH THE BLUE ANGELS
Gulfside, Pensacola Beach   452-2583

Thousands congregate to witness the aerial artistry of the Pensacola-based Blues stunt-flying team. It's quite a good show (and free to boot), but be warned that you'll be stuck in traffic for a while afterwards. Better to plan a day at the beach so you won't have to move from your spot on the sand.

GALLERY NIGHTS
Downtown Pensacola   432-9906

Come be a part of this Friday evening

celebration of the arts in downtown Pensacola. Shops stay open until 9 PM and invite the public in for a free tour, refreshments and entertainment.

WINE FESTIVAL
Quietwater Beach Boardwalk
Pensacola Beach 934-3108

Pay one price and get your fill of more than 175 different wines from 150 wineries worldwide. Several winery representatives are on hand to talk to patrons about the wines. Each winery donates a magnum of wine with a signed label to be auctioned off, with all proceeds going to charity.

August

BUSHWACKER FESTIVAL
Quietwater Beach Boardwalk
Pensacola Beach 934-3108

The Bushwacker is a local drink that tastes something like a milkshake with a kick (there are a few kinds of alcohol tossed in). It's cold, frothy and refreshing, and that's about all you need to build a festival around. Pull in some local en-

tertainers, print up a few souvenir cups, add a few events such as the 5K Capt'n Fun Run for charity, invite 33,000 of your closest friends, and voila! A festival is born.

BAR-B-Q RIB BURNOFF
Pensacola Civic Center
Downtown Pensacola 432-0800

What can people be thinking? Fifteen barbecue grills all cranked up and cooking in the asphalt parking lot of the Civic Center in August? If you love barbecue so much that you're willing to put up with the heat, then don't miss this one. There are activities (in a grassy area we hope) and a raffle. There is no admission charge.

September

SANTA ROSA COUNTY FAIR
Santa Rosa Industrial Park
Milton 623-2339

The big draw to this fair is the two-day rodeo, where bronco-busting and calf roping elicit plenty of whoops and hollers from the enthusiastic audience. Carnival rides, food and live entertainment fill out the five-day celebration.

Photo: McDonnell Douglas Corp.

The Blue Angels perform for the hometown crowd on Pensacola Beach twice a year.

LABOR DAY FIREWORKS

Casino Beach, Santa Rosa Island 932-2259

Pick a beach or a boat for fireworks-watching the Sunday before Labor Day — you can see the display from all over the beach area. This event is sponsored by the Santa Rosa Island Authority.

INTERNATIONAL BILLFISH TOURNAMENT

Orange Beach Marina
Orange Beach, Ala. **(334) 981-4407**

Even if you don't care a whit for fishing, the Orange Beach Marina is a spectacle in itself and moreso during a fishing tournament. Slips are jammed with multimillion-dollar yachts and pleasure boats of all descriptions. Men and women run around in Izod polos sporting plenty of gold jewelry. In short, it's a tournament for the well-heeled and a spectator sport for the rest of us.

FAMILY EXPO

Pensacola Civic Center
Downtown Pensacola 432-1222

This is a trade show for families. Pick up information on various family-related topics, fill a shopping bag with giveaways, ask questions about particular services, sit in on demonstrations and short seminars. Topics range from "How to Talk to Your Teenager" to "Family Stress: Keeping it Under Control." Kids have a variety of activities of their own to keep them busy — costumed characters stroll around talking to children, and a special celebrity makes an appearance. Daycare is provided. The response to the first Expo was overwhelming, so the plan is to expand it

in upcoming years. The family-friendly expo is free.

BEACH AND SHORE CLEAN-UP

Big Lagoon State Recreation Area
Near Perdido Key 492-1595

Dedicated volunteers arrive at various coastal locations throughout Northwest Florida to pick up trash and learn more about the preservation of our delicate coastal environment. It may not sound like much fun, but it really can be. The park rangers keep track of how many bags of trash are collected and from where, what are the most unusual items collected, etc. The media almost always shows up to talk with volunteers and park rangers, and a very upbeat, positive atmosphere prevails. It's a great way for children to learn about ecology and preservation of our most precious natural resource.

JUBILEE LOBSTER FEST

Quietwater Beach Boardwalk
Pensacola Beach 934-3108

This is a mini-version of the blowout in June, featuring live Maine Lobsters cooked to perfection. Yummmm.

GNU ZOO ARTS REVIEW

The ZOO 939-2691
Hwy. 98 E., Gulf Breeze (800) 480-SAND

The area's most talented artists create their own images of zoo animals or flora from the extensive botanical gardens. The works are put on display, patrons purchase tickets and then enjoy wine and hors d'oeuvres while selecting that just-right zebra watercolor for the foyer.

Insiders' Tips

It is still customary in Pensacola for traffic to stop to allow funeral processions to pass.

SEAFOOD FESTIVAL
Quietwater Beach Boardwalk
Pensacola Beach   433-6512

The person who thought that setting up a bunch of food booths and barbecue grills in an asphalt parking lot on a hot September weekend was a good idea probably stayed in the sun too long. Yet, people still flock to the beach by the thousands for this event, perhaps to enjoy the weather and the free live entertainment. It doesn't cost anything to go, and if you get too hot, you can always jump in the water, which is never very far away.

SEAFOOD FESTIVAL
Seville Square, Pensacola   433-6512

Now, for folks who don't like sand in their shoes, this version of the popular festival is more like it — shade, giant oak trees and the pleasant and historic atmosphere of Seville Square. Bands set up in the quaint gazebo in the park, and folks tend to linger a little longer at the many arts and crafts booths when they're out of the hot sun. Besides the fresh seafood cooked many wonderful ways, there's a children's activity area, an antique show and a 5K run.

JUANA'S GOOD TIME REGATTA
Navarre Beach   939-2691, (800) 480-SAND

Juana's is a local hangout in a tiki hut, but most important is its location right on the Intracoastal Waterway. Come on down for three days of catamaran racing and beach competitions.

October

TERN FEST
Navarre Beach   939-2691, (800) 480-SAND

Navarre Beach is one of the last sanctuaries for the endangered Least Tern, so this celebration centers around enlightening the public about the little beach bird with a host of events and exhibits.

ST. ANNE'S ROUND-UP
St. Anne's Catholic Church, 5200 Saufley Field Rd., Pensacola   456-5966

Why this church's fund-raiser has become so popular is a mystery, but it must have something to do with good public relations. The grounds of the church are enormous, big enough to build an entire little western town on. During the three-day event, you can witness shoot-outs, stuff yourself with lots of rich food or listen to the many entertainers. Heather Locklear and John Ritter have graced the stage in past years. All it costs is a buck for parking.

GULF SHORES SHRIMP FESTIVAL
Gulf Shores, Ala.   (334) 968-7511

Barbecued, braised, broiled, buttered, battered and on-a-stick — eat shrimp to your heart's delight at this festival on the public beach area at the dead-end of Highway 59 in Gulf Shores. Entertainment, arts and crafts, a parade and other beach activities are interspersed between bouts of overeating. The activities are free.

HISPANIC HERITAGE FESTIVAL
Quietwater Beach Boardwalk
Pensacola Beach   932-3560

You'll enjoy this free festival with everything Latin — food, music and crafts — celebrating Pensacola's Hispanic heritage.

ELBERTA SAUSAGE FESTIVAL
Elberta City Park
Elberta, Ala.   (334) 986-5987

If you missed it in the spring, here's one more opportunity to savor the best German sausage in the South! Continuous live entertainment, dancing and arts and crafts are featured — for free. Bring a few bucks and a big appetite.

BEATLES ON THE
BEACH FALL FESTIVAL
Pensacola Beach   932-2259

Buttons, T-shirts, old records, Beatles look-alike contests, entertainers playing Beatles tunes and touring Beatles sound-alike bands highlight this free event.

INTERNATIONAL FALL FESTIVAL
St. Rose of Lima Parish
515 W. Park Ave., Milton   623-3600

This festival with its international flavor attracts hundreds of people from all over the area. Sample food from several countries, try your skill at Scottish or Greek games, listen to traditional music from other countries, or pick your merry way through the throngs of people to the crafts booths. No admission is charged.

GRAND FESTIVAL OF ART
Marriott's Grand Hotel, Hwy. 98
Point Clear, Ala.   (334) 928-2228

This is a grand celebration of art, with quality works for sale. There are also fun children's activities. Both the beautiful drive over from Pensacola (just follow Highway 98) and the historic Grand Hotel on Mobile Bay are worth the trip.

PENSACOLA INTERSTATE FAIR
Pensacola Fairgrounds, Mobile Hwy.
Pensacola   944-4500

More than just prize cattle and beets with thyroid conditions, this fair features an amazing number of rides for all ages, games of chance and skill, plenty of sweets and fatty foods, exhibit buildings and nationally known entertainers (mostly country acts). Lee Greenwood, The Judds, Kenny Rogers, Waylon Jennings, Ray Stevens and Diamond Rio have all performed in past years. The admission charge is $5 for adults, $3 for 3 to 11 year olds, $1 for parking. All proceeds go the Florida Highway Patrol. Six hundred thousand people a year attend the 10-day fair.

HAUNTED HOUSE WALKING
TOUR OF SEVILLE SQUARE
Seville Historic District
Downtown Pensacola   433-1559

This walking tour of the district's haunted places will send chills up your spine whether the weather outside is frightful or not. Listen to the tales of the Charbonier House (1885), whose family members suffered "rage, lunacy and torment." The local Jaycees, who used the house for their Halloween haunted house, reported doors closing, floating and exploding lights and other mystifying occurrences. At his house on Seville Square, the spirit of Thomas Moristo Gray paces the floors and drags his old sea bag up and down stairs. The architectural firm now occupying the house reports chairs rolling across the floor by themselves, strange smells, footsteps on the stairs and doors opening. Find out more by taking the tour, sponsored by the Pensacola Historical Society. Tickets are $3 for adults, $1.50 for children. Reservations are necessary for this popular tour!

November

GREAT GULFCOAST ARTS FESTIVAL
Seville Square, Pensacola   438-4081

This is absolutely the finest arts festival Northwest Florida has to offer. Two hundred artists are chosen from across the country for this juried show to display their wares in historic Seville Square. Artists are chosen for the quality of their work as well as for variety. On display are handmade instruments and furniture pieces, exquisite jewelry, whimsical toys, photography and ceramics — it's more diverse than most any other show on the

Photo: Dave Sanders

The Pensacola State Fair brings in top country music acts and Gooding's Million Dollar Midway each October.

Gulf Coast and a good time to start your Christmas shopping! Food, a children's area and continuous live entertainment (all free) could keep you there all day. If you choose only one festival to attend this year, make this the one.

VETERANS' DAY PARADE

Pensacola Beach   932-2259

Saluting veterans from World War I on, the parade is sponsored by the Pensacola Beach Elks Lodge and the Santa Rosa Island Authority.

GALLERY NIGHTS

Downtown Pensacola   432-9906

Downtown arts-related businesses open their doors to the public for a celebration of arts and culture. Free buses take gallery-goers to each stop along the tour. There is no admission charged.

POARCH CREEK INDIANS THANKSGIVING DAY POW WOW

Poarch Reservation
Near Atmore, Ala.   (334) 368-9136

The Poarch Creek and other regional tribes congregate on the Poarch Reservation to cook Thanksgiving dinner for visitors and share their culture, their songs and their dances. More than 8,000 show up for the Pow Wow, where tribes compete against one another for $5,000 in cash prizes. It's a rare opportunity to witness a culture vastly different from our own, enjoy the beautifully detailed costumes and cheer on the dancers.

Several booths are set up selling handmade jewelry, handwoven ponchos, toys and crafts. Tickets for the festivities are $3 for adults, with children 6 and younger admitted free. If you'd like to have Thanksgiving dinner, it's $4.50 for turkey and dressing, $3 for a chicken dinner. Seating is often a problem for dinner, so the festival organizers suggest you bring your own lawn chairs. There's free parking and shuttle service provided.

After a 5K run at 8 AM, the gates for the Pow Wow open at 9 AM. The festival continues until 5 PM. Take Highway 29 N. into Atmore and turn left at the Church's Chicken (Jack Springs Road). The reservation is on your left.

DEPOT DAYS

Henry St. at the Railroad Tracks
Milton   623-8493

The free two-day festival gets bigger

every year with the resurgence of interest in the restored Milton Depot as the West Florida Railroad Museum. Besides pony rides, continuous musical entertainment, crafts, a kiddie carousel and the Orbitron space exerciser, a restored L&N boxcar is open for public viewing. Three other railroad cars near the Depot await restoration funding.

BLUE ANGELS
HOMECOMING AIR SHOW
Sherman Field
Pensacola Naval Air Station   452-2583

The Blues perform on their own turf every November, a free show that concludes their season. The show begins at 11 AM but is tied in to other activities on the base, including a display of more than 60 military aircraft.

BAYOU HILLS RUN
Bayview Park, Pensacola   432-1768

The 10K course winds its way around Bayou Texar (pronounced Ta-HAR) beginning at 8 in the morning. If you're not that ambitious, there's a 2-miler at 9:30 AM. The run benefits the Creative Learning Center.

THE FRANK BROWN
INTERNATIONAL SONGWRITERS' FESTIVAL
Various Locations Along the Florida
and Alabama Gulf Coasts   (334) 981-7325

The week-long event celebrates noted songwriters (some Grammy winners) and many local writers performing at local lounges. Two Songwriters' Seminars are sponsored by BMI and ASCAP, a "Legends of Songwriters" concert is held at the end of the week, and two songwriters' contests award cash and college scholarships. What began as an event for local lounge lizards has exploded into a nationally recognized event. Sponsored by chambers of commerce of the Perdido Key Area, the Greater Gulf Coast and Orange Beach.

MARKETBASKET
Bayfront Auditorium
Pensacola   438-4040

It's a fund-raiser for the Junior League of Pensacola, but the show is a veritable wonderland of Christmas gifts. More than 50 local and national merchants display food items (lots of sampling), jewelry, art work, books, clothing and holiday decorations. If yours is one of the first 50 children to arrive, he or she will be treated to breakfast with Santa on Saturday. Tickets are $3 for adults, $1 for children 6 to 12; children younger than 6 get in free.

December

CHRISTMAS ON THE ISLAND
Island-wide, Pensacola Beach   932-2259

Highlights of this celebration are the annual Christmas Parade, a decorated Boat Procession and the Residential/Commercial Outdoor Decorating Contest. Call the Santa Rosa Island Authority for a complete schedule of events.

BLACKWATER HERITAGE TOUR
Milton Opera House, Willing St.
Milton   623-8493

The Heritage Tour takes you inside some of the restored businesses downtown as well as private residences throughout Milton's historic district. The first tour (5 PM) ends at the Imogene Theatre next to the Opera House, where a lavish dinner and live entertainment finish out the evening. The second tour begins at 2 PM Sunday. Tickets are $15 for both members of the Santa Rosa Historical Society and nonmembers.

MUSIC AT CHRIST CHURCH
Christ Episcopal Church, Wright
and Palafox Sts., Pensacola   432-5115

This free music series started in 1975, providing concerts of local and traveling performers. Although concerts are scheduled throughout the year, locals seem to flock to the annual Christmas concert series. Small orchestral ensembles, instrumental and vocal soloists and the Christ Church choir perform in the ethereal surroundings of this turn-of-the-century church. Donations are accepted and appreciated for the continuation of the concert series.

CHRISTMAS WALK
Seville Historic District
Pensacola   434-1234

The Seville area restaurants and merchants are decked out in Christmas finery to welcome visitors. Many feature great bargains, and most offer coffee, mulled wine or cider and cookies. The Pensacola Historical Museum is open to the public at no charge during the walk as are the house museums in Pensacola Historic Village.

WINTER WILDLIFE WONDERLAND
The ZOO
Hwy. 98 E.
Gulf Breeze   939-2691, (800) 480-SAND

The ZOO has never looked better than it does during the winter holidays, with a delightful light display of giant animals. Inside, holiday concerts and other festivities make it a great time to "Do the ZOO!"

DECEMBERFEST
Gulf Shores, Ala.   (334) 968-7511

You can get in shape for all the holiday partying at this month-long celebration featuring a Christmas tree lighting, fashion shows, boat parades and the Taste of the Tropics, a collection of food booths

and tasty delights from several area restaurants.

CHRISTMAS PARADES
Downtown Pensacola, Gulf Breeze and
Milton   434-1234

With downtowns decorated with twinkling lights and shop windows all aglow, the annual Christmas parades make their trek through downtown streets featuring marching bands, dance troupes, gaily decorated floats, gobs of parade throws and, of course, Santa.

PENSACOLA'S NUTCRACKER BALLET
Saenger Theatre
118 S. Palafox St., Pensacola   444-7686

A yearly event, the *Nutcracker* is a family favorite, performed by members of local dance troupes and other individuals fortunate enough to be selected in open auditions. The music, dancing and pageantry of the traditional holiday story will delight all ages. A special (shorter) children's performance happens on Saturday at 10 AM.

FIRST NIGHT PENSACOLA
Downtown Pensacola   434-2724

Music, dance, theater, improvisation, storytelling, workshops and a parade are just a small part of this alcohol-free New Year's Eve celebration encompassing most of downtown. Take the kids to the workshop where they can decorate hats and masks (so can grownups). Don your creations and get in line for the People's Procession down Palafox Street complete with giant puppets and other costumed revelers. Downtown businesses offer some kind of music or activity within, and the entire evening culminates with a spectacular laser light show at midnight to ring in the New Year. First Night buttons (your admission) are $5 in advance, $7 at the show.

Photo: Robin Rowan

Set sail in a Hobie Cat rented by the hour or the day.

Pensacola Area
Parks and Recreation

Taking on a subject as wide-ranging as recreation is a rather daunting task for a resort area. It seems any answer you'd get to "So, what do you do for fun around here?" qualifies for a listing. Herein, are some of the top picks for outdoor and indoor fun, which is by no means an exhaustive list. Some equipment rentals have been included to give you an idea of the vast amount of activities available to visitors.

New this year is the announcement of a possible minor league hockey team for Pensacola (yes, we said *hockey*), plus a $3 million soccer complex with 25 fields, which can accommodate up to 240 teams for tournaments. The complex, on the west side of town, opened in June 1995.

Golf

CLUB AT HIDDEN CREEK
3070 PGA Blvd., Holley-By-The-Sea
Navarre 939-4604

This semiprivate 18-hole, par 72 course is open to the public, off Highway 98 inside the Holley-By-The-Sea subdivision. Avail yourself of the pro shop, driving range, the restaurant and the snack bar. It's open from 6:30 AM to 6 PM every day.

CREEKSIDE GOLF
2355 W. Michigan Ave.
Pensacola 944-7969

Creekside is a fairly new 18-hole course on Pensacola's west side. Marcus Creek winds through the length of the course with oaks, cedars, pines and native wildlife all around. Creekside is open to the public starting at 8 AM every day and features a practice green, snack bar and a pro shop.

MARCUS POINTE GOLF CLUB
2500 Oak Pointe Dr.
Pensacola 484-9770

Tee off on 18 holes of championship golf, spread over 600 acres of rolling pine and oak woodlands with Bayou Marcus Creek bordering much of the course. Marcus Pointe hosted both the 1991 and 1992 PGA Pensacola Open tournaments. The full-service facility has practice greens and a clubhouse restaurant. The course is located off Highway 29 just 10 minutes north of downtown. The pro shop opens at 6 or 6:30 in the morning; tee times start at 7 AM.

THE MOORS
3220 Avalon Blvd.
Milton 995-4653

The Moors is one of the area's newest public golf courses, a mile north of I-10 at the Avalon Exit just 10 minutes from Pensacola. The Scottish- and Florida-style golf course features broad fairways and native grasses. The par 71 course is open to the public on a daily-fee basis every day except Christmas. There's a driving range and a lavish Tudor-style clubhouse with a pro shop, locker rooms and banquet facilities. Call three days in advance for tee times on weekends. The pro shop opens at 6:30 AM; tee times begin at 7 AM.

PERDIDO BAY RESORT
One Doug Ford Dr.
Pensacola   *492-1223, (800) 874-5355*

Home of the prestigious PGA Pensacola Open from 1978-1987, Perdido Bay Resort is just this side of Perdido Key. The resort encompasses a huge tract of land on the bay, an ideal setting for golf or just about anything else. Three of the back nine holes on this 7,154-yard tournament course were picked as some of the toughest on the 1987 PGA tour. Perdido Bay's pro shop opens at 6:30 AM; the practice range, putting and pitching greens and a snack bar are open starting with the first tee time at 7 AM.

TIGER POINT GOLF & COUNTRY CLUB
1255 Country Club Rd.
Gulf Breeze   *932-1333*

East and west facilities off Highway 98 offer 36 holes on Santa Rosa Sound. The newer east course highlights an island green on the fifth hole. The west course provides the nicest views and is especially challenging on the back nine.

The country club facility has two practice greens, a driving range, a pro shop and a good restaurant, all open to the public; tee times begin at 6:45 AM.

SCENIC HILLS COUNTRY CLUB
8891 Burning Tree Rd.
Pensacola   *476-0611*

An older semiprivate course recently updated by Jerry Pate, Scenic Hills is in an attractive residential area. Mature trees keep the links fairly shady even in the dregs of summer. The 6,689-yard, 18-hole course offers four sets of tees for all skill levels. A driving range, golf shop, clubhouse, swimming pool, children's pool and tennis courts are available to members and guests. Off of Nine-Mile Road in northeast Pensacola, the course is open to the public with the first tee time at 6:30 AM.

Golf Supplies and Equipment

EDWIN WATTS GOLF SHOP
5705 N. Davis Hwy.
Pensacola   *477-0519*

Nationally advertised proline golf equipment is Edwin Watts' forte. A golf expert is on staff to offer advice. It's open Monday through Friday 9:30 AM to 6 PM; Saturday 9 AM to 3 PM.

PLAY IT AGAIN SPORTS
6601 N. Davis Hwy., Tradewinds
Shopping Center
Pensacola   *477-7407*

Buy, sell or trade new and used equipment for golf and many other sports at

Insiders' Tips

Area community centers are packed with possibilities for recreation, crafts, games and field trips for all ages. If you're new to the community, your area rec center would be a great place to become involved and meet lots of neighbors!

Play It Again. It's open 10 AM to 7 PM Monday through Friday, 10 AM to 6 PM on Saturdays.

NEVADA BOB'S DISCOUNT GOLF
4350 Bayou Blvd., Pensacola   474-9844

Nevada Bob's features the best prices on proline golfing equipment, including clubs, clothing, balls, shoes, bags and accessories. They are also a full-service golf shop, offering club repair, custom club fitting, a putting green, even an indoor driving net. Look for them at the entrance to Cordova Square seven days a week from 9 AM to 7 PM Monday through Saturday and 12 to 4 PM on Sundays.

Charter Boats

SCUBA SHACK CHARTERS
719 S. Palafox St.
Pensacola   433-4319

Charter fishing trips, dive trips and moonlight excursions are offered courtesy of the 50-foot *Wet Dream* docked at Baylen Slip right behind the Scuba Shack. Trips are available year-round, weather permitting. Scuba Shack provides rod and reel, bait, ice and stringer for trolling or bottom fishing. Cost for a 6-hour trip is $50 per person; an 8-hour trip is $55. Pre-certified divers make visits to several sites out in the bay and the gulf. A typical two-tank dive is around $50 per person.

MORENO QUEEN
Perdido Pass Marina, Hwy. 182 E.
at Alabama Point Bridge   (334) 981-8499
Orange Beach, Ala.   (800) 981-4499

The *Moreno Queen* party boat takes individuals and groups out to try their luck in the Gulf of Mexico, for back bay fishing, trolling, bottom and inshore fishing. They supply everything you need to fish. Food and drink can be purchased on board. Half-day trips start at $35 for adults, $25 for children. If you don't care to fish, come along for the ride at the child's fare.

THE OUTCAST CHARTER DOCKS
Under the Perdido Pass Bridge
Orange Beach, Ala.   (334) 981-5453

Three boats are available for deep sea adventure: the 65-foot *Outcast*, the 52-foot *Adventure* or the 40-foot *Escape*. Six-hour trips are $50 per person for bottom fishing. Walk-ons and overnight trips are available too. They furnish bait, tackle, and ice — you bring the food and drinks.

DAEDALUS
Robert's Bayou, 6816 S. Bayou Dr.
Elberta, Ala.   (334) 986-7018

Take a tour of the extensive and scenic Perdido Bay from the 50-foot *Daedalus* sailboat. Salty Capt. Fred puts out the net to catch critters of all sorts, including shrimp and crabs, which are either set free or thrown into a delicious boil for all the riders to snack on! The good captain guarantees there will be no sea sickness and seems to have discovered the secret that he will be only too happy to pass along. Each sailing adventure can be personalized to the riders, from the music on board to the captain's stories of his own treks to Costa Rica, Mexico and Columbia to a moonlight tow where you're pulled along 200 feet behind the boat in a rubber raft! Nature tours and biology field trips are also available.

CHULAMAR
Docked at Boy On A Dolphin restaurant at the foot of the Pensacola Beach Bridge
Pensacola Beach   434-6977

Trips leave daily for individuals or groups. The *Chulamar* offers day and night fishing, party and moonlight cruises. All equipment and bait are furnished for fishing trips. During the winter months, full-day trips are required to get you far enough out to where the fish are biting. The 7 AM to 5 PM trip is $45 per person, $25 for children. The *Chulamar* will take your family or party out on a private chartered cruise for $250 for 2 hours; each additional hour is $75.

LO-BABY
Docked downtown at Pitt Slip Marina
Pensacola   *934-5285*

Fish, dive, cruise or frolic with the dolphins on this 22-passenger vessel. Captain G.K. Lough has been in the business for more than 20 years and loves to tell sea stories to his guests! Boating charters are tailor-made for your enjoyment. On board in the air conditioned cabin, you'll find music, a microwave and a coffee maker. From 2-hour boat rides to daylong fishing charters, the 40-foot *Lo-Baby* is ready to go. Capt. Lough recommends the 8- to 9-hour trolling and bottom fishing trip since it takes a few hours just to ride out to the reefs where

you can try your luck hooking snapper, grouper, triggerfish, Spanish mackerel, ling, ladyfish and bluefish. There's enough room in the front of the ship for "fifteen people who really like each other." All cruises are based on demand.

ROCKY TOP
Downtown at Pitt Slip Marina
Pensacola   *432-7536*

This one is especially for family fun, offering bottom fishing for king and Spanish mackerel, blue fish and little tunny. Half-day and all-day rates provide fishing for up to six passengers. Fishing license, bait and tackle are all included in the price. The *Rocky Top* runs spring to fall only; call for rates.

Amusement Centers

FAST EDDIE'S FUN CENTER
505 Michigan Ave. at "W" St.
Pensacola   *433-7735*

Get ready for a day your kids will thank you for. This is Pensacola's complete family fun park — rides, games, prizes, parties, food and snacks. Three

Photo: Bill Gonzalez

Southwind Marina on Perdido Key is one of many spots to refuel the boat — and the family. Several area marinas offer on-site restaurants and convenience items.

go-cart tracks, a gameroom with pool tables, air hockey and video games award high-scorers with redemption tickets that can be traded in for prizes. It's open during the summer months from noon until midnight; winter hours are 3 to 10 PM. There's no admission charge, just a cost to ride and play games.

GOOFY GOLF AMUSEMENT CENTER
3920 W. Navy Blvd.
Pensacola 456-6794

This peculiar amusement is decades old, but that's its charm. Windmills, goony birds and giant dinosaurs with glowing eyes lure you to try your luck at each of the nine-hole courses. There's a modern game room (with all the latest crash 'em/slash 'em video games) and batting cages in this small complex.

POPPY'S SUPERTRACK
Hwy. 98 E., Gulf Breeze 932-5487

Get ready to roll on this supercharged $1/8$-mile track! Besides the go-carts, Poppy's has volleyball courts and hosts birthday parties too. Pick up a brochure at any area visitor information center or hotel and get one free ride with the purchase of two regular rides. Poppy's is next to the ZOO.

Canoeing/Tubing

ADVENTURES UNLIMITED
Tomahawk Landing, 12 miles north of Milton, then 4 miles off Hwy. 87
Milton 623-6197, (800) 239-6864

You're really missing out on some of the best parts of Northwest Florida if you skip a trip down one of the inland rivers. Adventures Unlimited provides canoes, life jackets, paddles, camping gear, ice, refreshments and just about everything you could ever possibly need on a one-

day or overnight canoe trip. Cabins on Wolfe Creek and campsites are available for overnight stays; see our Pensacola Accommodations chapter for all the details. Canoe rentals start at $11 per person for a short trip; to completely outfit you for an overnight stay on the river is $40 per person.

BOB'S CANOES
On Munson Hwy. at the Coldwater
Creek Bridge 623-5457, (800) 892-4504

In business for more than two decades, Bob's Canoes sends you down the river in canoes, tubes, paddleboats and kayaks. Choose from Coldwater Creek, the East Fork of the Coldwater, Juniper Creek or the Blackwater River — all clear, cool and relatively shallow freshwater streams, perfect for beginners. A large waterfront pavilion at rental headquarters is available for picnics. Bob's provides canoes, paddles, life jackets, seat cushions and a trip up the river to your starting point. Rates start at $11 per person for a short trip, $12 for a day trip. Tube floats are $7 each, $4 for a cooler tube. Paddle boats, kayak trips and group rates are available.

BLACKWATER CANOE RENTAL
9 miles east of Milton
off Hwy. 90 623-0235, (800) 967-6789

Canoe, tube or kayak for a half-day or up to a three-day camping trip on the beautiful Blackwater River. Blackwater Canoe Rental provides all the necessities for getting you there; you supply your own camping equipment, eats and drinks. A short trip (1.5 hours paddling time plus stops) is $11 per person; a day trip (4 hours paddling) is $12. Children 12 and younger are free with two adults in one canoe. Overnight trips start at $17 per person. Call for reservations and directions.

Watersport Rentals

WAVERUNNER & JET SKI RENTALS
17100 Perdido Key Dr.
Perdido Key   492-7656

Rates here are by the hour and half-hour, and the staff will deliver to you! They're closed in the winter months.

CURIOSITY RENTALS
17100 Perdido Key Dr.
Perdido Key   492-2516, 492-1188

You may be curious about what some of these strange contraptions are, but the folks at Curiosity Rentals will explain all before you rent. Take the family out on a pontoon or ski boat, or pack the car for an outing with rods and reels, boogie boards and beach umbrellas. They offer one-stop rentals for outdoor adventure by the hour, half-day and daily. Curiosity Rentals is open 9 AM to 7 PM daily, earlier by appointment.

KEY SAILING
Quietwater Beach Boardwalk
Pensacola Beach   932-5520

Key Sailing is the watersports headquarters on the beach for parasailing, Waverunners, pontoon and sailboats. They close up shop in the winter.

RADICAL RIDES
444 Pensacola Beach Blvd. near the toll bridge
Pensacola Beach   934-9743

Take off on your own Jet Ski, jet boat, Waverunner, sailboat or sailboard from Radical Rides, advertised as the best rental bargains on the beach. Look for the tiny green hut (don't blink) next to Boy On A Dolphin restaurant. Radical Rides can also outfit you for volleyball or horseshoes and provides its own playground for the kids and a shady rest area for you. It's closed during the winter months.

Bike Rentals

PARADISE SCOOTER & BICYCLE RENTAL
715-A Pensacola Beach Blvd.
Pensacola Beach   934-0014

We call these bikes "beach cruisers," since they're especially made for the terrain on the beach: kind of short and squatty with big tires. Bike paths cover all of Pensacola Beach up to the Gulf Islands National Seashore boundaries. Riding into the Fort Pickens area comes highly recommended for some outstanding scenery and solitude. Motorized scooters are also available. Paradise is closed during the winter months; call for new rates by the hour, day or week.

Concert Halls and Arenas

The Pensacola area is truly blessed with a terrific variety of small, intimate theatres, coffeehouse clubs and auditoriums in addition to the Pensacola Civic Center, a 10,000-seat arena. Bob Dylan and Dan Fogelberg have both chosen the more intimate setting of the Bayfront Auditorium, while touring Broadway shows such as *Cats* and *Chicago* enjoy the plush surroundings of the historic Saenger Theatre. Jazz flutist Tim Weisberg likes the airy Blue Angels Atrium at the National Museum of Naval Aviation to stage a command performance.

The Pensacola Civic Center, in business for more than a decade, has played host to Pensacola's own basketball team, the Tornadoes (they have since moved their franchise elsewhere), but now hosts plenty of out-of-town visitors to its sporting events, roller and ice skating shows, monster truck exhibitions and trade shows. But where it really shines is in the sheer volume of concerts and big names Pensacola is able to draw. Pearl Jam performed their Rock for Choice concert here last year; Reba McIntyre has sold out two concerts in two years; the Civic Center was a stop on Traffic's comeback tour in 1994; Jimmy Page, Robert Plant, Van Halen and Tom Petty have all chosen Pensacola to first rehearse then kick off their international tours in 1995.

TICKETMASTER OUTLETS

Pensacola Civic Center Box Office	433-6311
Sound Shop Records	
University Mall	476-2533
Saenger Theatre Box Office	438-2787
NAS-Pensacola	452-4229

Community Centers

Many of these public recreational centers offer classes in dance, music, arts, crafts, sports or self-improvement. Most are located within area parks; all are available to residents. Please call 435-1770 for schedule information or hours of operation.

BAYVIEW COMMUNITY CENTER

Bayview Park, 20th Ave. and Lloyd. St.
Pensacola   435-1788

With a gorgeous view of Bayou Texar and a location right on the water in Bayview Park, this community center is popular for its dance classes (featuring jazz, tap, ballet, ballroom and belly!), gymnastics program, oil painting, after-school arts and crafts and Taekwondo classes in addition to many special events such as the annual Easter Egg Hunt.

BAYVIEW SENIOR CITIZENS CENTER

Bayview Park, 20th Ave. and Lloyd St.
Pensacola   435-1790

Right next to the community center, this senior center gets its members from AARP, Retired Railway Employees and other retiree groups, but is open to all seniors 50 and older. The building houses meeting rooms, a pool room (that's billiards), an art room, a music room, a social hall and a library/lounge area. Several programs and classes in activities such as stitchery, ballroom dancing and aerobics are offered.

BEACON CLUB

119 E. Church St., Pensacola   435-1791

The Beacon used to be a teen hangout in the '50s and '60s, and many high schools and social clubs use the old refurbished hall for reunions. The club, in the heart of the downtown historic district (across the street from Seville Quarter) has a large dance floor, a bar, a kitchen, an ice machine and a giant-screen TV with VCR hookup and a pool table. Rental is only $100 for a night.

E.S. COBB COMMUNITY CENTER

Sixth Ave. and Mallory St.
Pensacola   435-1792

Tumbling, cooking and baking, tennis, ceramics, Black History studies and Kid's Movie Nights are some of the activities available at this community center. Everybody can enjoy the free daily activities such as volleyball, shuffleboard, Ping-Pong, skating, basketball and video

Biking along the beach path down to Fort Pickens on Santa Rosa Island is a wonderful way to spend an afternoon. From Pensacola Beach, it's about a 9.5-mile journey, but the surroundings are exceptional, with both beachfront and wooded landscapes.

Insiders' Tips

Bayview Park, on Bayou Texar, is one of the Pensacola area's largest, with 30 acres of rolling hills, three playgrounds and several picnic shelters.

Photo: Rbain Rowan

games. Call about Cobb's many sports programs and special events.

CORINNE JONES CENTER
600 W. Government St., Pensacola   435-1793
This small center presents many programs for senior citizens, including ceramics, senior exercise, sewing and walking.

EAST PENSACOLA HEIGHTS CENTER
3208 E. Gonzalez St.
Pensacola   435-1794, 435-1770
Some of the classes offered in this refurbished 1919 recreational center are adult aerobics, folk dancing, quilting, art study and round dancing. The facility is also available for parties, meetings and receptions for just $15 an hour.

FRICKER CENTER
1121 W. DeSoto St., Pensacola   435-1795
Get fit with regular activities such as aerobics, jogging, weight training, karate, tumbling and basketball. Other offerings are arts and crafts for children,

gospel singing, adult basic education and bingo.

GULL POINT CENTER
7140 Old Spanish Tr. (at Creighton Rd.)
Pensacola   478-4301
Ladies' exercise, Walk for Life, Kenpo Karate, cheerleading and modeling are just as few of the offerings at Gull Point. Call about classes in art, special parents' nights out and recitals by the Gull Point Dancers.

SANDERS BEACH CENTER
913 S. "I" St., Pensacola   435-1798
With a beautiful view overlooking Pensacola Bay, Sanders Beach is in an older part of town with a public beach and picnic facilities nearby, two lighted tennis courts, a volleyball court, a boat ramp and a pier. Soccer classes, as well as classes in country and western dancing, tennis and ballroom dancing are available at the center.

SCOTT TENNIS CENTER

4601 Piedmont Dr. at Summit Blvd.
Pensacola 432-2939

Eighteen courts with lights, a pro shop, restrooms, lessons and major tournaments are all available to locals at this exceptional tennis facility in the Cordova Park area.

MALCOLM YONGE CENTER

925 E. Jackson St., Pensacola 435-1796

The Yonge center offers youth basketball, football, girls' slow pitch softball and many other youth programs throughout the year.

City Parks

There are nearly 100 parks within the city limits, featuring old fort sites, swimming pools, scenic overlooks on the bay and more. Below, just a few of our top picks.

BAYVIEW PARK

20th Ave. and Mallory St., Pensacola

This 30-acre park overlooks Bayou Texar and is probably the city's very best park, located in the heart of East Hill. Three separate playground areas provide enough equipment for a hoard of kiddies; covered picnic pavilions with barbecue grills are just perfect for family reunions or Sunday outings. There are four tennis courts lit for night play, a boat ramp, a huge over-the-water deck with piers (these are great for either fishing or duck feeding) and a recreation center.

CECIL T. HUNTER MUNICIPAL POOL

200 E. Blount St., Pensacola 435-1797

This public pool under the I-10 spur is open daily May through September from noon until 8 PM. Lessons are offered during the summer by Red Cross-certified instructors. Admission fee to the pool is $1 for adults (18 and older), 50¢ for children 4 to 17 and free for children younger than 4. Children younger than 10 must be accompanied by an adult. Season passes are available.

ADMIRAL MASON PARK

Ninth Ave. and Romana St., Pensacola

Wide and open and right on the bayfront, Admiral Mason is tops for kite flying. It is here where you'll find the Wall South, the half-scale replica of the Vietnam Veteran's Memorial in Washington, D.C.

PLAZA FERDINAND

Bounded by Government, Palafox, Zaragoza and Jefferson Sts., Pensacola

Plaza Ferdinand is the very centerpiece of the downtown historic district. It was here in a somber ceremony in 1821 that Andrew Jackson accepted Florida from Spain. This "passive" park (meaning there are no ball fields or playground equipment) with its lovely fountain also

---

The Pensacola Civic Center celebrates 10 years of great success in 1995 by bringing in some of the best names in the biz such as Reba McIntyre, Nine Inch Nails and Tom Petty. Reba McIntyre, Van Halen and Led Zeppelin pals Jimmy Page and Robert Plant spent time rehearsing in Pensacola before kicking off tours here.

Insiders' Tips

Marinas and Fish Camps

BAYOU CHICO MARINA
806 Lakewood Rd.
Pensacola   455-4552

BERKINS MARINA
3009 Barrancas Ave.
Pensacola   453-2031

BOY ON A DOLPHIN MARINA
400 Pensacola Beach Blvd.
Pensacola Beach   932-7954

HARBOR VIEW MARINE
1220 Mahogany Mill Rd.
Pensacola   453-3435

HARBOUR VILLAGE MARINA
600 S. Barracks St.
Pensacola   432-9620

HOLIDAY HARBOR MARINA
14500 Canal-A-Way
Perdido Key   492-0555

DUANE HOODLESS MARINE
110 Quinn St., Milton   623-3751

JIM'S FISH CAMP
3100 Highway 90, Pace   994-7500

LAFITTE COVE MARINA
1010 Fort Pickens Rd.
Pensacola Beach   932-9241

THE MARINA
715 Pensacola Beach Blvd.
Pensacola Beach   932-5700

MAC'S MARINA
2 Marietta Ave.
Pensacola   453-3775

MEL'S MARINA
300 Pensacola Beach Blvd.
Gulf Breeze   934-1005

MOORINGS OF PENSACOLA BEACH
655 Pensacola Beach Blvd.
Pensa cola Beach   932-0305

NICHOLS SEAFOOD AND MARINA
Baines Dr, off Robinson Point Rd.
Bagdad   623-3410

ORANGE BEACH MARINA
27075 Marina Rd.
Orange Beach, Ala.   (205) 981-4207

OYSTER BAR MARINA
13700 River Rd.
Perdido Key   492-3162

PENSACOLA SHIPYARD
700 S. Myrick St. on Bayou Chico
Pensacola   434-3548

PERDIDO PASS MARINA
27501 Perdido Beach Blvd.
Orange Beach, Ala.   (205) 981-6481

PORT ROYAL MARINA
Baylen St., Pensacola   438-8400

ROD AND REEL MARINA
10045 Sinton Dr., Pensacola   492-0100

RUBY'S FISH CAMP
Mobile Hwy. at Perdido River Bridge
Pensacola   no phone

SMITH'S FISH CAMP
E. Hwy. 90 at Escambia River Bridge
Pensacola   no phone

SOUTHWIND MARINA
10121 Sinton Dr.
Pensacola   492-0333

THE SWAMPHOUSE MARINA & LANDING
E. Hwy. 90, southwest of Escambia River Bridge
Pensacola   478-9906

THE LANDING MARINA
665 Palomar Dr.
Pensacola   456-0331

THE MOORINGS MARINA
655 Pensacola Beach Blvd.
Pensacola Beach   932-0305

hosts Picnics in the Plaza each Friday during lunch in October and May.

SEVILLE SQUARE
Bounded by Government, Adams, Zaragoza and Alcaniz Sts., Pensacola

The original city square, the Seville area is a virtual hub of festival activity throughout the year with its charming gazebo, giant oaks and shady sidewalks.

BARTRAM PARK
South of Seville Square, Pensacola

The small bayfront park just south of the main park at Seville Square is used primarily for smaller festivals such as the Crawfish Festival and as an overflow for larger festivals such as the Great Gulfcoast Arts Festival.

BAY BLUFFS PARK
Scenic Hwy. and Summit Blvd., Pensacola

Pensacola is fortunate enough to be the only city in Florida with its own bluffs — most likely because most of Florida is completely flat! These bluffs are gorgeous and now have scenic overlooks and stairs

built all the way to the foot of the bay (huff, huff).

JOHN HITZMAN/OPTIMIST PARK
Langley Ave. and Buford, Pensacola

This is a fine 16-acre park in northeast Pensacola with plenty of room to run. Since the Optimists had a hand in funding this park, the playground equipment is really first-class; ball fields with stadium bleachers and lots of large trees beckon visitors to linger.

EXCHANGE PARK
Lakeview Ave. and Watson, Pensacola

National softball tournaments are held at this large fenced-in park complete with good playground equipment, lights for night play, restrooms and a concession stand.

FORT GEORGE
Palafox and LaRua Sts., Pensacola

This is more of a historic site than a park, but it's worth a stop to read about the great 61-day siege of Pensacola in 1781, part of which took place right under where you're standing. Only a tiny

Public Boat Ramps

- 17th Avenue at Bayou Texar, Pensacola
- Cervantes St. bridge at Bayou Texar, Pensacola
- Bayview Park at Bayou Texar, Pensacola
- Hilliard St. on Bayou Chico, Pensacola
- Navy Point ramp on Bayou Grande at Sunset Bridge access road, Pensacola
- Sherman Cove ramp at Pensacola Naval Air Station, Pensacola
- Big Lagoon State Park on Gulf Beach Highway, Pensacola
- South end of Bob Sikes Bridge, Pensacola Beach
- Shoreline Park, Shoreline Drive, Gulf Breeze
- Fort Pickens Rd., Fort Pickens, Pensacola Beach
- Hwy. 184 at Quintet Bridge on Escambia River, Milton
- Cotton Lake Rd. off U.S. Hwy. 29 on Escambia River, Molino
- Carpenter Park, Munson and Broad St., Milton
- Fairground Rd. off Hwy. 182 on Escambia River, Molino

portion of the land was saved, and a few representative parts of the original fort are reproduced. The view of the entire down-town area to the bay from here gives you an idea of why this location was chosen to build a fort.

Pensacola Area
Arts and Culture

Since so many Pensacolians have moved here from other places, and many from major metropolitan areas, they are used to attending the ballet, the opera and the symphony. Our cultural awareness has been expanded by these new residents who see the need for a particular group and take it upon themselves to start one.

How very fortunate we are, too, to have the facilities and the savvy to attract Broadway productions, top-name entertainment and nationally recognized musicians and soloists to perform with our many choral, opera and symphony groups.

The following list of cultural groups is so extensive, you might think you're reading our Atlanta book! But, they're all vibrant parts of the Pensacola community. Enjoy!

Crafts

GULF COAST WEAVERS GUILD
9200 Chisholm Rd., Pensacola   477-0240

This guild provides an opportunity to learn or further your knowledge of weaving, spinning and basket-making through workshops, demonstrations and community exhibitions. Call for class schedules.

Dance

EXPRESSIONS IN DANCE
9708 N. Palafox St. (Ensley)
Pensacola   478-4749

Want to move those feet in graceful, joyous fashion? Then this group can help

Photo: Arts Council of NW Florida

The Choral Society never disappoints with their exhiliarating performance of The Messiah *each year.*

with dance instruction in tap, ballet and jazz for dancers from 4 years old to adult.

GULL POINT PERFORMING DANCERS, INC.
Gull Point Community Center, 7140 Old Spanish Trail Rd.
Pensacola   432-8965, 478-4301

Between 10 and 20 students, ages 10 to 17, are either invited or recommended to become part of this performing troupe, which is privately funded. The Gull Point Dance program serves its members by offering dance instruction in a variety of styles and educational and performance opportunities. Instruction at the Gull Point Community Center paves the way for three scheduled performances each year, one of those in conjunction with the Pensacola Junior College Dance Theater. All performances are free and open to the public.

KALEIDOSCOPE DANCE THEATRE/BALLET PENSACOLA
400 S. Jefferson, Pensacola 432-9546

This nonprofit school, headquartered at the Pensacola Cultural Center, seeks to educate its young dancers in a variety of dance styles, offering performances through Ballet Pensacola. Performances are held three times a year at the Saenger Theatre. Kaleidoscope also offers classes for your budding ballet dancers, both boys and girls, from age 3 on up. Kaleidoscope brings the magic of *The Nutcracker* to the Saenger Theatre each December.

PENSACOLA JUNIOR COLLEGE DANCE THEATRE
1000 College Blvd., Pensacola   484-1330

Students may earn college credit while they learn about dance as a performance art and have the opportunity to perform themselves. Call the number above for registration information.

OLD WORLD FOLKDANCERS
1218 E. Moreno St., Pensacola   433-1405

Revival of recreational folk dancing with an emphasis on Eastern Europe is the thrust of this teaching group. Folkdance demonstrations in wonderfully vivid traditional costumes are held at various festivals and events throughout the year.

PENSACOLA SPECIAL STEPPERS, INC.
P.O. Box 11313, Pensacola 32524 455-6052

This square dance club is specifically set up for people who are mentally handicapped. The Special Steppers have performed at many national conventions and have received recognition for their efforts, including a Presidential Citation.

ST. ANDREW'S SOCIETY OF PENSACOLA SCOTTISH COUNTRY DANCERS
5642 Leesway Blvd., Pensacola   477-7136

The Society offers weekly classes for beginners and more advanced dancers and was organized to maintain the standards set up by the Royal Scottish Dance Society of Edinburgh, Scotland.

Ethnic/Cultural

AFRICAN-AMERICAN HERITAGE SOCIETY, INC.
400 S. Jefferson St., Pensacola   469-1299

Besides its yearly festival, this group seeks to promote and encourage the development of African-American cultural heritage in Northwest Florida. *When Black Folks Was Colored*, a collection of memoirs and poems by local African-Americans, was such a hit in 1993 that the group has published its second edition. The Society meets monthly at the Pensacola Cultural Center.

HANSA CLUB/GERMAN-AMERICAN SOCIETY OF PENSACOLA
P.O. Box 552,
Gulf Breeze 32562   932-2326

Camaraderie and a chance to practice your German is offered to those of German-American, German, Austrian and Swiss heritage.

ITALIAN CULTURAL SOCIETY OF NORTHWEST FLORIDA, INC.
P.O. Box 4142, 6555 Mobile Hwy.
Pensacola 32507   839-9443

This group is trying to organize an Italian-American museum to promote Italian heritage. It offers grants, scholarships and endowments to Italian-Americans or to groups promoting Italian-American culture. The group usually meets for lunch but is not on a regular schedule. Call for meeting place and time.

ITALIAN CULTURAL SOCIETY OF PENSACOLA, INC.
P.O. Box 1811
Pensacola 32598   932-7062

This cultural society promotes the Italian culture through nonprofit activities and scholarships.

THE JAPAN CULTURAL SOCIETY OF NORTHWEST FLORIDA, INC.
P.O. Box 11512
Pensacola 32598   944-1164

The Japan Cultural Society promotes understanding of Far Eastern culture through a series of cultural events and public performances.

NORTHWEST FLORIDA CREEK INDIAN COUNCIL
3300 N. Pace Blvd.
Pensacola   444-8410

The Creek Indian Council is set up to ensure that all Creek Indians and their descendants take advantage of all state, local and federal benefits currently available. Group members also offer educational programs for schools and civic groups.

PHILIPPINE CULTURAL SOCIETY, INC.
8113 Westbourne Dr., Pensacola 453-9240

Filipino-Americans interested in becoming more involved with Escambia County schools and cultivating native customs through exhibits, a performing arts series and presentations will find this group helpful.

ST. ANDREW'S SOCIETY OF PENSACOLA, FLORIDA, INC.
302 Camellia St., Pensacola 932-3605

Monthly dinner meetings are held the second Friday of the month at the Seville Inn. Discussions center around promotion of Scottish culture and heritage.

Literary

FRIENDS OF THE PENSACOLA PUBLIC LIBRARY
200 W. Gregory St., Pensacola   435-1760

The Friends is a volunteer nonprofit group promoting library services to the community. The group's annual book sale raises money for the continuation and enhancement of library services.

WEST FLORIDA
LITERARY FEDERATION, INC.
Pensacola Cultural Center
400 S. Jefferson St., Ste. 212
Pensacola　　　　　　　435-0942

This diverse group offers several sub-groups in the promotion of West Florida writers. The Readers Showcase performs local and well-known writers' works at the Pensacola Cultural Center. The Back Door Poets meets once a month in a coffeehouse atmosphere to read poetry, and the Writer's Workshop and Student Writer's Network meet monthly to develop the writing technique of published and unpublished authors. Another program, Writers in Service to Education (WISE), puts local writers in the public schools to talk about their craft. The federation publishes an annual anthology, the *Emerald Coast Review*, containing the best works of West Florida writers.

WEST FLORIDA REGIONAL LIBRARY
Headquarters: Pensacola Public Library
200 W. Government St.
Pensacola　　　　　435-1760, 435-1763

The library system serves residents of Escambia and Santa Rosa counties with

Traditional and contemporary dance performances thrill audiences of the Northwest Florida Ballet.

Photo: Arts Cuoncil of NW Florida

branches in Northwest Pensacola, Milton, Gulf Breeze and Jay. Bookmobile and Outreach Van service reach the more rural areas of Escambia County. There's even a Sub-regional Talking Books Library for visually and physically handicapped residents.

Music

AMERICAN THEATRE ORGAN SOCIETY
Saenger Theatre, 118 S. Palafox Pl.
Pensacola   *444-7696*
A magnificent 1925 Robert Morton pipe organ, built especially to accompany silent movies at the Saenger Theatre, now comes out of storage for recitals and concerts by prominent organists.

THE CHORAL SOCIETY OF PENSACOLA
1000 College Blvd., Pensacola   484-1800
This group performs "serious" music in grand style, both at Pensacola Junior College's Ashmore Fine Arts Auditorium and at the Cokesbury Methodist Church right across the street. The Choral Society focuses on all musical styles and periods, often accompanied by the Pensacola Symphony Orchestra. Locals look forward to the stirring annual performance of Handel's *Messiah* at Easter or Christmas.

THE EARLY MUSIC CONSORT
5106 Treahna Rd., Pensacola   455-1500
This recorder group performs traditional and contemporary works, many times in period costume, for festivals and private functions.

GULF COAST CHORALE
412 Dolphin St.
Gulf Breeze   932-9248, 932-6209
Limited to 40 members, the Gulf Coast Chorale's four yearly concerts (in mid-October, mid-December, mid-March and the end of April) focus almost entirely on the classics: Mozart, Bach, Haydn, Beethoven and Handel. Vocalists must audition for a slot in the Chorale; membership dues are $40 yearly. Performances are at St. Anne's Catholic Church, 100 Daniels Drive in Gulf Breeze.

JAZZ SOCIETY OF PENSACOLA, INC.
P.O. Box 18337
Pensacola 32523   433-8382
The Jazz Society founded the *Pensacola JazzFest*, a weekend festival held each April in Seville Square combining local, regional and national jazz performers. Group members also make themselves available to schools and civic groups for lectures, discussions and performances. The group also sponsors some delightful Sunday afternoon concerts at Seville Quarter.

JOE OCCHIPINTI'S BIG BAND
P.O. Box 4068   433-6287
Pensacola 32507   (800) 447-8532
Strictly a performance band (that means for hire), the five-piece ensemble's

---

Insiders' Tips

From its name, The Pensacola Mining and Water Ballet Authority might seem to be a little unusual. They are basically an improv group, staging impromptu performances whenever called upon, including a rendition of *How the Grinch Stole Christmas* on the front lawn of a private residence!

repertoire offers all the best of the Big Band era.

MUSIC AT CHRIST CHURCH
18 W. Wright St., Pensacola   432-5115

Sit back, relax and enjoy organ, vocal and chamber music presented in the gilded opulence of Christ Church downtown. Performances are held throughout the year, with groups and soloists brought in from all over the world. The highlight of the year is the Pensacola Summer Music Festival, which showcases the church's Gabrial Key pipe organ. All concerts are open to the public. There is no admission charge, but donations are accepted to continue these outstanding programs.

MUSIC STUDY CLUB OF PENSACOLA
400 Jefferson St., Pensacola   434-3770

The Music Study Club seeks to enhance the love of music by encouraging young musicians to hone their skills and perform publicly. The club meets monthly at the Pensacola Cultural Center.

PENSACOLA FIESTA BARBERSHOP CHORUS
8349 Pilgrim Rd., Pensacola   476-5922

These delightful gentlemen, clad in festive red-and-white-striped vests, perform traditional and contemporary barbershop tunes every time they get the chance. They are part of a larger organization called The Society for the Preservation and Encouragement of Barbershop Quartet Singing in America, or SPEBSQSA for short(!).

PENSACOLA JUNIOR COLLEGE GUITAR ASSOCIATION/PENSACOLA GUITAR ENSEMBLE AND SOCIETY
Department of Music and Drama - PJC
1000 College Blvd., Pensacola   484-1805

Under the direction of Joe Stallings, the Association sponsors concerts and recitals throughout the community, some-times bringing in outside masters to enhance students' education. The classical Guitar Ensemble performs a wide range of music, from Renaissance to contemporary. Call for scheduled concert information.

PENSACOLA MUSIC TEACHERS ASSOCIATION
726 Bay Blvd., Pensacola   433-5206

These are the folks to call to set up lessons for your child prodigy. Area music teachers in piano, voice and other instruments teach applied music, sponsor sonata contests and work with students who must audition for scholarships. Stop by Reynalds Music House, Garden and Jefferson streets in Pensacola, or Dollarhide Music Center, Palafox Place in Pensacola, for listings of music teachers who take students as young as 6 or 7 right up to college age. Other members of the association can be contacted through the University of West Florida or Pensacola Junior College.

PENSACOLA SYMPHONY CHILDREN'S CHORUS
400 S. Jefferson St., Pensacola   434-7760

Weekly rehearsals are held at the Pensacola Cultural Center for children ages 9 through 13. The competition is fierce for placement in the group, and only the most musically talented are accepted. But the benefits are great: These kids get to sing with the Pensacola Symphony Orchestra, and the results will take your breath away. They're good.

PENSACOLA SYMPHONY ORCHESTRA
321 S. Palafox St., Pensacola   435-2533

This very professional volunteer group seeks to promote symphonic music by bringing it to the people several times a year. Annual auditions are held. The or-

Photo: Pensacola Little Theater

The Pensacola Little Theater is one of several area groups performing musicals, dramas and comedies throughout the year. The PLT will occupy a new 600-seat theater in the Pensacola Cultural Center in 1996.

chestral performances, all at the Saenger Theatre, at times combine with the talents of the Pensacola Symphony Children's Chorus, The Choral Society or nationally known guest soloists and conductors for many memorable evenings of first-rate entertainment. Tickets are available at the Saenger Theatre box office.

Science/History

ESCAMBIA AMATEUR ASTRONOMER'S ASSOCIATION

c/o Professor Wayne Wooten484-1152
6235 Omie Cr., Pensacola   477-8859

Search out shooting stars, meteor showers and other strange lights in the sky at public stargazings offered at area schools and during the summer at Fort Pickens on Santa Rosa Island. Regular meetings are in the Geology Lab at Pensacola Junior College the last Friday of the month. The Science & Space Theatre at Pensacola Junior College is the site of the association's monthly labs, but it also holds regular planetarium shows, which are open to the public Thursday

through Saturday. Admission charge is $3 for adults; $2 for students; children younger than 5 are not admitted. Call 484-1150 for a complete schedule of shows.

HISTORIC PENSACOLA PRESERVATION BOARD

120 E. Church St.
Pensacola   444-8905

This lavish art deco office, formerly home to a very hip ad agency, seems an odd home base for a group interested in the preservation of historic landmarks. But the HPPB has accomplished some remarkable feats, first among them the Historic Pensacola Village and the Pensacola Colonial Archaeological Trail (see listings under Pensacola Attractions). If you live in the North Hill or Seville Historic districts, you may be able to locate and search through a file with your home's address to find original blueprints, old photographs of your house and a listing of all former owners and their occupations.

NATIONAL MUSEUM
OF NAVAL AVIATION
Naval Air Station, Pensacola   453-2389

Here is a one-of-a-kind museum, which is a must-see even for nonmilitary personnel. Pensacola got the first-ever Naval Air Station, hence yet another nickname, "The Cradle of Naval Aviation." But the museum is crammed with fascinating displays, exhibits and rare full-size aircraft incorporating Navy, Marine Corps and Coast Guard aviation. The new *Blue Angel Atrium*, used for concerts and lectures, displays four of the retired planes hanging overhead in perfect formation. Kids can climb into the cockpits of vintage aircraft, onto the deck of an aircraft carrier, or walk through a WWII-era encampment in the South Pacific.

PENSACOLA HISTORICAL SOCIETY
405 S. Adams St.
Pensacola   433-1559,434-5455

Pensacolians find this phone number easy to memorize — it's the date when Don Tristan de Luna first landed on Pensacola shores (1559). The historical museum is housed in Old Christ Church, the oldest church in Florida (1832). Its many displays and artifacts detail life from the earliest tribes of American Indians through the lumber boom of the late 19th century and beyond. It's open 10 AM to 4:30 PM Monday through Saturday; admission is $2.

Theater

MINI-MASQUERS, INC.
4241 Morelia Pl., Pensacola   432-2042

Performing twice yearly in the fall and spring at the Pensacola Little Theatre, the Mini-Masquers' focus is family entertainment. One of the group's recent productions was the holiday children's show *The Snow Queen.*

PENSACOLA LITTLE THEATRE, INC.
186 N. Palafox St.
Pensacola 432-2042, 432-8621, 434-6703

The Little Theatre, now in its 58th season, cranks out eight shows a year: musicals, comedies, dramas, you name it. Whatever the group performs, the community attends in force to support it. Once the third phase of the Pensacola Cultural Center is completed, the PLT will have a new permanent home with a 600-seat theater. The Pensacola Little Theatre Guild is the fund-raising arm and staffs the box office.

PENSACOLA MINING AND
WATER BALLET AUTHORITY
P.O. Box 10570
Pensacola 32514   474-0034

Marc Peterson and his troupe of happy revelers produce plays, one acts and reviews for special events, as well as improvisational theater, which seems to be the group's first love.

The troupe doesn't have a real home but performs at several locations, among them the Imogene Theater in Milton, the Pensacola Cultural Center, First Night Pensacola on New Year's Eve and several performances al fresco, such as *How the Grinch Stole Christmas,* acted out on the front lawn of a private residence!

PENSACOLA OPERA, INC.
321 S. Palafox St., Pensacola   433-6737

Here is a group of real opera aficionados who saw a need to bring good opera performances to the people and started this group. They do more than just perform, however; one goal of the Opera is to provide an opportunity for students and other talented individuals to perform in complete opera productions. The group has a performing arts series and provides lectures, demonstrations, workshops and tours of its Scenic Design Studio. In 1994, the opera performed *The Barber of Seville* and *La Traviata* at the Saenger Theatre in downtown Pensacola. *La Boheme* and *Il Trovatore* are featured productions for '95.

PUPPET FACTORY
8804 Jernigan Rd., Pensacola   484-8494

Yes, they perform traveling puppet shows, but what the group enjoys doing most is workshops for children from kindergarten through the 8th grade on designing and building puppets and stages and learning how to become puppeteers. Find them at the weekly "Picnics in the Plaza" at Plaza Fredinand in the fall and spring, at the First Night Pensacola Celebration on New Year's Eve, at the Family Expo at the Pensacola Civic Center in the spring and at many schools and other events all year long.

ST. MARY'S PRODUCTIONS
8019 Coronet Dr., Pensacola   484-1400

Yet another Pensacola-based theater group, St. Mary's produces one show per year, usually a musical, at the Saenger Theatre, with auditions open to the public. *The Sound of Music* was 1995's show-stopper.

UNIVERSITY THEATRE/
THEATRE DEPARTMENT
University of West Florida
11000 University Pkwy., Pensacola   474-2146

This is a thriving theater community, staging three or four full productions an-

nually, student productions and the Northwest Florida Young Playwright's Society during the summer.

Visual Arts

ARTEL GALLERY
22 N. Palafox St., Pensacola   432-4080

Local artists exhibit their work here, as well as hold exhibitions of local, regional and national contemporary art. All artwork is offered for sale.

CASA DE COSAS
210 E. Garden St., Pensacola   433-5921

This candy factory-turned-gallery in the heart of downtown features several rooms filled with paintings, pottery, jewelry, sculpture and crafts.

GALLERY OF LOVELY THINGS
280 N. Palafox St., Pensacola   434-9044

This unusual gallery features African-American sculpture and art mostly, but not always, by African Americans. Visit them between 10 AM and 6 PM Monday through Saturday.

SOHO GALLERY
23 S. Palafox St., Pensacola   435-7646

Both fine art and artsy gifts blanket the walls, shelves and tables of Soho, one of Pensacola's newest galleries. The works of both local and national artists are well represented. Bet you can't tell one from the other (except maybe for the price tag!).

Insiders' Tips

For a complete listing of art galleries, concerts, dance and theater performances and meetings of various area groups, look for the weekly magazine *The Weekender* in Friday's *Pensacola News Journal*.

Photo: Arts Council of NW Florida

The Great Gulfcoast Arts Festival brings the talents of 200 artists from across the country to Historic Seville Square each November.

BAYFRONT GALLERY
713 S. Palafox St., Pensacola   438-7556

Art in the Pensacola area is thriving, as are Pensacola area artists, with quite a few galleries at their disposal in which to showcase their talents. Bayfront is one of the best, displaying the works of more than 400 artists from 45 states. Beautiful copper fountains, burled wood clocks, unusual jewelry boxes with swing-out drawers and whimsical children's toys highlight this downtown gallery.

FLORIDA FIVE
4535 LaVallet Ln., Pensacola   434-7398

Florida Five is a group of talented artists whose sole purpose is to bring their combined knowledge to the schools and the community through exhibitions, classes, lectures and demonstrations.

GARTH'S ANTIQUES
& AUCTION GALLERY
3930 Navy Blvd., Pensacola   456-7192

Winston Garth and his staff conduct fine arts showings four times yearly for school children. You'll enjoy arts charity auctions at his shop on Navy Boulevard.

GULF BREEZE ARTS, INC.
312 Smith Cr., Gulf Breeze   932-5691

A group of artists got together five years ago and now are 50 strong. Monthly meetings are held at the Gulf Breeze Library; speakers lecture on some aspect of the visual arts. Gulf Breeze Arts members award a scholarship each year to a deserving high school student and every October exhibit their work at the Santa Rosa Recreation Center.

NORTHWEST FLORIDA
PORCELAIN ARTISTS
P.O. Box 34405
Pensacola 32507   492-9501

Here is a unique art form that this group seeks to expand by learning how to better create it. The emphasis on their work is china painting, but members create other art pieces as well. The porcelain is displayed once a year in November at the East Pensacola Heights Center and at the Garden Center on Ninth Avenue in Pensacola. Meetings are moved around so no one member always has to travel; they are held the second Friday of each month. Dues are just $5 a year.

PENSACOLA MUSEUM OF ART

407 S. Jefferson St., Pensacola   432-6247

This is the old City Jail building, where art pieces are exhibited in cell blocks with bars on the windows. The surroundings are nearly as interesting as the exhibits. Some of the art is local, and monthly exhibitions showcase some outstanding work. The museum also brings in really terrific exhibitions from all over the world: Chinese porcelain, Dutch Masters, photography and contemporary art.

SANTA ROSA ART ASSOCIATION

P.O. Box 4256
Milton 32572   623-6686, 623-1256

These artists enjoy promoting their craft in any way they can: by bringing in guest artists for workshops, by exhibiting at their annual Members' Show (held at the Milton Depot during November's Depot Days Festival), and by getting their work selected for the juried Riverwalk Fine Arts Show in Milton, which is held in late March or early April. Regular meetings are the last Saturday of the month at the Milton Depot on Henry Street.

UNIVERSITY OF WEST FLORIDA ART GALLERY

11000 University Pkwy.,
Pensacola   474-2482

Since this is a university studio, it calls for diversity. And that's what you'll find — to educate, to keep an eye on new trends, to display the avant garde.

UNTITLED II

1904 E. Moreno St., Pensacola   438-1572

Untitled II is comprised of feminist artists who provide programs of readings and critiques on current issues and topics. Once a year, the group exhibits its work in the University of West Florida art gallery.

Multidisciplinary

THE CREATIVE GUILD

106 E. Gregory St., Pensacola   433-2400

Now here's a diverse group: photographers, illustrators, copywriters, graphic artists, fine artists, sign artists, sculptors, video and audio production people, voice talent, you name it. The Guild is an organization of creative professionals brought together to promote their creative abilities, to network with other creative folks and to let businesses know they're out there, waiting to be hired. Look for a directory of creative services from the Guild in 1995. They meet the first Thursday of every month.

DOWNTOWN ARTS DISTRICT ASSOCIATION (DADA)

P.O. Box 731
Pensacola 32594   432-9906

Organized to increase awareness of the arts in downtown Pensacola and sponsored by the Arts Council of Northwest Florida, the Downtown Arts District Association puts on the ritz three times a year in March, July and November with a gallery tour. Pottery shops, bookstores, frame shops, art galleries and studios, museums and music stores provide exhibitions, entertainment and refreshments to the public free of charge.

FIRST NIGHT PENSACOLA

803 N. Palafox St., Pensacola   434-2724

Looking for an alternative to the traditional New Year's Eve celebrations? This night of alcohol-free family entertainment might be just the ticket. Events and entertainment take place all over downtown Pensacola, featuring storytellers, musicians, dancers, actors, singers, a giant puppet parade, magicians, mimes, great food and lots of surprises, including a laser-light show at midnight to welcome in the new year.

GREAT GULFCOAST ARTS FESTIVAL
P.O. Box 731
Pensacola 32584   432-9906

An annual event for more than two decades, the GGAF might just be the best festival in Northwest Florida. The juried show attracts artists from all over the country to exhibit in historic Seville Square. Only the top 200 are chosen in a wide variety of mediums including ceramics, torn rice paper, batik, jewelry and woodworking. Dance and musical performances, a children's area and heritage arts are also part of this popular celebration.

WEST FLORIDA ADVERTISING COUNCIL
P.O. Box 12491
Pensacola 32573   474-7940

The ad council is a group of advertising folks who get together once a month over lunch to hear one of their peers speak about some aspect of "the biz." Once a year, the Advertising Council stages the ADDY Awards, a fund-raiser to reward the best in local advertising.

PENSACOLA HERITAGE FOUNDATION
P.O. Box 12424
Pensacola 32582   438-6505

Started almost 30 years ago, the Heritage Foundation promotes the history and preservation of this area through entertainment and recreational fund-raisers.

PENSACOLA JUNIOR COLLEGE LYCEUM
Music and Drama Department
1000 College Blvd., Pensacola   484-1800

Throughout the school year (September through May), the artist series holds regular exhibitions either at the PJC Ashmore Fine Arts Auditorium on campus or the Saenger Theatre downtown.

SANTA ROSA HISTORICAL SOCIETY, INC.
814 Caroline St. S.E.
Milton   623-8493, 626-9830

The historical society oversees the preservation and restoration of several historical buildings and sites. The society owns the Milton L&N Depot and the Arcadia Mill. It also owns the Milton Opera House, which is home to the Imogene Theatre, the Historical Society's headquarters and Museum of Local History.

SOCIETY FOR CREATIVE ANACHRONISM
SCA c/o 10279 Sugar Creek Dr.
Pensacola 32514   479-1680

Need a historical reenactment? These are the folks to call, but only if you need something from the Medieval Period (600-1600 A.D.). Lots of people do, so the society gets out into the community to provide it with exhibitions, classes, lectures and demonstrations. Members design and create their own costumes and weaponry and can stage quite a good swordfight. Look for them at the annual British Festival held in May in Seville Square.

Pensacola Area
Retirement

The positive side of so many military personnel constantly coming through Pensacola for a two-, three- or four-year tour of duty is that when they leave, they take the good word about Pensacola with them. Nearly all of them return at some point, for a military reunion or a vacation. Or they come to find their place in the sun to retire. With plenty of sunshine and housing, an affordable cost of living and water at every turn for fishing or boating, the Pensacola area seems an ideal place for empty nesters to put down permanent roots. Although many retirees opt for beach condominiums, some like the comfort and camaraderie afforded by retirement communities. The carefree lifestyle frees up time spent on yard maintenance, household repairs and a host of mundane chores for relaxation, a wealth of planned activities and time to get to know their neighbors.

Retirement Communities/
Independent Residential Facilities

THE ELITE GUEST HOUSE
1120 N. Palafox St.
Pensacola   438-8368
You'll fall in love with this turn-of-the-century Queen Anne home the moment you see it. The 1909 Elite Guest House is located in Pensacola's North Hill Preservation District, and the owners have done a magnificent restoration job, doubling the size of the original house a few years ago with an attached addition in back. Original stained- and leaded-glass windows, turned balusters and a gazebo connected to the shady front porch bring back memories of simpler times. It's only about 2 miles from Baptist Hospital and less than that from the heart of downtown. Choose from 18 private or semiprivate rooms or two-room suites with cabinets, a sink, a microwave and a small refrigerator. Residents have their medications supervised and administered, menus are individually planned with special dietary needs in mind and the home has a wanderguard system for residents with Alzheimer's.

AZALEA TRACE
10100 Hillview Rd.
Pensacola   478-5200
This 56-acre campus in north Pensacola offers more choices in residential units than any other retirement community in the area — 25 floor plans! It is near Escambia Bay and a population center with excellent medical facilities and shopping malls. Towering pines, nature trails, a pond and four seasons of flowering plants provide a well-tended and re-

Shady gazebos and landscaped walkways characterize Carpenter's Creek Community in Pensacola.

laxing environment away from the bustle of the city.

Choose the type of unit that suits your lifestyle, from master studios to spacious two-bedroom units in the Garden, Midrise or Terrace apartments. All feature complete kitchens, safety-equipped baths, security and complete privacy. If you'd like to prepare a gourmet meal for close friends, you have the facilities at your disposal. If you choose not to cook, have your meals in the comfortable dining area, and invite your friends if you wish. On the grounds are a library, sewing room, woodworking shop and an indoor swimming pool. Azalea Trace's Health Care Center offers 24-hour emergency, recuperative and unlimited long-term care.

BAY BREEZE NURSING & RETIREMENT CENTER
3375 Gulf Breeze Pkwy.
Gulf Breeze 932-9257

Freedom, privacy and independent living are the keys to the Bay Breeze lifestyle. This adult congregate living facility is spacious and decorated with con-

temporary furnishings in warm pastels. In addition to pleasant surroundings, Bay Breeze provides social and recreational activities, a comfortable, airy dining facility and assistance with medication, bathing, dressing and housekeeping on a daily basis or as needed. Physical therapy, occupational therapy and speech therapy are also offered as part of the rehabilitation program.

If further care is needed, the Bay Breeze Nursing Center, adjacent to the retirement center, is available for 24-hour restorative nursing care. A registered dietician plans all meals with regard to physician recommendations for each patient. The facility is a member of the Florida Health Care Association.

CARPENTER'S CREEK COMMUNITY
5918 N. Davis Hwy.
Pensacola 477-8998

Ninety-six one-bedroom, efficiency and studio units center around an attractive Southern-tinged facility in the heart of Pensacola. A tin-roofed main building, with a cupola and weather vane, wrapped porches, arched windows and vaulted ceilings, lends an air of comfort and hospitality. Mennonite-style cooking is a favorite of the residents. In addition to a full country breakfast each morning, Carpenter's Creek serves complete Southern meals such as country fried steak, fried mullet, fried chicken and short ribs, greens, hushpuppies and okra with homemade bread, rolls and desserts daily.

Private baths, small in-room refrigerators, a 24-hour snack and juice bar and CCC's own country store are just a few of the special touches that make it feel like home. Rentals are by the month with no endowment fees. Ten assisted living units for residents and nonresidents provide 24-hour medical assistance, private baths, cable TV connections and rentals by the day, week or month.

BAYOU VILLAS
201 S. Stillman St.
Pensacola   *434-1504*

Tranquil waterfront retirement living is the hallmark of this facility on the shore of Bayou Chico, one block off of Navy Boulevard on Pensacola's west side. Private and semiprivate units are available with or without waterfront views. Two-room suites have separate living and bedroom accommodations and are specially suited to couples. Enjoy the company of friends and a lovely view of the bayou in the large dining room. A full-time recreation director provides for field trips, shopping, arts and crafts, lectures, movies and special social hours, among other activities. Limited nursing services provide assistance with bathing, grooming, dressing and medications on a 24-hour basis. Counseling is offered to residents for respiratory, physical and speech therapies.

THE HOMESTEAD VILLAGE
7830 Pine Forest Rd.
Pensacola   944-4366, (800) 937-1735

Although fairly new, this well-planned development is already one of the most popular retirement communities in the area. It could have something to do with the delicious Mennonite recipes used in the dining area or the fresh breads and rolls made right here daily. Several living options are available to residents. Choose from a large custom-designed two-bedroom, two-bath patio home at The Homestead Estates; a studio, one- or two-bedroom, two-bath unit with a Jacuzzi at The Homestead Garden Apartments; one of the new Homestead Villas with nine spacious floor plans in one, two or three bedrooms with access to the dining room and common areas and a 24-hour nurse call; or one of four apartment styles in The Homestead Retirement Center, a cluster-design building featuring special 24-hour assistance with personal care, medications and recuperation. Fees are by the month with no endowment.

Homestead Village is licensed to provide extended care, should the need arise.

They're so certain you're going to love it that they've extended an invitation for a free lunch and a tour of the grounds; just call for an appointment.

Senior Support Services

ESCAMBIA COUNTY
COUNCIL ON AGING, INC.
21 S. Tarragona St.
Pensacola 432-1475

The Council on Aging provides many services to seniors in Escambia County. Among them are Meals on Wheels, hot meals delivered to elderly people; a retired senior volunteer program; and a foster grandparent and senior companion program. Staff members can assist with home-care services, Alzheimer's respite care, transportation or choosing a retirement community. The Council truly provides full-service support to all residents of the county 55 or older. Satellite offices offer many of these services in Cantonment, 132 Mintz Lane, 968-6259; and Century, 1600 Mayo Street, 256-1012.

AMERICAN ASSOCIATION
OF RETIRED PERSONS
904 N. 57th Ave.
Pensacola 455-3794

Assisting with everything from tax forms to travel, the AARP has become a powerful voice for seniors. Get an AARP card for discounts on hotels, tickets to special attractions and even restaurants. The Pensacola Chapter 3564 will guide you to the services and programs available in this area.

BAYVIEW SENIOR CITIZENS CENTER
Bayview Park, 20th Ave. and Lloyd St.
Pensacola 435-1790

Right next to the community center, this senior center gets its members from AARP, Retired Railway Employees and other retiree groups but is open to all seniors 50 and older. The building houses meeting rooms, a pool room (that's billiards), an art room, a music room, a social hall and a library/lounge area. Several programs and classes in activities such as stitchery, ballroom dancing and aerobics are offered.

Pensacola Area
Military

It's a comfort to the people of Pensacola, and a good selling point to real estate and tourism folks, that Pensacola remains a top pick for Navy personnel. At the time the Navy Yard was established in 1825, the government pretty much had its pick of coastal lands for establishing military strongholds. Pensacola was an obvious choice with its easily defensible bay system, deep-water harbor and ample timber reserves.

Shipbuilding was what the Pensacola Navy Yard did best, turning out some of the finest warships of all time, including the USS *Pensacola*, a player in Civil War battles in both Mobile Bay and New Orleans.

Confederate troops abandoned the Navy Yard in 1862 after the fall of New Orleans, burning and destroying almost everything of value. The Navy Yard received a major blow, literally, in 1906 when a hurricane of tremendous power flattened most of what was left. In less than two years, an epidemic of yellow fever brought a reconstruction effort to an end and signed the yard's death warrant; it was decommissioned in 1911.

Naval Air Station

Meanwhile, wheels were turning in the area of naval aviation. The value of the airplane had been demonstrated to the Navy, and in 1914, the surprised residents of Pensacola got the news that the country's first Naval Air Station would be built on the site of the old Navy Yard. And, shall we say, the rest . . . is history.

Although its function has shifted somewhat (Pensacola NAS no longer has a homeported training carrier, and flight training is now shared with other bases), its relevance to Pensacola, both as a tourist draw and a base for economic development, cannot be disputed.

In 1914, the abandoned naval yard at Pensacola became the site of the first U.S. Naval Air Station, which immediately proved its worth by training more than 1,000 aviators who served in World War I. By the time World War II rolled around, military experts were already calling the station the "Annapolis of the Air." The base expanded in preparation for American's entry into WWII, and pilots trained at the Naval Air Station displayed a stunning 14-to-1 air superiority over Japanese planes.

After the war, the station was actively involved in furthering the field of naval aviation, and soon jets and helicopters filled the skies along with airplanes. The Naval Air Station has served in both a combat and noncombat capacity in the Korean War, the Vietnam War and more recently the Persian Gulf War.

Several training programs call Naval Air Station Pensacola home, including the

Naval Aviation Schools Command, the Chief of Naval Education and Training and training squadrons VT-4, VT-10 and VT-86. There are actually three schools under the umbrella of the Naval Aviation Schools Command. These schools prepare officer candidates for commissioned status as well as aviation indoctrination and ground training for officer candidates, student officers and naval aircrew trainees.

The **Naval Aviation Depot**, which had a work force of nearly 3,000 people, will close in September 1995. To the area's credit, the depot is being replaced with a training center that will accommodate thousands of student aviators as two or three bases are consolidated in Pensacola.

The Pensacola Naval Air Station makes a huge contribution to the area's economy, employing nearly 10,000 military personnel and 9,000 civilians. Though the current trend toward military downsizing will certainly have effects on the Naval Air Station, its presence is certain to remain strong and able in the years to come.

NAS Sites of Interest

NATIONAL MUSEUM OF NAVAL AVIATION
452-3604

The National Museum of Naval Aviation is one huge time capsule displaying the history of Navy, Marine Corps and Coast Guard aircraft from the past 80 years. It's one of the largest air and space museums in the world, and more than half a million visitors pass through its doors each year. You can see the entire lineage of aircraft here, from WWI-era biplanes to advanced spacecraft and everything in between, including a replica of a WWII flight deck, the NC-4 Flying Boat (the first plane to cross the Atlantic) and F-14 Flying Tomcat (used in the movie *Top Gun*). The **Flight Adventure Deck** gives kids the chance to climb into real cockpits from vintage aircraft for some hands-on exploration of flight.

One of the museum's showpieces is the seven-story glass-and-steel **Blue Angels Atrium** with four of the retired A-4 Skyhawks suspended in diamond formation.

The museum is open daily from 9 AM to 5 PM except on Thanksgiving, Christmas and New Year's day. Be sure to browse through the **Flight Deck Museum Shop** for model planes and aircraft carriers, bomber jackets and a terrific selection of coffee table books. Admission to the museum is free.

FORT BARRANCAS

Although officially part of the Gulf Islands National Seashore, Fort Barrancas sits on the Pensacola NAS property and is open to the public. It is the third fort built on this site, and the first for the United States. More information about the fort is contained in the Gulf Islands National Seashore chapter.

The Pensacola lighthouse on the Naval Air Station can be recognized by its color scheme — two-thirds black at the top and one-third white. Every lighthouse in America can be identified by color alone.

Insiders' Tips

BLUE ANGELS

There are many squadrons based at the station, but the best-known is probably the Blue Angels, the Navy's Flight Demonstration Squadron, home-based at **Sherman Field**. Though this elite squad of fighter pilots is based here, they're often on the road — or in the air — traveling around the country with their fantastic air show. They usually return for a special demonstration in Pensacola in November and have been known to buzz the beach in July as well. You might want to check and see if they're going to be taking their thrilling aerial ballet to the skies when you visit. You can call the Blue Angels' Public Affairs Officer at 452-4784.

Other Military Facilities in the Pensacola Area

Corry Station

Naval Technical Training Center Corry Station in Warrington, 640 Roberts Avenue, 452-6381, graduates nearly 7,000 naval students each year in the fields of cryptology, electronic warfare and photography. Corry Field started life as an

Photo: U.S. Navy

Many Change of Command ceremonies and other special events take place in the Blue Angels Atrium, part of the National Museum of Naval Aviation.

aviation command but was recommissioned in 1960 as a training center.

Saufley Field

Saufley Field, Saufley Field Road, 452-1788, Pensacola, is home to the Naval Education and Training Program Management Support Activity, the Naval Training Systems Center, the Naval Reserve Center and a Federal Prison Camp. It's been part of the supporting cast for Pensacola NAS for more than 50 years.

U.S. Coast Guard Station

The U.S. Coast Guard Station, located on Big Lagoon just west of Pensacola Pass, is officially a subunit of the Coast Guard Group in Mobile, Alabama, but they're also an important player at the Naval Air Station.

Whiting Field

Just because it's located 7 miles north of Milton in Santa Rosa County certainly doesn't belie its importance to the military. Whiting, 7550 USS Essex Street, Milton, 623-7651, accounts for fully 10 percent of all Navy and Marine flight operations, doing about 80 percent of its fixed-wing training and *all* of its helicopter training. Navy pilots are broken in on the T-34 "Turbo Mentor" aircraft; helicopter pilots learn the ropes on the TH-57 "Sea Ranger" helicopter. This is *the* busiest air space in America; more than 2 million takeoffs and landings take place at Whiting every year. Locals are trying hard right now to keep the operation here; the government is looking to consolidate helicopter training at Fort Rucker, Alabama.

The Pensacola Lighthouse: Beckoning Ships Home for More Than A Century

Photo: U.S. Navy

In the fading light, the beacon shines out to sea for many miles, beckoning ships like a mother herding her brood toward home in the gathering darkness. The Pensacola lighthouse on the Naval Air Station grounds was the first one built on the Gulf Coast. The

The Pensacola Lighthouse

original 80-foot light, built in 1824, eventually had to be moved because trees were obstructing the view of the light. The first beams from the new structure (191 feet above sea level) shone out on January 1, 1859.

The tales of the lighthouse are fascinating, told with fervor and eloquence by members of the Coast Guard Auxiliary. Each one of the 178 steps (huff, puff) was hand cast of wrought iron, since each is a slightly different size, becoming narrower near the top. The first keepers lugged a pail of whale oil from the tiny brick quarters near the bottom to the top every two hours to refuel the lamp and pull up the weights that turned the lens. When the first lightkeeper died, his wife took on the task for another 15 years.

During the Civil War, Union troops took possession of the lighthouse but found its lens dismantled and missing. What may be local legend still fascinates in the retelling: The magnificent Le Paite lens, made in Paris, was buried in the sand for protection from the enemy. Although the lighthouse was repeatedly bombarded, it remained intact, and the lens was reinstalled after the war.

The light was automated in 1965 and now shines out 27 miles. One 1000-watt bulb does the job, the light being refracted over and over again by the powerful room-size lens that never stops turning.

Free tours are offered every weekend from May to September. Be sure to take one; the view from the top is nothing short of spectacular. The lighthouse Keeper's Quarters have been restored and are open to the public. For information on the lighthouse and the tours, please call 492-0310.

Pensacola Daytrips
Mobile and the Alabama Gulf Coast

Although only 50 miles separate Mobile from Pensacola, the two cities remain vastly dissimilar in landscape, long-held traditions and the forces driving their economies. While many may know of Pensacola for its beautiful beaches and strong military presence, Mobile's recognition stems from its many gracious Southern homes and thriving port.

This bustling city by the bay introduced azaleas to the United States in the mid-1700s. The roots of Mardi Gras come not from New Orleans but right here in Mobile starting with the "Cowbellions" some time around 1830. And while so much of the South has become homogenized, where cities lose their character and become no more than strings of con-

dominiums and fast food restaurants, Mobile has retained much of its Southern-ness, highlighted by events such as the Azalea Trail Festival, the Blessing of the Fleet and the Historic Homes Tour.

At the end of this chapter, take a look at what else awaits you just over the border: Gulf Shores, Orange Beach, the Fort Morgan area along the gulf and scenic Point Clear and Fairhope on Mobile Bay.

Getting Around

Quick, before you come, you've got to learn to say it correctly: mow-BEEL. Now you're talking like a native. From Florida, I-10 will bring you right into the heart of the city. While you will be traveling almost due west, you'll find yourself

Photo: Alan Whitmann

Permission to come aboard granted on the U.S.S. Alabama docked at Battleship Park.

quite a ways inland from the Gulf of Mexico. The City of Mobile is built at the headwaters of Mobile Bay and on the Mobile River. The bay is nearly shallow enough to walk across at the point where the 8-mile-long Jubilee Parkway (I-10) crosses it. If you're just passing through, I-10 is the quickest way through town, but you won't see much. Take the exit at Government Street if you're planning to stop and explore. Both routes take you through tunnels under the Mobile River.

Once you get through the Bankhead Tunnel (named for Tallulah's daddy), you'll be right downtown on Government Street. Take a quick left onto Royal Street and stop first at the Fort Condé Welcome Center to pick up brochures, ask directions and get a tour of the fort. But more on that later. Since some of the area's best attractions are outside the city limits, it's best to have your own car to get to those. But in town, there are a few alternate modes of transportation you may wish to try. **Note: The area code for the lower half of Alabama has just changed to 334.** Please remember to use the area code when calling from Florida, since many Pensacola and Mobile numbers have the same prefixes!

Gulf Coast Carriage Service, 433-8601, will pick you up right at the front door of Fort Condé from 9 AM until 5 PM for a 35-minute tour through Mobile's historic downtown district. The tour is $30 per couple, or $40 for a family of four.

Gray Line Tours, 432-2228, (800) 338-5597, provides four different scenic tours where they do the driving and you relax in air-conditioned comfort! A two-hour tour of Historic Mobile is $15 and includes one historic home tour. An hour-long Historic Districts tour is $8 per person; it's $12 for a tour of the battleship

U.S.S. *Alabama*; to tour the Bellingrath Gardens and Home, you'll pay $26 ($18.50 for the gardens only). All tours depart from Fort Condé at 10:30 AM and 2 PM (Sundays 2 PM only). Children receive half off the admission fee.

The Mobile Bay Ferry, (904) 434-7345 in Florida, (334) 421-6420 or (800) 634-4027, takes you and your car from Dauphin Island south of Mobile Bay to Fort Morgan, which is built on a peninsula between the bay and the gulf. Ferry service began in 1979 after Hurricane Frederic wiped out the old drawbridge connecting Dauphin Island with the mainland. There's a new bridge now, so the ferry provides a pleasurable shortcut across the bay. Cost to ride is $13 for trucks and cars (round trip is $20); motorcycles pay $6; walk-ons are charged $1. Ferries leave from Fort Morgan every 1½ hours from 8:45 AM until 7:15 PM and from Dauphin Island from 8 AM until 6:30 PM.

Attractions

In town, Mobile's focus is on history in its many museums, walking and driving tours and grand houses. Discover famous forts, verdant gardens, rural wilderness and Gulf Coast beaches within a short drive. Mobile Bay's eastern shore offers plentiful pleasures for yet another day's outing.

THE DE TONTI SQUARE HISTORIC DISTRICT

Bounded by Adams, Claiborne, St. Anthony and Conception Sts.   *438-7011*

This nine-block historic district is just three blocks north of the central business district and is the oldest residential area in Mobile. All buildings are antebellum, from the 1830s through the 1850s. Most of these homes were built by cotton brokers, river pilots and traders in maritime

Photo: Mobile Chamber of Commerce

For a pleasant day's sojourn, venture to the tip of Pleasure Island to explore historic Fort Morgan.

supplies. Look for the architectural detailing of Italianate and Victorian styles as well as the classic lines represented by Gulf Coast, Greek Revival and Federal architecture.

CHURCH STREET EAST HISTORIC DISTRICT

Bounded by Broad, Canal, Conti, Eslava, Church and Royal Sts. 438-7011

Fifty-nine buildings of historical significance are found within this neighborhood, surpassed in age only by the De Tonti Square district. The buildings here serve many purposes — civic, commercial and religious as well as residential. Among these are the 1857 City Hall at 111 Royal Street, which began life as a one-story open market. A second story was designed in the Italianate style featuring bracketed cornices and the unusual polygonal cupola (in regular people's language, that's the round thing at the top with all the windows). This building is one of just a handful of city halls in the country still used for its original purpose.

The European influences of earlier neighborhoods were lost to fires in 1827 and 1839, replaced by American Federal, Greek Revival, Italianate, Queen Anne and Victorian. The district remains the largest and one of the most architecturally diverse of all the city's historic districts.

OAKLEIGH GARDEN HISTORIC DISTRICT

Bounded by Ann, Government, Texas and Broad Sts. 438-7011

Most of the 41 buildings in this mainly residential district are post-Civil War, reflecting a surge of new growth and economic prosperity in the South in the last quarter of the 19th century. Besides the magnificent architecture, the abundance of live oaks are striking. They were planted some 135 years ago and now form shady canopies over the streets.

OAKLEIGH MANSION

350 Oakleigh Pl. 432-1281

This simple yet striking 1833 home is the focal point of the Oakleigh Garden

Historic District. During the spring, the blush of azaleas combines with the majesty of the live oaks to produce a real Southern spectacle. The interior curving stairway is unique in Mobile homes. Currently operated as a house museum by the Historic Mobile Preservation Society (its headquarters are in the house), tours operate Monday through Saturday between 10 AM and 4 PM and Sunday between 2 and 4 PM. The admission charge is $5 for adults, $4.50 for seniors 65 and older, $3 for ages 12 to 18 and $2 for ages 6 to 11. You may purchase an admission pass to all four of the house museums for $10. These are available at any of the houses.

THE RICHARDS — DAR HOUSE
256 N. Joachim St.   434-7320

Inside the De Tonti Square district, this 1860s Italianate townhome stands out for its iron-lace detailing. Steamboat Captain Charles G. Richards built the house with Neoclassic figurines of the Four Seasons worked into the intricate arabesques and scrolls of the ironwork. Inside adornments show off the almost overdone tastes of the period: brass and bronze chandeliers sporting mythological figures, ruby Bohemian glass, Carrara marble mantels, silver bell pulls for calling servants and a garish crystal chandelier in the hexagonal dining room.

It's open Tuesday through Saturday, 10 AM to 4 PM, Sunday 1 to 4 PM. A $3 donation is requested from adults, $1 from children.

CONDÉ-CHARLOTTE MUSEUM HOUSE
104 Theatre St.   432-4722

The house, built as Mobile's first official jail around 1822-24, is considered Mobile's oldest. It stands adjacent to the Fort Condé Welcome Center in the Church Street East Historic District. About 10 years before Mobile joined the Confederacy, the jail was converted to a residence, now owned by the National Society of Colonial Dames of America in the State of Alabama. This society took it upon themselves to decorate the rooms in this house to reflect periods and nationalities — French Empire, 18th-century English, American Federal and the Confederate room (a Southern parlor, of course). Tour the house between 10 AM and 4 PM Tuesday through Saturday and Sunday by appointment. Admission is $3 for adults, $1 for children.

THE BRAGG-MITCHELL MANSION
1906 Springhill Ave.   471-6364

This 20-room showplace of the Old South is part of the Explore Center, which includes one of Alabama's oldest schoolhouses and the Exploreum/Museum of Discovery science museum. Judge John Bragg built the residence in 1855 using a combination of Greek Revival and Italianate styles. During the Civil War, all the massive oaks around the property were cut down, allowing the Confederate artillery a clear shot at Federal troops. Following the war, Judge Bragg replanted all of the oaks from acorns he'd saved from the original trees. During the home's renovation in 1986, workers discovered elaborate Victorian stenciling beneath layers of paint on the crown moldings. Every room in the house was then restored using the brilliant colored moldings. The Bragg-Mitchell Mansion is open for tours Monday through Friday from 10 AM until 4 PM; Sunday 1 to 4 PM. Admission is $4 for adults; $2 for students.

FORT CONDÉ
150 S. Royal St.   434-7304

This French fort, reconstructed from

original plans in 1975-76, is the third fort to be built on this site. The first Fort Condé was a 1711 wooden stockade, but it must not have held up well since another French fort, made from brick and mortar, went up between 1724 and 1735. It is this second Fort Condé to be re-created (and somewhat adapted into a welcome center).

The French, the English and the Spanish all laid claim to the fort at one time. In 1813 American troops bullied their way in to capture the fort from the Spanish. Just seven years later, Fort Condé was declared surplus by the government; its walls were blasted, its brick sold at public auction, its rubble used as fill for low-lying streets in the city. As you tour the fort, look for costumed guides and bits of 1720s fort life. Admission to the fort is free.

MAGNOLIA CEMETERY

Virginia and Ann sts.

Cemeteries seem to be the best place for people looking for clues to their past.

Photo: Mobile Chamber of Commerce

The towering oaks at Oakleigh Mansion were planted from seedlings after the Civil War.

This 120-acre cemetery, established in 1836 and listed on the National Register of Historic Places, is the final resting place of many notable Mobilians. Look for Confederate generals, Alabama governors, Civil War-era writers, Apache Indians and Coca-Cola magnates Walter D. and Bessie Morse Bellingrath. Gravestone architecture is appealing here as well as Victorian funerary art, unusual styles of mausoleums and intricately sculpted cast and wrought ironwork.

FINE ARTS MUSEUM
OF THE SOUTH (FAMOS)
4850 Museum Dr. off Springhill Ave.
in Langan Park
or at 300 Dauphin St. 343-2667, 694-0533

Two thousand years of cultural history are depicted in 4,500 works of art. Prestigious museums across the country provide the museum with traveling exhibits, strengthening and expanding the works on display. The 19th- and 20th-century exhibits of American art and Southern decorative art are some of the museum's best. FAMOS is open between 10 AM and 5 PM Tuesday through Sunday and is always free. The downtown museum is open 8:30 AM to 4:30 PM Monday through Friday.

MUSEUM OF THE CITY OF MOBILE
355 Government St.   434-7620

Showcased inside an 1872 Italianate townhouse, this history museum thoroughly details Mobile's heritage, beginning with its river-dwelling Indian tribes to today. Of special note are the Colonization Room, covering French, English, Spanish and American rule; the Civil War Room, with its mostly Confederate relics; the Rutherford Carriage Room's fine collection of horse-drawn buggies; the grand and glorious women's fashions in the Hammel Collection; and the unforgettable Staples Gallery tracing Mardi Gras' history in costumes and float designs. The City Museum is absolutely free (!) and open from 10 AM to 5 PM Tuesday through Saturday.

EICHOLD HEUSTIS MEDICAL
MUSEUM OF THE SOUTH
In the lobby of the Lafayette St. entrance at the University of South Alabama -
Springhill Ave. campus   434-5055

Two hundred years of medical history are traced in this free museum, which contains the largest collection of medical artifacts anywhere in the Southeast. Gaze in awe at the curious assortment of old machines and instruments, read about primitive techniques for treating tuberculosis and the ghastly practice of bloodletting or re-create a Civil War battlefield scene with photographs and a set of Army surgical instruments. Although quite fascinating, we recommend not doing this museum just before lunch! Open Monday through Friday from 8 AM until 5 PM.

THE EXPLOREUM
MUSEUM OF DISCOVERY
2½ miles east of the Springhill Ave.
Exit off I-65   476-MUSE

The Exploreum is a hands-on science museum geared to fun and learning. Send a message in the "whispering" chamber that a friend can hear from 50 feet away, build an arch like an ancient engineer and learn the secrets of defying gravity or watch the movement of the earth "draw" a picture! These plus many other stimulating exhibits teach youngsters and grownups about the laws of physics, the world of nature and our fascination with the humanities. Come and discover Tuesday through Friday from 9 AM to 5 PM or weekends 1 PM to 5 PM. There's a $3 admission for adults; $2 for children ages 2 to 17.

The Blessing of the Fleet at Bayou La Batre kicks off the fishing season along the Gulf Coast.

PHOENIX FIRE MUSEUM
203 S. Claiborne St.   *434-7554*

Imagine the bells clanging, horse hooves pounding and cries of men dressed in fire gear racing to the scene of a fire. Even now, the sight of a shiny red engine with its tense and stern-faced crew, its sirens and lights shouting out warnings to motorists, still plays out a thrilling drama for many.

The fire museum is actually in the old Phoenix Steam Fire Company No. 6's station house, built in 1859. Inside are old horse-drawn and steam fire engines and artifacts dating back to Mobile's first volunteer companies in 1819. The museum is free and open from 1 PM to 5 PM Tuesday through Sunday.

USS ALABAMA
BATTLESHIP MEMORIAL PARK
East on I-10 to Exit 27 at U.S. 90 (Battleship Pkwy.)   *433-2703*

Ready for inspection! The giant battleship floating in Mobile Bay once held a 2,500-member crew in the Pacific during World War II. Even after shooting down 22 enemy planes and earning nine battlestars, the USS *Alabama* remained un-touched. You can tour both the battleship and the USS *Drum* submarine, then visit the other military exhibits, which include a B-52 bomber, a gull-winged Corsair and the P-51 "Mustang" World War II fighter planes in the 100-acre park. On the grounds also are a nature observatory, where a boardwalk and a two-story observation deck provide views of natural wetlands; a snack bar; and a display of 1,700 varieties of roses. The tours and the park are free to the public, which is open every day but Christmas from 8 AM until sunset.

ALABAMA CRUISES
At Bellingrath Gardens
Theodore   *973-1244, (800) 247-8420*

Alabama Cruises has changed its location, its cruises and just about everything about it except the friendly, quality service and excellent meals! Formerly docked at Battleship Park, *The Commander* has now moved to the Fowl River at Bellingrath Gardens, undergoing a transformation into the *Southern Belle*. Sightseeing river cruises leave on the hour from 10 AM until 4 PM from April through August. Board right behind the

Bellingrath home. Tours last about 45 minutes.

Value packages for the gardens, the guided home tour and the river cruise are $18.95 for adults and $13.95 for children ages 5 through 11. For the river cruise only, tickets are $8.75 for adults and $5 for children. Remember that you must pay for a ticket to the gardens (see the following Bellingrath Gardens admission prices) to gain access to the river cruise.

Dinner cruises are great fun after a day of walking through the gardens and touring the magnificent Bellingrath home. A lavish three-entree Southern-tinged buffet awaits you aboard the boat, part of the 2½-hour cruise every Friday and Saturday April through August. Docking begins at 6:30 PM with departure time at 7 PM. Boarding is on the Bellingrath property at the Alabama Cruises office off of Rebel Road.

Bellingrath Gardens and Home
West of Mobile off I-10, 12401 Bellingrath Garden Rd., Theodore   973-2217

A most spectacular showplace, Bellingrath Gardens is one of the area's finest attractions. It's *way* out in the boonies, but if you follow the signs, you'll get there eventually. A tour of the 65-acre floral and landscaped paradise is worth a trip in itself. Seasonal flowers are in bloom all year long, but nothing compares with the spring azaleas. Enjoy a spring showing of more tulips and daffodils than you may have ever seen all in one place. At every turn is another incredible view eliciting gasps, squeals or shutter clicks. There's the Oriental American Garden, the Bridal Garden, the Rose Garden, the Exotica Conservatory and Mirror Lake, among many other sights. The home is built along the Fowl River, and a roofed pavilion with big porch swings affords

cooling breezes all year. Still to come is a wildlife exhibit and a hummingbird garden.

The Bellingrath home is grand as well, with a superb collection of antiques, but if you only have a few hours, spend them in the gardens; the rewards are great. The home and gardens are open every day from 7 AM until sunset. Admission to the gardens only is $7 per person, kids ages 5 to 11 $5. Tickets to both the gardens and the home are $13.95 for adults, $9.95 for children ages 5 to 11. Special value packages are available if you want to add a scenic cruise on the river. Ask about special senior prices.

Wildland Expeditions
Hwy. 43 at the Chickasaw Marina
Chickasaw   460-8206

Capt. Gene Burrell invites visitors out on his custom-built 22-passenger boat, the *Gator Bait*, for a tour of the swamps, tidal marshes and bayous of the Mobile-Tensaw Delta. Prepare yourself for adventure throughout the largest inland delta in the United States. Bring along a camera and a pair of binoculars to capture the flight of one of 250 species of birds or 200 species of fish and wildlife. You may even be fortunate enough, if the time is right, to spot a black bear munching clumps of palmetto. Other endangered species can be found in the dense woodlands including the bald eagle and the osprey, whose giant nests of twigs perch atop cypress trees.

It wouldn't be an adventure without an alligator or two . . . or two dozen, and Capt. Gene can almost promise that some of the leathery reptilians will surface for your cameras. Tours leave at 9 AM and 2 PM and take about 2½ hours. Prices for the expedition are $20 for large gator bait; $10 for bite-sized bait (12 and younger).

Take I-10 W. to I-65 N. Take Exit 13 (Highway 158) west for 2 miles. It intersects with Highway 43.

South of Mobile

DAUPHIN ISLAND
Off Hwy. 193 south of Mobile   861-5525

Dauphin Island suffered a direct hit from Hurricane Frederic back in 1979 but has come back to life with many fine public areas island-wide. There are a couple of nice little shopping areas with restaurants, a marina and charter boat cruises, six public boat ramps, two fishing piers, a 150-site campground, a ,pre-Civil War fort, the Dauphin Island Sea Lab, an 18-hole public golf course, the 160-acre Audubon Bird Sanctuary and an Indian shell mound, besides miles of white-sand beaches along the 15-mile-long island.

FORT GAINES
Exit I-10 at 193 S. to
Dauphin Island   861-6992

This 1821 fort marks the place where Admiral David Farragut shouted the oft-quoted command: "Damn the torpedoes. Full speed ahead!" during the Civil War Battle of Mobile Bay. Early French explorers dubbed the island "Massacre Island" for a curious pile of human skeletons they found there. The first wooden fort was built by the French in 1717 on the far eastern tip of the island.

It was 1813 when the Americans moved in to capture the island from the Spanish and establish a fort on this strategic spot of land guarding the entrance to the bay. The five-pointed design has walls 22½ feet high and 4½ feet thick. Soldiers lived and worked at Fort Gaines from the early 1800s up to 1946, when it became a historic site. The fort is open every day but Christmas and New Year's Day from 9 AM to 5 PM. Admission is $2 for adults, $1 for kids 7 to 12.

FORT MORGAN
Hwy. 180 at the tip of Pleasure Island
Fort Morgan   540-7125

It's a daytrip all by itself; the drive over to Fort Morgan is as much fun as being there. Our recommendation is to head out to Perdido Key from Pensacola and keep on going west along Highway 292 into Alabama. You'll pass by the famous Flora-Bama Lounge at the state line, then go on into the scenic coastal resort towns of Gulf Shores and Orange Beach. The trip to Fort Morgan will take about 1½ hours from Pensacola, but there's much to see and do along the way. You may want to stop for lunch in Gulf Shores or Orange Beach, since the Gulf Shore peninsula is rather devoid of commercialism. At the tip of the island, also known as Pleasure Island, is the fort, built between 1819 and 1834, which was one of the last Confederate forts to fall to Union forces in the Battle of Mobile Bay. Every fort seems to get in on the action with Admiral David Farragut's famous line (see Fort Gaines).

There's a controversy afoot with the old fort, stemming from new plans to build more houses, an inn, a restaurant and a marina on the 450-acre park site. The Fort Morgan Civic Association has other ideas and is talking to another developer about erecting replicas of a barracks, a hospital, a quarantine pier and officers' houses that were once at the fort. Right now the area is rather development deficient, with a few beach cottages and the undeveloped Bon Secour Wildlife Refuge along the two-lane road. Fort Morgan is open weekdays from 8 AM to 5 PM and weekends 9 to 5 year-round except for Thanksgiving, Christmas and

New Year's Day. People younger than 6 get in free; ages 7 to 12 pay $1; for anyone older than 12, it's $2. Seniors pay $1, and if you're 100 years old and have a note from your mom, you get in free.

Restaurants

Although it really isn't far enough away from Pensacola to have to spend the night, you will need sustenance to get you through the day. Whether beachside, bayside, islandside or on the bayous, restaurants throughout the Gulf Coast almost always offer some type of seafood fare, so dig in and savor the flavor of the Gulf Coast's best catches!

Price code for Alabama restaurants follow for a dinner for two with beverage and dessert (no tax, tip or cocktails). All restaurants accept major credit cards unless otherwise noted.

Less than $20	$
$21 to 40	$$
$41 to 60	$$$
More than $60	$$$$

ROUSSOS SEAFOOD RESTAURANT & CATERING

166 S. Royal St. in the
Fort Condé Village   433-3322
$$

The first Roussos on Battleship Parkway was obliterated by 1979's Hurricane Frederic, but the new restaurant is still making old favorites such as hot'n spicy Cajun shrimp, sauteed crabmeat, fried baby squid and fresh seafood cooked to your liking. Come on back to the kitchen to watch the preparation, ask questions and talk to one of the seven family members who works here. Roussos can be a romantic-night-out place or an in-and-out family spot — you choose. Kids' plates start at just $1.95. Roussos is open for lunch and dinner every day.

KORBET'S RESTAURANT OF MOBILE

At the loop in midtown Mobile
2029 Airport Blvd.   471-1000
$$$

Warm, comfortable surroundings are the hallmark of Korbet's, which has been here for decades. Just about every kind of

A late afternoon scene on Mobile Bay.

food imaginable is served at Korbet's, so nobody gets left out, and everybody goes home happy. Soups, salads, specialty sandwiches, burgers, steaks and chops, chicken entrees, eggs and omelets, seafood and spaghetti round out the list of tempting delights. Ever tried a lump crab omelet sandwich? This may be your only opportunity. How about a fresh Florida lobster stuffed with crabmeat dressing and served with lemon butter sauce . . . mmmmmm. You'll get your fill here and then some with sweet endings such as homemade pies, strawberry shortcake and hot fudge sundaes. The landmark restaurant is open every day for breakfast, lunch and dinner.

WEICHMAN'S ALL
SEASONS RESTAURANT

168 S. Beltline Hwy.   344-3961
$$$

OK, it's pretty hokey, and we hope some high-priced advertising exec didn't come up with it, but the All Seasons' slogan is: "The Quality is Rare, the Prices are Medium, and the Service is Well Done." Kind of makes you cringe, doesn't it? All that aside, the fresh seafood, prime rib, aged steaks, lamb, pasta and chicken specialties are absolutely first class, especially when served with one of the many fine wines offered by Weichman's. Be sure to try their gumbo. Dinners start at just $7.95. It's open for lunch and dinner every day; dinner only on Saturday.

WINTZELL'S OYSTER HOUSE

605 Dauphin St.   433-1004
$$

Fried, stewed and nude, get your oysters here. Just be careful about those raw ones — warnings should now be placed in every restaurant still serving raw oysters. But Wintzell's knows oysters probably better than anybody around here,

since they've been here longer than just about everybody (1938). This is a suck-'n'-slurp, good-times place; just looking at the walls as you come in will tell you that. It will take your entire visit here to read just the sayings within eyeshot. When you come back, ask to sit in a different spot so you can read something new! You don't have to be an oyster aficionado to eat here; Wintzell's promises some of the best fresh seafood on the Gulf Coast will be cooked any way you like it. It's open Monday through Saturday for lunch until late; Sundays for lunch only.

THE PILLARS

1757 Government St.   478-6341
$$$$

Another gourmet restaurant with a sterling reputation for quality, The Pillars' romantic setting in an antebellum Southern mansion exudes charm, style and a fairly steep price tag. The 12 dining rooms are each decorated with period antiques, fireplaces, chandeliers and candlelight. Chef Tim Ward is sometimes helped in the kitchen by the owner, Filippo Milone, who also likes to run quality control. Milone was trained in Europe as a chef himself, so he knows the business — from the kitchen to the food selection to the impeccable service to the extensive selection of wines from The Pillars' own cellar. Choose thick, sizzling steaks, fresh seafood, veal, lamb and pasta creations.

Menu specialties change daily; your server will be happy to explain the preparation of each. Fine dining commences at 5 PM Monday through Saturday.

HISTORIC DOWNTOWN DAUPHIN STREET

Dauphin St.
$

From Royal Street to Hamilton, several little eateries and food boutiques are

Southern Belles come out in force along the Mobile Azalea Trail.

Photo: Mobile Area Chamber of Commerce

making news. They're fun, trendy and inexpensive. **G.T. Henry's** at Dauphin and Hamilton, 432-0300, is a good local watering hole, featuring live music Wednesday through Saturday. Across the street, **South Side**, 438-5555, features blues, Cajun, reggae and rock, mixed with muffelattas, po-boys and pizza. Head three blocks west for a lively game of darts, foosball, cold beer and good company at **Hayley's**, 433-4970, where there's never a cover charge. Hayley's is open seven days from 3 PM to 3 AM.

Within every large city, there seems to be at least one great chocolatier, and **Three Georges Southern Chocolates** at 226 Dauphin is it in Mobile, 433-6725. Free samples, gift boxes and special offers make it a great souvenir (and dessert) stop. It's open Monday through Saturday between 9 AM and 6 PM. Look a few doors down the street toward the **Port City Brewery & Eatery**, 438-2739, which actually has its own microbrewery on the premises. So try a local brew and top it off with one of their great specialty sandwiches. Where would any tourist town be without its own Subway? This one, at

Dauphin and Joachim, is called **Subway Bienville**, 433-0571, most likely for the historic district.

Cafe au lait (half chickory coffee and half hot milk), bagels, beignets (French doughnuts), lunch specials and sandwiches are all made fresh at **Bagel Fanagle, Inc.,** 107 Dauphin, 694-0900. They also specialize in low-fat and no-fat cooking, then they go and make fattening gourmet desserts. Go figure. **Mostly Muffins**, 433-9855, is *mostly* muffins, but also croissants, cookies, coffee beans, shakes, yogurts and specialty coffees. Drink it there or take some home!

HEMINGWAY'S

1850 Airport Blvd. at the Loop (4 points), Mobile 479-3514
Orange Beach Marina, Orange Beach 981-9791
$$$

Nice atmosphere, great food, dependable service and the prices aren't too bad. We like the Orange Beach Hemingway's a little better for its waterfront location, but the in-town restaurant is cozy and comfortable and serves just as well for a business lunch as a night on the town. Try original creations such as the grilled grouper with lump crabmeat topping and grilled tomatoes on the side. A personal favorite is the crawfish-stuffed fillet — the fillet can be whatever was caught that day, and it's filled with crawfish tail stuffing (incredible) and ladled with Brandy Alexander sauce. No, it's not fat free, but you owe it to yourself. Hemingway's is open for lunch and dinner seven days a week.

THE TINY DINY
2159 Halls Mill Rd. at Pleasant Valley
Mobile   476-3880
$

OK, we like the name too, but ask around town, and this name will come up over and over for really good food for just a little pocket change. It's a homestyle menu, so expect gravies, sauces, biscuits and enough greens to choke a horse. The Tiny Diny (we love saying that) is also proud to serve a fresh seafood menu nightly. It's open all day until 9 PM.

Shopping

Factory outlets, antique stores and specialty boutiques are all the rage in the Mobile area; down south along the gulf, shops selling sundresses, floppy hats and resort-type beachwear line the shore. Flea markets are big business everywhere, and who knows what you'll uncover!

ROBERT MOORE & CO.
CHRISTMAS TOWN & VILLAGE
4213 Halls Mill Rd.   661-3608
Mobile   661-3693

If you just can't wait until Christmas, stop in here for that holiday feeling all year long. Beautifully decorated themed trees are everywhere, as are tiny lighted villages, crèches, beautiful doll displays and more lights and ornaments than you'll know what to do with! Also in the

village are a candy shop, a deli, a wine and cheese shop and a coffee and tea shop to make a day of it. A half-mile west of Azalea Road, just 10 minutes off I-65 or I-10, Christmas Town and Village is open Monday through Saturday from 10 AM to 6 PM, Sunday 1 PM to 6 PM. It's closed New Year's Day, Mardi Gras Day, Easter, 4th of July, Thanksgiving and — yes — Christmas! The little elves who work here can only take so much holiday spirit, you know.

RIVIERA CENTRE FACTORY STORES
2601 S. McKenzie St., Hwy. 59 S.
Foley   943-8888, (800) 5-CENTRE

People drive for hours to get here, so the savings and the selection must be worth the trip. Save as much as 70 percent every day from more than 110 manufacturers. Here's a small sampling: Arrow Shirts, Bugle Boy, Calvin Klein, Oshkosh B'Gosh, Oneida, West Point Pepperell, Bass, Reebok, American Tourister, Carter's, Ruff Hewn, L'eggs... you get the idea. Seven food court merchants provide quick lunches and dinners (so you can get back to shopping). It's open Monday through Saturday 9 AM to 9 PM, Sunday 10 AM to 6 PM daily except Easter, Thanksgiving and Christmas.

FLEA MARKET MOBILE
401 Schillinger Rd. N.   633-7533

You won't have time to look at everything with 700 — that's right, 700 — booths under cover. Besides what people have dug out of the attic or the root cellar, there are fair-type foods (you know, such as Auntie Peg's jams and Sister Lil's 'maters), fresh produce, fine and not-so-fine antiques, and the catch-all "collectibles," meaning everything from "Z-Man" comics to Hummel figurines. Up to 40,000 people pass through here every week! The Flea Market is on Schillinger Road just off Airport Boulevard. Market hours are Saturday and Sunday 9 AM to 5 PM.

COTTON CITY ANTIQUE MALL
2012 Airport Blvd. at the Loop   479-9747

Ninety dealer spaces showcase period furniture, accessories, glassware, jewelry, silver and more. The mall is open Monday through Saturday 10 AM to 5 PM, Sunday 1 to 5 PM.

VICTORIAN ROSE ANTIQUES
450 Dauphin Island Pkwy.
at the Loop   479-9119

Victorian Rose Antiques is not huge, but the priceless store of antiques makes up for volume. Shop, deal and haul it away Monday through Saturday from 9 AM to 5 PM, Sunday 1 to 5 PM.

WARD'S
2103 Airport Blvd. at the Loop
Mobile   479-9058

It started out to be an Army-Navy store, but since there are literally bezillions of private schools in Mobile (which we're not sure says more about the public schools or the mindset of the locals), Ward's is now in the business of selling school uniforms right along with camo and footlockers. Camping and sporting goods equipment can outfit you for just about any outdoor activity you mean to try.

... And While You're Daytripping

We can't send you over to Mobile without telling you about a couple of other scenic Alabama daytrips. The first begins on Highway 98 W. in Pensacola (the same one that stretches through most of Northwest Florida) and follows into Alabama over the Lillian bridge. Pass through the tiny German community of **Elberta**. Then go on into historic **Foley** (home of the **Riviera Centre Factory Stores** and **Stacey's Rexall Drugs** with its old-fashion soda fountain). Continue through scenic **Magnolia Springs**, where the mail is still delivered by boat, then swing northward into **Point Clear**. Stop at the **Punta Clara Kitchen** to watch wonderful candies and sweets being made, have lunch and don't forget to pick up some souvenirs in the 1897 Victorian home. You owe yourself a trip to **Marriott's Grand Hotel**, just a mile north of Punta Clara Kitchen to see what a real genteel Old South hotel is like. The grounds are immaculate (there may be a few folks playing croquet on the lawn), the view is lovely (right on Mobile Bay), and the hotel, which was first built in 1847, is a tribute to tradition and service. Continue north into the pretty little town of **Fairhope**, site of numerous arts and crafts festivals and historic homes along the waterfront.

A second trip follows the Florida Gulf Coast right onto the Alabama Gulf Coast. **Perdido Key** spans both states, with the landmark **Flora-Bama Lounge** as the dividing line. Cross over **Perdido Pass** on into **Orange Beach** (follow the signs to the **Orange Beach Marina** for some yacht ogling), then double back to the beach road into **Gulf Shores**, with its fancy beach homes, resort strip and **Gulf State Park**, complete with overnight accommodations on the gulf. Keep on going through this area known as **Pleasure Island**, and drive until you run out of road. That's when you'll be at **Fort Morgan**. From Perdido Key, the drive only takes about an hour, depending on how often you choose to stop. Have a great trip!

Pensacola Area
Community Information

Real Estate Companies

LEIB & ASSOCIATES REALTY
14620 Perdido Key Dr.
Perdido Key   492-0744, (800)553-1223

AQUATIC REALTY
14508 Perdido Key Dr.
Perdido Key   492-4632, (800)881-RENT

KEY CONCEPTS
13880 Perdido Key Dr.
Perdido Key   492-5462

TRISTAN REALTY, INC.
1010 Fort Pickens Rd.   932-7363
Pensacola Beach   (800)445-9931

PENSACOLA BEACH REALTY
649 Pensacola Beach Blvd.   932-5337
Pensacola Beach   (800)874-9243

REAL ESTATE HOUSE INC.
U.S. 98 and College Pkwy.
Gulf Breeze   934-8700, (800)239-4346

MONTGOMERY REALTORS
1388 Country Club Rd.
Gulf Breeze   932-9228, (800)445-2507

CENTURY 21 FOUR WINDS REALTY
2507 Gulf Breeze Pkwy.
Gulf Breeze   932-3513

Photo: Bill Gonzalez

*Looking down Perdido Key onto Johnson Beach, part of the Gulf Islands
National Seashore.*

ERA Navarre Beach Agency, Inc.
1804 Prado St.
Navarre   939-2020, (800)598-8428

Tidewater Realty
8095 Navarre Pkwy.
Navarre   939-0300

Bill Pullum Realty, Inc.
8494 Navarre Pkwy.
Navarre   939-2363

IFirst Choice Realty of Pensacola
7200 N. 9th Ave., Ste. A-1
Pensacola   476-2154, (800)405-HOME

Joseph M. Endry Realty Company
22-A Via de Luna Dr.
Pensacola Beach   932-5300
3232 Gulf Breeze Pkwy.
Gulf Breeze   932-1000
4301 Spanish Trail Rd.
Pensacola   432-5300
5601 Woodbine Rd., Pace   994-6128

Connell & Manziek Realty Inc.
2107 Airport Blvd.
Pensacola   478-4141

Re/Max Horizons Realty
1335 Creighton Rd.
Pensacola   476-6000, (800)947-3629

Rainbow Realty, Inc.
1212 Creighton Rd.
Pensacola   478-6116

Re/Max Horizons Realty
13335 Creighton Rd.
Pensacola   476-6000

Century 21 Classic Properties Gold, Inc.
524 E. Zaragoza St.
Pensacola   435-7600, (800)582-7105

Donovan Realty, Inc.
226 E. Government St.
Pensacola   432-6104, (800)228-7603

Health Care

Hospitals and Medical Centers

Sacred Heart Hospital
5151 N.Ninth Ave.
Pensacola   474-7000

Baptist Hospital
1000 W. Moreno St.
Pensacola   434-4011

Gulf Breeze Hospital
1110 Gulf Breeze Pkwy.
Gulf Breeze   934-2000

West Florida Regional Medical Center
8383 N. Davis Hwy.
Pensacola   494-4000

Immediate Care Centers

Carriage Hills Family Care Center
4929 Mobile Hwy., ½-mile north
of Fairfield Dr.
Pensacola   453-3281
Open 8 AM to 9 PM, seven days a week.

Insiders' Tips

Hot new areas for subdivisions are in Pace, north of Pensacola and east of Gulf Breeze, stretching to Navarre and beyond. What 10 years ago was wilderness and acres of pine forest is now an ever-expanding population base, essentially blurring the divisions between "here" and "there."

PERDIDO BAY FAMILY CARE CENTER
*13139 Sorrento Rd., one mile north
of the Intracoastal Waterway Bridge
near Perdido Key   492-0543
Open 8 AM to 6 PM, Monday through Friday;
Saturdays from 8 AM to 1 PM.*

PENSACOLA BOULEVARD
FAMILY CARE CENTER
*6950 Pensacola Blvd.,north of Car City
Pensacola   478-4357
Open 8 AM to 8 PM Monday through Saturday;
Sundays 2 to 8 PM.*

PINE FOREST FAMILY CARE CENTER
*7284 Pine Forest Rd., ½-mile south of I-10
Pensacola   944-4686
Open 7 to 6 Monday through Friday; 8 AM to 1
PM on weekends.*

TIGER POINT FAMILY CARE CENTER
*3370 Gulf Breeze Pkwy., across from
Pizza Hut
Gulf Breeze   932-9251
Open 8 AM to 7 PM Monday through Friday;
weekends from 8 AM to 1 PM.*

NORTH DAVIS
FAMILY MEDICINE CENTER
*6330 N. Davis Hwy.
Pensacola   478-3336
Open 8 AM to 6 PM Monday through Saturday.*

WARRINGTON PRIMARY CARE
*4045 Barrancas Ave.
Pensacola   455-0314
Open 9 AM to 5 PM Monday through Friday.*

NAVARRE FAMILY MEDICINE CENTER
*7964 Navarre Pkwy.
Navarre   939-6110
Open 8 AM to 5 PM Monday through Friday.*

SCENIC HIGHWAY
FAMILY MEDICINE CENTER
*8105 Scenic Hwy.
Pensacola   484-9435
Open 7:30 AM to 5:30 PM Monday through
Friday.*

WEST SIDE
FAMILY MEDICINE CENTER
*6715 Hwy. 98 W.
Pensacola   453-6737
Open 8 AM to 5 PM Monday through Friday.*

SPANISH TRAIL
FAMILY MEDICAL CENTER
*4601 Spanish Tr.
Pensacola   433-9911
Open 8 AM to 5 PM Monday through Friday.*

GULF BREEZE
FAMILY MEDICAL CENTER
*85 Baybridge
Gulf Breeze   932-2251
Open 8 AM to 5 PM Monday through Friday.*

WARRINGTON FAMILY
MEDICAL CENTER
*30 S. Third St.
Pensacola   455-4516
Open 8:30 AM to 4:30 PM Monday through
Friday; ½ day on Wednesday.*

Whenever possible, new uses are being found for historic buildings. Two such successes are the old Sacred Heart Hospital on 12th Avenue in East Hill, now converted into restaurants, offices and shops; and the P.K. Yonge School in the North Hill neighborhood. The building, which sat empty and vandalized for years, has a facelift and a new life as the Florida Department of Law Enforcement.

Insiders' Tips

Photo:Sacred Heart Hospital

The Health Performance Center is more than a gym, it's an overall health-maintenance program.

CANTONMENT FAMILY MEDICAL CENTER

748 Hwy. 29, ¼-mile north of Champion Paper Mill
Cantonment   968-0763
Open 7 AM to 5 PM Monday through Friday.

WEST PENSACOLA MEDICAL CENTER

321 S. Fairfield Dr.
Pensacola   456-6696
Open 7:30 AM to 5 PM Monday through Friday.

Support Services

THE HEALTH PERFORMANCE CENTER

1601 Airport Blvd.
Pensacola   474-6150

PEDIATRIC EXTRA HOURS AT SACRED HEART

Children's Medical Services Building
5177 N. Ninth Ave.
Pensacola   474-7299
Open Monday through Friday 5 to 10 PM; weekends from 2 to 9 PM.

SACRED HEART SURGICAL CENTER

5147 N. Ninth Ave., Ste. 301
Pensacola   474-7120

THE REHABILITATION INSTITUTE OF WEST FLORIDA

8391 N. Davis Hwy.
Pensacola   474-5358

MEDICAL CENTER CLINIC, P.A.

8333 N. Davis Hwy.
Pensacola   474-8000

SURGICARE

1000 W. Moreno St.
Pensacola   469-2169

THE NORTH FLORIDA SURGERY CENTER

4600 N. Davis Hwy.
Pensacola   494-0048

Physician Referral Services

CALL SACRED HEART

Offered by Sacred Heart Hospital   474-7500
Open 8 AM to 4 PM Monday through Friday.

Call Sacred Heart
474-7500

A free physician referral and appointment service

We have the experience and resources to help you find a physician who meets your special needs. With just one phone call, you have...

☐ easy access to over 200 physicians in the Call Sacred Heart network.

☐ up-to-date information on physician specialties, office fees, accepted insurance plans, office hours and more.

☐ prompt help in making an appointment.

Call Sacred Heart, Monday-Friday 8 a.m.-4 p.m.

MDLINE
Offered by Baptist Health Care   434-4080
Open 9 AM to 5 PM Monday through Friday.

PHYSICIAN ON CALL
Offered by West Florida Regional Medical Center   474-8200
Open 8 AM to 4:30 PM Monday through Friday.

Substance Abuse/Mental Health/Geriatric Services

TWELVE OAKS
2068 Healthcare Ave.
Navarre   939-1200, (800)622-1255

THE PAVILION
2191 Johnson Ave.
Pensacola   494-5000

BEHAVIORAL MEDICINE CENTER
1000 W. Moreno St.
Pensacola   434-4866

LAKEVIEW CENTER INC.
1221 W. Lakeview Ave.
Pensacola   432-1222

THE FRIARY OF BAPTIST HEALTH CARE
4400 Hickory Shores Blvd.
Gulf Breeze   932-9375, (800)332-2271

Higher Education

Colleges and Universities

UNIVERSITY OF WEST FLORIDA
11000 University Pkwy.
Pensacola   474-2000

The local public radio station, WUWF (88.1 FM), broadcasts from new facilities at the University of West Florida, playing classical, jazz and alternative music, as well as sponsoring or cosponsoring numerous community events such as the annual Jazzfest, Springfest and the Great Gulfcoast Arts Festival.

Insiders' Tips

PENSACOLA JUNIOR COLLEGE

Main Campus, 1000 College Blvd.
Pensacola   484-1000

Naval Air Station Center, Bldg. 679, West Wing
Pensacola Naval Air Station   453-7526
                                     452-4520

Downtown Center, 19 W. Garden St.
Pensacola   434-8411

Warrington Campus, 5555 W. Hwy. 98
Pensacola   457-2200

Milton Campus, 1130 U.S. Hwy. 90
West Milton   626-1010

PENSACOLA CHRISTIAN COLLEGE

250 Brent Ln.
Pensacola   478-8496

Vocational-Technical Schools

GEORGE STONE AREA
VOCATIONAL-TECHNICAL CENTER

2400 Longleaf Dr.
Pensacola   944-1424

Inside
Gulf Islands
National Seashore

Stretched out from Perdido Key on the west to Mexico Beach on the east is almost 100 miles of coastline. In the past few decades, much of what hadn't been snatched up by the military had become industrial waterfront or had fallen to haphazard development. Gulf Coast residents became anxious over places like Port St. Joe, its coastline almost completely given over to the timber industry, and Pensacola Beach, where blocks of cheap cinder block homes were hastily constructed as "summer cottages" in the 1950s.

By the 1960s, more and more people were discovering Gulf Coast beaches — people who needed places to stay and places to eat and other diversions besides the beaches. Not only was encroaching development threatening the remaining pristine shoreline, but Fort Pickens on Santa Rosa Island and Fort Barrancas on Pensacola Naval Air Station were in shambles. A prehistoric Indian site at the Naval Live Oaks Reservation near Gulf Breeze had been vandalized.

Finally, spurred by radio and newspaper editorials in Pensacola, U.S. Representative Bob Sikes introduced a bill to create a national seashore. President Richard Nixon signed the bill into law in January 1971.

The Gulf Islands National Seashore, GINS, effectively preserves portions of islands and keys from Horn Island in Mis-

Photo: Robin Rowan

Salt air, intense heat and lots of bugs were a way of life for Civil War soldiers at Fort Pickens.

sissippi to Okaloosa Island near Destin — a stretch of 150 miles. Fifty-two of those miles are in Northwest Florida, the largest tract of protected shoreline in the state. Twelve more miles will be added when the Air Force vacates its property at Eglin between Fort Walton Beach and Navarre Beach.

The Seashore, with its historic forts, white beaches, hiking trails and campgrounds, is a destination in itself; therefore, all facets of the park will be discussed here (one exception: detailed camping information can be found in the chapter on Pensacola Accommodations). For more information on the Gulf Islands National Seashore, call 934-2600.

The Beaches

Come to our beaches. Wiggle your toes into the powdery white sand. Gaze out over the waves crashing at sea, then breaking gently on the shore. Listen to the surf, the sea gull cries, the wind whistling through the dune grasses and sea oats and you'll come to understand why we've worked so hard to preserve this natural splendor.

All Gulf Islands National Seashore beaches are open to the public all year. At the Fort Pickens and Perdido Key areas, there is an admission charge of $4 per car, $2 for bicycles and foot traffic (good for seven days). A yearly pass can be bought for $10. All other areas are free.

Perdido Key

Almost 7 miles of gulf-front on Perdido Key is part of the Gulf Islands National Seashore; 9.5 more miles line Big Lagoon. A 2-mile paved road allows visitors direct access to the beach. Beyond that, 5 additional miles of shoreline bar all but foot and water traffic. There's a picnic area with shelters and showers, a nature trail, restrooms and a boat launch for very small sailboats and skiffs. Perdido Key is off Gulf Beach Highway, 15 miles west of Pensacola.

Santa Rosa Island

The entire western tip of Santa Rosa Island, called the Fort Pickens Area, is under GINS jurisdiction, and what a magnificent piece of property it is. The drive toward Fort Pickens is nothing short of spectacular — huge grass and scrub-covered white dunes frame emerald and turquoise gulf water. A few miles down the road, ancient batteries jut from the landscape, nearly covered over with vegetation sculpted by the wind. And out of the brilliant white sand grow magnolias and slash pines, lending an appearance of a forest after a snowfall.

For preservation of the dunes and beach grasses, you're encouraged to use boardwalks and dune walk-overs whenever possible. There are plenty of parking areas along the road, but if you must park on the shoulder, watch that powdery sand!

As you near the western end of Santa Rosa Island, Fort Pickens looms out of the tall grasses and pines. There's ample parking here, so pick your spot and start walking. On the sound side, about 100 yards east of the fishing pier, is some of the best snorkeling in the area. Concrete chunks from fort construction were left along the shoreline, attracting scads of unusual marine life. It's best to bring gloves and a net for poking around — the gloves are handy for holding onto a piece of rock when the current's strong. On the other side of the fishing pier is a favorite dive spot, but be aware that the current coming from Pensacola Pass is much too strong for even the best swimmers without a weight belt. The shoreline at the pass is terrific both for watching the sun sink into the watery depths and for spotting schools of dolphin.

The next tract of National Seashore is a few miles east of the main commercial beach area (Pensacola Beach) on Santa Rosa Island. Just keep driving until you run out of houses. The coastline here is the longest continuous stretch of protected beach in Northwest Florida — some 16 miles (if you count both gulf and sound sides) between Pensacola Beach and Navarre Beach. Although the gulf side is what sunners and swimmers prefer, the soundside offers plenty of natural sub-tropical wilderness for anyone in a mood to explore. Dunes on this side tend to be taller and laden with more vegetation, since they are better protected from harsh winds and tidal action (and feet) than their sisters across the highway. These are some wide-open spaces, perfect for birders and shutterbugs (but bring along some heavy-duty insect repellant!).

Along Route 399 (the beach road) is the Santa Rosa Day-Use Area with picnic pavilions, a snack bar, showers (inside and outside) and an exhibit room with displays of natural and cultural history. It's open 8 AM until sunset every day.

Okaloosa Island

Okaloosa Island is really just another name for the eastern end of Santa Rosa Island, but the flavor of this area is far removed from the remoteness of the beaches farther west. Besides an expanse of public beach on Choctawhatchee Bay,

the Okaloosa Area of GINS, located on U.S. Highway 98 just east of Fort Walton Beach near the Eglin Air Force reservation, offers picnic tables, restrooms and outdoor showers. There is no admission charge.

Naval Live Oaks Area

This 1,400-acre tract of gnarled live oaks along Highway 98 east of Gulf Breeze was set aside in 1828 by then-President John Quincy Adams. The wood from the oaks, called "ironwood," is much stronger than most other types of timber, and its natural curves are more easily shaped for hulls and bows in shipbuilding.

The Naval Live Oaks Area, which is also the Seashore headquarters, offers peaceful walks through dense woodlands and along the sound, harboring abundant marine, animal and bird life. Remember that here, as well as in other preserved areas, all plants, animals and artifacts are protected by the National Park Service and must not be disturbed.

A visitor's center displays Indian artifacts and runs a free orientation slide show on the Gulf Islands National Seashore. Several nature trails and a shady picnic area make this area a delightful respite from all that bright sand and sun.

The Forts

Around the 1820s and 1830s, three forts were constructed forming a triangle to guard the entrance to Pensacola Bay: Fort Pickens at the tip of Santa Rosa Island, Fort Barrancas at the Naval Air Station and Fort McRee on Perdido Key. In ruins after a Civil War battle and due to shifting sands over a century, Fort McRee has crumbled into the water, but Pickens

Can You Eat This Stuff Or What?

It's a gorgeous day in early June. You pack up the family, head for the Gulf of Mexico, and there, clogging the water and spread out for miles on the beach like giant mounds of Brillo pads is — SEAWEED!! The annual migration of Sargassum seaweed, like the ebb and flow of the tides, is an inevitable but natural part of the Gulf Coast environment.

This sand-colored, scratchy seaweed was first described in the journal of Christopher Columbus while sailing the Sargasso Sea. Perhaps the worst year for the weed here in Northwest Florida was 1991. Violent winter storms kept the gulf in constant motion, causing the weed, which grows on the sandy gulf bottom, to be uprooted and sent sometimes hundreds of miles toward the shore. Bulldozers were used to move gigantic mountains of the weed away from public swimming areas. Besides spoiling an otherwise pristine view, the odor of dead fish permeated the air, sending beachgoers fleeing to inland waterways.

Photo: E. S. Clark

A filefish finds a safe haven among clumps of Sargassum weed.

Swimmers and surfers find Sargassum weed to be merely a nuisance, but the real threat is to boaters. Motors can become suddenly entangled in the weed, stopping them dead. If Sargassum weed has been spotted in the gulf, boaters are warned to steer clear.

But microbiologists, coastal scientists and park rangers see the weed as an asset to coastal ecology. The weed provides protection for hundreds of species of tiny fish, shrimp, baby sea turtles and other organisms. Marine creatures will lay their eggs in the weed, knowing the young have a better chance at survival if hidden from predators' view.

And the weed could one day provide a benefit to humans: Navy and Coast Guard trainees are instructed to seek out patches of Sargassum weed and fill their helmets. Just that amount of weed can provide enough nourishment from the instant supply of fish, shrimp and other edibles to keep a person alive until rescued.

and Barrancas remain intact and still have many fascinating stories to tell. More detailed historical information is included in the Pensacola History chapter.

Fort Pickens

The most colorful fort historically of the three mentioned above, Fort Pickens made a name for itself during the Civil War (Union troops had control of Pickens, while McRee and Barrancas stayed under Confederate command) and during the incarceration of Apache medicine man Geronimo (again, see the Pensacola History chapter for more information).

After the National Park Service took over, Fort Pickens received a heavy overhaul to repair the decades of neglect and constant battering by harsh sun, wind and salt air. One corner of the fort, blown to bits by an exploding magazine in 1899, was never rebuilt.

The fort is open from 9:30 AM to 5 PM daily from April through October; from November through March hours are 8:30 AM to 4 PM. Park rangers narrate guided tours Monday through Friday at 2 PM and at 11 AM and 2 PM on weekends. The tours are free and come highly recommended. After a tour, be sure to take some time to explore on your own — the fort is chock-full of dark, damp passageways, small rooms and underground tunnels that aren't part of the tour.

Just inside the main fort entrance is the Visitor Center. In the clump of green and white buildings near the fishing pier you'll find the Fort Pickens Museum (same hours as the fort) and the Fort Pickens Auditorium, which shows a movie or provides some type of program on the fort, the island, weather, local history, marine life or the like, at scheduled times during the year.

Near the fort is an exceptionally good fishing pier, and within a few miles are picnic shelters, swimming areas, nature trails, RV dump stations and campgrounds.

Just past the red-roofed ranger's station and up until the fort pops into view are several strangely shaped concrete structures poking out of the brush. These eight concrete batteries scattered throughout the area were built long after the fort to house various types of gunnery for coastal defense during the Spanish-American War and the two World Wars.

Fort Barrancas and the Advanced Redoubt

The fort that sits proudly overlooking the bayfront at Pensacola Naval Air Station played a vital role in Pensacola's coastal defense but was the last in a string of forts built on that site. The Spanish take credit for the first fortification, Fort San Carlos de Austria, built at the end of the 17th century, east of the current fort. That fort was destroyed when the French took possession of Pensacola more than 20 years later. Some ruins of this early fort may have recently been located.

French occupation was brief (only three years), and the Spanish were again in control when another country sought the strategic coastal position. The British docked at Pensacola after signing the Treaty of Paris in 1763. They built their

Both the USS *Pensacola* and the USS *Seminole* were constructed with the hard wood from the Naval Live Oaks Preserve, called "ironwood," the same wood that gave the U.S.S. *Constitution* the nickname "Old Ironsides."

Insiders' Tips

own fort on top of a mainland bluff, or "barranca," first called Red Cliffs, then renamed the British Royal Navy Redoubt. You guessed it, this one didn't last either. And neither did the Brits. They were ousted by the Spanish in 1781, changing the fort's name to Fort San Carlos de Barrancas. After just 25 years, this structure was decaying badly, so a new Fort San Carlos de Barrancas was built on the bluff (barranca), with a water level battery, Bateria de San Antonio, below it.

The British returned in the War of 1812, destroying the fort. Not to be intimidated, the Spanish charged ahead with a third Fort San Carlos de Barrancas in 1817. Four years later the American flag was raised over this fort, but the entire fort was razed in 1838 to make way for the present Fort Barrancas, which was actually built into the bluff this time. Bateria de San Antonio was somehow spared and is now connected to Fort Barrancas by an underground tunnel.

Early in 1861, a few musket shots were fired by Federal troops, which some claim were the first shots of the Civil War. For the remainder of the war, though, Federal troops moved to Fort Pickens; Barrancas remained a Confederate stronghold until troops departed in May of 1862. Adjacent to Fort Barrancas is the Advanced Redoubt, a small fortification built between 1845 and 1859, designed to protect Fort Barrancas from land attack.

Today the fort makes a great place for exploration, open from 9:30 AM to 5 PM daily April through September. From here on in hours get fairly complicated; call 934-2600 for hours during the remainder of the year (guided tour times tend to vary as well). Outside the visitors center, a ranger does a program on artillery at 9:30 AM. The 65 acres surrounding the forts contain oak and pine forests, a picnic area and a nature trail. Fort Barrancas is on Naval Air Station Pensacola and is free to the public.

Inside
Fort Walton Beach/Destin/
Beaches of South Walton

Huddled together smack in the middle of Northwest Florida, these three coastal resort areas are separated by only a few miles yet differ immensely in atmosphere. Beach activities range from rowdy Spring Breakers swilling beer and engaging in a rousing game of volleyball to a family oriented arts festival and a classy wine-tasting extravaganza complete with a concert pianist. It is rife with amusement parks and T-shirt shops, multimillion-dollar yachts and penthouse condos, peaceful gardens and seaside cottages.

To experience the real flavor of the place, you have to get off the main road. Highway 98 is the fastest way to travel from Point A to Point B, but it's also the most commercial. Savor the little inland communities, the beach hamlets along Route 30-A. It's scenic, engaging and worth the time to discover your own favorite spots.

Fort Walton Beach

Although only 10 miles separate Fort Walton Beach from Destin, the two resort destinations have distinct personalities, catering to a different clientele. Fort Walton Beach had a rather bawdy upbringing and is still looked upon as the stepchild in an area dubbed the "Emerald Coast."

First named Camp Walton during the Civil War for a military outpost there, by the turn of the century the tiny town was already gaining a reputation as a

Photo: Robin Rowan

Welcome to paradise.

pleasant vacation retreat. No matter that the number of black bears outnumbered the year-round residents, people flocked here for the fishing, stayed in rental cottages or the two downtown hotels and ferried across Santa Rosa Sound to the beach.

Real promotion of the area's amenities began in earnest by the 1930s, prompting a name change to Fort Walton. U.S. Highway 98 and the Brooks Bridge brought more automobile traffic in, but dirt roads and wayward livestock still made getting around a bit tricky.

But forward-thinking locals had a desire to offer visitors more than simply a place in the sun. They needed an attraction, something people would come back for again and again. They found it in gambling. Slot machines appeared in general stores, hotels, gas stations and restaurants. It brought the people in, all right, but with them came a sleazy reputation as a "Little Las Vegas." After some bad press from South Florida newspapers, the slot machines and the entire gambling industry faded into history.

But better news waited on the horizon, which eventually expanded and defined this little town perhaps even more than tourism. Until the 1930s, when Eglin Field was established as a bombing and gunnery base, much of Fort Walton was still wilderness. A good-sized expansion after World War II plus the addition of a Climatic Laboratory solidified Eglin's notoriety as a test center, pulling in military families and defense contractors.

By the late '40s and early '50s, tourism was in full swing. Fort Walton's population swelled between Memorial Day and Labor Day, and locals could barely keep up with construction of new restaurants, hotels and cottages. "Beach" was added to the city charter about the same time an enterprising newspaperman began calling the area the "Miracle Strip." Over the next 20 years, Fort Walton Beach saw a population surge, but the little town had no place to expand.

Today, Fort Walton Beach is a mismatched sprawl of residential areas, souvenir shops, military bases and strip shopping centers. Wayward development of past decades has been reined in with local zoning ordinances for both commercial and residential construction. Still, the downtown area with its many wooded parks, pink buildings and neon signs has a real feeling of the "Old Florida" — a town on the brink of a tourism explosion. The bridge onto Okaloosa Island, the *beach* part of Fort Walton Beach, carries you over to the city's alter-ego — resort hotels, beach bars, mini-golf courses, amusement parks and the Gulfarium, one of north Florida's oldest attractions.

Destin

Destin was the last beach area in Northwest Florida to make a name for itself as a resort destination. The reason

Visitor Information

**EMERALD COAST
CONVENTION AND VISITORS BUREAU**
P.O. Box 609, Fort Walton Beach 32549
651-7131, (800) 322-3319

**FORT WALTON BEACH
CHAMBER OF COMMERCE**
P.O. Box 640, Fort Walton Beach 32549
244-8191

**CRESTVIEW AREA
CHAMBER OF COMMERCE**
502 S. Main St., Crestview
682-3212

**NICEVILLE-VALPARAISO-BAY
CHAMBER OF COMMERCE**
170 John Sims Pkwy., Valparaiso
678-2323

DESTIN CHAMBER OF COMMERCE
P.O. Box 8, Destin 32541
837-6241

**BEACHES OF SOUTH WALTON
TOURIST DEVELOPMENT COUNCIL**
P.O. Box 1248, Santa Rosa Beach 32459
267-1216 or (800) 822-6877

could be that until a bridge was erected over Destin Pass in the 1930s, it was literally cut off from the rest of the world. The families who lived here thrived on the bounty of the gulf, and, until word reached the outside about the "World's Luckiest Fishing Village," it seemed enough.

There's no complete written history of Destin, so the real story of exactly how and when the town started depends on who you talk to. What *is* known is that Leonard Destin left New England to settle along the East Pass peninsula some-time around 1850. He hired young men from all over to build fishing seines and learn the life of the sea. The names of those that settled here themselves are well-known to Destin residents: Marler, Melvin, Jones, Maltezos. The town's name pays homage to Leonard Destin, the man who provided many men with lifelong skills and a love for this area.

Now, the identity of the first boat captain to turn from commercial fishing to sport charter fishing is a little fuzzy. There are a few old-timers left who remember the boats taking tourists out fishing in the '20s and '30s, but they all seem to remember it in a different way. No matter. A new industry was born in Destin, and sport fishing is still what makes it such a popular place to vacation.

The view of the Pass, with its emerald waters, white sand, high-rise condos and sea of charter boats may be one of the prettiest in Florida.

Beaches of South Walton

Cross the Walton County line and almost right away you'll feel a change in atmosphere. One reason is that it's more spread out; the toe-to-toe development drops off dramatically. Gone are the amusement parks, the bungee jumping and the mini-golf courses. The Beaches of South Walton are mostly that — 26 miles of pure white sand with scattered beach communities dotting the piney landscape.

Most communities sprang up in the last 20 years; the internationally acclaimed village of **Seaside** only recently celebrated its 10th birthday. But in parts of the county, such as Seagrove Beach, Point Washington and Grayton Beach, pockets of weather-worn cottages and historic community buildings provide the essence of the seaside lifestyle of decades past.

Point Washington started as a sawmill community in the latter part of the last century, built up around the Wesley Lumber Company. The Wesley mansion is now the centerpiece of Eden State Gardens.

Santa Rosa (not to be confused with Santa Rosa Beach) remains sparsely populated, although it once had about 1,000 residents. Citrus groves brought families in to grow oranges; around 1915, an outbreak of citrus canker meant the trees had to be destroyed. The industry, and the community, went with them.

Grayton Beach is probably the oldest community in South Walton, starting with just one house around 1880. That house is still standing. The Louisville & Nashville Railroad did its part to advertise the beauty and appeal of South Walton County by printing up postcards featuring fashionably dressed couples with hats and parasols strolling Grayton Beach.

The railroad line extended 25 miles north into **DeFuniak Springs**, which, perhaps because of its accessibility (and a few land concessions from railroad magnate W.D. Chipley), became the winter assembly of the Chautauqua. More likely, though, one of the residents of Lake Chautauqua, New York, owned a piece of land near here and started a southern version of the cultural and educational festival. The **Chautauqua Festival** continues in DeFuniak Springs each year on Lake de Funiak.

Rails and roads brought more people to the area, and by the 1950s and '60s some small communities offered year-round diversions for vacationers. By the '70s, developers caught wind of this magnificent piece of Florida that was just *sitting* there! One by one, condominiums, resorts and golf courses began filling the empty acres. Development here, though, seems to be more tightly controlled, so natural beauty still reigns.

Fort Walton Beach/Destin/ Beaches of South Walton
Restaurants and Nightlife

Salt air, saltwater and fresh seafood ...the mix provides for some of the finest eating anywhere. Try some of the local favorites such as grouper, amberjack, blue crab and red snapper. Come down to the docks near sunset when the fishing fleets return from their day's work. Watching crews unload and huge catches being taken directly from the boat to the restaurant's back door gives you an idea of what fresh really is.

Casual dress is the mode of the day, all day, all year in most restaurants in the area (the exceptions are noted), so relax and have a great time.

The pricing code below is to use as a general guide to a dinner for two. Prices listed include appetizer, entree, beverage and dessert but not cocktails, sales tax or gratuity. All establishments accept major credit cards unless otherwise noted.

Less than $20	$
$21 to $40	$$
$41 to $60	$$$
More than $60	$$$$

Fort Walton Beach

FUDPUCKER'S BEACHSIDE BAR & GRILL
On Okaloosa Island across from the
Holiday Inn   243-3833
Hwy. 98 2 miles east of downtown
Destin   654-4200
$$

Fudpucker's is about as far from serious as you can get — dressed up in weath-

Sure you'll love the architecture at Grand Isle Grill, but wait'll you taste the food!

ered wood with early attic accessories inside and out, Fudpucker's offers patrons a choice of dining on several levels, bands featuring classic rock 'n' roll, cool jazz and reggae and a tabloid newspaper menu filled with silliness. Seafood, burgers, steaks and sandwiches make up the standard beach fare, and there are plenty of cold drinks to wash them down. There's a kids' menu too. You can come away from Fudpucker's spending a lot or a little, since many menu items (except house specialties) are à la carte. The owners (and the patrons) seem to enjoy the funky atmosphere, which blends in well with the beach party crowd. Fud Stuff such as glasses, T-shirts, key chains and other memorabilia is available at the restaurant or through the mail. It's open every day for lunch and dinner until real late.

TEXAS SALOON AND DANCE HALL
West of the Brooks Bridge on
Eglin Pkwy.   664-6255
$

Round up the cowpokes, pardner, and head on down to Texas! The two-steppin', foot-stompin', hand-clappin' nightspot has become one of the more popular nightspots on the coast. Get a lesson in country dancing on Tuesdays and Thursdays from 8 to 10 PM. Drinks are just a buck from 8 to 11 PM, and there's no cover charge on those nights. There are only two requirements necessary to pay a visit to Texas; one, that you're at least 18 years old to party, 21 to drink, and two, that you *love* country music! Texas hosts some of the hottest country acts in the United States. Call the concert line at 664-5255. One night a week is Family Night, where kids of all ages are welcome. Learn to dance or rope a calf, or feast on pizza, hot dogs, nachos and

nonalcoholic specialty drinks. It opens nightly at 8 PM, 6 PM on Sundays.

JUDY'S GARDEN CAFE
334 N. Eglin Pkwy.   862-6210
$$

Judy's is a lunch place, which makes it popular with business folks who need a great place to take clients but have to get in and out in a reasonable amount of time. The restaurant decor makes you feel as if you're in a garden setting, with lots of cool blues and greens, open-backed wrought-iron furniture and plants, plants and more plants. Salads, soups and sandwiches are typical lunchtime fare. Sandwiches are served on fresh bread and rolls; salads are topped with one of 10 house dressings. Weekly specials include muffelettas (a giant New Orleans-style concoction of cheeses and meats with olive dressing) and chicken fettuccine. It's open for lunch Monday through Friday.

THE SOUND RESTAURANT AND LOUNGE
108 W. Hwy. 98   243-2722
$$$

Great sunsets, seafood, dining and dancing are yours for the taking at this Fort Walton Beach landmark across from City Hall. Begin your evening with cocktails in the lounge as sunset colors paint the water and cast golden light through the large windows. For dinner, you'll feel as comfortable in a dinner jacket as you will in walking shorts and polos as you settle into large rattan chairs with oversize cushions. Shrimp, scallops, snapper, grouper and soft-shell crab are absolutely fresh and cooked just the way you like. Or give in to temptation and order a sizzling chargrilled steak or cut-to-order prime rib. Linger a little over dessert, then head back to the lounge for late-night dancing and romancing on the water. It's open for lunch, dinner and cocktails seven days a week.

PERRI'S ITALIAN RESTAURANT
300 Eglin Pkwy.   862-4421
$$$

Perri's is off the main drag, but word-of-mouth regulars will tell you it's worth finding. Both Northern and Southern Italian favorites offer diners enough choices for many return visits. For the uninitiated, Southern Italian cooking is probably most familiar to you; lasagna, spaghetti, rigatoni and tortellini are served with a rich meat sauce that's been cooking for hours to blend the ingredients perfectly. Entrees from Northern Italy pride themselves on being a bit lighter: Sauces are cooked on the spot and served immediately. Both are outstanding, but you're not required to buy a one-way ticket to Italy just to eat here. Fresh gulf seafood is on every good Gulf Coast menu, as are chargrilled steaks, cooked just the way you like. It's open for dinner; reservations are suggested.

HIGHTIDE RESTAURANT, LOUNGE & OYSTER BAR
At the foot of the Brooks Bridge
Okaloosa Island   244-2624
$$

Walk in off the beach and, please, don't dress up! Here's where to get your *fresh*-shucked, absolutely ice-cold oysters, falling-off-the-plate burgers, and all types of fresh seafood steamed, fried or chargrilled. A tall icy mug of brew goes down good with this "barefoot" atmo-sphere. Nightly entertainment and drink specials make Hightide appealing after dark too. It opens at 11 AM daily just over the bridge from Fort Walton Beach on the island.

HOG'S BREATH SALOON & CAFE
1239 Siebert Ave.
Okaloosa Island   243-4646
541 E. Hwy. 98, Destin   837-5620
$

"Hog's Breath is better than no breath at all" and, if you believe that, you're in for a fun evening out at this giant lounge on the island and in Destin. It's all in fun, and what a time you'll have with $5 lunch and dinner specials, live entertainment and friendly clientele. Take home a Hog's Breath souvenir T-Shirt (they're world famous, you know). Suck in a little Hog's Breath daily beginning at 11 AM.

THE MELTING POT
225 Miracle Strip Pkwy.   664-7685
$$$

Do you fondue? Dunking and dipping are required at The Melting Pot, and so are about three hours to cook and eat your meal! Choose an appetizer of bread, carrots and apples dipped in a blend of beer and cheeses. Next, order up your batter-dipped chicken or beef entree, then have fun cooking it yourself at your table, interspersing bites with quiet conversation. The decor is dark wood with several private booths; The Melting Pot staff *expects* you to take your time. Fondue can be a welcome change of pace from standard steak and seafood fare and lots of

Insiders' Tips

Do as the locals do: Dine on the harbor in Destin at sunset and watch the fishing fleets unload the day's catch.

fun! It's open for a traditional lunch; fondue dinners begin at 5 PM.

SAM'S OYSTER HOUSE
1214 Siebert St.
Okaloosa Island   244-3474
$$

Get a grip on a jumbo "Sam"wich, a real meal on a bun, with fish, oysters, shrimp, soft shell crab, chicken or even ground beef! Sam's has passed these last 25 years serving hearty fare and cold drinks in a comfortable setting. It's a stripped-down, no-frills kind of place, but the food is inexpensive and you won't leave hungry! Bring the family for the seafood buffet, served every night from 5 until 9 PM for $10.95. It's open for lunch, happy hour and dinner daily except Monday.

JELLY ROLL'S JAZZ CLUB
209 Ferry Rd.
Downtown Fort Walton Beach   664-5159

Throughout Northwest Florida, there seems to be a resurgence of the old-time coffeehouse type of club, a place not only to hear some great music, but to come in and express yourself as well! Jelly Roll's offers up something different every night, from an evening of great jazz videos on the big screen to karaoke to an open mic night for poetry and reader's theater to rock 'n' roll. It opens at 2 PM Tuesday through Saturday.

THE BOARDWALK
Hwy. 98 E. next to the Ramada Beach Resort
Okaloosa Island   243-5500

You can't miss this wildly colorful monstrosity cuddled up to the dunes on the island. The colors we can't say we're too wild about (kind of a neon salmon and deep teal), but the entire complex gives a much-needed image boost to the island. Here you'll find shops and restaurants tied together by wooden boardwalks leading directly to the beach. Your favorite cocktails and snacks come with a smile, whether you eat inside or out on the deck at the Soggy Dollar Saloon. Harpoon Hanna's features "casual coastal cuisine" — or, to translate, burgers, sandwiches, prime rib, chicken and seafood, plus some rather luscious pies such as Bourbon Street Pecan or Chocolate Peanut Butter topped with chunks of Reese's Peanut Butter Cups — can you save room? Eat inside or out on the deck overlooking the water. Boardwalk merchants are open seasonally.

Destin

Destin restaurants do not require any special type of dress, so come on in, bring the family, dress casually and settle in for some great Gulf Coast hospitality.

MAGNOLIA CAFÉ
Shoreline Village Mall
824 Hwy. 98 E. at Gulfshore Dr.   837-7900

Make a right turn on your way to Holiday Isle and you'll see this pretty little cafe on your left. Come for a really special dinner out, then stay for dancing and live entertainment! Treat yourself to Crab Norfolk, fresh jumbo lump crabmeat baked in a light cream sauce, then topped with Monterey Jack and Gouda cheese, sprinkled with fresh parsley and baked. Or dig into the Shrimp Magnolia, jumbo gulf shrimp dusted in seasoned flour or the Magnolia Cafe's own coconut breading for an authentic Gulf Coast dish. A few entrees are half-price between 5 and 7 PM; all dinners come with a salad, angel hair pasta Alfredo and a fresh veggie on the side. Don't pack yourself too full to pass up a quick trip around the dance floor! It's open for dinner Tuesday through Saturday.

The Elephant Walk at Sandestin Resort was modeled after a plantation home in the 1954 movie of the same name.

BELLISSIMO PASTA & PIZZA

707 Hwy. 98 E. 654-3838
$

Forget that diet! Come sample (oh, alright, pig out on) great local pizza with at least *30* toppings to choose from! Check these out: artichoke hearts, goat cheese, pine nuts, amberjack, broccoli, pineapple and cauliflower! Or try one of Bellissimo's own concoctions, such as New Orleans Spicy Shrimp Pizza with marinated fresh shrimp, onions, garlic, peppers and jalapenos. The South of the Border Pizza is heaped with refried beans and chili, tomato sauce (with or without beef), cheddar and Monterey jack cheese, lettuce and tomato.

In just a few years, Bellissimo has risen to the top for favorite pizza spots in the area, but don't overlook the other great offerings — sandwiches and subs, pastas and entire dinners of chicken, amberjack, shrimp and pork chops. Bring the kids for a hearty, affordable meal. Carry out and free delivery also are available. It's open for lunch and dinner every day.

HARRY T'S

320 E. Hwy. 98 at the
Destin Yacht Club 654-6555
$$

Harrison T. Baben ("The Flying Harry T") was a circus trapeze artist, but really became known for his feats of bravery in the real world, such as saving the lives of Turkish soldiers who had imprisoned him during World War I, and later, saving more than 2,000 passengers from a sinking luxury liner. The boathouse no longer exists, and this restaurant bearing his name overlooks the Destin Harbor. Harry T. owned the boathouse back in the 1920s; some of his own collection of circus memorabilia plus shipwreck salvage graces the interior, making for interesting conversation pieces.

Choose from more than 120 menu items for lunch, dinner and Sunday brunch. Sandwiches, seafood, steaks, soups, salads and more are complemented by live music most nights. Kids eat free between 4 and 5 PM Sunday through Thursday; dinner entrees can be as inexpensive as $5.95 and run up to $15.45.

Look for Harry T's a mile east of the Destin bridge at the Destin Yacht Club.

HARBOR DOCKS

538 Hwy. 98 E.   837-2506
$$$

Perched on a bluff overlooking Destin Harbor, you can't beat Harbor Docks for a great view. On chilly winter evenings, they stoke up the potbellied stove, adding to the already warm atmosphere. Nautical antiques and historic photos line the walls that *don't* have a view; no spot is wasted at Harbor Docks, with plants and partitions and different levels to create an intimate dining experience.

Harbor Docks has its own fish market (next door), so while you dine you can watch the fishing fleet unload. Chefs Long and Dang dish up such delicacies as sauteed red snapper with artichoke hearts, broiled red snapper with lemon caper sauce and chargrilled marinated yellowfin tuna, as well as sizzling steaks and Thai specialties.

The downstairs Sporting Club is filled with the strains of live jazz, where you can belly up to the sushi bar. Come by land or sea, there are boat slips and valet parking. It's open seven days for lunch and dinner.

AJ'S SEAFOOD & OYSTER BAR

Hwy. 98 E.   837-1913
$$

There's always a party going on at AJ's in the heart of Destin on the harbor. Watch the boats unload their catches, then have a seat inside or out to enjoy the gulf's bounty — seafood comes chargrilled, fried, steamed or raw. Landlubbers and kids can order up sandwiches and burgers. Upstairs is Club Bimini with a complete hibachi menu. AJ's is about as comfortable as you can get, and the kids will really like all the saltwater aquariums. Things can get pretty wild on the weekends during the summer months, especially upstairs in the area's largest outdoor lounge, where bands perform seasonally. It's open 11 AM until . . . every day.

MARINA CAFE

404 Hwy. 98 E.   837-7960
$$$

Park your own boat at the back door and enjoy the remarkable view from every table. Inside and out, the Marina Cafe blends with its waterfront surroundings. Colorful underwater sculptures and a mosaic tile archway lend a seafaring air to this comfortable dining area centered around a two-story lighthouse sculpture. Entrees can be as kid-pleasing as pizza, as gourmet as Classic Creole or Pacific Rim cuisine. It's open for dinner daily; reservations are suggested.

THE BACK PORCH

Old Hwy. 98 E.   837-2022
$$

The restaurant dates back 20 years when it was no more than a concession stand; customers had to order at a tiny window. Now that it's expanded to about three or four times its original size, there's room for the throngs of diners looking for great views, great prices and great seafood. This is Destin's only "open air" full-service restaurant. Upstairs, the Appetizer Bar serves lighter menu items such as seafood nachos and freshly made cold smoked tuna dip, as well as delicious frozen concoctions. It doubles as a fine place to wait for dinner seating.

By day, walk in right off the beach and have a casual lunch. Watch carefully out the huge open windows for schools of dolphin playing in the surf. By night, the seafood is sensational. The Back Porch originated chargrilled amberjack, now a staple item on the Gulf Coast. Heart Healthy entrees use only pure vegetable oil and are either broiled or chargrilled. Everything from sauces to salads to desserts are made fresh every day in the Back Porch kitchen. And they haven't forgotten the kids! They have their own menu, and waitpeople are sure to fuss over them to make sure they're having as much fun as mom and dad! It's open every day for lunch and dinner.

THE CRAB TRAP

At James Lee Park, Beach Rd. 98
between Destin and Sandestin   654-2722
$$

A crab-lover's delight — soft shell crab sandwiches, She-Crab soup, snow crab, tender crab claws, New Orleans-style crab cakes, crab salad, gumbo (with crab, naturally!). But don't turn your back on this restaurant if you're *not* particularly fond of the little crustacean. There's "fresh-off-the-boat" shrimp broiled in a butter and garlic sauce with Cajun spices, juicy burgers, hearty sandwiches and a souvenir sports bottle filled with your favorite

daiquiri! The Crab Trap caters to the younger set, serving favorites such as shrimp and fries, burgers and hot dogs in a souvenir beach pail complete with a shovel! (No, the shovel's not to *eat* with, kids.) They'll stay busy with coloring books and crayons, giant ice cream cones, something sweet from The Parrot Sweet Shop or a Destin souvenir from Boardwalk Gifts. Dine inside or out in one of the tropical gazebos, or get it to go and eat on the beach! Plan to spend a little time here if you come during daylight hours; the setting is worth a few photos and a quick stroll along the boardwalks or the beach. It's open every day for lunch and dinner.

CAPTAIN DAVE'S RESTAURANT & MARINA ON THE HARBOR

314 E. Hwy. 98   837-6357
$$$

Yep, there really *is* a Captain Dave ... Captain Dave Marler, a gruff old salt who grew up on the water here. He turned in his rig for a restaurant long ago, but Captain Dave's is still the oldest seafood restaurant around; in fact, you may have seen it in *Jaws II*. The movie crew liked the atmosphere with its stuffed trophy fish, nautical knickknacks and historic photos and shot several scenes here. They also liked the food, returning again and again to savor huge overflowing platters of shrimp, oysters, scallops, fish and deviled crab. Captain Dave still oversees his fleet behind the restaurant, ensuring that only the freshest, top-quality catches wind up on diners' tables. Steaks, prime rib and chicken dishes will ensnare non-seafood lovers. It's open every day for lunch in the Oyster Bar; dinner is served in the main restaurant. It's closed from December to mid-February.

CAPTAIN DAVE'S ON THE GULF

3796 Old Hwy. 98   *837-2627*
$$$

A Destin original, this restaurant built in the '50s still has the old tunnel built under the highway for customers crossing from the parking lot. Now the tunnel just serves as a slice of Old Florida, since Old Hwy. 98 has had to make way for the newer version, which gets most of the traffic. But Captain Dave's sees that as a plus. Setting off the gorgeous gulf view are old curved greenhouse windows within the nautically themed dining room. A rustic Oyster Bar is outside downstairs, a casual spot for gulping oysters, peeling boiled shrimp and sipping cocktails and beer. For the main attraction, try chargrilled tuna with a green chile salsa, Snapper Dijon or fresh swordfish and scallops marinated in teriyaki sauce. It's open daily for dinner and closed between December 1 and mid-February.

LOUISIANA LAGNIAPPE

775 Gulf Shore Dr. at Sandpiper Cove
Holiday Isle   *837-0881*
$$$

"Lagniappe" (lan-yap) is a Cajun word meaning "a little something extra."

From the seafood gumbo, where the seafood is cooked and added just before serving, to the authentic Cajun recipes and homemade bread pudding with whiskey, Louisiana Lagniappe is noted for its attention to detail. The chargrilled tuna steak is wrapped in bacon and topped with flaky white jumbo lump crabmeat, then finished with a splash of hollandaise. Grouper Pontchartrain takes a heapin' helpin' of pan-sauteed grouper filet, tops it with a fried jumbo softshell crab, honey-roasted nuts and hollandaise. Is your mouth watering yet? This is a casual, family-style restaurant, where shorts are fine, smiles are plentiful and service is exceptional. There's only one selection on the kid's menu; if they don't like hamburgers (and you don't like spending seven bucks for it), leave them home. It's open daily for dinner from March through October. No reservations are accepted.

NIGHTOWN

Two blocks north of
Palmetto Plaza   *837-6448*
$

Nightown is a jumpin' joint featuring a variety of entertainment every night of the week. The Other Bar has a New Orleans feel, where live entertainment cranks out nearly every night. Play pool or foosball in a room bedecked in shipwreck salvage. The Beer Bar offers beer from around the world. And the main attraction, The Main Room, sports a 1958 Mack Truck in it's own garage overlooking the massive dance floor. This is the party room, where a sound and light extravaganza keeps you on your feet. Check out the surfboards, sailboards, Jet Skis and *real records* lining the walls. A Ferris wheel hangs from the ceiling, as does another dance floor, nine feet over your head, surrounded by neon palms.

You can't beat Harry T's for harbor views.

Two island bars in the Main Room offer cocktails, and the Smart Bar specializes in nonalcoholic drinks for the Designated Drivers. Let's see . . . a Foreign Bar with domestic and imported beer, lava lamps, a French Fry Bar, a comedy club . . . Yikes! You'll just have to come and see the rest for yourself. There's a cover charge, and it opens at 8 PM every night of the week.

FISH HEADS

543 Hwy. 98 E. across from
Harbor Docks   837-4848
$

Are you up past midnight on a regular basis? Then this is probably just the spot you've been looking for to mingle with the other night owls. Nightly specials, a daily happy hour, a DJ playing top hits for dancing, an outdoor patio deck . . . what more could you want? It opens at 11 AM daily.

DONUT HOLE CAFE & BAKERY

635 Hwy. 98 E.   837-8824
$

Here's the Insiders' tip of the day: Eat Here! Truly, you can't find better food for less money. You can certainly find lower calorie food, though, but oh, mama! What good eatin'! Try the Destin omelet, with a mouthful of lump crabmeat in every bite, served with homestyle potatoes, fresh biscuits, even gravy if you ask for it. Huge homestyle dinners start around $5, and dinner is served all day long. The service is terrific, baked goods are out of this world, and the old shots of Destin are just plain fun! It's open for breakfast, lunch and dinner every day.

DESTIN DINER

Hwy. 98 at Airport Rd.   654-5843
$

Right out of a '50s flashback, the Destin Diner is a burgers-and-malteds kind of place. It's a real chrome diner with vinyl-covered stools and booths and jukeboxes. Prices aren't quite out of that era, but they're not bad. The diner serves up omelets (12 varieties), breakfast sandwiches such as ham and egg served with two pickle slices, pancakes, soups, shakes, burgers, Coke floats and even banana splits!

You can eat here fairly cheaply — the most expensive menu item is a complete country-style dinner for $5.75. Choose from grilled pork chops, roast beef with gravy, chicken fried steak with gravy, grilled liver and onions or a grilled chicken breast, then add on two vegetables (corn, fries, greens, green beans, cole slaw or mashed potatoes) and soup or salad. The food is out of the days when you didn't even know what cholesterol was. Pop a quarter in the jukebox and hearken back to the days of tail fins and saddle shoes. The Destin Diner is serving up great food 24 hours every day.

SCAMPI'S SEAFOOD & SPIRITS
Old Hwy. 98 E.
Across from the Back Porch   837-7686
$$

Kinda fun, kinda rustic with its weathered wood exterior and seafaring decor, Scampi's does seafood better than almost anybody. Start with a dozen oysters or a steaming bowl of spicy gumbo. For your main course, we recommend the day's fresh catch, perhaps amberjack or yellowfin tuna perfectly chargrilled to bring out the full flavor of these meaty white fish. The fanciest offering is Shrimp Jeunelot, giant shrimp sauteed in wine and butter then served over pasta with a white Chardonnay cream sauce and sprinkled with Parmesan. For those with seafood burnout (*is* there such a thing?), try a thick portion of prime rib or a New York Strip,

which comes with hushpuppies, salad and a veggie of the day or baked potato. Another alternative is the seafood buffet, chock-full of steamed, fried, broiled and baked seafood, plus ribs, chicken and steak, veggies, pasta, salad bar and desserts. It's open nightly for dinner.

FAT TUESDAY
2 Hwy. 98 E. next to Boogie's Water Sports
At the foot of the Destin Bridge   654-9378
$

Stop in for a quick bite or a cold cocktail on a lazy afternoon. Frozen daiquiris and a panoramic waterfront view are the house specialties. Weekdays, happy hour specials are in effect from 4 until 7 PM. Fat Tuesday opens at 11 AM daily.

FLAMINGO CAFE
414 Hwy. 98 E.   837-0961
$$$

Make way for something completely different when you step through the doors of this delightful Key West-style cafe. The spacious dining room overlooks the Destin Harbor, a view that's hard to improve upon. But with the view comes some unusually creative cuisine, a nice change from the broiled seafood standards. The menu changes seasonally, but allow us to offer a preview of dining attractions anyway.

April 12, 1927: A distress call goes out that the luxury liner *Thracia* is sinking off the coast of Destin. Harry T. Baben, "The Flying Harry T", a former circus trapeze artist, is first to heed the call. In his boat *The Flying Harry T*, Baben forms an armada. Together, the boats rescue all 2,113 people aboard. Later, Baben opened a popular restaurant: The original Harry T's Boathouse, built in 1914, was destroyed in the 1933 hurricane.

Insiders' Tips

Try out a combination of jumbo shrimp and lump crabmeat baked in phyllo dough with two butter sauces to whet your appetite. Specialty salads get fairly fancy — the Spicy Fried Tiger Prawn salad starts with seasonal baby greens, adds some vegetables, crumbled Roquefort, tropical fruit jam, then a mixed herb vinaigrette. Flamingo's Sunset Features are two-for-one dinners served between 5 and 6 PM for around $17 (entree only). The two of you can order corn-mustard fried whole catfish with fresh house smoked sausage slow cooked with five beans and rice, rosemary roast chicken, or something called Choctawhatchee Shrimp Maque Choux. Fortunately, you don't have to pronounce it, just savor this dish that starts with fresh roasted corn, tricolor peppers, sweet onions and fresh shrimp stirred into a dark Southern bisque and served with fresh jalapeno-corn cake and steamed rice. You get the idea.

It's open for dinner nightly, with live entertainment Thursday through Saturday.

GRAND ISLE GRILL

1771 Hwy. 98 E.   *837-7475*
$$

We just love the architecture, the decor, the location, the view, and the *food*! Dine on many different levels, have fun gazing at either the white sand outside your window (or below from the deck) or at the unusual memorabilia gracing the walls. Now, a sampling of what you came for . . . grilled and fried seafood, steaks and chicken dishes, terrific pasta tossed with chicken, crawfish or shrimp. Try one of the tangy sauces atop your dinner, such as crab meat with Bearnaise sauce, mango salsa or Italian-style. *All* entrees are just $9.99 if you come in between 5 and 6:30

PM. Dinner is served nightly; enjoy live entertainers on the weekends.

SWEET BASIL'S BISTRO

104 Hwy. 98 E.   *654-5124*
$$

This casual Italian-inspired restaurant features hand-tossed pizzas and homemade pastas as its lure. Oh, lest you fret over there not being enough seafood, not to worry. Seafood is delicately blended into some tasteful Italian dishes, as is chicken. Find your favorites such as manicotti, rigatoni and fettuccine Alfredo. Children younger than 12 have five yummy choices, but when there's pizza available, it may be all they need to know! Sweet Basil's is open for lunch on weekdays and dinner every day.

HATTERAS CAFE

1 mile east of Destin Bridge
at the Destin Yacht Club   *837-1441*
$$$$

You know it's going to be special when you are offered valet parking (for boats too!). Pull your boat into one of the slips out back and step inside for an evening of quiet, romantic dining on the Destin Harbor. We don't really recommend you bring the kids this time so you can put your full concentration on these marvelous dishes . . . and each other! Menus change with the seasons, but a quick sampling includes Hatteras snapper amandine, certified Black Angus filet and lobster tail, Costa Rican tilapia and Hatteras fire-seared sushi-grade rare tuna. Take advantage of special dinner prices between 5:30 and 6:30 PM every night.

LUCKY SNAPPER GRILL & BAR

76 Hwy. 98 E.   *654-0900*
$$$

You'll find this fun wharf restaurant and nightspot right over the Destin Bridge

Seafood Facts

A quick guide for those who haven't yet been initiated:

• Grouper, triggerfish, snapper, amberjack and mahi-mahi (dolphin) are considered to be whitefish — fleshy, meaty and un-fishy.

• Shrimp can be about any size, from the microscopic ones in your shrimp salad to the super deluxe jumbo gulf shrimp that are half as big as your arm. If you're buying them to take home and boil, use Zatarain's or any type of Cajun boil (use sparingly) to bring out the flavor.

• Crawfish are not usually local, but if you see them alive before they appear on your plate, they're nice and fresh.

• Mullet appears on lots of menus, but it's an acquired taste. Breaded in cornmeal and fried, mullet is what you'll get at almost every fish fry you attend in Northwest Florida. Try it smoked too; it's delicious.

• Oysters are still a bargain everywhere, but warning signs are now posted at all raw oyster-serving establishments that they can possibly carry some strain of bacteria that could ruin your vacation. You're safe if you order them fried, broiled, Rockefellered or cooked in some way.

Photo: Robin Rowan

You ain't tasted fresh 'til you've tasted it here.

near the Harborwalk. There's water, water all around, and, again, seafood is tops. The restaurant downstairs is decidedly upscale in flavor, but don't feel intimidated about bringing the kids or about wearing shorts — this *is* a resort town, after all! While you're waiting for a table (it's inevitable, they don't take reservations), pop in for a cocktail at the little bar downstairs just to spend some time roaming and learning a bit about Destin history. There are some great old fishing photographs as well as some 1940s- and '50s-era advertisements (definitely *not* politically correct). Grab yourself one of the paper take-home menus to keep ordering time to a minimum.

If you're feeling especially spunky, you might go for conch fritters (made famous in Key West) or the gator tail appetizer, which is wrapped in bacon, deep fried, then served with a honey mustard dip. Seafood dishes are subject to whatever the boats brought in that particular day, so be assertive and order something different if your favorite isn't featured. Besides an endless variety of fish and shellfish, steaks and chops, pasta and sandwiches round out the menu. Kids get their own menu with crayons to color it.

Please don't leave without a trip to the upstairs lounge — it's open-air with plenty of seating inside and out. There aren't any walls to speak of; in the cooler weather, large plastic sheeting is simply zipped down around most of the area. The view from here is terrific by day or night. Lucky Snapper is also a stop on the Harbor Queen Water Taxi route if you'd like to take a quick tour of the harbor.

Beaches of South Walton

Fast food restaurants are about as scarce as snowstorms in South Walton County. What you will find, however, are several cozy gathering places — stop in not just for hearty homemade fare, but news and gossip from the locals. South Walton also prides itself on some of the best gourmet restaurants in Northwest Florida, impeccably presented against a backdrop of white dunes and emerald waters.

Some of the fancier restaurants will allow patrons to wear collared shirts and dressy walking shorts in lieu of coats and ties; those will be noted. Shirts and shoes are required everywhere.

BAYOU BILL'S CRABHOUSE

Hwy. 98 E., Santa Rosa Beach   267-3849
Hwy. 30-A, Seagrove Beach   231-1400
$$

Two locations along the Beaches of South Walton serve up heaps of blue crabs and steaming seafood buckets. The Seagrove Beach location on Eastern Lake has a special oyster bar. Any place that serves a crustacean that has to be hand-cracked and peeled and dipped and eaten with the fingers is bound to be unpretentious. Bayou Bill's welcomes all comers to its friendly and comfortable surroundings. It's open daily for lunch and dinner.

BUSTER'S BAR & GRILL

Delchamps Plaza near Sandestin   837-4399
$$

Buster's specializes in seafood — fried, chargrilled, steamed or broiled — in a casual hometown lounge atmosphere. Giant sandwiches, frosty spirits and a big-screen TV keep the locals happy. Lunch and dinner specials are daily features, ranging from oyster dishes to juicy steaks. Buster's won the first Great Southern Gumbo Cookoff, so its gumbo is sure to be a winner. There's a daily oyster happy hour; the restaurant is open for lunch and dinner every day.

CRIOLLA'S

County Rd. 30-A
Grayton Beach   267-1267
$$$$

Criolla's keeps its prestigious designation as a Golden Spoon Award-winner, meaning it's one of Florida's top-10 restaurants according to *Florida Trend* magazine. Criolla's unique Creole/Caribbean cuisine is a gourmet's delight and unbelievably wonderful, even for someone who's pretty picky (like yours truly). Some of the menu items are unpronounceable and fairly exotic, so you might want to ask your server to recommend something. One memorable dish was the Criolla Colado, grilled tenderloin chili between layers of masa, steamed in banana leaves and served with ancho tomato sauce. Chef and owner Johnny Earles changes the menu seasonally, depending on what's available (and what is absolutely fresh), so expect Criolla's to be a different experience every time.

Muted shades of melon and dark green, antiques and paintings and Caribbean-flavored-what-have-yous all around create a warm and pleasing environment for diners to hunker down and prepare for an evening they'll long remember. Resort dress attire is requested. It's open for dinner Monday through Saturday.

ELEPHANT WALK

Hwy. 98 E. at the Sandestin
Beach Resort   267-4800
$$$$

Save the Elephant Walk for a really special night out, like a night when you can get a babysitter. It's all candlelight and crystal and linen and four-waitpeople-per-table service, where you wouldn't want to worry about less than perfect behavior from your offspring. So, now that you've settled into the business of eating, start with an appetizer of chargrilled shrimp and scallops with lump crabmeat served chilled on a bed of lettuce with a brandy cocktail sauce or twin cakes of lump crabmeat seasoned with fresh herbs. Since a dinner at the Elephant Walk constitutes an entire evening out (expect to spend a couple of hours enjoying this meal), feel free to walk out on the deck in between courses. The building itself was modeled after a plantation home in the 1954 movie *Elephant Walk*.

Ready for the main course? Try the Grouper Elizabeth, a sauteed fillet with seasoned jumbo lump crabmeat with toasted almonds and a white wine cream sauce, a chargrilled fillet of beef with Bearnaise sauce served with potato cakes or Georgia mountain trout (one of the

nightly specials) stuffed with crawfish tails and red onions served with black bean and okra sauce. Coats and ties are not required, but most folks like to dress up to dine in such splendor. Elephant Walk is open Tuesday through Saturday for dinner and on Mondays during the summer season.

BUD & ALLEYS

County Rd. 30-A, Seaside   231-5900
$$$

One of the original Seaside eateries, Bud & Alley's features its own herb garden, so you know you're getting the freshest ingredients possible in dishes including chicken, seafood and sushi. The old 1955 Airstream trailer, formerly housing the restaurant's grill, has been replaced with a spacious and fully equipped outbuilding. You can enjoy live jazz on weekends in the summer. Lunch and dinner are served daily at this cozy white-tableclothed establishment. Dine under the stars in the new gazebo or up on the rooftop deck when the weather's nice. It's closed Tuesdays in the off-season.

SHADES

County Rd. 30-A, Seaside   231-1950
$$

Look for the neon shades in the window. Shades is frivolous and about as laid-back as Seaside gets. Ribs, crab cakes, barbecued shrimp, burgers and indoor and outdoor seating set the mood; shoes are not required. It's open for lunch daily and dinner every day but Sunday.

JOSEPHINE'S DINING ROOM

Inside Josephine's Bed & Breakfast
Seaside   231-1939
$$$$

Since the bed and breakfast is so tastefully decorated, the turn-of-the-century charm so thick, the Southern style so el-

Buy tonight's dinner just-off-the-boat fresh at one of the area's seafood markets.

egant, Josephine's Dining Room has a tough act to follow. But from the moment you step into this comfortable oasis, Bruce and Judy Albert, your evening's hosts, will make you feel like you've come to a very special place. Rich burgundies, deep greens and dark wood set the mood for dining on fresh seafood, thick steaks, lamb and chicken entrees.

Try something as offbeat as New Zealand Rack of Lamb with fresh rosemary, served with a northern bean ragout. Six other entrees are just as enticing. Chef Douglas Alley along with apprentice chef Aaron Wolfe stir up a kettle of soup daily featuring handpicked herbs with fresh vegetables and a stock they prepare fresh daily. All dinner entrees come with a salad of wild greens with creole mustard vinaigrette, sauteed vegetables and a potato du jour. Expect to spend the better part of your evening partaking of all of these delights. At Seaside, there's no need to rush. A full wine list is available; ask your server for recommendations. Reservations are suggested. Josephine's is open for dinner Wednesday through Sunday.

BASMATI'S
C-30A, Blue Mountain Beach 231-1366
$$$

Looking for some place that's really intimate? Basmati's only has room for about 30 guests, so you're sure to get some individualized attention here. Basmati's takes popular Asian-Pacific cuisine and gives it a Gulf Coast twist with *lots* of fresh seafood. One spin on a local favorite is lump crabmeat stir-fried with asparagus, basil and somen noodles. Or try a meaty fillet of pompano pan-seared in ginger with a fig sweet and sour sauce served with a combination of Chinese rice noodles, shrimp, scallops, spinach and plum tomatoes. Very unusual, but folks staying in this neck of the woods are open to new tastes, which makes Basmati's quite popular. No credit cards are accepted but reservations are. The entire dining room is nonsmoking. It's open every evening but Wednesday.

SILVER BUCKET
On the Gulf, Seaside 231-1190
$

When you're out on the beach or shopping in the open-air market at Seaside, the Silver Bucket's the place to stop for inexpensive treats, quick meals or mid-day snacks. Six different sandwiches include Vermont Cheddar with sliced green apple on sourdough bread, smoked turkey with roasted pepper and coarse grain mustard on multi-grain bread and grilled marinated chicken breast with lettuce and fresh pesto on a baguette. There's nothing run-of-the-mill for this place, except for the kid-size grilled cheese and peanut butter and jelly sandwich buckets. Stop in for take-out every day but Monday.

DONUT HOLE II CAFE & BAKERY
32459 Hwy. 98 E.
Santa Rosa Beach   267-3239
$

As you might imagine, doughnuts are a specialty (and at 44¢ apiece are a good deal), but fresh-baked muffins and stacks of flapjacks will lure you in again and again. "Country dinners" are hearty, tasty and about five bucks, and sandwiches and soups are stick-to-your-ribs yummy. A full bakery features danish, fruit cobblers, cookies, pies and fresh breads daily. It's open for breakfast, lunch and dinner (dinner menu begins around 11:30 AM) daily. Bring cash 'cause it's all they take.

AJ'S SEAFOOD & OYSTER BAR
Corner of Hwy. 30A and Hwy. 283
Grayton Beach   231-4102
$$

Good, cheap, and plenty — what more do you need to lure you except to tell you "come as you are?" AJ's pours on the seafood, both fresh-from-the-gulf and some favorite imports, such as stone crabs from Key West, Pacific Dungenous Crab and Alaskan Snow Crab. Now have it

your way — steamed, grilled or fried in a sandwich or in a salad. Kids meals don't get too exotic, so they'll be happy. This AJ's isn't quite the wild place like its sister in Destin, so expect casual, friendly and maybe even quiet. It's open for lunch and dinner daily.

THE GRAYTON CORNER CAFE
Off County Rd. 283 on the corner
Grayton Beach   231-1211
$

These folks practically have a corner on the market, since there are only about two restaurants in all of Grayton Beach. The Grayton Corner Cafe is directly across the street from that beautiful beach and serves basic sandwiches. You're in Grayton Beach, a wonderfully old seaside community without much flash, and that's why people like it. An example of the "mañana" spirit of the town is a sign posted outside the Grayton Corner Cafe: "Hours may vary depending on the quality of the surf." Generally it's open for lunch and dinner Tuesday through Sunday. Cash-only is the policy.

GOATFEATHERS RAW BAR & RESTAURANT
Hwy. 30-A between dune Allen
and Blue Mountain Beach   267-3342
$$

Steam buckets, steak, soups, sandwiches and kid's baskets fill tummies and warm hearts at this fun and friendly eatery. The open-air deck offers spectacular gulf views, and the seafood comes from downstairs at Goatfeathers' own seafood market. It's open for lunch and dinner daily. It's another cash only place.

Photo: Robin Rowan

Cool tiled fountains and native flora separate condominiums at Hidden Dunes.

Fort Walton Beach/Destin/ Beaches of South Walton
Accommodations

Residents of Fort Walton Beach and Destin may wince at this, but it's quite likely that Florida's Great Northwest is becoming more well known because of Seaside. Articles on the little village's architecture, its planned community and its ambiance have appeared in hundreds of national and international magazines. As far as getting good press goes, Seaside could be right up there with Disney World. But what's been good for that little community has been good for the entire area. New visitors from all over the United States and many foreign countries are trying us on for size — and liking the fit.

Along this 30-mile stretch of U.S. 98, visitors can shop around for good deals before they ever leave home. Fort Walton Beach caters to singles and families and probably offers more hotel and motel accommodations than the other destinations. Destin is condo heaven, with most high-rises right on the water. The Beaches of South Walton are a mix — interior-designed cottages, luxury condos, quaint bed and breakfast inns and backwater cabins.

Put your money down on cottage and resort reservations; most require a deposit before your reservation can be confirmed. Before you sign on the dotted line, ask about added costs such as a pet deposit or a post-visit flea spray (although most do not accept pets), bed taxes and cleaning fees.

Fort Walton Beach

Fort Walton Beach doesn't try to be all things to all people. Compared to Panama City Beach, it's peaceful; compared to Destin or Seaside, it's affordable. Stay on Okaloosa Island and you're near all the action — amusements, beaches and recreation. Families especially will find Fort Walton Beach a friendly and accommodating place where locals love to stop and chat with out-of-towners and take great pride in the place they call home.

Note: Okaloosa Island properties are just over the Brooks Bridge from Fort Walton Beach.

Hotels and Motels

The giant Holiday Inn and Ramada Resort on Okaloosa Island are just what you'd expect — large, spacious rooms, restaurants and lounges on the grounds, beautiful lobbies, atriums and a high-rise view of the gulf. But if you'd rather spend your money taking a charter fishing trip or dining in a gourmet restaurant, we've included a few of the local motels too, which may not have fancy shampoos and blow dryers, but they're inexpensive, and nice enough to at least offer the basics. Price structure is based on double occupancy for one night and does not include tax.

$80 or less	*$*
$81 to 100	*$$*
$101 to 150	*$$$*
$151 or more	*$$$$*

HOLIDAY INN — OKALOOSA ISLAND

1110 Santa Rosa Blvd.　　　　*243-9181*
Okaloosa Island　　　*(800) 732-GULF*
$$$

A full-service, 385-room hotel right on the gulf, this all-inclusive property offers three landscaped swimming pools, two lighted tennis courts, a poolside snack bar and a restaurant. Children's activities and seasonal beach rentals are available through the hotel's resort services. Double-room rates depend on location and range from $110 (parking lot view) to $135 (gulf view) per night. Junior suites and executive suites facing the gulf include more amenities and cost extra.

BLUEWATER BAY RESORT

1950 Bluewater Blvd.　　　　*897-3613*
Niceville　　　　*(800) 874-2128*
$-$$$

Residents and guests are welcome to enjoy 36 holes of golf, 21 tennis courts, a 120-slip marina, swimming pools, playgrounds, a bayside beach, bike and nature trails. Both nightly and weekly rates are available on three-story hotel units, condominiums and villas. Since lots of folks live here year round, you get in on all the luxuries they enjoy every day. Bluewater Bay is a Northwest Florida gem; the units are spacious, the grounds immaculate and the sunset views across the bay outstanding.

BEACHMARK INN

573 Santa Rosa Blvd.　　　　*244-8686*
Okaloosa Island　　　*(800) 433-7736*
$$

One-bedroom suites overlooking the gulf include separate living and bedroom areas and kitchens. All rooms have sliding patio doors leading to private patios or balconies; interiors are contemporary

Photo: Steven Brooke

Cool breezes, paddle fans and porch swings invite you to linger at Seaside.

with beach-inspired pastels. You're within walking distance of restaurants, shopping, nightlife and amusements on Okaloosa Island. These units are pleasant and functional without the high price.

PIRATES' BAY
CONDO & HOTEL MARINA
214 Miracle Strip Pkwy.   243-3154
$$$ (800) 356-1861

Studio and one-bedroom suites are geared toward both tourists and business travelers. All units have sofas and work areas, microwaves, refrigerators and private wraparound balconies. All units offer free local calls. Dock your boat at the 121-slip marina, or dive into one of two large free-form pools. Pirates' Bay is on the Intracoastal Waterway in the heart of Fort Walton Beach.

CONQUISTADOR INN
874 Venus Ct.   244-6155
Okaloosa Island   (800) 824-7112
$-$$

The Conquistador Inn gives its guests plenty of options when it comes to accommodations with 87 units, both double hotel rooms and one- and two-bedroom condos on the gulf. All rooms are Old Florida tropical in shades of aqua and pastels. A pool, boardwalk to the beach and volleyball courts are on the property.

RAMADA BEACH RESORT
1599 Miracle Strip Pkwy. U.S. 98 E.
Okaloosa Island   243-9161
$$-$$$ (800) 874-8962

With 454 rooms, the Ramada offers everything a vacation is meant to include: pools indoors and out (we think the kids will love the giant fake rock formations and you'll like the swim-up "rock" bar), a hot tub/whirlpool, kiddie pools, three restaurants, two lounges, a courtyard garden area, a health spa, tennis courts and

a picnic area — it's all handicapped accessible. Room rates depend on location; choose from a parking lot view ($95) up to a room right on the gulf ($125).

ISLANDER BEACH RESORT
790 Santa Rosa Blvd.   244-4137
$$-$$$ (800) 523-0209

This renovated high-rise on the gulf offers standard hotel rooms, efficiency units, and one- or two-bedroom units with full kitchens. All rooms have either a private patio or balcony. There's an outdoor heated pool for everyone's use, an onsite gift shop and a bit of beachfront. Enjoy Jamaica Joe's Lounge, the tiki bar and Hurricane's Poolside Grill, all on the property.

LEESIDE INN & MARINA
1350 Hwy. 98 E.   243-7359
Okaloosa Island   (800) 824-2747
$

An older hotel on the bay side, Leeside has been upgraded to be handicapped accessible. With 107 units, every other room offers a small kitchenette; that is, a small refrigerator, a two-burner stove and service for four. Rooms have either two queen- or one king-size bed. Nothin' fancy, but if you plan to spend your days taking in the sights of the area, all you'll require at night is a comfortable place to sleep!

SHERATON INN
11325 Miracle Strip Pkwy.   243-8116
Okaloosa Island   *(in Fla.)*   *(800) 843-8720*
$$$ *(in the U.S.)(800) 874-8104*

Deliciously verdant foliage frames the walkways leading to the Sheraton's entrance, instantly transporting you to the tropics of northern Florida. Step into a lobby with beach-inspired wicker, tile floors and skylights throughout. Many rooms face the gulf, but even courtyard views are lush and private. Try the outdoor pool, slip into the whirlpool, have a hot shower (with complimentary shampoo and lotion), then dress for dinner in whatever you please and enjoy your meal relaxing beachside at the Plantation Grill. Gulf-front rooms are most expensive, followed by a room with a dune view, pool view and parking lot view.

Condominiums/Townhomes/ Vacation Cottages

Gulfside, bayside, or soundside, just about every condo in a two-county area is on the water, affording splendid all-around views. Check the neighbors to the east (that's Destin and The Beaches of South Walton) for additional accommodations. Prices reflect the average weekly cost of a two-bedroom/two-bath condo or house during the peak summer season and do not include tax.

$500 to $750	$
$751 to $900	$$
$901 to $1,100	$$$
More than $1,101	$$$$

BLUEWATER BAY RESORT
1950 Bluewater Blvd.   897-3613
Niceville   (800) 874-2128
$-$$

Bluewater Bay masterfully melds residential community and resort living. The 2,000-acre property on Choctawhatchee Bay takes special care to leave some spaces in their natural state, to insist upon stringent building codes and to preserve every tree possible.

Spacious condominium units offer many extras; each is individually owned and suited to the owner's taste and lifestyle. Resort extras abound; see the listing under hotels for a rundown.

EMERALD ISLE CONDOMINIUM
770 Sundial Ct.
Okaloosa Island   (800) 336-GULF
$$$$

By the day, the week or the month, Emerald Isle is a favorite of vacationing families. Gulfside, this seven-story high-rise is nicely landscaped with private beach boardwalks, a large pool with sundeck and tennis courts. All rooms have private balconies; indoors, look for all the comforts of home.

The Beaches of South Walton
We talk about them often enough, but do you really know how *many* beaches there are in South Walton? Try 18! And heeeerrrre they are:

Frangista Beach	dune Allen
Seascape	Blue Mountain Beach
Surfside	Gulf Trace
Edgewater	Grayton Beach
Miramar	Seaside
Mainsail	Seagrove Beach
Hidden Dunes	Camp Creek
Sandestin	Inlet Beach
Tops'l	Santa Rosa Beach

SEA OATS CONDOMINIUM

1114 Santa Rosa Blvd.
Okaloosa Island   (800) 336-GULF
$$-$$$$

With views of the gulf or the Intracoastal Waterway from every room, Sea Oats is on that spit of land over the bridge from Fort Walton Beach known as Okaloosa Island. You're close to all the best stuff — The Gulfarium, mini-golf, amusement parks, restaurants, shopping. Tennis and shuffleboard courts, pool, game room and 24-hour security are all onsite.

SEASPRAY CONDOMINIUMS

1530 Hwy. 98 E.   244-1108
Okaloosa Island   (800) 428-2726
$$-$$$

These one-, two- and three-bedroom low-rise townhomes front the gulf on Okaloosa Island. The units are arranged in a horseshoe design with a courtyard opening on the gulf beach. An athletic club, sauna and large courtyard pool provide recreational opportunities. Some pets are welcome, but check first. This is a family-oriented property, meaning no Spring Breakers or student groups. Nightly and monthly rates are available.

Destin

Next to the remarkably emerald green water and huge fleets of fishing boats, some of the first things you'll notice upon crossing the Destin Bridge are the tall rows of shimmering condos lining the water in every direction. The success of charter fishing brought tourism and a resort lifestyle along with it, summoning a new era more suited to the comfort and convenience of visitors.

Reasonable year-round rates get even better in the slower fall and winter seasons, with some rates dropping by one-third after Labor Day, lower than in the winter months.

Check both the Fort Walton Beach and Beaches of South Walton listings for an even wider range of prices and unit availability.

Hotels and Motels

One of the hotel chain's slogans is "The Best Surprise Is No Surprise," and if you make reservations at a hotel you're already familiar with, you won't be disappointed when you get there. Condos are king in Destin, but the chain hotels provide a nice alternative, usually for less money.

DAYS INN — DESTIN

1029 Hwy. 98 E.   837-2599
$-$$

One of the newer motels in Destin, the Days Inn offers regular rooms, suites and efficiencies with in-room Jacuzzis and cable TV with Showtime. There's a nice pool here, but you won't need it, since you're right across from the gulf. Both nonsmoking and handicapped accessible rooms are available. A continental breakfast of coffee, doughnuts and orange juice comes with the price of a room. Call for special corporate, military, AAA and senior discounts.

CLUB DESTIN RESORT

1085 Hwy. 98 E.   654-4700
$$-$$$

This timeshare resort also offers nightly rates on hotel rooms and efficiencies. The entire resort encompasses 4.5 acres near Sandestin with a large heated swimming pool, a putting green, shuffleboard courts and Stoney's restaurant and lounge. Club Destin opened a couple of years ago, so expect upbeat, contemporary furnishings and lots of little extras. A few rooms on the first floor are designated as handicapped accessible.

SUMMERSPELL

3881 Scenic Beach Hwy. 98 E.   *654-4747*
$$$ *(800) 336-9669*

All the comforts of a privately owned condominium are found at Summerspell, with the affordability of an in-town hotel. Although rentals by the week and month are available, these are all one-bedroom, one-bath units, so for our purposes we've included them in the hotel listings. French doors open onto balconies, affording gulf views. A heated pool, gazebo, onsite laundry and beach service (in season) are available to guests as are nonsmoking units. Each unit is designed to sleep six.

Bed and Breakfast Inns

HENDERSON PARK INN

2700 Scenic Beach Hwy. 98 E.
$$$$ *(800) 336-GULF*

The Queen-Anne-style Henderson Park Inn is celebrated as the Emerald Coast's first bed and breakfast. Thirty-nine suites and apartment villas provide all of the daily necessities, and its only western neighbor is the new Henderson Beach State Park. The structure oozes Victorian charm, featuring Shaker-style siding, a cupola and a widow's walk, plus the benefit of being right on the water.

Complimentary breakfast, evening social hour, heated pool, sundeck, beach gazebo, outdoor grills and beach rentals in-season are all part of the package. Most rooms in the main building come with Jacuzzis. Weekly rentals and handicapped accessible rooms are available.

Condos/Townhomes/ Vacation Cottages

Condominiums and cottages, with their full kitchens and multiple bedrooms, seem perfect for families who don't want to eat out every night or couples desiring a romantic respite from workday pressures.

Prices reflect the weekly cost of a two-bedroom/two-bath condo or house during the peak summer season. Since prices are a bit higher than in the Fort Walton Beach area, the pricing structure below reflects that increase. Most rental agencies want a deposit up front, which can be up to a third of the week's rental. The rest is due upon check-in. Prices do not include tax. Please be sure to check both Fort Walton Beach and the Beaches of South Walton accommodations for a full area listing; many realty companies offer properties throughout the entire area.

$750 to $950	*$*
$951 to $1,100	*$$*
$1,101 to $1,500	*$$$*
More than $1,501	*$$$$*

Photo: Sugar Beach Inn

With only three guest rooms, the Sugar Beach Inn exudes charm in every corner.

ABBOTT REALTY SERVICES, INC.

35000 Emerald Coast Pkwy.   837-4853
$-$$$$ (800) 874-8914

Abbott is one of the largest realty companies in the area, offering more than 80 resort properties from high- and low-rise condominiums to townhomes and beach cottages throughout the Fort Walton Beach, Destin and Beaches of South Walton area.

EDGEWATER SERVICES, INC.

Palm Plaza   654-1113
5160 Hwy. 98 E.   (800) 322-7263
$$$

Edgewater manages units in 12 properties in Destin and the Beaches of South Walton. Since they're smaller, you might get more individualized attention. Some of the properties available are at Edgewater Beach Resort, the unusual stepped structure that provides a nice family atmosphere; Hidden Dunes, which has both high-rise and secluded low-rise units and the Beachside Towers at Sandestin. Nightly and weekly rates are available, as are monthly rentals in the off-season.

SHORELINE TOWERS

Off Hwy. 98   837-6100
Holiday Isle   (800) 223-1561
$$$

Streamlined high-rises set on 500 feet of gulf-front, these two- and three-bedroom condominiums are huge — 1,400 and 1,600 square feet. Guests have a clubhouse, tennis and racquetball courts and a swimming pool at their service. Some units have fireplaces; all have private balconies. Ramps are provided for wheelchair access.

DESTIN HOLIDAY BEACH RESORT

1006 Hwy. 98 E.   (800) 874-0402
$$$

Your own private beach highlights this all-inclusive resort. Boardwalks, a pool, an outdoor hot tub, lighted tennis courts, an exercise room, shuffleboard courts, a putting green, a kiddie pool and outdoor grills make for a great family place to play.

There's a $200 deposit required; nightly rates are available.

HENDERSON PARK TOWNHOMES
2701 Scenic Beach Hwy. 98 E. (800) 336-GULF
$

Newly renovated, these rustic-style townhomes are on the eastern boundary of Henderson Beach State Park and across from the Henderson Inn B&B. Many floor plans and square footage layouts are available. The view from the third floor decks is nothing short of spectacular. If you don't like paying for health clubs and golf courses that you'll never use anyway, these townhomes are a perfect alternative and are only a short walk to the beaches.

SUNDESTIN
1040 Hwy. 98 E.   *654-4747*
$$$ *(800) 336-9669*

Another of Destin's sun spots, this high-rise condo-hotel beach resort on the gulf offers one-, two- and three-bedroom floor plans with a full palate of amenities. Exercise equipment, a steam room, sauna, whirlpool, shuffleboard and a party room are part of the all-inclusive health club. You'll enjoy an outdoor and an indoor heated pool, an onsite restaurant and lounge and in-season beach service. All rooms are handicapped accessible. You're close to everything in Destin and right across the street from Big Kahuna's Water Park.

SANDPIPER COVE
775 Gulfshore Dr.   *837-9121*
$$

Sandpiper Cove is a Destin landmark on Holiday Isle, popular because of its homey low-rise look and the zillion and one extras offered with your rental. Start with studio, one- or three-bedroom gulf-front, gulf view or street-side units, a private beach boardwalk with gazebo, six tennis courts (three night lighted), four pools open 8 AM to 10 PM, beach equipment, a marina and boat ramp, picnic pavilions and barbecue pits, a nine-hole, par 3 golf course, a beach bar and restaurant . . . shall we go on? Talk about your full service! Needless to say, you'll probably like it.

SEAVIEW COTTAGES
316 E. Hwy. 98   *837-6211*
$

The fact that these tiny but charming older cottages seldom have vacancies — even in the off-season — might clue you in that they're great cottages at a great price. These two- and three-room cottages were probably some of the first to be built here, and now with all of the new construction crowded around them, they seem a bit out of place. The neon sign is right out of a 1950's B movie, which is actually why we were tempted to try it in the first place. All of the cottages have been recently refurbished and come with all the basics for sleeping and cooking. They're very close to the Destin Harbor, but the cottages don't actually have a view; a short walkway will take you down to the water. The best parts here, though, are the location (next to the Destin Yacht Club and right in the middle of the action in central Destin) and the price. Peak season rates are around $115 per night; if you rent for a week, your seventh night is free. Winter rates can't be beat: $400 to $500 per *month*.

Beaches of South Walton

Views, luxury, golf and tennis galore and quaint charm all describe the variety of accommodations in the Beaches of South Walton. You'll see many Mercedes, BMWs and Jaguars on the road here too; affluent visitors from the Midwest and

East Coast are discovering Florida's last frontier and wondering why they ever bothered going farther south!

Resort Properties

With all this sprawling, undeveloped beachfront, why opt for just a hotel room when you can have golf, tennis, spas, fitness centers and restaurants right at your fingertips?

So you won't have to refer back to the price code chart at the start of this chapter, here it is again:

$80 or less	$
$81 to 100	$$
$101 to 150	$$$
$151 or more	$$$$

SANDESTIN RESORT

5500 Hwy. 98 E.   267-8150
Emerald Coast Pkwy.   (800) 874-3950
$$$$

Spanning both sides of the highway and fronting both the Gulf of Mexico and Choctawhatchee Bay, Sandestin is a city unto itself. Twenty-three hundred acres offer condos, hotel rooms and villas (from one to four bedrooms), 45 holes of golf, 14 tennis courts, a 98-slip marina, 10 swimming pools, bike and watersport rentals, two full-service restaurants, an upscale festival marketplace, children's programs and a spa and salon. You want a great view? There are many more options than just a high-rise on the gulf — choose a bay view, a golf fairway, a lagoon or the wildlife sanctuary. If you're looking to really live it up on your vacation, you can't beat it for a place to be pampered!

SANDESTIN BEACH HILTON GOLF & TENNIS RESORT

5540 Hwy. 98 E.
Destin   267-9500, (800) 367-1271
$$$$

Towering over almost everything in the resort, the all-suite Hilton rises above the gulf within the confines of the Sandestin Beach Resort. All 400 junior suites have gulf views, bunk beds, wet bars and private balconies. Heated indoor and

Photo: Robin Rowan

The Henderson Park Inn provides visitors with turn-of-the-century charm right on the beach.

outdoor swimming pools, a gourmet restaurant and all the amenities of the Sandestin Resort (previous entry) are included. Room rates begin at around $200 per night for a partial beach view and go up from there; the most expensive room faces the gulf. A $5 per night resort fee is added to the price of any room.

SEASCAPE RESORT
& CONFERENCE CENTER

100 Seascape Dr.   837-9181
$$$ (800) 874-9141

Seascape is a nicely landscaped, 230-acre beach resort with an 18-hole championship golf course, five swimming pools, eight tennis courts and one full-service restaurant. These one-, two- and three-bedroom low-rise condos with private balconies and all the trimmings offer either golf course or beach views.

Bed and Breakfast Inns

SUGAR BEACH INN

3501 Scenic 30-A
Seagrove Beach   231-1577
$-$$

Still fairly new, this three-room inn might be just what you're looking for a weekend or week-long getaway. Seagrove Beach is just down the road from Seaside, but the ambiance is much different, much slower — people are never in a hurry. Choose from the Sunflower, Rose or Magnolia rooms on the second floor, all with spectacular views of the gulf. French doors, a wrapped veranda, brass and poster queen beds, private baths, English and American antiques and fireplaces grace the interior. Breakfast is served daily at 9 AM. Due to its small size, children are discouraged and pets are not allowed.

PATRONES BED & BRUNCH

Rt. 2, Box 7230
Santa Rosa Beach 32459   231-1606
$

This off-the-highway hideaway has grown and changed a great deal (for the better) since we first visited several years ago. The bed and breakfast cottages are new in just the last couple of years, and what they lack in waterfront views they make up for in atmosphere and decor. You'll see in less than a minute that artists must live and work here, since there are so many personal touches and hand-painted furnishings. We especially like the two units upstairs and downstairs set off in a building by themselves. These have their own sun porches, and the morning light is exquisite. Breakfast consists of coffee, juice and muffins, so if you need more than that, you'll have to go shopping the night before. There's a two-night minimum stay on the weekends, but you'll find plenty of browsing time with all of the artists' shops and animals on the grounds. It's truly a one-of-a-kind place; you'll just have to go and see it for yourself.

BAY VIEW HOUSE

Rt. 1, Box 2120
Santa Rosa Beach 32459   267-1202
$

Can this possibly be true? Seventy dollars for a suite for two people, a private bath and breakfast daily on the water? It isn't the Gulf of Mexico, but Bay View House is right on Choctawhatchee Bay, and the sunsets are unforgettable. This small bed and breakfast is nearly lost amidst the palms and magnolias shading the large deck. You've also got a nice white sandy beach out your door plus all of the wonderful amenities the area holds. Sit out on the giant porch swing to catch a cooling afternoon breeze, or spend a few quiet hours browsing through the library. Pets are sometimes welcome (call ahead), and children older than 4 are OK too. It's open from April 1 to the end of October.

JOSEPHINE'S BED AND BREAKFAST
101 Seaside Ave.
Seaside   231-1940, (800) 848-1840
$$$-$$$$

Like everything at Seaside, Josephine's does an exquisite job of capturing the mannerly Southern feel of a seaside retreat. Every room is perfectly furnished in period antiques or reproductions, topped off with balloon curtains, Battenburg lace comforters, settees, fireplaces and claw-foot tubs. No cookie-cutter hotel here, though; each room has its own color scheme — and its own surprises. All include wet bars, coffee makers and small refrigerators. Brunch is included in the comfort and privacy of your room (perhaps on your own veranda?) or Josephine's private dining room. The dining room is open for breakfast, lunch and dinner daily.

A HIGHLANDS HOUSE
10 Bullard Rd.
Dune Allen Beach   267-0110
$

Sit back and enjoy this taste of the Old South — a summer home with wide porches and gentle gulf breezes right on the beach. Rooms are individually furnished with four-poster rice carved beds, wing-backed chairs and wicker furniture on outdoor porches. An expanded continental breakfast comes with your room and is served in the dining room. Children younger than 10 stay free with parents. Credit cards are not accepted. A Highlands House harkens back to the time when families rented tiny cottages

along the beach, and there were maybe two restaurants, one store and one gas station within 30 miles. It's pretty far out there, but it's quiet; the beach is beautiful, and the price is great!

FRANGISTA BEACH INN
4150 Old Hwy. 98 E.   837-1071
$$ 837-9878, (800) 225-7652

Frangista (Fran-GEE-sta) began life back in the 1940s, when people came to this part of Florida to *really* get away, since there were no gas stations, no stores, no bridges and few roads. A Greek couple named their cottage after the Greek village from which their family descended and maintained a small apartment below their living quarters for friends. Later, they added a few rooms to let to travelers, and the tiny hotel was born. What you'll find here is a feeling for the old and rustic with clay tile floors, tongue and groove paneling and Adirondack chairs, together with resort conveniences such as gourmet dining and many types of water recreation. Cottages rent weekly as well as nightly and range from a single room on the gulf to one with four beds and four baths (one tub for each person?). With your room comes beach service, a morning newspaper and daily coffee.

Condominiums/Townhomes/ Vacation Cottages

Please be sure to check Destin accommodations for a full area listing; many realty companies offer properties throughout the entire area. Prices, which follow the same code as those in Destin, reflect the average weekly cost of a two-bedroom/two-bath condo or house during the peak summer season. Most rental agencies want a deposit up front, which can be up to a third of the week's rental. The rest is due upon check-in. Prices do not include tax.

$750 to 950	$
$951 to 1,100	$$
$1,101 to 1,500	$$$
More than $1,501	$$$$

ABBOTT REALTY SERVICES, INC.
35000 Emerald Coast Pkwy.   *837-4853*
$-$$$$ *(800) 874-8914*

Abbott is one of the largest realty companies in the area, offering more than 80 resort properties from high- and low-rise condominiums to townhomes and beach cottages. If you're not sure exactly where in the area might be best for you and your entourage, Abbott can explain the huge variety of options, both beachfront and inland, family-friendly or couples only, luxury at every turn or basic lodging.

EDGEWATER BEACH CONDOMINIUM
5000 Hwy. 98 E.
$$$ *837-1550, (800) 882-4929*

All units were decorated by designers, so each has its own special touches in addition to marble baths, views of the gulf and private balconies. Three swimming pools, a wading pool, a hot tub, shuffleboard, a putting hole and a playground are available to guests.

TOPS'L BEACH & RACQUET CLUB
5550 Hwy. 98 E.
$$$$ *267-9222, (800) 476-9222*

Lose yourself in 52 acres of rolling dunes and hills with two- and three-bedroom gulf-front and tennis villa accommodations. Twelve tennis courts, three racquetball courts, an indoor/outdoor pool, a fitness center, a full-service salon and a 1.7-mile nature and fitness trail are surrounded by some of the area's best natural woodlands. Your individually decorated unit comes furnished with

dishes, linens, a washer and dryer, disposal and ice maker. If for some reason you want to leave all of this luxury to venture out, Tops'l's private tram can escort you all around the property.

RIVARD OF SOUTH WALTON
2100 Magnolia St.
Santa Rosa Beach   *267-1255*
$$-$$$$ *(800) 423-3215*

Rivard manages a wealth of private home, condominium and townhouse rentals throughout the many communities of South Walton County. Many offer water views or are directly at the foot of the gulf. Where your rental unit sits in relation to the water can make hundreds of dollars of difference in the price. If the view doesn't matter all that much, be sure to ask for one a bit inland. The beach is never far away.

MONARCH REALTY AT SEASIDE
At Josephine's Bed & Breakfast, Seaside
Cottages   *(800) 475-1841*
Josephine's   *(800) 848-1840*
$$$-$$$$

Monarch rents all sorts of pristine cottages and townhomes at Seaside, which can't be beat for ambiance and seaside resort atmosphere. Park your car and leave it for the length of your stay; all shops, restaurants and the beach are just steps away. But there's a price for all that "atmosphere" — a two-bedroom/two-bath cottage starts around $1,500 a week. Reservations for Josephine's Bed & Breakfast can also be made through Monarch.

HIDDEN DUNES
BEACH & TENNIS RESORT
5394 Hwy. 98 E. 837-3521, (800) 824-6335
$$-$$$

A great getaway place, Hidden Dunes features secluded one-, two- and three-bedroom condos centered around man-made tiled pools with fountains. Private screened porches with ceiling fans keep out the bugs while letting you relax or dine in comfort. Hidden Dunes is a large property (27 acres) but was designed with privacy and relaxation in mind; walkways lead you around but not to the units (main entrances face the parking lot). You're never face-to-face with someone else's bathroom window. Strolling around the grounds at night is peaceful, well-lit and safe. On the grounds are swimming pools, Jacuzzis and one high-rise condo on the gulf, if that's your style. Other buildings have two stories.

SEASIDE

County Rd. 30-A
between Grayton Beach and Seagrove Beach,
Seaside   231-4224, (800) 635-0296
$$$$

A tiny beach community rising out of the scrub on the Gulf of Mexico, Seaside is an architect's dream. Brightly painted cottages sport wrapped porches with swings and rockers, widow's walks, gazebos and gingerbread of every description. White picket fences mark property lines, and community playgrounds and beach pavilions allow residents and visitors to meet and mingle.

Northwest Florida is fortunate and privileged to have this internationally acclaimed community in its midst. The word is out, the trend has caught on. Copycat communities have sprung up throughout the area and the Southeast. But Seaside was the first, and people still flock here to buy vacation homes or just spend a week or two in this idyllic setting.

People from Atlanta, New Jersey, New York and just about every other place have bought property here — people who are used to paying high prices. Consequently, Seaside is one of the most expensive places to stay in Northwest Florida. A two-bedroom/two-bath cottage for a week at high season will run you somewhere between $1,600 and $3,500. The difference in price is not the space — most cottages are fairly small — but whether there's a view of the gulf (only the honeymoon cottages are directly *on* the gulf).

Campgrounds/RV Parks

EMERALD COAST RV RESORT

Hwy. 30-A   267-2808
Santa Rosa Beach   (800) BEACH-RV

Plain and simple, this is the prettiest, cleanest RV park you may ever lay eyes on, with more amenities than some luxury resorts. Try these on for size: 30 concrete pads with patios, a heated pool, cable TV, phones, LP gas, tennis, a laundry facility, a country store, a clubhouse, picnic tables, a security gate, nature trails and fishing in stocked lakes. A complimentary shuttle takes you to the beach from May through September. No tents or pop-ups are allowed since this is strictly an RV resort. Summertime daily rates start at $28 for a full hookup (that includes electric and cable). Weekly rates are $172. Prices do not include tax.

GRAYTON BEACH
STATE RECREATION AREA

County Rd. 30-A near
Grayton Beach   231-4210

This exquisite state park with its rolling white dunes and forests of pine is perfect for camping, picnicking, swimming and hiking on the nature trail. Canoes are available for rent. No pets are allowed. RV hookup sites are $10.86 until March 1; without electricity $8.72. In-season rates are $15.26; $17.40 with electricity, which includes tax. Some of the 37 sites back up to the freshwater Western Lake, just a stone's throw from the gulf.

HOLIDAY TRAVEL PARK

5380 Hwy. 98 E.   *837-6334*

Camp right on gulf beaches or in grassy, shaded sites. Two hundred-fifty RV and primitive sites are available. Off-season rates are terrific, just $10 a night for any site or $50 a week. From March 1 through November, the park charges per-night fees of only $27 for water and electric hookups, $29 for a full hookup and $37 if you want to camp on the beach. A pool and convenience store are on the grounds.

WILLOWS CAMPGROUND

Hwy. 98, Santa Rosa Beach   *267-2183*

Stands of palmetto, slash pine, oaks and magnolia grace the surroundings of this small right-on-the-highway RV campground. A few willows are thrown in for scenery (and to provide this campground with its name). Sites start at just $15 per night plus tax, $60 a week or $180 for a month. On the grounds are a pool, telephones and a bath house. Look for Willows Campground a half-mile east of the flashing yellow light in Santa Rosa Beach.

Fort Walton Beach/Destin/ Beaches of South Walton
Shopping

Beach Ts, souvenirs, airbrush art, swimwear, footwear, beachwear and enough little sculptures, nightlights, boxes and bangles created from the gulf's treasures to leave you "shell" shocked. Most everyone gets a new hat, swimsuit or pair of sunglasses from one of these shops, and boy, they're out there. In fact, they're everywhere. But so are some terrific outlets in Fort Walton Beach, Destin and Graceville; gorgeous restored antiques, boutiques and original works of art throughout the Beaches of South Walton; and some pretty unusual finds in between.

Fort Walton Beach

ALVIN'S ISLAND
TROPICAL DEPARTMENT STORES
1204 E. Hwy. 98 on the corner of
Santa Rosa Blvd., Okaloosa Island   244-3913
1079 E. Hwy. 98, Destin   837-5178

You'll find everything you could ever want in the way of beachwear, airbrush art, postcards, souvenirs and jewelry.

MANUFACTURERS OUTLET CENTER
127 S.W. and
255 Miracle Strip Pkwy.   244-2744

In the mood for some real outlet shopping, with savings of 30 percent to 70 percent? With the bargains you'll find here, you may want to buy yourself an extra suitcase to haul it all home! Check out these brand names: Russell, Van Heusen,

Converse, Corning/Revere, Bass Shoes, Carter's and many more. And since they're open seven days a week, you can shop to your heart's content. The stores here expanded so rapidly that a second Manufacturers Outlet Center had to be built about 1.5 miles down the road, hence the two addresses. There's a free trolley that runs between the two; for now, it just runs on weekends.

SANTA ROSA MALL
300 Mary Esther Blvd., Mary Esther   244-2172

One of the more popular area malls, Santa Rosa Mall has 120 shops including anchors Gayfers, McRae's, Sears and JCPenney. Shop here for fashions, sporting goods, footwear, books, toys, music and electronics, eyewear, jewelry, cellular phones, furniture, flowers . . . have we missed anything? Oh yes, *food* — there are sit-down restaurants, snack shops and a fast-food food court mecca of 11 eateries.

ISLANDER'S SURF & SPORT
Hwy. 98, downtown   244-0451
Shoreline Village Mall, Destin   837-5735
Hwy. 98 at The Market at Sandestin   654-4141

Islander's offers a most excellent selection of beach and swimwear including Patagonia, Nike, Quicksilver, Oakley and more. You'll find T-shirts, flops, tanks and plenty of accessories too. When the surf's up, Islander's is ready with a great

Talk about diversity! Look for fashions and gifts you'll find nowhere else at The Market at Sandestin.

selection of surf boards and boogie boards for sale and for rent.

SMITH'S

123 Miracle Strip Pkwy. S.E.   243-1714
                                   243-6215

With clothing and accessories catering to women only, Smith's is as trusted as an old friend in Fort Walton Beach. Find not just sportswear and beachwear, but a full line of shoes, hosiery, lingerie, jewelry, formals and unique gifts for your favorite lady (even if that's *you*!).

BEACH AVE. T-SHIRT FACTORY

196 Miracle Strip Pkwy. S.E.   664-6765

Along U.S. 98 (called Miracle Strip Parkway here) is a short strip of shops, many of them geared to tourists. Strategically placed *before* you hit the beach, the "Miracle Strip" can get you just about anything you might need, and sometimes for a lower price than you'll find on the island. This store you can't miss, and not just because it's *hot pink*. Here are T's of every sort, screen printed, airbrushed or with a handpicked, custom transfer. The

T-Shirt Factory also has plenty of those coordinated pants-and-tunic sets with tropical motifs, mostly birds.

VF FACTORY OUTLET

950 Prim Ave., Ste. 12
Graceville   263-3207

Is it worth going well out of your way to save up to 50 percent on everything you buy? Let's do a little name dropping: Lee, Health-Tex, Jantzen, Vanity Fair and Wrangler. There are many more. Happy shopping!

THE SHOWTOWN SWAP SHOP & FLEA MARKET

2 miles north of the Mary Esther cutoff
on Beal Pkwy.   863-9034

Flea markets are big in Northwest Florida. If you've never been to one, you owe it to yourself to go just to see the incredible array of stuff offered at ridiculously low prices. It's fun to browse and bargain, even if you end up with something you can't possibly use but just had to have! Shop for your treasures on Saturday 7 AM until and Sunday from 8 AM until . . .

Destin

SHORELINE VILLAGE MALL

Hwy. 98 and Gulf Shore Dr.

Several specialty shops center around a courtyard and The Lighthouse Restaurant. **The Mole Hole** and **Gifts of Joy** offer an assortment of unique gift items, and Gifts of Joy also has gourmet gift baskets and flowers for all occasions. **Maxine's of Destin** sells beach sportswear and collectibles such as lead crystal, Dickens village and Andrea Sadek pieces. An airbrush artist is on staff for custom T's, visors and car tags. **Tooley Street** is a rather sophisticated clothing

store for women, while **Destin T-Shirt & Supply Co.** is more low key for casual and beach wear. **Lindz's A Place of Christmas** lets you browse through a winter wonderland all year long. **Streetwear** is another clothing shop for men and women with casual styles and affordable prices. **Islander's Surf & Sport** is a local favorite for casual wear from the beaches to the outback.

JAN'S BOOK NOOK AND HALLMARK

867 Shores Shopping Center   837-7461

Find your favorite vacation reading among the shelves at Jan's — sports, fiction, Florida information and adventure as well as terrific souvenirs, gifts and cards. Jan's is a full Hallmark store, so also look for gift wrap, cards and accessories to make someone's special day even better. Jan's Book Nook is right along Highway 98 on the same strip as the Delchamp's and Eckerd's.

BUMIN' IN THE SUN BEACHWEAR

1655 E. Hwy. 98   654-4622

The stuff inside is as good as the name — beachwear, swimwear, jewelry, beach accessories and just about everything you could want to outfit you for vacation. You've just got to splurge on yourself once during your visit, maybe with a new hat, a daring swimsuit or a night-on-the-town sundress. They're right across the street from The Back Porch Restaurant.

SILVER SANDS FACTORY STORES

5101 Hwy. 98 E., 1 mile west
of Sandestin   942-6685

Calling these upscale exclusive shops "factory stores" is like calling Dom Perignon just another drink. Anne Klein, Brooks Brothers, Calvin Klein, Dansk, Donna Karan, Flapoodles, Laura Ashley, Nautica and

Ruff Hewn might whet your appetite for more. And there is more! A whole new section of the complex opened in March 1995 to bring the total number of stores to 63.

GALLERY OF FINE ART
Palmetto Plaza at the corner of U.S. 98
and Palmetto 837-3993, 837-3488

Richard and Dorothy Williams invite you to come in and browse through their collection of fine art by local and nationally known artists. An artist's studio is upstairs, where watercolor classes are taught by Richard during the winter months. The Gallery of Fine Art will not only help you select a painting, but assist in framing it as well.

THE CANDYMAKER
Old Hwy. 98 E. across from The Back
Porch Restaurant 654-0833

You not only get to sample some of the finest saltwater taffy, creamy fudge, walnut toffee and juicy caramel apples north of the Gulf of Mexico, but you get to watch it all being made! The Candymaker may be more of an attraction than merely a place to shop. Passersby can stop in front of the huge front window and marvel as the taffy-pulling machine works its magic. Hand-dipped ice cream cones, frozen yogurt, floats and shakes will make you save a trip to The Candymaker for a scrumptious dessert!

DESTIN ICE SEAFOOD MARKET
Hwy. 98, a half-mile east of the
Destin Bridge 837-8333

Fishing put Destin on the map, so here, laid out before you, is the abundance of the sea, done in fine fashion by Destin Ice Seafood Market. The market started 25 years ago as a little business supplying ice to commercial fishing vessels, and now they've entered the seafood business themselves, supplying seafood to many of the area's fine restaurants.

If you've never bought fresh fish before, try a mild, white flaky fish such as grouper, triggerfish, red snapper, scampi or flounder. If you buy it already filleted, about a half-pound a person is the rule. This kind of fish is best broiled, baked or fried. For backyard grilling, try amberjack, yellowfin tuna, cobia, swordfish or — shark! Shrimp, a Gulf Coast favorite, is available in several sizes, either with "heads-on" or "heads-off," depending on your preference. Crab meat and lobster come in many varieties, and the Destin Ice Seafood Market has all the accompanying spices and sauces to make your meal complete. They can even pack fresh seafood for shipping!

Marine Supplies

YACHTIES'
200 Hwy. 98 E. 837-4900

It's affordable because it's been

Floppy hats, funky jewelry and hand-painted attire dress up the open-air marketplace at Seaside.

used before! This is a classy, quality place for new and used marine equipment, nautical clothing, gifts, jewelry and other items for sea and land. A quarter mile east of the Destin Bridge, Yachties' is open 9 AM to 5 PM Monday through Saturday.

THE SHIPS CHANDLER
646 Hwy. 98 E. 837-9306

This marine store is also a complete boating equipment and fishing tackle shop. Get a good buy on safety equipment, marine paints, topsider shoes and nautical sportswear. Rod and reel repair, fishing information and guide service make it a one-stop shop.

Beaches of South Walton

BEACH BUMS
Hwy. 98 west of Sandestin 837-7111

In the incredibly *pink* building that you can't miss, Beach Bums has between 5,000 and 10,000 swimsuits. Even if you're only looking for one, Beach Bums is a fun place to browse.

SEASIDE
C.R. 30-A, Seaside

Spanning both sides of the two-lane highway, Seaside offers an eclectic collection of outdoor markets, gourmet food shops and galleries. Beginning with the gulfside shops, there's **Sue Vaneer's** (Get it? Sou-ven-irs), selling all forms of Seaside memorabilia, which, of course, sells like crazy! Beach reading is popular at Seaside, and **Sundog Books** provides great Southern literature, children's books and timeless classics (including this one!). Whimsical clothing describes **4 Kids**, with a full complement of accessories, toys and novelties.

Donna Burgess' watercolors grace the homes of many a Seaside visitor and resident, and one can be yours by stopping by **Artz**, Burgess' Seaside gallery. No animals were harmed to create the line of skin care products and cosmetics at **Patchouli's**. And, Patchouli's can create a custom fragrance to blend with your body's own chemistry. **Per-spi-cas-ity** might be hard to pronounce, but it's not hard

Antiques, History and Country Weddings

If you need statuary for your garden, a lesson in watercolor painting, some history on the area or a place to hold a wedding, Chick Huettel is happy to provide. His shop, Bayou Arts & Antiques, 267-1404, is one of those rare,

one-of-a-kind finds that seem to abound in Northwest Florida. A winding dirt road at Cessna Park and Highway 393 takes you past pines and scrub to Huettel's acreage in the midst of dense marshlands on Hogstown Bayou.

A portion of the Santa Rosa cannery has been incorporated into the Bayou Arts & Antiques complex.

The simple outbuildings welcome in the afternoon sunlight, displaying everything from bird baths and arbors to hand-carved fish and exquisitely rendered wood and iron antique furniture. Take the wooden outdoor staircase to admire the lovely water view while Chick proudly explains that his property once housed the old Santa Rosa sugarcane factory. Although the town was wiped off the map by a citrus canker sometime around 1910, it was a thriving community of about 2,000 people at its peak. A small map attached to the upstairs porch railing shows a layout of what was once the town's center along the bayou.

Follow a narrow dirt path from the main antiques shop to a miniature house painted with animals and scenes of local lore. Inside, several benches and a modest altar

The now vanished town of Santa Rosa once bustled along Hogtown Bayou.

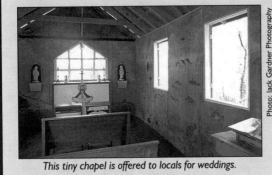

create a makeshift wedding chapel. "We mostly get local fishermen coming in here to get married," says Chick in his slow drawl. "Cathy and I don't charge 'em anything. We kind of get a kick out of it." Seems as though that's the Huettels' whole reason for being here.

This tiny chapel is offered to locals for weddings.

to find something wonderful in this outdoor marketplace, filled with casual clothing, baskets, glassware and accessories.

A couple of new shops round out the Seaside fun: **Flicks 'N' Clicks** offers camera supplies, video rentals and sales; **Peepers & Timekeepers** sells clocks, watches, sunglasses, and rents giant three-wheeled bikes; **Frost Bite** is a great place to go on a hot summer's day for shave ice, icy drinks, and snacks; the old-timey tin signs inside take you back. **The Fitness Fetish** is brand new, but is already expanding into larger quarters. Besides sales of sports apparel and nutritional products, owner Laurie Olshefski heads up fitness classes right here at Seaside in the meeting hall. The last new spot on this side of the street is **Surfer Girl**, which is filled with delightfully colorful tropical women's clothing.

Jump across the highway to Central Square and begin your shopping adventure with **iiis**, featuring designer eyewear. **Azure** is for men, with sports and casual wear and accessories. **L. Pizitz & Co.** is the "purveyor of Seaside style" (read: pricey) in dinnerware, handpainted pottery and linens. Some antiques, some new pieces, jewelry, pewter and sterling, all handpicked for you are at **Fernleigh Ltd.** And don't miss an opportunity to see some outstanding watercolor work by artist **Nina Fritz**. Her interpretations of jazz musicians and singers are dead-on perfect; her style is that of a well-seasoned, first-class pro. Travel a ways down Ruskin Place to the artist's colony. The **Martha Green Gallery** offers fine art and interior furnishings, jewelry, hand-blown glass and many other home furnishings, all handmade. Works by well-known and emerging artists are featured at **Newbill Collection by the Sea**, and **The Keeping Room** sells popular Folk Art and American reproductions. One new place of note is **Studio 210** at Ruskin Place, a bona fide coffee house. Linger over a steaming cup of java while you peruse some of the short stories by local authors scattered about, or take time to pet Squatter, the resident mouser.

PATRONE'S

Off Hwy. 98, Grayton Beach   231-1606

This is one of those unusual gems in Walton County that seems interesting enough from the road to stop and take a closer look. It's *kind* of an artist's colony mixed in with several animals on display in a giant pen, a barbecue place and a pretty view of the water. Joe Elmore, an artist who used to create huge wood carvings (some were used in the film *The Lost Boys*) evidently has found fame (if not fortune) and moved out, but he's left a few carvings behind to draw folks in to other artists' shops. Much of the work being done here, such as custom-made cypress and whimsical hand-painted furniture, hand-painted children's clothing, Florida paintings, jewelry and hats, is of wonderful quality and offered at *very* reasonable prices. Keep in mind, the artists are ready to bargain. Patrone's is open 9 AM to 5 PM daily. Ask to look at the delightful overnight cottages; staying in one of these could be a good introduction to this quirky part of Florida's Great Northwest.

THE MARKET AT SANDESTIN

Sandestin Beach Resort, Hwy. 98

You could spend a good part of a day here with thirty-eight specialty shops to tempt and delight you. And here's just a sampling: **Benetton** international fashions, **Black-n-White** "uncolorized" clothing, **Classic Cargo** fine porcelain and crystal, **Infinity** bed, bath, and linen shop with a Victorian flair; **Tis the Season** year-round Christmas shop; **Summer Rain** home furnishings and gifts with an environmental theme; and **Tarzana's** trendy swimwear for toddlers to size 18. The Market at Sandestin is located at the entrance to Sandestin Beach Resort.

CLEMENT'S ANTIQUES

U.S. 98, 7 miles east of Destin   837-1473

Although there are numerous antique shops throughout the Beaches of South Walton, this is still the largest (23,000 square feet), specializing in estate quality antiques and some of the best 17th- and 18th-century antiques in the state.

SMITH'S ANTIQUES MALL

12500 Emerald Coast Pkwy.   654-1484

You could spend hours browsing the enormous quantity of antiques and collectibles such as hand-painted screens and furniture, porcelain, Spanish paintings, glass and brass and much more. You'll find Smith's between the bay and the gulf on Highway 98. It's the giant *red* metal building just three minutes west of Sandestin.

Fort Walton Beach/Destin/ Beaches of South Walton
Historic Sites and Attractions

So you maybe thought that all Northwest Florida had going for it was a few pearly white beaches? Insiders have spread out far and wide, traversing the beaches, the water and farther inland to find you, our reader, absolutely up-to-the-minute data on the area's many attractions. Here it is, all in one place, your guide to the ordinary, the unusual and the downright strange — diversity galore. Attractions marked with an asterisk (*) are centered around family fun.

Fort Walton Beach

*THE GULFARIUM

U.S. 98 on Okaloosa Island   244-5169

Florida, 1955 ... before Disney World, Busch Gardens and world-class resorts, opening day at The Gulfarium was making front-page news. As the second-oldest marine show aquarium in the world, The Gulfarium's focus is primarily on family entertainment, but it also serves as an introduction to the wonders of marine life. Dolphin shows demonstrate the grace and agility of these gentle creatures and educate audiences on the dolphins' eco-locators (to find food or fellow dolphins when it's too dark to see) and their uncanny eyesight and strength.

Sea lions are visitors from the "left" coast, but have adapted well to their more humid surroundings. As they slap and splash and clap and howl, trainers explain how the bristly whiskers allow them to balance objects in or out of the water.

Enter the dark arena of The Living Sea, where a trained diver glides through a 10,000-gallon tank for a close encounter with alligator gars, sting rays and sharks as well as colorful tropical fish and a loggerhead turtle well more than a century old!

The diverse services offered by The Gulfarium include a captive breeding program, environmental education and The National Marine Mammal Stranding Network. The Network is set up to rescue and care for stranded dolphins, whales, turtles and birds. Admission charge is $12.72; $8.48 for children 4 to 11, $10.60 for seniors, plus tax.

*THE FOCUS CENTER

139 Brooks St.   664-1261

Here's a touchy feely museum, but not in the way your parents might think. Touchable, workable exhibits demonstrate natural phenomena and basic scientific principles. Kids can make a gigantic four-foot bubble and believe they're just having fun instead of experimenting with fluid dynamics and surface tension. Come face-to-face with yourself in skeleton form to learn about bones and joints and how they are adapted to work together on command. There's a Try On A

Cool down in one of Northwest Florida's scenic inland rivers.

Career Room where youngsters can climb into a space suit or fire-fighting garb. Traveling exhibits, such as a mini-planetarium dome called the Starlab, rotate with other exhibits on a yearly basis. Schedule your child's birthday party at The FOCUS Center and Focusaurus, the museum's dinosaur mascot, may stop in for a visit. During the school year, the FOCUS Center is open on weekends only from 1 to 5 PM; summer hours are 1 to 5 PM daily. Admission is $2, younger than 3 free.

*ROCKY BAYOU
STATE RECREATION AREA
State Rd. 20, Niceville   833-9144

Mature sandpine forests tower over scrub vegetation and shade Rocky Bayou, an offshoot of Choctawhatchee Bay. This area was a favorite of long-ago Native Americans; exhibits attest to their occupation. A mile of bayou shoreline runs within the park, which is especially nice for saltwater fishing and boating. There's freshwater fishing in Puddin Head Lake, where Rocky Creek flows into the bay. (Please remember that licenses are re-

quired for either type of fishing.) Three nature trails are explained in a self-guided booklet available at the park, and ranger-guided walks and campfire programs are offered seasonally. Admission is $3.25 per vehicle (up to 8 people); $1 for bikers or walkers.

DOOLITTLE MEMORIAL
193 John Sims Pkwy., Valparaiso

A memorial marks the site where Doolittle's Raiders, headed up by Gen. James Doolittle, trained for bombing missions over Japan in WWII.

*HISTORICAL SOCIETY MUSEUM
115 Westview Ave., Valparaiso   678-2615

Start with an exhibit of stone tools, found right here in Northwest Florida, that were used by Paleolithic and Archaic Indians more than 8,000 years ago. More recent local history displays huge iron kettles and pots slung by pioneer women in the 19th century and instruments of the turpentine industry of the 1920s. Heritage craft classes teach old-time methods of quilting, tatting, bobbin lace and needlepoint. A Youth Settlers program introduces pioneer life to 9 and 10 year olds. More than a two-week session, they learn to fashion corn husk dolls, dip candles and weave as well as doing without the conveniences of modern life. The museum is open Tuesday through Saturday from 11 AM until 4 PM, and admission is free.

*INDIAN TEMPLE MOUND MUSEUM
U.S. 98,Downtown   243-6521

Exhibits and dioramas date Native American tribes in this area back 10,000 years. All 4,000 Native American artifacts were found in a 40-mile radius of downtown. Designated a National Historic Landmark, the temple mound, just outside the museum, was used by Native Americans for political and religious ceremonies and has been restored to its original configuration. Admission is 75¢ for adults; kids are free. The museum is closed Mondays.

FORT WALTON BEACH ART MUSEUM
38 Robinson Dr. S.W.   244-5319

This is a pleasant place to spend an hour or so, examining the American paintings and sculptures, many by local artists, and the Thai and Cambodian relics. The museum is open Sundays from 1 to 5 PM and weekdays by appointment. Admission is free.

*AIR FORCE ARMAMENT MUSEUM
West gate of Eglin AFB on State Rd. 85
near State Rd. 189   882-4062, 882-4063

The SR-71 Blackbird, the fastest plane ever built, welcomes you to the museum. Inside, look for four full-size aircraft representing WWII, the Korean Conflict and Vietnam. For those interested in weaponry, you'll find a huge exhibit of bombs, missiles, rockets and guns. A 32-minute movie, *Arming the Air Force*, is shown continuously. Other aircraft and missiles dot the museum grounds. The museum is open daily from 9:30 AM to 4:30 PM and is closed Thanksgiving, Christmas and New Year's. Admission is free.

*PLEASURE ISLAND WATERPARK
Hwy. 98 on Okaloosa Island   243-9738

In the heat of summer, there's no better way to cool off! Seven waterslides and an activity pool, let you and the kids float, slide and splash to your heart's content. Go-carts, an arcade, an ice cream shop, restaurant and gift shop let you cool off out of the water. Pleasure Island tickets are $8 plus tax for people less than 85 pounds; $12 plus tax for those 85 pounds or more. Go-carts are $4.50 per ride plus tax. The park is open 10 AM to 10 PM.

Destin

Fishing is right at the top of the charts in Destin, and most activities center around the water. Since it's a resort area, some family-type attractions are slowly creeping in, which is to be expected — and welcomed. Be

The sun rises *and* sets over the gulf along the Emerald Coast!

Insiders' Tips

sure to check the Recreation chapter for Destin as well; charter boat fishing and sightseeing offer a unique perspective on this scenic area, as do Destin's historical museums.

*THE GLASS BOTTOM BOAT II
Capt. Dave's Marina,
304 E. U.S. 98   654-7787

Billed as "A Sightseeing Adventure," *The Glass Bottom Boat II* offers scenic wonders above — and below — the surface! Your adventure begins with a pleasant sojourn through Destin Pass and Choctowhatchee Bay as you head into the Gulf of Mexico. Be sure to bring your camera, not only to capture that emerald water (the folks back home won't quite believe it), but the remarkable scenery and flocks of sea gulls and pelicans escorting the boat to sea (and anticipating a handout). Schools of dolphin, almost as if on command, appear alongside the vessel, racing and jumping and having almost as much fun as the people on board.

Get set for a close-up encounter with fish, crabs, rays and other creatures of the deep through the large viewing window as the boat glides over the shallows of Choctowhatchee Bay and the pass. The captain and crew will point out the different species and tell you a little about them. Shrimp nets or crab traps may be pulled onboard to show guests the intricacies and varieties of marine life as well

as the different methods of obtaining tonight's dinner!

As soon as the weather's warmed up a bit (as early as January), *The Glass Bottom Boat II* is off and running on Wednesdays and Saturdays with trips from 1 to 3:15 PM. Cost is $12 for adults, $7 for children. Call for summer cruises.

*THE TRACK FAMILY RECREATION CENTER
Hwy. 98   654-4668

A clean, affordable family place, The Track is loaded with entertainment for teens, tots and even grown-ups. Go-carts, bumper boats and the Surfin' Safari Mini-Golf courses will appeal to everybody. The teens will love to "hang" at the arcade or get courageous and go bungee jumping, and the tiniest among you will thrill to "Kids Kountry" with its pint-sized Rio Grande Railroad, small-fry Ferris wheel, swing ride, spinning top (like a small-scale Tilt-A-Whirl) and Noah's Lark (a giant swinging boat ride).

Tickets for go-carts, bumper boats and bumper cars are $4.50 each (one ticket per ride); five rides cost $20; 10 rides cost $38; 15 rides cost $54. Kids Kountry rides are $2.25 each.

Value packages are available at four rides for $8, eight rides for $15.50 and twelve rides for $22.50. One round of mini-golf is $5.75 for adults, 12 and younger $4.25; for four or more adults it's $5 each. *If you must . . .*

Insiders' Tips

The Florida Park Service is issuing vacation passes good for up to 15 days. A Family Entrance Permit (up to eight people) covers admission to any of Florida's State Parks and costs $20. You can purchase the passes at any Florida State Park.

The Legacy of "Uncle Billy"

William Marler, a longtime Destin resident, was a pretty special man in the eyes of this tiny fishing community and maybe did more than any other resident to make it a better place. Known to everyone as "Uncle Billy," Marler moved to East Pass in 1879 to fish with Captain Leonard Destin and quickly became one of the best fishermen in the area. He built his own sloop for fishing and hauling supplies. He built a wharf and a store because they were needed. And in his lifetime, he built more than 100 boats.

Although he loved boat building, Uncle Billy had other concerns for his adopted home. He became the village coffin maker and the undertaker, charging nothing because he did it as a public service.

The first school for area children was held in the Marler living room, and the first church services in the Marler home until a community church could be built.

In 1897, he set up the first post office in the parlor of his home and became the self-proclaimed postmaster, serving in that capacity until his retirement in 1945. Some time during his first years as postmaster, Marler named the village "Destin" in honor of his first boss. The Marler tradition of handling mail was passed on, first to his daughter, Willie Mae Marler Taylor, then to his two nephews. A great-grandson still works at the Destin post office.

Photo: Willie Mae Taylor Family Archives

"Uncle Billy" Marler made more contributions to the Destin area than perhaps any other citizen.

bungee jumping costs $15. The Track is open from 10 AM until 10 PM from March to September, 9 AM to midnight in the summer and 10 AM to 5 PM in the winter.

MUSEUM OF THE SEA AND INDIAN
8 miles east of Destin on
Beach Hwy. 837-6625

This one plays strictly for fun, one of those delightfully tacky old-Florida tourist attractions. Strange and unusual marine exhibits have been amassed from all corners of the world (if you believe the signs). Look for the drunken fish, the walking catfish, the mola mola (all head-no brains), Native-American exhibits and a spook house. For the kids, there's a little zoo, but these creatures are not for petting — alligators, peacocks and monkeys are among the assemblage. This unique place is open 8 AM until 7 PM daily in the summer; 9 AM to 4 PM in winter. Admission is $3.75 for adults, $3.45 for seniors and $2 for kids 5 to 16.

*HENDERSON BEACH STATE PARK

17000 Emerald Coast Pkwy. 837-7550

More than 200 acres of beachfront were acquired for this new park as part of the Save Our Coast program. A nature trail winds through the white sand, dotted with Southern magnolias and native wildflowers. Six dune walkovers put you almost toe-to-toe with the gulf, while two tin-roofed picnic pavilions and bathhouses with outdoor showers provide families with all the amenities to enjoy a day at the beach. The site is handicapped accessible. Admission is $3.25 per vehicle (up to eight people), $1 for bikers and walk-ins.

*OLD DESTIN POST OFFICE MUSEUM

Stahlman Ave. across from the
Destin Library 837-8572

Artifacts and photos tell the story of early culture and standards of area pioneers. Destin's first post office was set up in the parlor of "Uncle Billy" Marler's home in 1897 (see sidebar). Admission is free, and guided tours are available. The museum is open Monday and Wednesday from 1:30 to 4 PM.

*DESTIN FISHING MUSEUM

Moreno Plaza, one block east of
Destin Bridge 654-1011

Old photographs and fishing artifacts demonstrate how Destin became the fishing capital of the world. Most of the museum is a "dry" underwater scene, complete with lighting and sound effects. It's open Tuesday through Sunday 11 AM until 4 PM, and there is no admission charge.

*BIG KAHUNA'S WATERPARK

1007 Hwy. 98 E. 837-4061

Big Kahuna's is chock-full of water slides, one with a multilevel activity pool with a Shamu the killer whale slide. It's water fun for everyone. Older kids will thrill to the new **Tunnel of Doom** and **Cave of No Return**! The **Grand Prix** racetrack and tropical golf course are open 10 AM until 10 PM; the water park is open until 5 PM. The waterpark is open Memorial Day to Labor Day. Call for admission prices.

Beaches of South Walton

Beaches and leisure-time activities are the top draw along the Beaches of South Walton. Slip through a shady wooded trail on horseback, imagine the bustle of a long-ago timber mill on the grounds of the Wesley mansion or head inland for a close-up look at how award-winning wine is made. Don't look for any high-traffic amusements here; folks spend their time playing golf, tennis and croquet. Shopping in South Walton's many boutiques can net the bargain hunter some one-of-a-kind finds.

Insiders' Tips

A favorite spot for divers off Destin's coast is called Timber Hole, a submerged petrified forest brimming with lobsters, sponges, shells and other fascinating types of marine life.

Even more fun than touring the Chautauqua winery and learning how wine is made is the free tasting session at the end.

*EDEN STATE GARDENS

Off Hwy. 98
Point Washington   231-4214

These neatly manicured grounds no longer echo with the laughter of children, the drone of a buzz saw or the chorus of voices intermingled with the sounds of a busy lumber mill. The old Wesley mansion, once the hub of the 12-acre site, stands majestically framed by gnarled oaks, colorful azaleas and garden walks of camellias. A century ago, the Wesley Lumber Company did a brisk business in yellow pine, building a dock out into Tucker Bayou for loading the lumber onto barges. From here the pine traveled to northern and western states, Europe and parts of South America. At its peak, the acreage was filled with a saw mill, planer mill, dry kiln, about 20 company-owned houses for employees and their families and a company commissary. The home is open for tours daily (admission is $4). The gardens and picnic area are open from 8 AM until sundown. Peak flowering season is around mid-March, but Eden is a delightful spot to set a-spell any time of year. Admission to the park is free.

*GRAYTON BEACH
STATE RECREATION AREA

State Road 30-A near
Grayton Beach   231-4210

You cannot leave South Walton County without standing on the beach that was rated No. 1 in the United States! Wide and flat, with scrub-covered rolling dunes, Grayton Beach is a Northwest Florida gem. After a visit, you may not want to leave at all. The park is heavily wooded with pine flatwoods and scrub oak. An inland lake is ringed by a salt marsh, a perfect nesting habitat for shorebirds and sea turtles. Camping and nature trails are offered in the park. Admission is $3.25 per vehicle (up to eight people), $1 for bikers and walkers.

CHAUTAUQUA VINEYARDS

I-10 at U.S. 331
DeFuniak Springs   892-5887

It's out of your way, but worth the drive, not only for a winery tour but for the lovely historic town of DeFuniak Springs nearby. The several varieties of wines grown, produced and bottled here are made from muscadine grapes, giving the wines an unusual flavor. Although the winery is small and has been in operation only a few years, several Chautauqua wines have racked up top honors at international wine competitions. The tour is really fascinating; you may ask questions of the people who actually *make* the wine (called vintners). Now comes the fun part. When the tour is over, you may spend some time in the tasting room (only those 21 and older, please) deciding which of the several varieties you like best. Most visitors buy at least one souvenir bottle if only for the tastefully designed label; there's a discount on cases. Admission is free.

Fort Walton Beach/Destin/ Beaches of South Walton
Annual Events and Festivals

Balmy weather emphasizes outdoor frolicking, so both visitors and locals take to the beaches and the water for year-round pleasure-hunting. Seasonal events add some extra zest to the good-times recipe. The events and festivals listed in this chapter are only a small part of the total pie; these get a listing because they occur annually. Note that a few of our festivals and events are in north Walton County, a pleasant daytrip away from the beaches, with plenty of scenic and historic diversions along the way.

Fort Walton Beach

April

EGLIN AIR SHOW
Eglin AFB, Hwy. 85 north of   882-3931
Fort Walton Beach

Eglin is the free world's largest military installation, and once a year it opens its gates to the public. Watch the aerial acrobatics of the Thunderbirds, simulated dogfights from the Desert Storm 33rd Tactical Fighter Wing and flightline displays of military power.

AMERICAN INDIAN SPRING FESTIVAL
E-CHOTA Cherokee Reservation
at Mossy Head   892-2562, 892-2875

Native American (Cherokee) arts and crafts, intertribal dancing, native dance competitions and demonstrations combine to make this twice-yearly event fun as well as educational. Admission is just $1.

OLD SPANISH TRAIL FESTIVAL
Spanish Trail Park, Crestview   689-6783

A rodeo, arts and crafts, food booths, trail rides, beauty pageants, carnival rides, a parade and musical entertainment commemorate the area's heritage and the 16th-century trade route between El Paso, Texas, and Jacksonville, Florida.

SATURDAY IN THE PARK
Perrine Park, Valparaiso   678-2323

Sponsored by the Okaloosa-Walton Historical Society, the free festival attracts thousands from surrounding communities to shop at arts and crafts booths, listen to continuous live entertainment, watch demonstrations of pioneer crafts and eat!

June

BILLY BOWLEGS FESTIVAL
Fort Walton Beach Landing   244-8191

A 500-boat parade brimming with costumed ruffians "captures" the Emerald Coast to celebrate the landing of the notorious pirate Billy Bowlegs. Fireworks, a triathlon, volleyball, food booths, crafts, a torchlight parade and many other fun activities highlight the week-long event.

• **203**

July

NICEVILLE/VALPARAISO
FIREWORKS DISPLAY

Boggy Bayou, Niceville   678-2323

The beautiful Boggy Bayou is the setting for this annual pyrotechnic display. Fireworks-watchers line the bayou or anchor out in the water for this brilliant free entertainment.

October

OKTOBERFEST

Niceville   897-3338

Every community worth its sauerbraten has a version of this German celebration. Niceville hosts this yearly bash with authentic German beer, music, ethnic foods, beer, arts and crafts and, of course, beer. Admission is free.

FESTA ITALIANA

Fort Walton Square   243-9055

Festa Italiana is a one-day festival celebrating Columbus and everything Italian — an Italian-flavored parade, Italian cuisine and continuous live entertainment. No admission is charged. Pass the pesto.

BOGGY BAYOU MULLET FESTIVAL

Old Sawmill Site, Hwy. 85 N.
and College Rd., Niceville   678-1615

Mullet is considered a "trash fish" by Northerners, but that's just because they've never tried it! The folks down here find the mighty mullet good eatin' fried up in cornmeal batter. About 11 tons of the plentiful fish are consumed each year. Sixty food booths, 80 arts and crafts vendors, clown shows, pony rides and live entertainment should keep the family busy for at least one of the two festival days. A few entertainers of regional or

national notoriety seem to show up each year, maybe just to get in on some of that mullet eating! You can get in on it too — admission to the festival is free (*you* buy the fish).

November

AMERICAN INDIAN FALL FESTIVAL

E-CHOTA Cherokee Reservation
at Mossy Head   892-2562, 892-2875

If you missed it in the spring, it's back in the fall — Native American (Cherokee) arts and crafts, intertribal dancing, native dance competitions and demonstrations. Admission is just $1. Call for directions; Mossy Head is *way* out there.

December

NICEVILLE/VALPARAISO
CHRISTMAS PARADE

John Sims Pkwy., Niceville   678-2323

The main street of downtown Niceville provides an idyllic hometown setting for marching bands, scouts, dance classes, drill teams and float-riders throwing candy to spectators.

CHRISTMAS FESTIVAL

Okaloosa Courthouse, Crestview   682-3212

This one-day festival is a highlight for Crestview residents. Centered around a bazaar with arts, crafts, wares, food and entertainment, a grand parade marches past the courthouse; elementary school choruses sing their hearts out at the Courthouse Terrace, and everybody enjoys the music and steaming cups of cocoa. There's a special Kid's Korner where grown-ups are not allowed; children can shop here for special gifts for mom, dad and other favorite people at prices especially suited to the younger-than-12 set. No admission is charged.

Photo: Destin/Fort Walton Beach TDC

And they're off ! The Destin Fishing Rodeo lasts the entire month of October.

Destin

Almost every one of Destin's events is some sort of fishing tournament, but you don't have to fish for something to do! Check listings for Fort Walton Beach and the Beaches of South Walton too; they're close by and ready for a festival almost anytime you are!

May

MAYFEST

837-6241

It's a celebration of spring, centered around the arts. This Cajun-flavored festival features enough spicy food and music to make a bayou-dweller feel right at home.

June

HARBOR DOCKS SUMMER OPEN

Harbor Docks Restaurant
Hwy. 98   *837-2506*

This is a small tournament with regard to boat entries (about 20 boats participate), but anglers vie for prizes of up to $2,000 for the elusive blue marlin.

July

DESTIN FIREWORKS

East Pass   *837-4242*

Here's another extraordinary fireworks spectacle, held at the pass for landlubbers and boaters. Bring a blanket, some popcorn and a few sparklers and you'll be ready for some free front-row entertainment over the beautiful Destin Pass.

DESTIN SHARK FISHING TOURNAMENT
654-1011

This is like a real fishing tournament, only ... sharks are the main catch. Now, some people actually *eat* shark and, we hope, many of these fearsome fish will end up on somebody's plate. You might guess the shark-infested docks attract a wild crowd; some catches weigh in at more than 800 pounds!

August

DESTIN KING MACKEREL TOURNAMENT
654-1011

Sponsored by the Destin Fishing Museum, anglers fan out into the gulf for three days, fishing for the silver-striped king of the deep. Weigh-ins are held at Harbor Docks Restaurant.

October

DESTIN SEAFOOD FESTIVAL
Harborwalk at the foot of the
Destin Bridge   837-6241

It's the kickoff to the fishing rodeo, a warmup for the fresh catches yet to be caught. Alligator, crawfish, shrimp, shark, mullet, amberjack, pompano and a zillion varieties of marine life are barbecued, kebabed, fried, battered and broiled to the accompaniment of beach bands and a backdrop of the picturesque Destin harbor. The eats and drinks are for sale, but the merrymaking is free.

DESTIN FISHING RODEO
Harborwalk
at the foot of the Destin Bridge   837-6734

Hook 'em, little doggie! Leave your spurs and chaps at home and pick up a rod and reel, 'cause this is the big one ... a month-long inshore, offshore, bay and bayou frenzy where everybody can vie for prizes in more than 100 categories and more than $100,000 in cash and prizes. The rodeo started more than 40 years ago, and the dock parties have become legendary. While private and charter boats head out hoping to reel in the big one, those left on shore can partake in parades, regattas, dances, art shows and much more.

Beaches of South Walton

Perhaps more than anywhere else in Northwest Florida, the Beaches of South Walton have got something cooking. With sporting events, writ-

---

Insiders' Tips

The Florida version of the New York Chautauqua began on Lake de Funiak in 1885. Since most Americans were sadly lacking in formal education and school was not mandatory, the Chautauqua emphasized religious training and educational activities for both children and adults. The three-week intellectual summer camp focused on philosophy, theology, art, music, elocution and cookery. That festival ended in the mid-1920s, but local residents are working to revive a contemporary version of the Florida Chautauqua.

Photo: Steven Brooke

Can you imagine a more idyllic environment for a writer's retreat?

ers' retreats, wine tasting and arts festivals a-plenty, the pleasure of these man-made diversions is heightened by the quiet surroundings of some of the world's most scenic beaches.

January

GREAT SOUTHERN GUMBO COOK-OFF
Market at Sandestin
Sandestin Resort 267-8092, (800) 277-0800

Fifteen area restaurants compete for the best gumbo and recognition by their peers in this deliciously enticing event. All proceeds go to the United Way of Okaloosa and Walton Counties, so eat, eat, eat, vote for your favorite, and feel good inside and out! Tickets are $7 per person; $10 the day of the event.

ESCAPE TO CREATE
Seaside 231-2421

Is that creative urge surging? Then attend this week-long residency program featuring readings, concerts, exhibits, lectures and more scholarly pursuits. The magical surroundings of Seaside will inspire you!

February

ESCAPE TO CREATE
Seaside 231-2421

This is a weekend version of the artistic retreat in January.

March

EMERALD COAST CHEF'S TASTING
Sandestin Beach Resort
Hwy. 98 E. (800) 277-0800

Some of the area's finest culinary delights are prepared for discriminating palates at this tasty event. Proceeds benefit the American Cancer Society. Call Sandestin Resort for ticket information.

April

CHAUTAUQUA FESTIVAL
Around Lake de Funiak
DeFuniak Springs 892-9494

This one-day family festival includes arts, crafts, food, an antique and classic car show, a parade, a children's activity area, live entertainment and a fireworks

Killer Trash

Your fishing line gets tangled around a floating log. You snip the line off and start fresh. You finish your six-pack and toss the plastic rings into the water. You dump your bag of ice into the cooler and leave the bag on the beach. If you've ever done any of these things, you could be a killer.

Marine debris contributes to the higher-than-normal death rates for seals, seabirds, turtles and many species of fish. Uncaring, or in some cases simply unknowing, people dump plastic nets and lines off of boats or near the shore, a lethal trap for all inhabitants of the coastal environment. Turtles that become entangled in fishing line are unable to break free and quickly drown. Ospreys, gulls and other birds sometimes collect pieces of line for nesting material, creating death traps for their young. Beyond the threat to sealife, fishing line can easily become wrapped around boat propellers, crippling the vessels.

Plastic bags can be mistaken for jellyfish by turtles who ingest them and suffocate, a slow and agonizing death. Plastic six-pack rings are a threat to all kinds of marine animals. Fish, birds and sea lions have been found entangled in the rings.

Since these items are created and used only by people, it is up to all of us to dispose of them properly. It is illegal to dump *any* type of debris over the side of a boat, and it's so simple to save your trash until you get back to shore.

Northwest Florida is fortunate to be blessed with a thriving marine ecosystem and a wealth of natural beauty. We all need to take the steps necessary to help preserve the gulf and beaches, not only for ourselves, but for the creatures who inhabit them.

Photo: Center for Marine Conservation

An escaped balloon proves deadly for this marine bird.

show over the lake at day's end. A $1 donation is charged.

SPRING WINE AND MUSIC FESTIVAL
Seaside   231-5424

Jazz and blues performers provide the musical backdrop for aficionados of fine wines to sample, swirl and select from vineyards throughout the Southeast. Saturday is the wine tasting, but Sunday is reserved for the music — blues, jazz and soul. Tickets for Saturday only are $30. Sunday late afternoon combines a tour of Seaside homes, a silent auction and a wine and cheese reception for $20. Packages may be available.

May

GRAYTON BEACH
FINE ARTS FESTIVAL
Grayton Beach   231-5141

This old Florida resort community has grown into a haven for the arts and artists. There are many historic buildings in the tiny town, which is so small you can park and just walk to your heart's content. Artists from throughout the United States will have works on display and for sale at this juried show, and all attendees may vote on their favorites for the People's Choice Award. Admission is free.

MEMORIAL DAY SAILING REGATTA
Seaside   231-5424

Hoist the sails, mate, and join in the fun! The regatta starts at high noon Saturday in conjunction with a sandcastle building contest. Sunday's activities include a Memorial Day Sunset Serenade. Enjoy an old-fashioned Seaside cookout on Monday.

June

SANDESTIN PROFESSIONAL GRASS
COURT TOURNAMENT CHAMPIONSHIPS
5500 Hwy. 98 E. at
Sandestin Beach Resort   267-7110

Avid tennis aficionados hit it off on the sprawling grass courts of Sandestin in both singles and doubles divisions. The event is free to spectators.

SUMMER FILM FESTIVAL SERIES
Seaside amphitheater
Downtown Seaside   231-5424

The Downtown Seaside Association presents its Summer Film Festival Series every Friday from June through August at 8:30 PM. Bring a blanket and a cooler, and enjoy some classic family and art films. Admission is free, and the event is open to the public.

July

STAR SPANGLED SANDESTIN
FAMILY FUN FOURTH FEST
Sandestin Beach Resort
Hwy. 98 E.   267-8150,   (800) 277-8100

Grab the troops for a weekend of star-spangled fun! Start with a July 4th cook-

Since many charter boat captains prefer a scaled-back schedule in the winter months to shutting down completely, you may be able to swing some outstanding deals in the off-season on sightseeing and charter fishing trips as well as dive charters.

Insiders' Tips

Photo: Destin/Fort Walton Beach TDC

Join in the festivities as these "pirates" capture The Emerald Coast during the Billy Bowlegs Festival in Fort Walton Beach.

out on the pool deck with live entertainment, a giant seafood buffet, and to top it off, a fireworks extravaganza on the beach.

THE SEASIDE
JULY 4TH CELEBRATION

Seaside   231-5424

Not to be outdone by all this patriotic flag-waving, Seaside puts on a party of its own, beginning with a parade at 8 AM in front of Seagrove Plaza. A beach barbecue with all the fixins, watermelon eating

and apple bobbing are topped off with a beach dance party beginning at 6:30 PM.

TURTLE WATCH

Grayton Beach State Recreation Area
Grayton Beach   231-4210

This watchdog volunteer group monitors nesting loggerhead sea turtles from July through August. The tiny newborns are subject to predators, vandals and a host of other dangers. Anyone spotting a nest or an egg-laying female is encouraged to immediately report it to one of the park rangers so protective measures can be taken.

WALTON COUNTY FOURTH OF JULY

Lake deFuniak
DeFuniak Springs 892-2821

Beginning with a parade around the lake at 5 PM, the celebration includes music, food and a fireworks display over the lake. Admission is free.

August

ELEPHANT WALK TRIATHLON & BAYTOWNE DUATHLON

Sandestin Resort
Sandestin 267-7000, (800) 277-0800

This competition has grown into one of the most popular sporting events (maybe next to fishing) in the area. More than 500 men and women from across the United States sign up for the event, part of the Grand Prix Series Events.

September

THE SEASIDE INSTITUTE FALL CONCERT SERIES

Seaside Amphitheater, Seaside 231-2421

Nationally acclaimed singers and musicians perform three weekends in September and October. Call Seaside for dates and season tickets.

SEEING RED WINE AND MUSIC FESTIVAL

Seaside 231-5424

The formerly one-day wine tasting festival (you guessed it, *red* wine this time), has become so popular that it now encompasses three full days. Events are centered around jazz and blues performers and an art exhibition. Stick around for the fancy fund-raising dinner for the Seaside Institute, or just come back the following day for more music and art.

October

MONARCH MIGRATION

Grayton Beach State Recreation Area
Grayton Beach 231-4210

Each year, tens of thousands of Monarch butterflies migrate from northern states to Mexico, stopping off in Northwest Florida for a week or so every October. The Monarchs seem particularly attracted to Grayton Beach's salt myrtle bushes, where thousands might cover one particular bush at a time. Monarchs have been spotted throughout Northwest Florida during this time, at Fort Pickens and other places along the coast in late October. Call the parks to find out approximate dates . . . and don't forget your camera! Admission to the park is $3.25 per car.

FIU/SEASIDE INSTITUTE WRITER'S CONFERENCE

Seaside 231-2421

What perfectly inspirational surroundings for aspiring screenwriters, novelists and playwrights! The Seaside Institute, in conjunction with Florida International University, brings in top instructors who peek over your shoulder during workshops. Lectures and evening public readings are also part of the weekend.

THE MONARCH FESTIVAL

Seaside 267-8150

The festival, which may or may not become an annual thing (this all depends on the monarchs, of course), celebrates the migration of thousands of the colorful butterflies to the Beaches of South Walton. Attend environmental seminars as well as musical and sporting events. It's sponsored by Monarch Realty at Seaside (naturally).

SOUTH WALTON SPORTFEST WEEKENDS

Various locations throughout the Beaches of South Walton   267-1216, (800) 822-6877

Held on three consecutive weekends in October and November, Sportfest is South Walton's biggest event; participants double in number every year. Events include a triathlon, duathlon, 10K run, half-marathon, bike race, century bike tour and a beach to bay volksmarch. The event is free to spectators. Call for entry forms, then start practicing!

ARCHITECT'S HOUSE TOUR

Seaside   231-2421

Oh, take me, take me! Once you see the outside of some of the stunning Seaside homes, you long to prowl within, and during this tour, you get your chance. Not only do you get to gawk to your heart's content, you can talk to the architects responsible for the homes' designs. Please call to preregister.

November

JAZZ BY THE SEA

Seaside   231-5424

Spyro Gyra, Tuck & Patti and the Subdudes have been featured in past concerts; this year's performers are still under wraps. What you can expect, however, is a wonderful weekend of main-stream jazz, great eats and lots of surprises. Call for ticket information.

EMERALD COAST GOLF TOUR FALL CHAMPIONSHIP PRO-AM

The Garden and Emerald Bay Golf Courses Hwy. 98 E.   862-0803

Both The Garden and Emerald Bay courses host this pro-am tournament, now in its fourth year.

December

CANDLELIGHT CHRISTMAS TOUR AT EDEN MANSION

Eden State Gardens Point Washington   267-2166

The stately Wesley mansion, formerly part of the Wesley Lumber Company property, is decked out in holiday splendor for candlelight tours. There is a $4 admission to the house; there is no charge to tour the gardens, which in December are awash in a lavish display of camellias.

A SEASIDE CHRISTMAS

Seaside   231-5424

Spend a spectacular season sunning at Seaside. Special packages for families are offered during this time, plus a full calendar of activities such as the Christmas tree lighting ceremony, a Christmas parade and a tour of homes.

Fort Walton Beach/Destin/ Beaches of South Walton
Parks and Recreation

Northwest Floridians love spending their leisure time outdoors enjoying the area's natural as well as man-made attractions. The sun shines more than 340 days a year, and there's no snow (well, hardly ever); locals take advantage of recreational pursuits by creating their own playgrounds.

This entire area from Fort Walton Beach to the Beaches of South Walton is only about a 20-mile drive, so don't limit yourself! Check listings in the other sections; many overlap or may be listed twice because of locations in more than one area. Some activities, such as charter boat cruises, may be listed as attractions, so be sure to skip around here before you venture out in your car.

Fort Walton Beach

Golf

BLUEWATER BAY GOLF CLUB
2000 Bluewater Blvd.
Niceville   897-3241

Recently named one of the top-25 courses in Florida by *Golfweek* magazine, Bluewater Bay is a golfer's dream — dense woodlands, marshes and alternating rolling and flat terrain running along Choctawhatchee Bay create opportunities for challenging play. The four nine-hole courses were home to the Bluewater Bay International Invitational, welcom-

ing players from 18 countries. It's open every day from 7:30 AM until dark. The pro shop opens at 7:15 AM and closes at 5 PM.

EGLIN AIR FORCE BASE
John Sims Pkwy.
Niceville   882-2949

Within Eglin Air Force Base, these 18 holes are open to those with active and retired military ID. A driving range, pro shop and snack bar are part of the facility. The course is open 6:30 AM to 5:30 PM daily.

FOXWOOD COUNTRY CLUB OF CRESTVIEW
Antioch Rd. off State Rd. 85
South of Crestview   682-2012

This is an 18-hole semiprivate course (public welcome) where water comes into play on six holes. The country club offers its own driving range, restaurant and snack bar. The course and the pro shop open at 7 AM; closing is an hour after the last golfer leaves the course, usually around 6 or 7 PM.

FORT WALTON BEACH MUNICIPAL COURSE
Off Lewis Turner Blvd.   862-3314

Across from the fairgrounds, this city course has two public 18-hole courses, two putting greens and a driving range. Golf aficionados agree it's one of Florida's finest municipal courses appealing to the

Photo: Destin/Fort Walton Beach TDC

Of all the man-made activities provided by the Emerald Coast, nothing can compare with the area's best natural attraction.

average golfer. It's open daylight until dark daily; the pro shop is open from 6:30 AM to 6 PM.

HURLBURT AIR FORCE BASE

On Hurlburt AFB   884-6940

The Hurlburt course is open to active and retired military with government ID. Water surrounds 14 holes, interspersed with forests and bunkers. The course is open from 6:30 AM to 5 PM daily. Other facilities for your convenience include a driving range, putting greens and a pro shop.

ISLAND GOLF CENTER & LOST LAGOON MINI-GOLF

1306 Miracle Strip Pkwy. (Hwy. 98)
Okaloosa Island   244-1612

This huge complex includes nine holes of pitch-n-putt, two 18-hole mini-courses, nine-hole and par 3 courses lit for night play. Lost Lagoon features 36 holes of miniature golf and a game room with a pool table and videos. This family-oriented attraction is good for at least a few hours of your vacation time. It's open 7:30 AM until dark.

SHALIMAR POINTE GOLF AND COUNTRY CLUB

2 Country Club Rd.
Shalimar   651-1416 , (800) 964-2833

The rolling dunes and stands of magnolia, pine and oak make for tricky set-ups; keep your eyes peeled on the 11th and 17th holes. A driving range, putting green, snack bar and a restaurant are part of the Shalimar Pointe package. *Golfweek* magazine calls this course "One of the Southeast's Top 50 Development Courses." The pro shop is open from 6 AM to 6 PM every day; tee times start at 6:30 AM.

SHOAL RIVER COUNTRY CLUB

1104 Shoal River Dr.
Crestview   689-1010

Semiprivate, the 7,000-plus yard Shoal River course changes elevation constantly. Natural landscaping of trees and grasses creates navigational problems throughout. The country club has a lounge, snack bar, putting green and practice green. It's open 7 AM until dark; the pro shop closes around 6 PM.

Tennis

FORT WALTON RACQUET CLUB
23 Hurlburt Field Rd.   862-2023

Nine courts, both clay and hard, are open to all. Since many players prefer to wait out the heat of the day to play, four courts are lit for night play. It's open 8:30 AM to 9 PM Monday through Friday, 8:30 AM to 6 PM on weekends.

BLUEWATER BAY TENNIS CENTER
Bay Dr. at Bluewater Bay Resort
Niceville   897-3664

Twelve courts are at the tennis center, and seven others are sprinkled throughout the resort. Clay courts are $7.50 per person per hour; hard courts at Bay Drive are $3.50 per hour per person. The tennis center is open daily from 8 AM until 9 PM.

FORT WALTON BEACH
MUNICIPAL TENNIS CENTER
45 W. Audrey   243-8789

Twelve lighted Laykold surfaced courts and four practice walls are open to the public on a first-come, first-served basis. The clubhouse has lockers, showers and a lounge area. It's open Monday through Thursday 8 AM to 9 PM; 8 AM to 5 PM Friday and 9 AM to 5 PM Saturday and Sunday.

SHALIMAR POINTE TENNIS CENTER
2 Country Club Rd., Shalimar   651-8872

In addition to its lavish golf facilities, Shalimar Pointe offers six outdoor Rubico courts, four of them lighted. Lessons are also available and must be set up in advance. Fees are $8 per person per hour, then $4 for every additional hour. The center opens at 8:30 AM; closing time varies depending on the weather.

Scuba/Snorkeling Trips

CHUCK'S DIVE WORLD
116 Meadow Woods Ln.
Niceville   897-3405

Once they teach you the open water PADI certification, you can scuba dive in a crystal clear spring where the freshwater fish are tame enough to eat from your hand. The dive shop offers flexible scheduling and supplies dive gear; financing is available.

Watersport Rentals

ADVENTURE WATERSPORTS
Next to Toucans
Okaloosa Island   244-5222

Water toys abound! A three-seat Sea-Doo zips across the water at lightning speed. The Waverunner takes you on a two-hour excursion with a guide. Sailboats and wet or dry parasailing also are available.

PARADISE WATERSPORTS
Six locations on Hwy. 98 in
Fort Walton Beach and Destin   664-7872

Why not learn a new watersport while you're here? Rent Jet Skis, Waverunners, sailboats, pontoon

---

"The World's Luckiest Fishing Village" really *is* lucky, and here's why: There's an offshore shelf that dips straight from Destin's East Pass to 100-foot depths within 10 miles of shore — the speediest deep-water access on the Gulf of Mexico!

Insiders' Tips

boats, jet boats, sailboards and water trikes. The rental staff will instruct you on their safe operation before you head out. Parasailing on the bay and beach is probably best reserved for the more adventurous. Paradise Watersports locations are at the seawall between Destin and Fort Walton Beach, The Hut (across from The Ramada on Okaloosa Island), the Destin Bridge, behind Pleasure Island, behind the Back Porch and the parasail beach pickup.

PONTOON BOAT RENTALS

Hwy. 98, a mile west of Fort Walton Beach in Mary Esther at Consigned RVs   243-4488

For a true Insider, this is the only way to go. It's a little noisy, but it's easy, flat and sturdy, and you're the captain! Bring a few friends and make it a fun and inexpensive day on the water. An 18-foot pontoon boat rents for $70 for a half-day; all day rental is $120 (up to four passengers). Twenty-footers go for $90 (half-day) and $150 (all day), taking up to eight passengers. The two largest are 24- and 28-feet and will accommodate wheelchairs. Those rates are $110 and $175, respectively. You pay for fuel, bring a cooler, lots of friends and family and have a ball!

Canoeing/Tubing

ADVENTURES UNLIMITED

Tomahawk Landing, 12 miles north of Milton, then 4 miles
off Fla. 87   623-6197, (800) 239-6864

You're really missing out on some of the best parts of Northwest Florida if you skip a trip down one of the inland rivers. Adventures Unlimited provides canoes, life jackets, paddles, camping gear, ice, refreshments and just about everything you could ever possibly need on a one-

day or overnight canoe trip. Cabins on Wolfe Creek and campsites are available for overnight stays (see our Pensacola Accommodations chapter). Canoe rentals start at $12 per person (two people per canoe) for a short trip; to completely outfit you for an overnight stay on the river is $41 per person.

BOB'S CANOES

On Munson Hwy. at the Coldwater
Creek Bridge   623-5457, (800) 892-4504

In business for more than two decades, Bob's Canoes sends you down the river in canoes, tubes, paddleboats and kayaks. Choose from Coldwater Creek, Juniper Creek or the Blackwater River — all clear, cool and relatively shallow freshwater streams, perfect for beginners. A large waterfront pavilion at rental headquarters is available for picnics. Canoe trips start at $11 per person (two people per canoe). Paddleboats, kayak trips (one person per kayak) and group rates are available.

BLACKWATER CANOE RENTAL

Nine miles east of Milton off
U.S. 90   623-0235, (800) 967-6789

Canoe, tube, kayak and camp for a half-day or up to three-days on the beautiful Blackwater River. Blackwater Canoe Rental provides all the necessities for getting you there; you supply your own camping equipment, eats and drinks. A short trip (1½-hours paddling time plus stops) is $11 per person; a day trip (four hours paddling) is $12. Children 12 and younger are free with two adults in one canoe. Overnight trips start at $17 per person. Call for reservations and directions.

Beyond the Bay

If you tried this trip yourself, you might never be heard from again. But Captain Frank Harris handles this incredible network of rivers and bayous like he grew up here. In the fall of 1994, Captain Frank began his Cypress Wilderness Trek into the pristine waterways off Choctawhatchee Bay.

Leaving from the Baytowne Marina at Sandestin Resort, *The Osprey* is nearly filled to its 15-person capacity this bright March morning. Harris begins the adventure with a few safety measures, then warns that we're in for a rollicking 30-minute ride across open water to Choctawhatchee Bay's easternmost shore. He asks if we're ready to "plane up," then kicks *The Osprey* into high gear, and away we go!

Just prior to entering the mouth of the Indian River, we motor slowly past hundreds — maybe thousands — of pilings sticking a few feet above the water. Captain Frank explains that during World War II, the top of each of these pilings was equipped with a radar mechanism, an effective decoy to lure enemy planes into thinking that this stretch of uninhabited wilderness was indeed Eglin Air Force Base. The real base lies several miles to the north and west.

Most of the 3½-hour trip is spent within the boundaries of the Cypress Wilderness Preserve, a 50,000-acre tract owned by the state of Florida. Rivers widen and narrow at will, branching off into yet another smaller tributary. Giant cypress, some hundreds of years old, lean over the water, forming a shady canopy.

From this point, directions start getting a little fuzzy. We traverse the Indian, Mitchell, Cypress and Choctawhatchee rivers, pass a few man-made canals lined with a few rather rustic residences and navigate into tiny waterways with names such as the Live Oak Cutoff, Watermelon Bayou and Smoke House Run. Harris provides his guests with a map and is good about telling us where we are.

"We'll be going up Live Oak Cutoff to Mitchell River for about a quarter-mile," Harris says confidently. "There's a true swamp up here, and I know the place where a 12-foot gator hangs out." After turning up this river and down that bayou, doubling back to search for gators, circling around waiting for an osprey to return to its nest . . . well, the map became useless. We put our faith in Captain Frank instead; he pulled us through without a hitch — all 62 miles!

EGLIN RESERVATION

Entry gate at Jackson guard on Hwy. 85 N.
Niceville 882-4164

Freshwater lakes, the Yellow River and several other canoe and dirt bike trails are inside the base. You must first get permits to enter and use the facilities. Camping permits are $5 for five consecutive days and can be purchased by mail by sending a photocopy of your driver's license and a check to: Eglin Natural Resources Branch, 107 Hwy. 85 N., Niceville, Florida 32578. It should take about three weeks to obtain your permit.

Bottom Fishing

OKALOOSA ISLAND PIER

Okaloosa Island
east of Fort Walton Beach

Cast off from this extra-long pier, which juts 1,261 feet into the gulf.

Community Centers

Classes in dance, crafts and music, as well as competitive sports come in adult and child versions at the city's five recreation centers. Call the recreation coordinator, 243-3119, for a schedule of classes and events.

THEO DOCIE BASS RECREATION CENTER

54 Ferry Rd. NE, Ferry Park, Fort Walton Beach
off Hollywood Blvd. 243-8911

The gym and meeting room host a soccer program, after-school program, a Tot's Time program and many special events including the Greater Fort Walton Beach Talent Contest, the Annual Track Meet, a Halloween Carnival and a Kid's Day Out.

FORT WALTON BEACH CIVIC AUDITORIUM

U.S. 98, Fort Walton Beach 243-3119

This auditorium, right in the heart of town, is home to the Okaloosa Symphony Orchestra and hosts many other concerts and school productions.

FRED B. HEDRICK RECREATION CENTER

132 Jet Dr. (take Beal Pkwy. to Hollywood
Blvd., then west on Hollywood to Jefferson),
Fort Walton Beach 243-3119

This center is headquarters to the Parks and Recreation Department and also has a gym, ceramic workshop, exercise room and two meeting/classrooms.

CHESTER PRUITT RECREATION CENTER

24 Carson Ave. 244-0534

Inside are a gym and two meeting rooms for a variety of classes and activi-

Insiders' Tips

Eglin Air Force Base is home to several threatened and endangered species: the red-cockaded woodpecker, the Florida black bear, the Okaloosa darter, the least tern, loggerhead and green sea turtles, the gopher tortoise, alligators and the indigo snake. Besides these, you may likely come across deer, wild hogs, beavers, coyotes, skunks and armadillos. And you say you want to go *camping* there?

ties; outside is a playground area. There's a summer recreation program at the center every year.

CREATIVE SENIOR CENTER

31 Memorial Pkwy. S.W.   *244-1511*

Classes, programs, special activities and luncheons are held here for residents 55 and older. The center's facilities are extensive, including a meeting hall, a pool room, a library, shuffleboard courts, a ceramic workshop and horseshoe pits!

City/County Parks

JOHN BEASLEY WAYSIDE PARK

Hwy. 98, Okaloosa Island

Right on the gulf, this public beach area comes with picnic tables, barbecue grills and restrooms.

BRACKIN WAYSIDE PARK

Hwy. 98, Okaloosa Island

Just down Highway 98 on the gulf side, the public beach area provides beachgoers with picnic tables, barbecue grills, a bathhouse with showers, dressing rooms and restrooms.

BRIARWOOD PARK

Briarwood Cir.

On Briarwood Circle off Beal Parkway on Cinco Bayou, the small park has playground equipment and its own "tot lot."

FERRY PARK

Ferry Rd. and Hughes St.

In addition to the a recreation center, the park has a Little League field and four tennis courts lit for night play.

FORT WALTON LANDING

Brooks St.

Just off Highway 98, this is another waterfront park with a boardwalk, a stage

area, a gazebo, picnic tables and a boat ramp.

GARNIER'S BEACH PARK

Beachview Dr. off Eglin Pkwy.

Right where Cinco Bayou empties into Choctawhatchee Bay is a great public beach area with 240 feet of waterfront, a boat ramp, a playground and, of course, restrooms.

HOLLYWOOD AND MEMORIAL PARK

Hollywood Blvd. and Memorial Pkwy.

This is just a teeny weeny park with a few benches for watching the world go by.

LIZA JACKSON PARK

Hwy. 98 next to the Howard Johnson's

This large city park sits on Santa Rosa Sound and is one of the first things you see as you drive into Fort Walton Beach. It's got 1,000 feet of waterfront, boat ramps, a fishing pier, open-air pavilions for picnicking, barbecue grills and lots of playground equipment and large shade trees.

JET DRIVE PARK

Jet Dr. and Holmes Blvd.

Just past the Hedrick Recreation Center, the small park has a fenced playground area, basketball and tennis courts.

MARIER MEMORIAL PARK

Okaloosa Island

Marier is on the bay side of the island off Santa Rosa Boulevard and offers picnic tables, barbecue grills, a boat ramp and a bathhouse.

MIMOSA PARK

Mimosa St.

Named for the flowering tree, not the drink, this small park near the bayou has picnic tables and a playground.

CHESTER PRUITT PARK

Hollywood Blvd., Harbeson Ave. and McGriff
St. next to the Head Start Center

With the recreation center as its focal point, this large park also provides a basketball court, tennis courts, a playground area, a softball field and two picnic pavilions.

VESTA HEIGHTS PARK

Memorial Pkwy.

This little neighborhood park within the Vesta Heights subdivision has a jogging track, two playground areas, picnic tables and park benches.

VILLA RUSS PARK

Elliott Rd.

This little triangular park is not more than a block or two from the bay going either east or south. You'll find park benches and playground equipment here.

SEABREEZE PARK

Memorial Pkwy.

Travel north on Memorial Parkway from Highway 98 to find this small park, which may not be close enough to the water to catch a sea breeze but does provide a playground, picnic tables and restroom facilities.

Destin

Golf

EMERALD BAY GOLF CLUB

40001 Emerald Coast Pkwy.   *837-5197*

Wound around and through a residential community, Emerald Bay's semiprivate 18-hole championship course features pine-rimmed fairways and a tough slope rating of 135 from the championship tees. The pro shop hours are 7 AM to 5:30 PM; tee times begin at 7:30 and last until it's too dark to see the ball!

THE GARDEN

40091 Emerald Coast Pkwy.   *837-7422*

Lush landscaping surrounds the nine-hole lighted executive golf course (seven par 3s and two par 4s). The practice range is 10 acres with putting greens, a sand trap and a driving range. It's open seven days a week, 7:30 AM to 4 PM off-season; 7:30 AM to 9 PM in-season.

INDIAN BAYOU GOLF AND COUNTRY CLUB

Off Hwy. 98 and Airport Rd.   *837-6192*

Indian Bayou is predominantly a flat course with undulating greens and seven water holes. All nine holes of the Creek course wind through natural swamp surrounded by a residential community. Semiprivate, Indian Bayou has 27 holes of golf, a driving range, putting greens and a restaurant. It's open 6:45 AM all year; closing is seasonal, usually around 5:30 or 6 PM.

Tennis

DESTIN RACQUET & FITNESS CENTER

995 Airport Rd.   *837-7300*

This is an all-inclusive center, with six Rubico courts, four of them lit for night play. Guest fees are $10 per person for singles and $8 per person for doubles, which will get you about 1½ hours on the courts. If you'd like to avail yourself of the fitness center, there's a full range of Nautilus equipment, stationary bikes, StairMasters, aerobics classes and racquetball courts. The one-time fee for equipment use and courts is $10 per person. It's open from 6 AM until 9 PM.

Charter Boats

FLYING EAGLE
74 Stingray St.   *837-4986, 654-6931*

The tops'l steel schooner *Flying Eagle* sets sail daily from the docks at Capt. Dave's Restaurant and Marina in Destin Harbor. Boarding is a half-mile east of the Destin Bridge on Highway 98. The *Flying Eagle* takes up to three 2½-hour cruises daily on a space available basis; reservations are preferred. Beer, wine, soda, T-shirts and hats are all available on board. Tickets are $25 per person for adults, $15 for kids younger than 15 and free for kids younger than 3.

THE LADY EVENTHIA
½-mile east of the Destin Bridge   837-6212,
837-8729

Go fishing or sightseeing on *The Lady Eventhia*, a 70-passenger deep sea fishing party boat. Electronic equipment for locating running fish, a ship's galley and an indoor lounge offer guests every convenience for a day on the water. Six-hour fishing trips are $34 for adults, $16.50 for ages 12 and younger; 8-hour trips cost $39.50 and $16.50 respectively. Just want to ride? That's only $11 for either trip. *The Lady* runs from March to November.

MOODY'S
194 Hwy. 98   *837-1293*

Tom Moody captains the *America II* for five-hour fishing trips year round. Charters and cruises are available as well.

Refreshments and an indoor area that's either heated or air conditioned are de rigueur for most boats, but this one throws in free fish cleaning as one of its services. Trips are $35, $25 during the off-season.

SAILING SOUTH
Hwy. 98 at Benning Dr.   *837-7245*

Take an afternoon or sunset sail for $35 per person (a captain is included, of course). Private parties can rent out the *High Noon* for $175 (3½ hours). Sailing South rents 19-, 25- and 30-foot sailboats for $35 an hour or starting at $150 a day.

BLACKBEARD SAILING CHARTERS
¼-mile east of the Destin Bridge
behind AJ's Restaurant   *837-2793*

Welcome aboard, me hearties! This 54-foot gaff-rigged schooner sails three times daily at 11 AM, 2 PM and 5 PM just for the thrill of the wind in your face, the salt in your hair and a unique perspective on the Gulf Coast as seen from the water. The luxury sailboat accommodates up to 25 people, with the trip lasting about 2½ hours. Tickets are $25 per person; $15 for kids 4 to 12.

CAPT. DUKES PARTY BOAT
Destin Harbor   *837-6152*

For fishing or sightseeing, the *Capt. Dukes* will be happy to take you where you want to go. This 65-foot charter boat, with its own galley and lounge, heads out for five-hour fishing trips for $30 per person or $28 for seniors and active military.

More billfish are caught each year on the Emerald Coast than all other gulf ports combined. Prime months run April to October for sailfish, white marlin, blue marlin, dolphin and wahoo.

Insiders' Tips

One of Florida's most scenic wild rivers is the beautiful Blackwater.

Children can fish for $18; riders cost $15. A 4-hour trip on the 42-foot "scrimshaw" (called the "six pack" because it accommodates six people) is $300. Fish cleaning, bait and tackle are included.

MINDY LOU

*Behind Captain Dave's Restaurant
on Destin Harbor*   *837-1790,
(800) MINDY LOU*

Trolling, bottom fishing, sport and billfishing trips are hosted by owners Bill and Mindy McDonald. The *Mindy Lou* takes up to six passengers for up to 12 hours — even overnight! Prices start at $300 (extra riders are $35) and include license, tackle, bait and ice.

LIN-C-ANN

East Pass Marina   864-3880, 654-2022

For deep sea fishing, trolling, bottom fishing, billfishing, dive trips or sightseeing tours, the Lin-C-Ann is your ticket to over- and underwater fun. No license is required, but certification is necessary for dives. The boat runs seasonally; call for dates, times and prices.

OLIN MARLER'S CHARTER SERVICE

*Olin Marler Dock across from
Sweet Basil's Restaurant   243-1769*

All types of fishing are offered on a fleet of charter boats. Bottom fishing for snapper, grouper and amberjack is popular in the cooler months, and eight-hour trips are required to get far enough out to where the fish are biting. Bait, ice, tackle and a fishing license comes with your ticket. Bring your own food and drink. Eight-hour trips are $99 per person; half-day trips cost $49.

SWEET JODY 5

*¼ mile east of the Destin Bridge   837-2222
next to AJ's Restaurant   654-0088,
(800) 531-9386*

It's a fishing boat, it's a party boat, it's a private charter, it's whatever you want it to be. This 65-foot beauty of the sea is fully equipped with navigational and fish-finding electronics, a snack bar and an observation deck. Half-day trips are $27 for grown-ups; $13.50 for kids and riders (plus tax). During the summer months, the *Sweet Jody 5* runs a

$22 special for a 2:30 PM to 6:30 PM trip; kids and riders are $11. They'll clean your fish for you, keep your drinks on ice for you and pick up the tab for the fishing license.

SEA SCREAMER

No. 2 Hwy. 98 E.
at Boogie's Restaurant   654-2996

Here's something everyone in the family can enjoy. The *Sea Screamer*, the world's largest speedboat, is docked under the Destin/Fort Walton Beach Bridge. You get two rides in one: first, a narrated cruise of the Destin Harbor and Choctawhatchee Bay, where birds, dolphin and other marine life are clearly visible in the air or through the crystal waters. Then, the *Sea Screamer* revs up for an exhilarating flight through the open waters of the gulf! Casual clothes or swimsuits are preferred for this venture because you may get wet! The *Sea Screamer* departs April 1 through May 27 at noon, 2 and 4 PM every day but Monday and Tuesday. From May 28 through September 12, trips go out at 10 AM, noon, 2 PM, 4 PM and 6 PM every day. September 13 through October 31, trips are at noon, 2 PM and 4 PM; it's closed Monday and Tuesday. Cruises last about an hour. Tickets go on sale at the dock 30 minutes prior to departure. Cost is $9 for adults, $6 for children 6 to 12; children 5 and younger are free.

NEW FLORIDA GIRL

Captain Dave's Marina
½ mile east of the Destin Bridge   837-6422

At a whopping 85 feet, the *New Florida Girl* may be the biggest in Destin. On board, find all the latest technology, not only to find the fish, but to steer you through foggy weather or night travel.

Meals are available, or you may bring your own. Five-hour trips run Monday, Wednesday and Friday for $27 per person; kids younger than 12 are admitted for $14, riders and child riders are $10 and $5. Eight-hour trips are $35, or for just $5 more, take an all-day trip (Saturdays and Tuesdays only).

HARBOR QUEEN WATER TAXI

Destin Harbor   boat 585-3321
                        office 654-5566

Park your car and take the water way! For just $3 (or $1.50 for children younger than 12), you can ride the *Harbor Queen* to any Destin Harbor location, including restaurants, lounges and waterfront homesites. Pickup and drop-off is right at your door; either call ahead or just wave and Captain Cathi Jones will pick you up! Harbor cruises are $5 for adults and $3 for children. Look for the little yellow boat with the blue and yellow awning.

Scuba/Snorkeling Trips

FANTASEA SCUBA HEADQUARTERS

At the foot of the
Destin Bridge   837-0732, 837-6943

Week-long courses allow you to become certified while on vacation. Daily dive trips are offered with all gear included. Snorkeling gear comes with a map for just $10. Non-divers are welcome to snorkel, sunbathe or sightsee.

AQUANAUT SCUBA CENTER, INC.

24 Hwy. 98   837-0359

Family-owned for more than 20 years, the Aquanaut Scuba Center takes passengers out on dive trips, sunset cruises and snorkeling cruises; instruction and week-long classes get you into the world of diving while you're still on vacation.

Dive trips begin at about $40 plus tax; snorkeling tours are $20 per person; the sunset cruise is $10.

ADVENTURES ON THE KOKOMO

500 Hwy. 98 E. at the Kokomo Motel & Marina   837-9029, 837-6171

Two boats are offered, a 50-foot, 49-passenger or a cigarette boat that holds six. Snorkeling trips are $20 with gear included; sunset cruises are $10. Capt. Brown has been diving these waters since 1957 and promises a delightful, fun time for everyone. Snorkeling trips run May to October only.

EMERALD COAST SCUBA SCHOOL

127 Hwy. 98 E., Ste. 10A   837-0955

The one-day resort course promises you'll get your first taste of diving in just one afternoon! A three-hour session includes a pool lesson, your scuba dive and an underwater photo to show the folks back home. Regular four-day certifications, rescue, advanced and specialty courses are also offered.

CAPTAIN J'S DIVE SHOP

301 Hwy. 98 E.   654-5300, 654-1616
*   (800) 677-DIVE

Two beautiful boats fill the bill for underwater adventure. The *Diamond Lady*, which is perfect for cruises and snorkeling trips, takes you out to the jetties to view tropical fish species, rays, blue crabs and other marine life. Grass beds on the

bay side are great for spotting scallops, crabs, and brackish water inhabitants. A two to 2½-hour trip is only $20 per person. Cruises of the bay, harbor and coast are also available.

For pre-certified divers, the *M/V Kenniann H.* speeds you to your choice of more than 20 dive sites within 15 minutes of the dock. Dives are generally from 2 to 10 miles offshore in depths from 60 to 90 feet. Two-tank dives are $40 plus tax per diver and $65 for a three-tank dive. Equipment rental is $45. As a diver, you are pre-licensed for underwater photography, spearfishing and shell collecting.

Watersport Rentals

HARBOR COVE CHARTERS

Behind AJ's on Destin Harbor   837-2222

You take the boat, you navigate, you go where you want to go — cruising, crabbing, fishing, snorkeling or swimming for a few hours, a half-day or a full day. Rates start at $100 for a 4-hour trip or $175 for all day (fuel is included) plus tax.

BOOGIE'S WATERSPORTS

At the foot of the Destin Bridge
Destin   654-6043

Waverunners, Jet Skis, Jet-n-Cats (rides three), winch boat parasails, pontoon boats, sailboats, cruises and champagne sunset cruises and dive trips make Boogie's practically one-stop for beach

Insiders' Tips

There's something special about a ribboning limestone reef off the Emerald Coast — the reef's ability to capture seashells makes this area one of the top-five shelling destinations in the world. Divers and snorkelers can make the 3 mile trek from shore to find lion's paw, tulips, horse conchs and hundreds of other species.

fun — just add water! Take a Discover Dive with no experience necessary!

PARADISE WATERSPORTS
Six locations on Hwy. 98 in
Fort Walton Beach and Destin   664-7872

You've reached Paradise — now get out there and enjoy it! Rent Jet Skis, Waverunners, sailboats, pontoon boats, jet boats, sailboards or water trikes. The friendly staff will be happy to show you the safe operation of all equipment. Parasailing combines the best of water skiing and skydiving, with takeoff locations on the bay and the beach. Paradise Watersports has locations at the seawall between Destin and Fort Walton Beach, The Hut (across from The Ramada on Okaloosa Island), the Destin Bridge, behind Pleasure Island, behind the Back Porch and the parasail beach pickup.

Bottom Fishing

DESTIN BRIDGE CATWALK

Hook tonight's dinner along 3,000 feet of catwalk on the south side of the East Pass Bridge.

Destin Community Centers

DESTIN COMMUNITY CENTER
Corner of Stahlman Ave.
and Zerbe St.   654-5184

Here's a building that really gets a workout with basketball courts, a platform stage and auditorium, a game room and meeting rooms for various community programs for everyone from senior citizens to Girl Scouts keeping the center bustling year round. Lobby displays reveal aspects of Destin's colorful past both in paintings and artifacts.

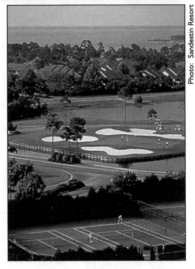

Photo: Sandestin Resort

Challenging courses await you at Sandestin Resort.

Beaches of South Walton

These little gulfside beach communities can range from really ritzy to downright down home. Some resorts don't look that different from ones on Hilton Head, South Carolina, or the Outer Banks in North Carolina. Other areas, such as Seaside and Grayton Beach, are one-of-a-kind.

You'll keep seeing the name "Sandestin" crop up in directions. Sandestin is not a town, but a gigantic, sprawling resort along Highway 98. The street address for Sandestin Resort, the Sandestin Beach Hilton, etc., is Destin, but we've broken it out here under the Beaches of South Walton because it's actually over the Walton County line. It was a bit confusing for us deciding which Destin addresses to include where, but it won't be for you, since most everything is right along Highway 98.

Golf

SANDESTIN BEACH RESORT/
SANDESTIN BEACH HILTON
5500 Hwy. 98 E., 12 miles east of Destin

Both courses are open to the public; however, priority is given to resort guests. Baytowne, 267-8155, has 27 holes and is open 7 AM to 7 PM daily; the Links Course, 267-8144, has 18 holes and is open 7 AM to 6 PM daily.

SANTA ROSA GOLF & BEACH CLUB
County Rd. 30-A
Santa Rosa Beach　　　　　267-2229

This 18-hole course is open to the public. A driving range, putting green, pro shop and a snack bar add to the enjoyment. It's open 7 AM to 7:30 PM daily.

SEASCAPE GOLF & RACQUET CLUB
100 Seascape Dr., Old Hwy. 98
2 miles west of Sandestin　　　837-9181

Here's a short, tight public 18-hole course with driving range and putting greens open from 7:30 AM to 6 PM daily.

EMERALD BAY GOLF
& COUNTRY CLUB
241 Ellis Dr., Ste.15　　　　837-5197

Emerald Bay gives you a beautiful 18-hole course 6 miles east of Destin. It's open to the public, and hours are from 7:30 in the morning until 6:30 in the evening daily.

THE GARDEN
Hwy. 98, 2 miles west of
Sandestin　　　　　　　　837-7422

This nine-hole executive course also offers a driving range and is open from 7 AM until 10 PM daily.

Tennis

HIDDEN DUNES
5394 Hwy. 98 E.
½ mile west of Sandestin　　　837-3521

Six Rubico courts are lighted for night play and open to guests only. There's a resident tennis pro and a pro shop. Hidden Dunes is open from 8 AM to 10 PM daily.

SANDESTIN TENNIS CENTER
5500 Hwy. 98 E.
Emerald Coast Pkwy.　　　　267-7060

One of the America's top-50 tennis resorts according to *Tennis* magazine, Sandestin offers 14 grass, hard and clay courts on both the gulf and bay side of the resort. The facility is open to the public, but resort guests get top priority. Hours are 8 AM to 7 PM daily.

SANTA ROSA GOLF & BEACH CLUB
County Rd. 30-A
Santa Rosa Beach　　　　　267-2229

Two hard courts are open to the public from 7 AM to 7:30 PM daily.

Insiders' Tips

And you thought the Gulf of Mexico was the end-all, be-all of water-related recreation around here? Slip yourself onto a giant inner tube, tie a rope onto a smaller tube for your cooler and lazily float down one of Northwest Florida's many scenic rivers! There's no experience necessary, and even the littlest family members find the cool, shallow water one of the best ways to keep cool!

SEASCAPE GOLF & RACQUET CLUB

100 Seascape Dr.   *837-9181 ext. 3535*

Eight clay and hard courts provide play from 8:30 AM to 6:30 PM.

SEASIDE

County Rd. 30-A, Seaside   *231-4224*

At these six clay and hard courts, Seaside guests play for free. If you want to get out there early, it opens at 7:30 in the morning and stays active until 6 in the evening on a daily basis.

TOPS'L BEACH AND RACQUET CLUB

5500 Hwy. 98 E.   *267-9222*

Ten Rubico and two hard courts, plus three racquetball courts will keep you on your toes and working on that wrist action. Fees are included in membership or guest-room rates. Hours depend on court availability. Tournaments, round robins, group and individual clinics, lessons and a pro shop make this a fun and active spot.

Dive Trips/Sightseeing Cruises

SCUBA TECH

5371 Hwy. 98 E.
Half-mile west of Sandestin   *837-1933*

Explore the wonders underwater or learn how to dive aboard the 45-foot *Sea Cobra*, which accommodates up to 29 passengers. Onboard are tank racks, bench seats, drop-down ladders and giant stride entry points. Pick up your rental equipment from the main store (address above) or at the *Sea Cobra*, docked at Captain Dave's on the Harbor, 312 E. Highway 98, a half-mile east of the Destin Bridge. Four diving charters are available daily: a four-hour, two-tank reef or wreck dive (65- to 90-foot depth); a six-hour, two-tank reef or wreck dive (65- to — gulp — 110-foot depth); an eight-hour, three-tank reef or wreck dive (same depth as the six-hour

dive); and a one-tank reef or wreck night dive. If you want to go diving at night with all that *stuff* out there, you go right ahead. These dive trips are fairly popular all year long, but remember you can't just go renting equipment and jump in. Prior certification is required, and Scuba Tech can help with that too.

CYPRESS WILDERNESS TREK

Baytowne Marina at Sandestin   *837-7245*

Tucked back into the easternmost reaches of Choctawhatchee Bay is the little-known Cypress Wilderness Area, where four rivers converge. What a nice break from the bustle of vacationland! Your trek begins aboard the *Osprey* power boat, whipping across the surface of the bay at racing speed! Suddenly, you lose sight of beaches and condos and become immersed in a quieter, completely natural environment. Bring a camera and a good pair of binoculars for spotting bald eagles, ospreys, alligators and wading heron. The flora here is spectacular too: Dozens of varieties of wildflowers grace your path, while the twisted bark of the bald cypress rises out of the swamp. The trip takes about 3½ hours, so be sure to allow the better part of the day for travel time to and from Baytowne Marina. Two trips are offered daily for $38 per person and $29 for children younger than 10.

Beach/Bike Rentals

CABANA MAN

C-30A, Village of Seaside   *231-5046*

The Cabana Man will take care of all your beach needs, from chairs and umbrellas to sailboats, aqua trikes, rafts and boogie boards. A 16-foot Hobie Cat is also ready to take out. Weekly rentals are available.

SANDESTIN BIKE RENTAL
Sandestin Resort near
Elephant Walk Restaurant   267-7077

Two-wheel it for $6 per hour for the public, $12 for two to four hours, or $17 all day. Three-day, weekly and monthly rentals also available. It's open 9 AM to 6 PM daily.

SEASIDE BIKE RENTAL
County Rd. 30-A, Seaside   231-2279

At the north end of Savannah Street,

Seaside Bike Rental's fees are $4 per hour plus tax, $10 for half a day, $15 for a full 24 hours. Seaside is open 8 AM to 4 PM daily.

SANDESTIN RESORT RENTALS
Baytowne Marina at
Sandestin Resort   267-7777, 267-8166

Waverunners, ski boats, Bayliner deck boats, Hobie Cats, aqua-cycles, boogie boards — if you want to be on the water,

Marinas

BLUEWATER BAY MARINA
300 Yacht Club Dr. on Bluewater Bay
Niceville   897-2821

THE BOAT MARINA & BOATING CENTER
32 Hwy. 98 S.W., Fort Walton Beach
on the Intracoastal Waterway   243-2628

DECKHANDS MARINA
1352 Hwy. 98 E.
Miracle Strip Pkwy. at Leeside Inn
Fort Walton Beach   243-1598

FORT WALTON LODGE & YACHT BASIN
104 Miracle Strip Pkwy.
Fort Walton Beach   244-5725

HERB'S EXECUTIVE EXXON MARINA
22 S.W. Miracle Strip Pkwy.
Fort Walton Beach   243-6535

HOWARD JOHNSON'S MOTOR LODGE
314 Miracle Strip Pkwy. S.W.
Fort Walton Beach
on Intracoastal Waterway   243-6162

HUDSON MARINA
9 Marina Dr., off Racetrack Rd.
Fort Walton Beach   862-3165

LIGHTHOUSE KEY MARINA
115 John Sims Pkwy.
Niceville   729-2000

MARINA BAY RESORT MARINA
80 Miracle Strip Pkwy., on Intracoastal Waterway
Fort Walton Beach   244-5132

Pirate's Bay Marina
214 S.W. Miracle Strip Pkwy.
Fort Walton Beach   243-3154

SHALIMAR YACHT BASIN
100 Old Ferry Rd. (on Choctawhatchee Bay)
Shalimar   651-0510

they have a way to get you there. The marina location is open from 7 AM to 7 PM daily; off-season hours vary. The beach location is open 9 AM to 6 PM daily.

SANDESTIN BEACH HILTON RESORT RENTALS
Sandestin Resort on Hwy. 98   267-9500

They've got 'em all — Hobie cats, Waverunners, kayaks, aqua-cycles and boogie boards. Daily hours are from 9 AM to 5 PM; winter hours vary.

SEASIDE BEACH RENTALS
County Rd. 30-A, Seaside   231-2214

Seaside also offers Hobie Cats, kayaks, aqua-cycles and boogie boards. They're open 9 AM to 6 PM in the summer, 9 AM to 5 PM in the spring and fall. (Open March through November 15.)

Hiking/Horseback Trails

GRAYTON BEACH STATE RECREATION AREA
County Rd. 30-A, near
Grayton Beach   231-4210

Encounter native Northwest Florida terrain in the pine flatwoods, sand dunes and scrub of the Grayton Beach Nature Trail in the park. Pick up a self-guided tour brochure as you enter. It's open daily from 8 AM to sundown. Admission is $3.25 per vehicle.

CASSINE GARDENS
County Rd. 30-A, near
Grayton Beach   231-5721

Explore the nature trail by foot or on horseback. A portion of the trail behind the Cassine Gardens townhomes is on a raised boardwalk over marshland, bringing visitors eye-to-eye with waterfowl and native vegetation, such as the garden's namesake, the Ilex Cassine, or holly tree. There's no charge for this brush with nature.

Fort Walton Beach/Destin/ Beaches of South Walton
Arts and Culture

Most of the cultural activities in this area are headquartered in the Fort Walton Beach area, but check this entire coastal region for some offbeat performances. One of the area's highlights is the outstanding Chautauqua Festival in DeFuniak Springs in North Walton County, a celebration of art, music, history and literature around Lake deFuniak each April. Although not a separate cultural group per se, the village of Seaside provides visitors and residents with year-round cultural activities, from writers' retreats to fine art shows. Check the Beaches of South Walton section of this chapter for more information.

Dance

NORTHWEST FLORIDA BALLET
P.O. Box 964
Fort Walton Beach 32549   664-7787

This professional ballet company performs throughout Northwest Florida and offers a training program for gifted students seeking a career in dance.

Music

THE CHORAL SOCIETY OF NORTHWEST FLORIDA
121 Bayou Dr.
Fort Walton Beach   863-1718

Although auditions are held for mem-

Photo: Arts Council of NW Florida

The laid-back, fun style of bluesman Steve Gunter is a popular favorite.

bership in the Choral Society, the group is mostly for fun and fellowship. These are folks who enjoy singing for the pure joy of it, but occasionally they will perform at public functions.

EMERALD COAST
CONCERT ASSOCIATION
P.O. Box 815
Fort Walton Beach 32549   243-3359

This is a nonprofit volunteer group dedicated to bringing the best possible local, regional and national entertainment into the area. Concert tickets are sold at several locations throughout Destin and Fort Walton Beach.

FORT WALTON BEACH
COMMUNITY CHORUS
P.O. Box 2221
Fort Walton Beach 32549   863-3900

Besides performing twice yearly, the 50-to-75-member Community Chorus sponsors a scholarship for high school or college students interested in becoming professional singers.

NORTHWEST FLORIDA
SYMPHONY ORCHESTRA
100 College Blvd.
Niceville   729-5283

The orchestra is made up of members of all ages and skill ranges from the Okaloosa and Walton County areas who perform quality music at five annual concerts.

OKALOOSA SYMPHONY ORCHESTRA
P.O. Box 2109
Fort Walton Beach 32549   244-3308

This year marks the 18th season of the orchestra. For the last seven years, musicians have been paid professionals. The 50-plus members perform four times per year at the Fort Walton Beach Civic Auditorium under the direction of Brian Sullivan, a talented young conductor from Orlando who travels to the area for several intensive rehearsals prior to each performance. The Symphony League is set up as a fund-raising organization; the remainder of the annual budget comes from grants and donations from public and private sources.

Visual Arts

ARTIST'S SHOWROOM
542 Hwy. 98 E., Destin   837-7606

More than 2,500 oil paintings and other artwork, much of it by local artists, are displayed in this wholesale/retail gallery on the harbor.

ARTS & DESIGN SOCIETY (ADSO)
P.O. Box 4963
Fort Walton Beach 32549   244-1271

The nonprofit artist's group holds exhibitions, demonstrations, workshops and art shows to educate the community and enhance appreciation of art in its many

The Northwest Florida/Okaloosa Film Commission stays busy bringing national and international productions to the area. Among its many accomplishments are the movies *Grand Isle* with Kelly McGillis and *Frogs*; two episodes of *Rescue 911;* a variety of music videos; and Spiegel, Oshkosh B'gosh and Land's End catalogs.

Insiders' Tips

Photo: Arts Council of NW Florida

The spirited bluegrass of The White Sands Panhandle Band can be heard at festivals all over Northwest Florida.

forms. The gallery is open Sundays from 1 to 4 PM.

CULTURAL ARTS ASSOCIATION

P.O. Box 4958
Santa Rosa Beach 32459   231-5141

The Association funds and awards scholarships in the visual arts and provides after-school arts experiences for children. They sponsor the Grayton Beach Fine Arts Festival in May, Scholarship Arts and Crafts in October and a Beaux Arts Ball in November.

THE PASTEL SOCIETY OF NORTH FLORIDA

P.O. Box 5133
Fort Walton Beach 32549   581-2550

Soft colors are the emphasis of this chapter of the Pastel Society of America, now in its seventh year. April is the one time of the year when the group gets to shine — the Members Show and the National Show, both at the Fort Walton Beach Art Museum, showcase the pastel work of artists from 32 states. This year, the group has organized the International Association of Pastel Societies. A July workshop in Denver will feature artists from China, England, Canada and Australia. The local chapter meets infrequently for lunch, so if you'd like to be invited or need information about upcoming exhibitions, contact the Pastel Society of North Florida for inclusion on their mailing list. Yearly dues are $25.

Insiders' Tips

The 80-year-old Chautauqua Ritz Theater in historic DeFuniak Springs stages four productions a year, including one children's theater production.

Multidisciplinary

CHAUTAUQUA FESTIVAL
P.O. Box 847
DeFuniak Springs 32433   892-9494

Years ago, some folks moved from upstate New York, where the original Chautauqua is held every year, to deFuniak Springs and decided to start a smaller version of the festival here. Chautauqua, held around Lake DeFuniak in the historic district, promotes the heritage of Walton County with a flurry of educational and cultural activities — dances, lectures, poetry readings and storytelling, among others. It is now a one-day festival in April each year that has grown steadily. The name "Chautauqua" has been linked to many other cultural events held at Lake deFuniak throughout the year. Please see the Beaches of South Walton section of the Fort Walton Beach Area Festivals and Special Events chapter for additional information.

NORTHWEST FLORIDA/ OKALOOSA FILM COMMISSION
P.O. Box 4097,
Fort Walton Beach 32549   651-7374

This is the local liaison office to try to bring film productions into Northwest Florida. The commission works with location scouts and provides technical and talent assistance.

Contact Film Commissioner Christine Pincince for more information.

Fort Walton Beach/Destin/
Beaches of South Walton
Retirement

When you make a decision to retire in Florida's Great Northwest, you'll find much more than clean and comfortable retirement communities and new friends who share your enthusiasm for the good life. There are a host of services offered to seniors to make the transition to retirement living go smoothly.

Retirement Communities

WESTWOOD RETIREMENT COMMUNITIES
1001 Mar-Walt Dr.
Fort Walton Beach   863-5174

Westwood spends a lot of time promoting itself as a rental community focusing on independent living. Residents live privately in their own studio and one-

or two-bedroom apartments, which are available on a yearly lease. No endowment or large entry fees are required. Amenities include restaurant-style dining, free scheduled transportation, recreational and social activities, a library, beauty and barber salon, swimming pool, country store, greenhouse, 24-hour security, maintenance and housekeeping. Westwood is next door to Fort Walton Beach Medical Center.

WHITE SANDS MANOR
40 Windham Ave. S.E.
Fort Walton Beach   244-7162

White Sands is an HUD-subsidized retirement apartment project designed specifically for elderly residents. Ninety-

When you live at Crystal Cove, you can also take advantage of all Sandestin Resort amenities.

five one-bedroom apartments are available with an emergency call system.

BOB HOPE VILLAGE
30 Holly Ave., Shalimar　　　*651-5770*
TERESA VILLAGE
321 Woodrow St.
Fort Walton Beach　　　*862-8778*

Both of these retirement villages are set up primarily for widows of Air Force enlisted personnel. Bob Hope Village has 256 one-bedroom apartments, and Teresa Village offers 123 one-bedroom units, both with scheduled transportation and activities. The facilities are operated by the Air Force Enlisted Men's Widows and Dependents Home Foundation, Inc., 92 Sunset Lane, Shalimar, 863-4113 or 863-4114.

CRYSTAL COVE AT SANDESTIN
2400 Crystal Cove Ln.
Destin　　　*267-1600, (800) 359-7809*

This sprawling retirement community centers around the spring-fed Crystal Lake 8 miles east of Destin between the Gulf of Mexico and Choctawhatchee Bay. The 2,600-acre property has several stocked lakes with fountains, a gazebo and walking paths. Other resort amenities such as 45 holes of championship golf, tennis courts, a 98-slip marina, a clubhouse, restaurants and shopping are within easy reach inside the Sandestin Beach Resort. Apartments in each of the three-story buildings come with fully equipped kitchens, washer and dryer hookups, cable TV, smoke detectors, spacious balconies and an emergency response system. Services provided with your lease fees include meals, housekeeping, linen service, security, maintenance, utilities and transportation. Adjacent to Crystal Cove is an assisted-living facility, Sandcastle Shores.

EDGEWOOD TERRACE
S. R. 393, Santa Rosa Beach　　　*267-1755*

This unusual retirement community will one day be filled with double-wide manufactured homes. Buy the land only or choose from a two- or three-bedroom model (some of these are already in place). Each home comes complete with driveway, carport, screened-in porch, landscaping and maintenance. Since Edgewood Terrace is for seniors only, you can almost be assured of a quiet neighborhood and lots of new friends!

TWIN CITIES PAVILION
1053 John Sims Pkwy.
Niceville　　　*833-9212*

CRESTVIEW MANOR
601 N. Pearl St.
Crestview　　　*689-7850*
AUTUMN HOUSE
207 Hospital Dr.
Fort Walton Beach　　　*833-9165*

All three of these facilities were established by the Okaloosa County Council on Aging to provide alternatives to people who no longer feel secure enough to live by themselves. Although these facilities operate as Adult Congregate Living Facilities, additional assistance is available to all residents at any time. The pleasant home-like atmosphere fosters independence and self-worth at a moderate cost. Autumn Home, the newest of the ACLFs, is currently undergoing renovation.

Senior Support Services

FORT WALTON BEACH SENIOR CITIZEN'S CENTER
31 Memorial Pkwy. S.W.
Fort Walton Beach　　　*244-1511*

Classes in handicrafts, ceramics, oil painting, crochet, aerobics, Danse Orientale, Mah Jongg and bridge are fairly popular all year long. Weekly Bible study, bingo, bowling, bridge tournaments, square dancing and shuffleboard keep minds alert and bodies active, plus provide avenues for lasting friendships. Monthly parties, covered dish luncheons and pool tournaments add more fun to the social schedule. Call for a list of monthly scheduled activities.

AIR FORCE ENLISTED WIDOWS HOME FOUNDATION

92 Sunset Ln., Shalimar   651-9422

Exclusively for widows of Air Force enlisted personnel, the foundation provides a safe and comfortable home for women 55 and older.

OKALOOSA COORDINATED TRANSPORTATION

833-9173; bus rides, 833-9168

This system provides transportation to all programs receiving state or federal funds for transporting clients. Transportation arrangements must be made at least 24 hours in advance.

OKALOOSA COUNTY COUNCIL ON AGING

The Council on Aging provides a range of services to encourage indepen-dence and preserve dignity to all people over 55. Contact one of the following of-fices.

207 N.E. Hospital Dr.
Fort Walton Beach   833-9165

Crestview Senior Center
198 S. Wilson, Crestview   689-7807

Crestview Manor
601 N. Pearl St., Crestview   689-7850

Twin Cities Pavilion
1053 John Sims Pkwy.
Niceville   833-9212

Valparaiso Senior Center
268 Glenview Ave.
Valparaiso   833-9211

Crestview Senior Center
198 S. Wilson St., Crestview   689-7807

Valparaiso Senior Center
268 Glenview Ave., Valparaiso   833-9210

STATE OF FLORIDA AGING AND ADULT SERVICES

417 Racetrack Rd.
Fort Walton Beach   833-3700

Services for adults and the disabled include elderly home care, adult foster care and placement in a retirement com-munity.

Fort Walton Beach/Destin/ Beaches of South Walton
Military

Eglin Air Force Base spreads over more than 450,000 acres in Okaloosa County, making its operations, its personnel and its economic impact of vital concern to the people in this area. Unlike some military installations, Eglin allows the public to use its vast resources — we're not talking high-tech weaponry now, we're talking *natural* resources for hunting, fishing, camping, canoeing, hang gliding . . . you name it. Whatever disassembling the government decides to do with the military in the next several years, Eglin will probably always remain.

Eglin Air Force Base

Eglin Air Force Base is the largest military installation in the free world and a crucial player in America's national defense system. Insiders are quick to point out the economic and social value of having such a massive military base in the area, one whose presence is felt in almost every aspect of life. On the fiscal side of things, Eglin's total payroll amounts to more than a half-billion dollars each year, much of that going to the local and state economy. On the social front, consider not only the 10,000 active military personnel stationed there but also their 8,000 children who are schooled and raised in the area. Throw in the 30,000 military retirees drawn here by the attractive climate and facilities, stir in the nearly 5,000 civilians employed by the base, and you'll see why Eglin's impact on the area cannot be overestimated.

Photo: US Air Force

The SR-71 Blackbird, the fastest plane ever built, is on display at the Air Force Armament Museum on the Elgin Air Force Base.

The base was established in the early 1930s and occupied a total area of fewer than 2,000 acres. It was named Eglin Field in 1937 after Lt. Col. Frederick I. Eglin, a U.S. Air Corps officer who died in an airplane crash.

During World War II, Eglin became an extremely important testing ground for aircraft and munitions. As the field's strategic importance grew, so did its size: In 1940 the War Department was given control of Florida's Choctawhatchee National Forest, whose land and water boundaries contained nearly 800 square miles.

Throughout the 1940s and 1950s, Eglin served as a vital test site for new advances in aircraft and weaponry, including the ground-breaking field of guided missiles. Several major defense programs were established at Eglin during the 1950s and 1960s, mostly in response to the Cold War. Many of these have grown into the Air Force Development Test Center, whose wide range of missions includes research and development, testing and acquisition of non-nuclear air armaments, electronic combat systems and navigation/guidance systems.

During the Vietnam War, Eglin housed and processed more than 10,000 Vietnamese refugees in a tent city. In 1980, Eglin did the same for more than 10,000 Cuban refugees who fled to America.

During the Persian Gulf War in early 1991, Eglin played a large part in the success of that operation. The base sent fighter planes and more than 2,000 people to the Middle East.

Today Eglin remains an influential and valuable asset to America's defense. Among the 50 tenant units stationed there are the 728th Control Squadron, the Army's 6th Ranger Training Battalion, the 33rd Fighter Wing, the 919th Special Operations Wing and the 20th Space Surveillance Squadron, whose football field-size radar tracks more than 85 percent of all objects currently orbiting our planet.

There are 10 air fields on the Eglin reservation, but only three are active: Eglin Main, which contains the main testing, administrative and living facilities along with the major airfield; Duke Field, which serves the 728th Tactical Control Squadron and 919th Special Operations Wing; and Hurlburt Field, home to the Air Force Special Operations Command and the 1st Special Operations Wing.

Eglin's Armament Museum offers a stirring and educational look into the base's military history and accomplishments. It's a must for aviation buffs. Outdoor exhibits include the sleek SR-71 Blackbird, a B-52 bomber, a Russian MIG-21 fighter and the gigantic B-17 Flying Fortress Eagle. Inside you can see a P-51 Mustang that blazed the skies during World War II, an F-80 Shooting Star

Insiders' Tips

You may remember the AC-130 Gunship that crashed during Operation Desert Storm in the Persian Gulf in 1991; all 14 crew members of the 16th Special Operations Squadron died. There's a small chapel on the Hurlburt Field property housing a memorial to the Hurlburt heroes who gave their lives for their country.

Welcoming a visiting dignitary at Eglin Air Force Base

and even a restored World War II flight simulator. There's also a display of aircraft armament dating from World War I to the present.

The museum is open seven days a week from 9:30 AM to 4:30 PM. It's closed on Thanksgiving, Christmas and New Year's Day. Admission is free, and don't forget to stop by the gift shop and browse the great selection of airplane models, books and other related items.

Hurlburt Field

Hurlburt's main gate is 5 miles west of Fort Walton Beach right on Highway 98; you can't miss it if you're coming in from Pensacola. Most of these buildings have been here since it opened in 1940, and a fresh paint job can only slightly mask that fact.

Hurlburt, on the Eglin property, is headquarters for the Air Force Special Operations Command, begun back in the 1940s as Auxiliary Field No. 9, a small pilot and gunnery training field within the Eglin complex.

What may have set Hurlburt troops apart came in 1943, when American C-47s and British Dakotas formed an impenetrable aerial lifeline of food, ammo, clothing and medical supplies to Gen. Wingate's Raiders. More unconventional assignments followed, such as assisting in the Vice President's South Florida

Drug Task Force to help curb the flow of illegal drugs into the United States.

Personnel from the first Special Operations Wing took part in the aborted attempt in 1980 to rescue the hostages from Iran; five of the eight who died there were members of the 1st SOW at Hurlburt. Troops stationed at Hurlburt were also key players in the 1989 capture of Manuel Noriega in Panama, 1991's Operation Desert Storm and 1994's Operation Provide Hope in Somalia.

Fort Walton Beach/Destin/ Beaches of South Walton

Community Information

Real Estate Companies

CARRIAGE HILLS REALTY, INC.
1821 John Sims Pkwy.
Niceville   678-5178, (800)874-8929

VILLAGE REALTY EAST
4400 Hwy. 20 E. #109
Niceville   897-5000, (800)525-6006

SUNDANCE AGENCY INC.
1150 John Sims Pkwy, Unit 1
Niceville   678-1156, (800)874-0144

AMERICAN REALTY OF NORTHWEST FLORIDA, INC.
1270 N. Eglin Pkwy.
Shalimar   651-2454, (800)372-0044

ABBOTT REALTY SERVICES, INC.
676 Nautilus Ct. at Island Echos Condominium
Fort Walton Beach   243-3191

HOLIDAY ISLE PROPERTIES, INC.
904 Hwy. 98 E.
Destin   837-0009

LINDA WATSON REALTY INC.
106 Benning Dr., Ste. 7
Destin   837-3111

ABBOTT REALTY SERVICES, INC.
35000 Emerald Coast Pkwy.
Destin   (800)547-0805

NEWMAN-DAILEY RESORT PROPERTIES, INC.
5050 Hwy. 98 E., Ste. #210
Destin   837-1071, (800)225-7652

REALTY ONE SERVICES INC.
114 Palmetto
Destin   837-5447, (800)548-8026

DESTIN REALTY INC.
1150 Hwy. 98 E.
Destin   837-3484, (800)633-7846

DUNE-ALLEN REALTY INC.
5200 W. Hwy. C-30A,
Santa Rosa Beach   (800) 423-7433

ABBOTT REALTY SERVICES, INC.
Rt. 2, Box 4820
Santa Rosa Beach   267-2693

CARRIAGE HILLS REALTY SOUTH, INC.
Hwy. 98 W.
Santa Rosa Beach   267-2424
(800)521-2951

Just about every neighborhood in Fort Walton Beach, Destin and the Beaches of South Walton is somewhere near the water; if you don't yearn to have a water view (and pay for it!), inland neighborhoods offer substantial real estate savings.

GULF FRONT REALTY

6 miles east of Seaside/Seagrove Beach on
Scenic Rd. 30A   231-1300
                                  (800)624-2055

MONARCH REALTY AT SEASIDE

At Josephine's Bed & Breakfast
Seaside   231-1938
Cottages   (800)475-1841
Josephine's   (800)848-1840

Health Care

Hospitals/Medical Centers

FORT WALTON
BEACH MEDICAL CENTER

1000 Mar-Walt Dr.
Fort Walton Beach   862-1111

NORTH OKALOOSA MEDICAL CENTER

151 Redstone Ave. SE
Crestview   682-9731

HCA TWIN CITIES HOSPITAL

Hwy. 85 N. at College Blvd.
Niceville   678-4131

Support Services

WHITE-WILSON MEDICAL CENTER

1005 Mar -Walt Dr.
Fort Walton Beach   863-8100

DESTIN WHITE-WILSON MEDICAL CENTER

1000 Airport Rd.
Destin   837-3848

DESTIN MEDICAL CENTER

623 Hwy. 98
Destin   837-5181

AMERICAN HOMEPATIENT

99 Eglin Pkwy. NE, Ste. 8
Fort Walton Beach   243-9400

NORTHWEST FLORIDA
HOME HEALTH AGENCY

1326 Lewis Turner Blvd.
Fort Walton Beach   863-1161

DELTA MED OF FLORIDA

426 Government St.
Valparaiso   678-1832

PHYSICIANS' HOME CARE

922 Mar-Walt Dr.
Fort Walton Beach   862-3240

GULF COAST
IMMEDIATE CARE CENTER

420 Miracle Strip Pkwy. SW (U.S. Hwy. 98)
Mary Esther   244-3211

Physician Referral Services

THE PHYSICIAN AND SERVICE REFERRAL

A service of Fort Walton Beach Medical Center
                                   863-7568

PHYSICIAN HEALTHLINE/REFERRAL

A service of North Okaloosa Medical Center
682-9731, ext. 106.

PHYSICIAN REFERRAL

A service of HCA Twin Cities Hospital
729-7433

Treatment Centers

BRIDGEWAY CENTER

728 N. Ferdon Blvd.
Crestview   *689-7845*

HARBOR OAKS HOSPITAL

1015 Mar-Walt Dr.
Fort Walton Beach   *863-4160*

RIVENDELL

1015 Mar-Walt Dr.
Fort Walton Beach   *(800)543-2919*

Nursing and Convalescent Centers

BAY HERITAGE NURSING AND CONVALESCENT CENTER

Hart St., one block south of Twin Cities Hospital
Niceville   *678-6667*

FORT WALTON BEACH CARE CENTER

1 LBJ Senior Dr.
Fort Walton Beach   *863-2066*

GULF CONVALESCENT CENTER

114 Third St.
Fort Walton Beach   *243-6134*

VILLAGE AT SANDESTIN

5851 Hwy. 98 E.
Destin   *267-2887*

SANDCASTLE SHORES AT SANDESTIN

2400 Crystal Cove Ln.
Destin   *267-1600, (800)359-7809*

Hidden Dunes in Destin proves an exceptional place to live or vacation.

Higher Education

Colleges and Universities

**OKALOOSA-WALTON
COMMUNITY COLLEGE**

1000 College Blvd., Niceville   678-5111

OWCC/UWF Fort Walton Beach campus 1170
Freedom Way, Bldg. 1, Room 106
Fort Walton Beach   863-6501

OWCC/UWF Eglin Center, Bldg. 251
Eglin AFB   678-1717

OWCC Hurlburt Center, Bldg. 90309
Hurlburt Field   884-6296

OWCC at Chautauqua Neighborhood Center
U.S. Hwy. 90 W.
DeFuniak Springs   892-8100

UNIVERSITY OF WEST FLORIDA

Fort Walton Beach campus, 1170 Freedom
Way, Bldg. 1, Room 114
Fort Walton Beach   863-6565

Eglin Center, Bldg. 251
Eglin AFB   678-3727

TROY STATE UNIVERSITY

Florida Regional Branches at Eglin Air Force
Base Education Center, Bldg. 251   678-1865
Hurlburt Field, Bldg. 90312   581-3162

Vocational-Technical Schools

**BAY AREA
VOCATIONAL-TECHNICAL SCHOOL**

1976 Lewis Turner Blvd.
Fort Walton Beach   833-3500

**CRESTVIEW VOCATIONAL-
TECHNICAL CENTER**

1306 N. Ferdon Blvd., Crestview   689-7276

**WALTON COUNTY
VOCATIONAL-TECHNICAL SCHOOL**

850 N. 20th St.
DeFuniak Springs   892-8105, 892-8106

Photo: Robin Rowan

Inside
Panama City Beach Area

Panama City Beach stretches out over more than 27 miles of shimmering, glittering beachfront. If you came to Florida for beaches, look no farther than Panama City Beach. Driving in from northern states, it's the shortest trip to any Florida beach.

The Panama City Beach area is almost completely surrounded by water — St. Andrew Bay, West Bay, North Bay, East Bay, St. Andrew Sound, Grand Lagoon, the Gulf of Mexico and dozens of bayous. Anglers visit from all over, taking advantage of the gulf's "loop current" to catch marlin and sailfish, and fishing tournaments are held nearly every weekend from May until October.

With so much waterfront property, shops and restaurants are spaced farther apart than they seem on your first drive through; in other words, the tightly packed string of tourist-oriented businesses goes on for miles, thinning out only slightly when you hit Thomas Drive and Back Beach Road and 15th and 23rd streets (in town).

And yes, spring break is quite an event here. During March and early April, students flood the area — tens of thousands of them. If you're curious, check out MTV during March for an incisive and hard-hitting journalistic examination of the event. Whether this sort of thing is your speed or not, you should know that Spring Break is as short-lived as it is frenetic.

Panama City Beach's off-season lasts from November to March. Things slow down — *way* down — and some beach

Photo: Panama City Beach Visitors Bureau

Panama City's beaches are perfect for long walks with the one you love.

establishments even close their doors for a few months. The light but constant tourist traffic usually consists of people from much colder climes who consider Florida, even in winter, a tropical paradise.

There's much more to see in the area if you can drag yourself off the beach for a day or two. Panama City is blessed culturally with active theater, music, dance and visual arts groups. There's a new Arts District downtown that features the works of internationally recognized artists alongside talented locals. Take in a concert in McKenzie Park, lunch on oysters and Cokes in the bottle at Hilda's in Southport or drive up to Vernon to tour an ostrich farm.

It's a local quirk, but "beach" people don't cross the bridge into town, and "city" people stay on their side of the bridge. Consequently, both sides are missing out on a wealth of opportunities for culture, recreation and, let's face it, neighborliness. Panama City Beach is a huge resort area overrun with visitors, while Panama City is a small and unassuming Southern town. Can these two distinct environs ever find happiness together? They can in this book, and you can help break the mold by wisely crisscrossing the bridge many times during your visit.

As a resort area, Panama City Beach goes back as far as the big tourist meccas down south. The Miracle Strip Amusement Park celebrated its 30th birthday in 1993. In town, performances at the Martin Theatre were wowing crowds long before Tyndall Air Force Base began gearing up for World War II. And families such as the Andersons, whose descendants once provided fish to Confederate forces stationed here, may have piqued visitors' interest in charter fishing. The Andersons remain one of the area's most successful families, having stakes in both commercial and charter fishing.

Although it may be difficult to see past the resorts and visitor-related offerings, other equally influential forces are commercial fishing and the military. The three have grown up together and remain eternally intertwined, providing the ideal balance for both residents and visitors.

Visitor Information

**PANAMA CITY BEACH
CONVENTION & VISITORS BUREAU**
12015 Front Beach Rd.   233-6503
Panama City Beach   (800) PC BEACH

**BAY COUNTY TOURIST
DEVELOPMENT COUNCIL**
12015 Front Beach Rd.
Panama City Beach   233-5070

**PANAMA CITY BEACHES
CHAMBER OF COMMERCE**
415 Beckrich Rd.
Panama City Beach   234-3193

BAY COUNTY CHAMBER OF COMMERCE
235 W. Fifth St.
Panama City   785-5206

Panama City Beach Area
Restaurants and Nightlife

A laid-back beach bar with servers who are never in a hurry . . .

a thumping, bumping dance club with palm trees growing up through the floor and elbow-to-elbow crowds . . .

down-and-dirty oyster bars where slurping off the shells is expected and encouraged . . .

elegant oceanside dining with high standards and prices to match . . . the Panama City Beach area's restaurants and lounges are as diverse as the people who fill them. Seafood is the favorite again, followed by steaks, then sandwiches. And because all Insiders need to know, you're going to have a heck of a time finding a nice restaurant on the beach that's open for lunch. Fine dining establishments do a great dinner business but won't budge for lunch, even during Spring Break. Oyster bars and snack and sandwich shops, however, do most of the lunch business, so steer yourself to those. Just about every single dinner place takes major credit cards, but many of the more popular spots shy away from reservations, so ask about both when you call.

Two more words about the beach — nothing fancy. Dress casually, wear that spaghetti-strap sundress and sandals or that loud Hawaiian-print shirt you just bought, brush the sand off your feet and come on in.

Price codes for the Panama City Beach area, for a basic dinner for two, are as follows:

Less than $20	$
$21 to 40	$$
$41 to 60	$$$
More than $60	$$$$

Panama City Beach

HAMILTON'S SEAFOOD RESTAURANT & LOUNGE
5711 N. Lagoon Dr.
overlooking Grand Lagoon   234-1255
$$$

Mesquite grilling of steaks, ribs and seafood brings folks back here time and time again. Try Hamilton's Shrimp Christo, with grilled shrimp over angel hair pasta laden with fresh stewed tomatoes, onions, Feta cheese and spices. All the ingredients are fresh, fresh, fresh, and nothing is prepared ahead of time. Hamilton's uses only pure virgin olive oil, creamery butter, fresh cheeses and herbs, top choice meats and "from-the-dock" seafood. If you order scallops here, know that you're getting real Florida bay scallops; some restaurants try to pass off cut outs from stingray wings as "sea scallops." These tiny real scallops are so tasty and slightly sweet that they don't need any accompanying sauces. That mesquite grilling brings out their full flavor — real melt-in-your-mouth. The desserts, sauces, soups, even salad dressings are made fresh from Hamilton's own recipes.

The decor and unique atmosphere can't be overlooked. Inside, find polished wood, stained glass, period antiques and old photographs of Panama City and the beach. Watch your meal being cooked from a huge display window, or step onto the covered deck for cocktails and a sunset view. You can even eat outside, if you wish. Enjoy live jazz in the lounge nightly and remember, children are always welcome. Reservations are not necessary.

THE TREASURE SHIP
3605 Thomas Dr.   234-8881
$-$$$$

You'll probably have to stop at The Treasure Ship just to see what the heck it is. What it is is a huge restaurant complex, a reproduction of Sir Frances Drake's *Golden Hind* with a gift shop and lounges on four levels. The Hold Gift Shop is the first thing you see upon entering, so take a few minutes and look for nautical and beach souvenirs. The Brig is here too, with music and dancing and live entertainment until the wee hours. All of Level Two is the main dining room with big, comfortable booths and exquisite bay views. The Captain's Quarters and The Pirate's Pleasure can be found on Level Three, the first for cocktails and the second for more casual dining in a 17th-century atmosphere. There's outside dining available on The Decks way up at the top of The Treasure Ship, or for more romantic dining, try the delicate French cuisine created for you tableside at the Top of the Ship.

Dine early and pick up on some great savings. The Treasure Ship also hosts a truly gluttonous Sunday Brunch from 10 AM until 2 PM, and that's when you're likely to spot a few renegade pirates scouting about the ship. You're invited to stay awhile and tour the many levels or stroll the decks. Reservations are not accepted.

BREAKERS
12627 Front Beach Rd.   234-6060
$$$

Not *spring* Breakers . . . this place is upscale. It must be doing a fairly brisk business to be able to stay open for 23 years, but the view of the gulf, the warm, tropical atmosphere, wonderfully prepared food and nightly entertainment make Breakers a special night out. Chef Debra Griffin will be cooking up the day's catch in a number of your favorite ways, but try a lean cut of prime rib, baked fish with a lemon herb crust or the shrimp and scallops primavera for a healthy alternative without a healthy price: all just $10.95. Woody Green is the house entertainer, singer and piano player.

THE BEACH HOUSE
9850 S. Thomas Dr.   233-8800
$$

This is one of Panama City's newest restaurants and has already established an impressive reputation among locals and tourists alike. The reason is its elegant and tantalizing menu, featuring some of the finest gourmet offerings on the beach. We particularly liked the shrimp and scallop pasta served with sundried tomatoes and Indian chutney, as well as the swordfish au poivre, where a fresh swordfish steak is coated with sweet mustard cream sauce and sauteed a golden brown, then served with a mustard and cognac sauce. There's also a shrimp pasta dish with shitake mushroom sauce that is highly recommended. While seafood is the preferred choice here, meat-lovers will love the tenderloin or grilled beef served with peppercorn butter, as well as grilled pork medallions topped with a tangy dijon sauce. The Beach House sounds like a casual place, but it's perhaps a tad more classy than most other beach restaurants.

CAPT. ANDERSON'S
Dockside on Grand Lagoon
Thomas Dr. 234-2225
$$$

The "Golden Spoon" Award is a prestigious honor given annually by *Florida Trend* magazine, and for 13 years Capt. Anderson's Restaurant has been named one of Florida's top-20 restaurants. Jimmy and Johnny Patronis, owners of Capt. Anderson's, take their seafood seriously. You might find them out on the docks talking and bartering with the local fleet captains about the day's catch. When it's personally selected by the restaurant owners, you can be assured that only top-quality seafood ends up on your plate.

In keeping with the nautical decor inside Capt. Anderson's (named for the Anderson fishing fleet, incidentally, which is one of the Southeast's best), the emphasis is on seafood and plenty of it. Get yours char-grilled, broiled, fried or served any number of wonderful ways. Try a Feta-packed Greek salad or some fresh bread or desserts made right here in the Anderson's bakery. There's no better place to watch the fishing fleets unload the day's catch, either in the dining room, or in the Topside Lounge overlooking the lagoon. Come early for dinner; no reservations are taken.

SCHOONER'S
On the east end of Thomas Dr. 235-9074
$$$

It's the last local beach club, but nobody will tell us why. Is it the last one before you leave the beach, maybe? That seems more likely, with all the mom-and-pop places all along the beach. There isn't a great deal of atmosphere at Schooner's, just a lot of neon beer signs and old wood

Photo: Panama City Beach Visitors Bureau

The seafood doesn't get any fresher than what you'll find served in any of Panama City Beaches' fine restaurants.

paneling. This is one of the fine beach establishments that welcomes you in for lunch, so gorge yourself on giant burgers, grilled grouper, salads and sandwiches, washed down with an icy cold beer. For lunch, outdoor dining is best, since the inside tends to be dark and, well, empty. But what's really earned Schooner's its reputation happens at dusk. Now things get a little bit nicer, with open-air dining, tablecloths, candles and live entertainment.

MONTEGO BAY

On the curve of Thomas Dr.   234-8686
$$

It's a place for shuckin' and slurpin' and licking butter off your fingers. It's the beach, mon. Montego Bay has something of a Jamaican atmosphere, meaning everything is colorful, including the clientele. Prices are really pretty good for all you get, such as the Captain's Catch, a seafood platter with a cup of gumbo, chargrilled amberjack or Jamaican grilled chicken, all for less than $10. Lunch specials start at $4. Visit Montego Bay's four other locations: the intersection of Middle Beach, Front Beach and Thomas Drive, 235-3585; the Shoppes at Edgewater, 233-6033; the Y, 233-2900; and Montego Bay downtown, Highway 77 across from the mall, 872-0098.

CAPTAIN DAVIS
DOCKSIDE RESTAURANT & LOUNGE

At Captain Anderson's Marina
5550 N. Lagoon Dr. and Thomas Dr.
Panama City Beach   234-3608
$$$

Something about the lull of dining on the water, watching the boats, the sunset, the fishing fleets . . . tends to make a person hungry. It may be romantic, but you may also have your three children in tow. They'll like this place too, since it's

fun to watch the boats come in, and Captain Davis's friendly staff is always happy to see families. Fresh seafood can be grilled, broiled, blackened or fried. Thick-cut steaks, prime rib and delicious frosty cocktails provide enough variety for a few meals out during your vacation stay.

BOAR'S HEAD

17290 Front Beach Rd. just west of
Hwy. 79   234-6628
$$$

The Boar's Head is supposed to be Old English-style, but we're not talking Shepherd's Pie or crumpets or any of that bland-but-authentic food. The atmosphere is Old English, and the food is out of this world — roasted and chargrilled steaks and seafood, succulent prime rib, baby back pork ribs, fresh fish and shellfish creations, plus some served with pasta. Try the garlic shrimp with cream sauce and pasta for a real treat. The shrimp are sauteed in fresh garlic and olive oil, then finished with a light cream sauce and served over fresh fettuccine. There's the grouper and crayfish (or crawfish) meunière, which maybe you can't pronounce, but you can sure appreciate: a broiled grouper fillet topped with crayfish tails in a Paul Prudhomme-inspired sauce (he's the famous New Orleans chef).

The children's menu is extensive, offering more choices than most (eight entrees). Nightly dinner specials start at just $9.95. Reservations are accepted but not required. Enjoy live entertainment in The Tavern every weekend.

PINEAPPLE WILLIES BAR & GRILL

9900 S. Thomas Dr.   235-0928
$

It had to happen sooner or later — a nightspot designed especially for Baby Boomers. By day, Pineapple Willies caters to families, with seafood, ribs and deli specialties. Let us tell you a little about these ribs before you let your 8-year-old order them: They're coated with a "secret" Texas rub, slow cooked for eight hours, then basted with some sort of a special sauce featuring Jack Daniels. OK, so most of the alcohol probably burns off. What's left is pure perfection.

SPINNAKER

8795 Thomas Dr.   *234-7892*

If you're a member of Generation X, Spinnaker is a custom fit. Live concerts, a beachfront playground, nightly contests, live rock 'n' roll, something for the ladies, something for the men, great drinks and after-dark dancing to today's music in a colorful, rhythmic sound and light show fill the bill for the younger-than-30 set. Spinnaker sometimes has two or three bands playing at the same time. They have a swimming pool where pool volleyball is quite popular, 12 different levels, 19 different bars, a Panama Jack Miss Spinnaker contest on Saturdays, A Wet T-Shirt contest every Sunday, volleyball contests, male and female revues, Jet Ski and Hobie Cat rentals, Ladies' Night every Thursday, great deli food, music, lights and dancing.

Panama City

THE GREENHOUSE RESTAURANT

443 Grace Ave.
in the Grace Ave. Mini-Mall   *763-2245*
$$

Let us give you yet another reason to cross over the bridge into town. The prices are nice, the crowds are nonexistent, and the food is worth the trip. This little mini-mall has cobblestone streets and archways; the Greenhouse Restaurant is right at the end of the "road." Inside, several small rooms separated by trellises and stucco walls make for intimate dining; bare trees covered with tiny white lights give the feeling of dining outdoors.

The luncheon menu has a few unusual offerings: chargrilled chicken teriyaki, a chicken chimichanga, fried fish and Marie's Famous Crab Cakes (snow and lump crab). You can get away easily for less than $10. For dinner, order sauteed scallops in butter and herbs finished with white wine and heavy cream and served over fettuccine. The catch of the day can be blackened to order, or you might try a beef tenderloin, sauteed to order with sauce Bernaise. All chicken, fish and shrimp can be ordered baked with wine and lemon if you're one of the health-conscious.

CANOPIES

4423 W. Hwy. 98
on St. Andrew Bay   *872-8444*
$$$

This elegant restaurant is in town, on the water like many others and features the same gorgeous sunsets. But no beach restaurant can hope to match Canopies' graceful atmosphere inside a home built in 1902 and framed by ancient oaks or a lush lawn sloping to the water's edge.

Now, get ready for the feature attraction. How about a hearty slab of New Orleans Andouille sausage, sauteed with fresh gulf shrimp and served over fettuccine Alfredo? Or a couple of succulent St. Andrew Bay blue crabs simmering in rich cream and sherry for a steaming bowl of she crab soup? If you're needing a seafood break long about half way through vacation, order up a juicy chicken breast stuffed with Feta cheese, mozzarella and fresh herbs, covered with marinara sauce and served with pasta and a fresh vegetable. Other entrees let your taste decide with grilled tuna, gulf grouper, roast pork tenderloin, filet mignon and many others. Order one of the superb pastas as an appetizer or a main course. All entrees come with a house salad, a loaf of still-warm homemade bread and strawberry and herb butter. Save room for whatever they're making for dessert that night and one of their numerous coffee creations.

THE CHEESE BARN
425 and 440 Grace Ave.
Restaurant   769-3892
Bakery and Deli   763-4466
$$

Here's another of those delightful out-of-the-way places that makes you feel like you alone have discovered it. As an insider, it's a place you need to know about. Here, take your choice: French crepes, German knockwurst, Cajun jambalaya, Italian manicotti, pizza, salads, an incredible array of sandwiches (including a rather superb Muffeletta on a poppyseed bun), nachos, steaks, quiche and lots of cheese. Many of the sandwiches feature The Cheese Barn specialty cheeses, such as the Downtown Philly with Swiss and Cheddar, the Che' Che' Cheddar Beef, the Submarine and Super Duper with provolone and plenty of others. The variety of domestic and imported beers is staggering, as is the selection of wines, wine coolers, champagnes and sparkling wines. This charming little spot has a European feel to it with its aged stucco walls, white tablecloths, several small dining rooms and dim lights, even during the day. Be sure to visit the bakery for a take-home dessert.

TAXI'S DINER
23rd and Beck   763-5025
$

Hooray! A place with good grub that's open 24 hours a day. Taxi's advertises "Cheap Fare — Speedy Service." They're slinging Hubcap Pancakes there in the back (ever had beer with breakfast long about 3 AM?), the Big Tipper Redeye and Checker's Chili, all in a slick chrome-polished, jukebox-playing, malt-shop-mixing diner atmosphere. Take-out is available during the same hours, like all the time.

THUNDERBIRDS
1 mile east of the
Hathaway Bridge on Hwy. 98   785-7444
$

Sometimes grownups need their own place, so Thunderbirds was invented to let big people have their own fun. Your kids wouldn't like that "old" music, anyway, but you'll be boogeying 'til the cows come home. Once a week is Comedy Zone, with national touring comedians you may have seen on David Letterman or *The Tonight Show*. Thunderbirds also has a once-a-week Sadie Hawkins night where the gal who asks the most guys to dance gets $100 in Thunderbucks. There's Two Buck night, Casino Night, crazy giveaways in cash and prizes on the weekends, and at that point Thunderbirds has just about run out of nights. Hop in your Thunderbird (or more likely, your mini-van), and bop 'til you drop.

Panama City Beach Area
Accommodations

Sleep cheap or surround yourself in luxury in a full-service resort. This area was designed with families and couples in mind, with most resorts and hotels right on the beach, enhancing leisure-time activities. Many visitors prefer the campground route, which shows off some of the abundant wooded areas. It's almost difficult to find accommodations that aren't on or near the water. The Panama City Beach area is blessed with an outstanding system of bays, bayous, lakes and inlets so that every visitor can take advantage of fishing, boating, swimming or just enjoying the incredible scenery in every direction.

One more note: Panama City Beach, more than any other resort area in Northwest Florida, is literally bursting with resorts, hotels, motels, townhomes, condominiums, cottages and campsites. There are hundreds of places to stay, so our list below barely scrapes the surface. What we've tried to do for you is give a representative sampling of available accommodations in many different price ranges. And because of the number and variety of places to stay, rates are comparable with those in Pensacola — in other words, they're great!

Resorts/Hotels

Driving up and down the beach, you'd swear that every hotel chain in America is represented here. And that may be true. The 27 miles of beachfront is just the start. Many of the luxury resorts and condos front St. Andrew or one of the other bays and are every bit as scenic and accessible to restaurants, shopping and attractions. Below are top picks for the best Panama City Beach has to offer in all price ranges. Our price guide is for a double room for one night at the peak of the season; off-season rates can drop by as much as one third. Prices do not include tax.

$80 or less	$
$81 to 100	$$
$101 to 150	$$$
$151 or more	$$$$

BAY POINT YACHT & COUNTRY CLUB
100 Delwood Beach Rd.
Panama City Beach   235-6966
$$$ (800) 543-3307

Could there be a more perfect setting for this relative newcomer than on St. Andrew Bay, surrounded by water and shaded by tall pines? Bay Point is an all-inclusive 1,100-acre retreat from the workaday world with 36 holes of championship golf, a 147-slip marina, a health club and swimming pools. Guests may choose from one-, two- or three-bedroom condos and villas on Bay Point's golf courses, on the marina or overlooking Grand Lagoon. All feature large balconies for a tranquil brunch and open living and dining spaces. Right there on the property are the Terrace Court and Greenhouse restaurants or the more casual Sunset Grill and Pub.

There's one thing you can get at Bay Point that you can't find much of on the beach: shade. If it's important to you, you'll love all the trees and gentle wooded setting. And that beach is never far away. There is a two-night minimum stay at Bay Point; weekly rates for a two-bedroom condo at Lagoon Towers run about $700.

The Chateau Motel

12525 Front Beach Rd.
Panama City Beach   234-2174
$$-$$$ (800) 874-8826

Among the dozens of easily affordable motels along the beach, the Chateau stands out for a number of reasons. First off, its crazy-sticks architecture is straight out of the 1970s — you can easily imagine the Brady Bunch staying here on a vacation. Once you're inside, however, you'll find that this cozy place has a lot to offer. It's conveniently located just a few minutes' walk from the Miracle Strip

Amusement Park, the prices are reasonable, and the service is very friendly. The comfortable rooms offer mini-refrigerators, wide beds and great views of the beach. If you're looking for a great, low-cost place to stay so you can spend your money having fun, you'll want to check out the Chateau.

Edgewater Beach Resort

11212 Front Beach Rd.
Panama City Beach   235-4977
$$$$ (800) 239-4853

A landmark in the Panama City area, Edgewater offers enough recreational activities, walking trails, pools and amenities to keep you within the confines of the resort property for a week. All studio, one-, two- and three-bedroom units are decorated in a tropical motif with full kitchens, living and dining areas, private baths for each bedroom and washers and dryers. Stay in the fancy waterfront towers on the gulf or one of the more private Caribbean-style golf villas along the golf course. On the 110-acre, $100-million property is a nine-hole, par 3 golf course, 12 all-weather tennis courts, 20 shuffle-

Photo: Panama City Beach Visitors Bureau

Even during the winter months, people enjoy Panama City's gorgeous beaches.

board courts, a beauty salon, an arcade, and five heated spas. Wrapped around those niceties are fountains, ponds and enough tropical vegetation to make it feel like paradise. The nine pools include a 1,500-square-foot lagoon pool at the edge of the gulf. And just to wrap it all up in one incredible package are three restaurants on the property: the Bimini Sandbar Cafe, the Palapa Bar and Grill and the Upstairs Clubhouse and Lounge.

HAMPTON INN
11004 Front Beach Rd.
Panama City Beach   234-7334
$$ (800) 426-7866

Hampton Inns do a fine job in every location and pride themselves on all the little extras that make a stay here so special. Start with gulf-view rooms (the inn is 75 yards from the beach), free HBO, no charge for kids, nonsmoking rooms and free continental breakfast. This particular Hampton Inn also has an outstanding location just 10 miles from the airport, a half-mile from Miracle Strip Amusement Park and 1 mile from Hombre Golf Course. Double rooms have two double beds, and rooms with coffee makers and refrigerators are $10 more per night.

HOLIDAY INN BEACH RESORT
11127 Front Beach Rd.
Panama City Beach   234-1111
$$$$ (800) 633-0266

This may be one of the nicest Holidays Inns you've ever seen. All 342 rooms and suites overlook turquoise waters and white sands. The resort boasts a tropical oasis with waterfalls, swaying palms and exotic flora of every description. Spacious rooms all have private balconies, ice makers, refrigerators and coffee makers (with coffee). There's a fitness center with steam room and sauna. The Blue Marlin Restaurant is a fine place to hang your hat after a hard day in the sun, or you might enjoy a cocktail at the Starlite Lounge, a local favorite. Sunsets are especially appealing over drinks and dinner at Charlie's Grill and the Oasis Bar.

PIER 99 BEACHFRONT MOTEL
9900 S. Thomas Dr.
Panama City Beach   234-6657
$$ (800) 874-6657

It's right on the beach, right next to the pier, right in the middle of everything. Rooms are not especially fancy, but you won't have much time to spend lazing away the days there with so much to do! This is a fine families-only motel, since location is everything and rates are fairly inexpensive. There's a two-night minimum stay at Pier 99, with a discount for your third through sixth nights and a seventh night free. Kitchen units are a little more expensive but well worth the extra $10 or so a night if you can make some meals in your room. Off-the-beach units save you even more. There's a gulf-front pool, a hot tub and Pineapple Willies Bar & Grill, serving up ribs, seafood and great entertainment nightly. If you stay here between Sunday and Thursday, Pier 99 will take $5 per night off the cost of a room.

PORTER'S COURT
17013 Front Beach Rd.
Panama City Beach   234-2752
$$ (800) 421-9950

This is a pretty little place with your choice of whitewashed single-story cottages with red roofs or a three-story motel building by the pool and facing the gulf. Choose a one- or two-bedroom/one-bath unit featuring kitchen and dining areas, and sofa sleepers. The larger cottages have porches facing the gulf, while some units face an open courtyard area.

Some folks say there are more castles along Panama City Beach than anywhere else in the world — at least, until high tide rolls in.

Efficiencies, though small, still pack in their own patios and refrigerators. Since the two-bedroom cottages are only $115 a night, a family could be very comfortable there, or even in a one-bedroom with a sleeper sofa. If you want the best at Porter's Court, there's a one-bedroom rooftop penthouse condo with its own private patio garden on the gulf.

RAMADA INN BEACH
12907 Front Beach Rd.
Panama City Beach   234-1700
$$$ (800) 633-0266

The glitzy mirrored columns and reflective facade of the Ramada are right out of the '70s, but Ramada Inns grew by leaps and bounds during that decade, so many of the properties reflect the era of discos and mirror balls. But wait, there's more: The pool is something you'll want to photograph from all sides. Giant fake rocks create grottos, caves and waterfalls around the free-form gulf-front pool. There are aquariums built into the reception desk and some kind of nautical motif, but the rooms are large, clean and comfortable, and they all have water views

(that might mean pool views, but the pool's right on the gulf as well).

Condominiums/Townhomes/ Vacation Cottages

Some people just know how to live. Why not have all of the amenities of a resort plus the privacy and space of a home? Bringing home fresh seafood from the market and cooking it yourself is a great vacation pastime, aside from eating it all up! Prices reflect the average weekly cost of a two-bedroom/two-bath condo or house during the peak summer season. Most rental agencies want a deposit up front that can be up to a third of the week's rental. Prices do not include tax.

$750 to 950	$
$951 to 1,100	$$
$1,101 to 1,500	$$$
$1,501 and more	$$$$

ABBOTT REALTY SERVICES, INC.
35000 Emerald Coast Pkwy.
Destin   837-4853
$-$$$$ (800) 336-4853

Abbott is one of the largest realty companies in the area, offering more than 80 resort properties from high- and low-rise condominiums to townhomes and beach cottages. If you're unsure of where to start looking for your vacation retreat, Abbott can provide an excellent overview of the area and what's available.

SEACHASE CONDOMINIUMS

17351 Front Beach Rd., ¼-mile west of Hwy. 79
Panama City Beach   235-1300
$ *(800) 457-2051*

Seachase's reasonably priced condominiums directly overlook the gulf. Every unit, whether a condo or townhome, boasts a panoramic 60-foot-wide, floor-to-ceiling view. Twin high-rise towers have a gulfside pool and sundeck in between. Two-bedroom units have spacious 1,400-square-foot floor plans. A $200 deposit is required at the time you make your reservation; nightly rentals are also available. All units have washers, dryers, microwaves, free local calls and HBO movies and cable. You must be 25 or older to rent (now hear this: no Spring Breakers!).

LARGO MAR

5717 Thomas Dr.
Panama City Beach   234-5750
$ *(800) 645-2746*

Although some of these units are set quite a ways back, the entire development is on the gulf. Largo Mar is another fine place to take the family; buildings are only three stories (you can request a ground-floor unit), there's lots of landscaped acreage for the kids to run around and units are far enough from Thomas Drive so the sound of the surf is louder than the blare of car horns. Every unit has its own washer and dryer, dishwasher, garbage disposal, fully equipped kitchen, cable TV and private deck. Outside, buildings

are clustered around a large swimming pool. There's an outside Jacuzzi, a club room, saunas and barbecue grills. Most of the units overlook the pool.

THE SUMMERHOUSE

6505 Thomas Dr.
Panama City Beach   234-1112
$ *(800) 354-1112*

These very nice, very comfortable condos are laid out in a series of three high-rises. From your private balcony, you can see out over the gulf or clear to Grand Lagoon. The views are spectacular. Inside, Summerhouse is designed with families and couples in mind. All units are two bedrooms and feature washers and dryers, a fully equipped kitchen for microwave popcorn, fresh coffee, cable with HBO and everything to make your stay just as pleasant as can be. The two pools, hot tub and kiddie pool are nicely landscaped and center around a gazebo. Beach service is also available to guests — just ask for beach umbrellas, cabanas, water cycles, sail boats and more. For your smallest travelers, cribs and baby beds can be brought to your unit on request. Kids especially like the glass elevators and the game room! For a larger family, or one that likes its space, request one of the corner units. These are 1,888 square feet with views all around.

PORTSIDE RESORT

17620 Front Beach Rd.
Panama City Beach   234-7157
$ *(800) 443-2737*

It's hard to imagine all this beauty, all this luxury, all these great amenities, and paying for a week what a two-night stay would cost in South Florida! That's what so many people discover about this little corner of Florida . . . the most incredible resorts imaginable cost so little. Portside is one of the best. The development is long and skinny and spread out enough to make your unit very private. And since it isn't actually on the gulf, but across the street, they've gone overboard on amenities. Two-bedroom units are bedecked in casual Florida colors and furnishings that reflect the lifestyle so well. You can park right at your door. Palms, pampas grass, hibiscus and ginger surround the three pool areas (one is heated), and a giant palapa overlooks the waterfall pool. Take advantage of the kiddie pool, tennis courts, shuffleboard, heated spa and poolside clubhouse.

ST. ANDREW BAY RESORT MANAGEMENT, INC.
726 Thomas Dr.
Panama City Beach 235-4075, (800) 621-2462
$ (800) 621-2426, (800) 423-1889

These are the people who know Panama City Beach best and prove it with an amazing assortment of accommodations all up and down the beach and five check-in offices. Take your choice from Ramsgate Harbour townhomes, offering the most privacy in their own "neighborhood;" Endless Summer Condos, which are villas just steps from the beach; Premier Townhouses, low-rises that sit right on the beach; Dunes of Panama on Thomas Drive with huge balconies on the gulf; and Commodore Condominiums with a pool, a hot tub and within walking distance of St. Andrews State Park. Many other condos and beach houses are available with three bedrooms.

Campgrounds/RV Parks

ST. ANDREWS STATE RECREATION AREA
4415 Thomas Dr.
Panama City Beach   233-5140

"Back to nature" vacations are a trend throughout the United States, and St.

Andrews is poised and ready to respond to eager campers. More than half of the 176 campsites were booked for April 1995 alone, and the rest were snatched up quickly on a first-come, first-served basis, just to give an idea of how popular eco-tourism has become. Waterfront sites on Grand Lagoon are $20.67 per night; nonwaterfront go for $18.49. Obviously, reservations are recommended well in advance. For more information about St. Andrews, see the chapter on Panama City Beach Attractions.

PANAMA CITY BEACH KOA
8800 Thomas Dr.
Panama City Beach   234-5731

With something close to 300 campsites, KOA proves camping is as popular as ever. And to back that up (as if staying right on the Gulf of Mexico wasn't fun enough), KOA has a game room, a fishing lagoon, two pools, basketball, volleyball, a playground, picnic tables, a rec hall, a toy store and a gift shop! During the winter months, they add Ping Pong and shuffleboard to the lineup. Why, you can even have cable TV for an extra $2 a day! At the peak of the season (March 1 through Labor Day), KOA still offers a 10 percent discount for staying a week. The daily rate is $22.95 for a full hookup (water, electric, sewer), $18.95 for primitive (tent) camping with water only. If you don't wish to rough it, try one of the "Kamping Kabins," for $31.95 a night, year round. These have beds, kitchens, linens, heat, AC and just about everything you need to be comfortable except those little bottles of avocado body balm. And, heck, you can bring that yourself.

MAGNOLIA BEACH RV PARK
7800 Magnolia Beach Rd.
Panama City Beach   235-1581

This RV park is so pretty that many

folks choose to stay here all year. Of course, those that do snatch up some of the tastiest sites, but there are plenty of others. If you're an RVer worth your salt, you'll know that the designation of a "Good Sampark" makes it top notch. Giant magnolia, yellow pine and oak trees dripping with moss make the park a cool respite even in the heat of July. It may be one of the only shady places to hang out at the beach in midsummer. The St. Andrew Bay location means the water is usually warmer than the gulf, and the waves are easy to handle, even for the little ones. On the grounds are a rec room, air conditioned showers and baths, picnic tables and barbecue grills, a pier, a pool and a grocery store with camp supplies. For all this excitement, you pay about $20 a night during peak season (with cable!), about $125 if you stay all week.

RACCOON RIVER RESORT

12405 Middle Beach Rd.
Panama City Beach   234-0181

This is another "Good Sampark," but it's got to be an older one, first, because a raccoon probably hasn't been spotted on Panama City Beach since the '50s, and second, because it has all these cutesy names that somebody's grandpa probably coined such as Turtle Turn, Possum Pond, Alligator Alley and Hoot Owl Hollow. The tent camping sites go by such monikers as Hawk Heights, Otter Alley and Beaver Bend. It's within walking distance to the beach, there's a pond to fish in, a pool and a playground, lots of shade trees, log cabin restrooms and a general store. Besides, the days-gone-by monikers are appealing in a comfortable sort of way. Primitive sites go for $14 in the peak season; sites with full hookups (that's with cable too) are $19.50 per night, $117 per week.

Panama City Beach Area
Shopping

T-shirt, beachwear and souvenir shops are crammed into every available space along the beach for take-home memories, so only a few of those are listed here. For more serious buyers, look into downtown for everything from imported tobacco to English bone china and original objets d'art. If you're looking for the latest bestseller or other reading material, B. Dalton and Waldenbooks along with other bookstores provide offerings to satisfy the most avid of readers.

On the Beach

ALVIN'S BIG ISLAND TROPICAL DEPARTMENT STORE
Across from Miracle Strip Amusement Park plus 12 other locations along Panama City Beach   234-3048

It's pretty hard to have a corner on the T-shirt and beachwear market in a place as huge as Panama City Beach, but it seems Alvin's tries very hard to do just that with an amazing array of stores. The big one's the most fun, though, and could almost be considered a tourist attraction. Delightfully tacky and whimsical, Alvin's Big Island seems to be poking fun at itself with its fake rock exterior, cavernous interior (complete with stalactites and stalagmites), tank of small sharks, cages of tropical birds and outdoor alligator exhibit. It is somehow dismaying to find

giant macaws, parrots and cockatiels shoved in among T-shirt racks, too accessible to the whims of the mean-spirited. The alligator farm does a pretty good job; at least fencing somewhat distances the creatures from passersby. An aquarium of small sharks is set in the middle of the sales floor showcasing shell nightlights, shell sculptures, caricature artists, coffee mugs and huggies all around.

You could call the stuff they have for sale beach junk, and they might even agree with you, but it sells like crazy. Who wouldn't want to take home a key chain with a tiny scene of real water and real sand and real shells encased in it? Or a visor sporting "I Survived Spring Break"? Alvin's has hundreds of top-name swimsuits, bikinis and other types of beachwear, but most of it is, well, beach junk. We can almost guarantee you can't walk out of there empty-handed.

TRADER RICK'S SURF SHOP
12208 Front Beach Rd. at the pier 235-3243

If you need stuff for the beach, for surfing, for skating, for volleyball, for skateboarding or just for looking good, Trader Rick's is the beach authority. Beach gear, beachwear, beach equipment and most everything in between to outfit you for a great vacation is here.

For those late-risers who miss out on the beachcombing, the tourists shops along Panama City Beach are filled with beautiful shells.

SHIPWRECK SHIRTS

10570 Front Beach Rd.   233-6750

By a Shipwreck Shirt, we don't mean they're all dirty and torn, but, hey, if they were, some people would still buy them (grunge is still "in," at least for this month). Shipwreck has plenty of shirts, but also swimwear, sportswear and gifts to bring home.

NIGHT MOVES

9526 Front Beach Rd.   234-5223

Somewhere on the beach there had to be somebody who sells more than just beachwear and T-shirts and souvenirs, and we finally found one. Night Moves sells sexy lingerie, dancewear, legwear, accessories, jewelry, adult toys, novelties and games. Oh, and that goes for men too. Night Moves puts on a fashion show every week — if you're interested in seeing how this stuff looks on a real person, call for times.

THE BOOK WAREHOUSE

Holiday Plaza Shopping Center
6646 W. Hwy. 98   235-2950

Come pick up a little light summer reading for the beach with 50 percent to 90 percent off suggested retail. The Book Warehouse carries an assortment of children's books, cookbooks, craft books, how-to's, computer books, fiction and scads of books in other categories. Bring your postcards and letters here too; there's a post office inside the shop.

QUICK SNAPS

553 Shoppes at Edgewater
Front Beach Rd.   234-7160

Look just across from the Holiday Inn to have your precious vacation photos processed in just an hour at no extra charge. Quick Snaps offers same-day service on enlargements, slides and reprints. Don't wait until you get home to discover you left the lenscap on — hit Quick Snaps first.

THE JOINT, KILLER
BEADS AND THE T-SHIRT CELLAR
14600 Front Beach Rd. 233-2752, 234-6361

We promise, it's one of the brightest shops you'll find anywhere on the beach. You can't miss this bizarre 1960s-style mural splashed in Day-Glo colors across the front of the store. Inside, things get even stranger. Buy beads, T's, beachwear, tobacco pipes and accessories, jewelry and some of the very finest airbrush work in the county. The Joint would be worth stopping into just to admire the work of airbrush artist Troy Pierce — it's truly spectacular.

BARRON'S ANTIQUE MALL
1.5 miles west of the Hathaway Bridge
8010 Front Beach Rd. 230-0612

More than 100 dealer room settings in a 20,000-square-foot, air-conditioned showroom feature fine antiques and collectibles of all descriptions. You could lose yourself (and your spouse), but the Antique Mall has a place for you to find each other again, the "Husband Recovery Room." Barron's accepts layaways and will deliver locally or long distance.

Panama City

AGELESS BOOK SHOPPE
1090 Florida Ave. 763-5264

If you're going to visit bookstores when traveling, the Ageless Book Shoppe is a great reason to get off the beaten path, particularly if you're searching for older, rare books. The shelves at Ageless are packed with more than 150,000 books, with special emphasis on Civil War history, poetry, vintage novels and children's books. They also run a search service, if you're looking for an out-of-print title that's hard to find. You won't find any new magazines here, but if you want to rummage through stacks of ancient *Saturday Evening Posts*, this is the place. The Ageless does have a small selection of new books, including fiction and travel.

CORNING REVERE FACTORY STORE
105 23rd St., 1 mile west of Hwy. 231 in the
Manufacturer's Outlet Center 784-0288
950 Prim Ave. at the
Factory Stores of America
Graceville 263-3277

If you'd like a little variety in your shopping, then you'll just have to cross the bridge into town (or make the trek to Graceville), where you can pick up on some incredible bargains at Corning Revere. Look for more than just the famed Corning Ware — there's Visions cookware, Pyrex and Revere Ware, Corelle dinnerware, lots of open stock dishes and glassware, plus kitchen gadgets and accessories.

MANUFACTURER'S OUTLET CENTER
105 W. 23rd St., Panama City

For serious bargain hunters, here's true outlet shopping from about a dozen of your favorite name brands such as Russell, Van Heusen, Capezio, Bass, Polly Flinders, London Fog and Corning. Heck, you can save up to 70 percent just by crossing the bridge — a deal too good to pass up.

PANAMA CITY MALL
2150 Cove Blvd., Hwy. 77 at
Hwy. 231 and 23rd St. 785-9587

More than 90 stores including JCPenney, Gayfers and Sears plus lots of eateries, puppet shows, a four-screen cinema and a game room make for a pleasant day's wandering. Shop in air-conditioned comfort seven days a week.

PAUL BRENT STUDIO AND GALLERY
413 W. Fifth St.   *785-2684*

Here's one of the best Insiders' tips you'll get this year: Go visit Paul Brent's studio and take home a souvenir. It is something you will always treasure after you learn that Paul Brent is a local artist and his works are displayed all over the world. You may already have seen some of it, although you might not have known you were looking at a local artist's work; Brent's colorful watercolors are on display at Busch Gardens, Sea World and Disney World, as well as many other offices and galleries in exotic locales such as Australia, South Africa and the Caribbean. Now his designs have been transferred to linens, placemats, shower curtains, greeting and playing cards and many other items. This is a gallery, so of course you can still buy his original works, prints and works by other artists. If you happen to catch him at the gallery, he won't mind you asking him to autograph your print. Brent is still very active in the local community, providing T-shirt and poster art for many worthwhile causes.

FLORIDA LINEN OUTLET
At Stanford Station on 23rd St.   *769-0950*

Walk in with an idea, walk out with a carload of bargains on curtains, comforters, sheets, towels, placemats, napkins and accessories for your home. Martex, Fieldcrest, Kirsch and other name brands are there for the picking in more than 6,000 square feet of floor space. Coordinate an entire bath in the time it takes to pull the stuff off the shelves . . . tissue holders, towel racks, toothbrush holders, matching picture frames, hampers, wicker shelves and baskets, rugs . . . everything.

Panama City Beach Area
Historic Sites and Attractions

Like the bumpers in a pinball game, visitors to Panama City Beach can bounce from one diversion to the next and never miss a beat; amusements rub elbows with outdoor activities all along the beach. Attractions that are most fun for families and kids are so noted by an asterisk (*), while museums, art galleries and more tranquil pursuits await discovery inland. Be sure to check the chapters on Panama City Beach Area Recreation and Shopping for more to do!

*ST. ANDREWS STATE
RECREATION AREA
4415 Thomas Dr.
Panama City Beach   *233-5140*

This 1000-plus-acre jut of land surrounded by water on three sides might seem at first to be a private island paradise. Just when you think you're really starting to commune with nature one-on-one, 10 people pass you on the nature trail and scare off the raccoon you were watching. Not that you won't find places to be alone, but St. Andrews is one of Florida's most popular state parks, so prepare to share. Pine forests, marshes, flatwoods and great lines of white sand dunes characterize the terrain. Near Grand Lagoon, visit a reconstructed "Cracker" turpentine still, a remembrance of this area's once-thriving lumber industry. Cannon platforms still exist from World War II when the park was part of a military reservation. One of the platforms is now a pavilion; the other lies on the beach, a victim of constant buffeting by wind and waves.

Camping, picnicking and concessions are all available in the park, as are a number of water-related leisure activities. Fishing is probably the no. 1 attraction at St. Andrews, since there are so many opportunities to wet a line — including the surf, two piers, jetties and freshwater fishing in Gator Lake or one of the other small ponds. Take your boat out (the boat ramp is on Grand Lagoon near the fishing pier) for some deep sea excitement.

The park's nature trail may take you past alligators or wading birds, but for up-close marine life study, check out the jetties. Fish, crabs and other creatures love to congregate around the huge rocks. Please remember that all plant and animal life in the park is protected (yes, that includes the water). Please do not remove or disturb any living thing. Feeding the animals is also prohibited.

Right across the thin stretch of beach is the Intracoastal Waterway, and beyond that, Shell Island — 3 miles of totally undeveloped solitude — accessible only by boat. Daily trips to the island are $7 for adults, $5 for chil-

Photo: Panama City Beach Visitors Bureau

This happy dolphin is one of the friendlier creatures you can encounter at Panama City's Gulf World.

dren. Island visitors are welcome to stay for an hour or all day. One of the biggest draws is the great snorkeling and diving here, in a protected cove formed by rock jetties that extend to the gulf. For more information on island jaunts, contact the Jetty Concession Store, 233-0197. They'll be able to help you with scheduling as well as any gear rental you may need.

Many other boat cruises offer trips to the island as well. Entry to the park for one day is $3.25, which will admit up to eight people in one vehicle. For campground information, see the chapter on Panama City Beach Area Accommodations. St. Andrews is open from 8 AM until sunset all year.

*CYPRESS SPRINGS
Hwy. 79, Vernon   *535-2960*

Just 30 minutes from the fury of Panama City Beach is one of Florida's many natural wonders, carved from a landscape inhabited by Native Americans thousands of years ago. The water is some of the purest and clearest in the world. Just reach your hand down and scoop some up. You've never tasted water so

sweet and cold (68 degrees year round). Visibility is more than 200 feet, perfect for underwater photography and spelunking (cave diving).

You must be a certified spelunker to enter the underwater cavern through an oval-shaped vent. The flow of water is quite strong here, so be sure to wear a weight belt. The cave opens onto a room about 40 feet wide with a ceiling 14 feet high. Even at its deepest point, divers can see the surface, some 70 feet above!

Cypress Springs pumps out close to a million gallons of fresh water daily. Tubing and canoeing are leisurely ways to tour the adjoining creeks and springs for a few hours, or stay in the nearby RV park to explore the scenic wonders at your own pace. Call for information on float trips, dive trips and RV park sites.

EBRO DOG TRACK
Off Hwy. 20, East of Freeport   *234-3943*
                            (800) 345-4810

Bursting out of the starting gate with lightning speed, the greyhounds take center stage every night but Sunday year round. More than $1 million are paid out each week, and if you'd like to get in on some of that action, bring a friend, buy a tip sheet and get anxious with the rest of the crowd. Dine on prime rib, stuffed shrimp or Grecian grouper in the Ebro Dining Room overlooking the action. The restaurant opens at 6 PM, and reservations are required. Ebro brings you continuous action in the off-season with simulcast wagering on greyhounds and thoroughbreds on tracks a bit farther south. Live racing goes on rain or shine Monday through Saturday at 7 PM with matinees at 1 PM (no racing on Sunday). General admission is $1; children are free when accompanied by a parent. To get to Ebro from Panama City Beach, take Highway 79 N. to Highway 20 and follow the signs.

*THE GLASS-BOTTOM BOAT

Treasure Island Marina
3605 Thomas Dr. behind the Treasure Ship
Panama City Beach   234-8944

Take a cruise through gentle bay waters and out into the emerald gulf while your captain fills you in on the scenery, the bird life and what you're about to encounter. Observe friendly dolphins and pesky pelicans up close, look for unusual marine life through the huge underwater viewing windows, visit scenic and protected Shell Island and try to identify the creatures captured in the Glass Bottom Boat's shrimp net! Snacks are served inside the air conditioned cabin. Bring your camera and a good pair of binoculars for an adventure you'll treasure. The Sea School trip just described runs from 9 AM until noon or 1 to 4 PM daily all year long. Prices may vary a bit from time to time, but are regularly $9 for adults, $6 for kids 3 to 12, and 2 and younger are free.

Also docked at the marina is a 40-passenger catamaran to take you on a super shelling safari. Explore remote sand bars off the end of Shell Island and comb the beaches for shells and sand dollars. Prices for this trip are $11 for adults and $7 for kids. Call for times, since the trip depends so much on the weather and time of year.

SEA SCREAMER

Treasure Island Marina, 3605 Thomas Dr.
Panama City Beach   233-9107

The *Screamer* is the world's largest speedboat, and it just might be the fastest too. Climb aboard this 73-foot twin turbo-charged cruiser for a relaxing tour of Grand Lagoon, Shell Island and the pass. Then hang on, because once the Sea Screamer hits open water, you'll blast off into the Gulf for the wettest, most exhilierating ride of your life. You will want to wear a swimsuit for this one. Adult tickets are $8, $5 for children, kids younger than 6 ride free. The *Screamer* departs daily at 10 AM, noon, 2, 4 and 6 PM daily.

*GULF WORLD

Front Beach Rd., 15412 W. Hwy. 98-A
Panama City Beach   234-5271

Ever see a dolphin hula? Hear a sea lion applaud? Or feel the rough surface of a stingray? All this and much more kicks into high gear at Gulf World, one of Florida's most popular attractions. The action never stops with continuous dolphin, sea lion and dive demonstration shows. While you enjoy the antics, you'll also learn something about dolphins and sea lions from their trainers. After the show, you might even get a chance to pet one of the dolphins!

At the Coral Reef Theater, a diver plunges into a giant tank filled with creatures of the deep such as sharks, rays, barracuda and giant sea turtles. Although you may gasp in amazement when the diver grabs hold of a fierce looking shark, he's really in no danger, since all of the marine life are well-fed before the show.

Colorful tropical parrots squawk and talk and put on quite a performance of their own before posing for pictures with visitors. Don't miss Gulf World's other star attractions — penguins, alligators, ducks and tropical fish of every description. It's open rain or shine between February 1 and October 31 and for a few days around Thanksgiving and Christmas. Gates are open from 9 AM until 3 PM. To see all of the shows and attractions here, you should allow about two hours. Admission prices are $13.95 plus tax for adults, $7.95 for children 5 to 12 , and free for 4 and younger.

*EMERALD FALLS FAMILY ENTERTAINMENT CENTER

8602 Thomas Dr. at Joan Ave.
Panama City Beach   234-1049

You'll never hear the kids complain that there's nothing to do on the beach when they can spend a day at Emerald Falls. With four go-cart tracks, there's almost no waiting. Bumper boats are for everyone in the family — even the tiniest

tots get excited about getting splashed . . . and splashing back! The two 18-hole mini-golf courses wind through mysterious caverns, over bridges and past thundering waterfalls. If you get caught in one of the frequent summer showers here, don't worry; they rarely last long, and, hey, the kids can head to the arcade to play more than 40 games, and parents can get some well-deserved down time over ice cream or cool drinks.

Kid's Kingdom is an extravaganza for your little curtain climbers. Rides like the Red Baron Airplane Ride, the Spinning Top or the Rio Grande Express are low-key and high-flying pint-sized fun. Emerald Falls is open every day from 10 AM until around midnight. Ticket prices range from $2.25 for kiddie rides to $4.50 for adults; all rides require just one ticket.

*MIRACLE STRIP AMUSEMENT PARK

12000 Front Beach Rd.
Panama City Beach   234-5810

This is the biggie . . . the one that's been here more than 30 years and is still one of the area's best family attractions. Be sure you don't try the 2,000-foot roller coaster on a full stomach! The same goes

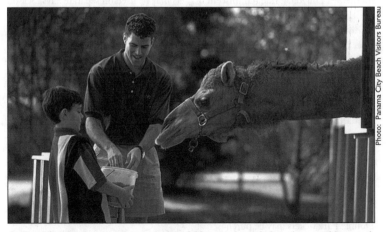

At Zoo World, you can meet more than 350 animals, including this amiable camel.

The Big Venture in Tiny Vernon

Charles and Glenda Camp took over a ranch from W.D. Whitehurst not too long ago, but this is not your typical ranch — they raise ostriches. Go

ahead and snicker if you want, but these big birds bring in big money. A good breeding pair is worth more than $50,000! The Camps have about 86 birds on their ranch, with new ones hatching every year. They also board birds for other residents in the area.

Glenda Camp says these ostriches get mighty big — sometimes as tall as nine feet — and they're not dirty or smelly "except maybe after a rain."

Most folks get into the bird biz as an investment. Bird pairs three to six months old go for about $7,000. The Camps started their ranch with six ostriches. Once a hens lay an egg, the Camps whisk it away to the warm and secure incubator. They claim that ostriches will lay eggs for 30 to 40 years and can live to be 60 or 70 years of age.

Photo: Grand Oaks Ostrich Ranch

Visitors flock to see these big birds at the Grand Oaks Ostrich Ranch in Vernon.

for the Sea Dragon, a ride reminiscent of a Viking ship rocking on the "waves" up to 70 feet in the air! With more than 30 rides in all, an all-new arcade and favorite kid foods such as Domino's Pizza, TCBY Yogurt and funnel cakes right here in the park, you may not see the kids until the vacation's over! But of course, you'll probably be right there with them chowing down on greasy, sticky foods and indulging your childlike tendencies with a corn dog and three trips on the Ferris wheel. Shipwreck Island Water Park is operated by the same folks that run Miracle Strip, so they offer a special deal: Double Park tickets may be purchased at either park for $27 per person. The tick-

ets may be used on separate days. Season passes are also available. Miracle Strip Amusement Park is closed all winter and reopens in late spring (too late for those Spring Breakers!) on Fridays from 6 to 11 PM and Saturdays from 1 to 11 PM. It's open daily during the summer season. Prices are $17 for those folks 50 inches tall and taller; $15 for anyone shorter than 50 inches.

*SHIPWRECK ISLAND WATER PARK
12000 Front Beach Rd.
Panama City Beach   234-0368

Shipwreck Island is the largest water park within 300 miles and has become something of a landmark with its giant sunken wreck as the park's centerpiece. Around that, splash, squirt, shoot and squeal on six acres of waterlogged madness! Fly down the Speed Slide at 35 miles per hour, ride the waves in the Wave Pool, shoot down the Rapid River's cascades or cruise along the Lazy River in a giant inner tube. Grab a rope and swing off the ship's bow into the pool or jump the waves in Ocean Motion, recreating the wave action in the Gulf. The Tadpole Hole is, you guessed it, for the preswim set, as are the Elephant Slide and the Kid Car Wash, but any age will find enough ways to get wet and make the trip worth their while.

Closed during the winter months, the park reopens in late spring on weekends between 10:30 AM and 5 PM. It's open daily in the summer months. Tickets are $17 for visitors 50 inches and taller; shorter than that, it's $15; ages 2 and younger are free. Seniors get in for just $5. A pass to both Shipwreck Island and Miracle Strip Amusement Park is $27.

*ZooWorld
9008 Front Beach Rd.
Panama City Beach 230-0096

Years ago, the place where ZooWorld now stands was a kind of funky, tacky, old Florida attraction, but you couldn't beat the name: The Snake-A-Torium. Thank goodness a local veterinarian took it over, cleaned it up and turned it into one of the area's nicest family attractions. Panama City Beach can be proud of this effort, a real first-class operation with more than 350 animals including orangutans, alligators and camels. A Petting Zoo with chickies and lambies and horsies will delight any preschooler. And the 250 different species of flora in the Botanical Gardens are lush, gorgeous and unusual at any time of year. A few of the former

occupant's slinky reptilians may still be around, but the glitzy snake charmers and snake wrestlers were packed off to South Florida long ago. ZooWorld stays open all year from 9 AM until dusk, longer in the summer. Adults get in for $8.95; kids younger than 11 for $6.50, and kiddies 3 or younger get in free.

*PIRATE's ISLAND ADVENTURE GOLF
9518 W. Hwy. 98
Panama City Beach 235-1171

Well, go ahead and swash your buckles or whatever it takes to set out on the path to high adventure! Pirate's Island is one of several mini-golf courses along the beach, so the more lavish, the better. Look for the tilted mast sticking out of the water and the overall nautical theme of these two 18-hole courses. You'll encounter Captain Kidd's Original Adventure (a par 42 course) and Blackbeard's Challenge (par 52) with a maze of caves, waterfalls, lagoons and islands. Mini-golf takes no particular skill to play, so even if you've never swung a club before, you'll thoroughly enjoy the challenge. Children as young as 3 can play with a small fry club of their own.

Admission to the Blackbeard's Challenge course is $6; Captain Kidd's Original Adventure costs $5. If you want to play both courses, it's $8 for all day. Kids 5 and younger play free. Pirate's Island is open all year, usually from 9 AM until 11 PM; midnight on the weekends. During the winter, hours are 10 AM to 10 PM.

*OCEAN OPRY
8400 Front Beach Rd.
Panama City Beach 234-5464

No need to pack the kiddies off to the hotel after dark, the Ocean Opry provides good-time, clean family entertainment just about every night. It's knee-slappin', hand-clappin', lighthearted, down-home fun featuring the best (or worst) of the South, depending on your point of view. You'll enjoy comedy bits, gospel, country and plenty of sing-a-longs that get everyone in on the show. There's no tellin' what kind of show you'll see, but the Rader family promises favorite tunes, color and spectacle, a little humor and smiles all around. Reservations are recommended for these popular shows but are not necessary. Most shows are $14.95 for adults; $13.95 for seniors; $7.50 for children. It's open every night except Sunday at 8 PM during the summer months; open at 7:30 PM at other times. The ticket office opens at 9 AM daily.

*MUSEUM OF MAN IN THE SEA
17314 Back Beach Rd.
Panama City Beach   235-4101

Here's a fascinating look back at man's final frontier. Exhibits cover topics such as the first diving bell (1690), sponge divers of the 19th century, Florida's many shipwrecks and rare diving equipment such as inflated animal skins and breathing tubes. Outside, take a look at some of the unusual vessels used by the Navy and others to learn more about life under the sea. A favorite part of the museum is the video on Mel Fisher's successful attempt, after 20 years and many tragedies, to recover the tremendous wealth from the Spanish galleon *Atocha*. Admission is $4 for adults, $2 for children 6 to 16; there's a 10-percent discount for seniors. It's open every day from 9 AM until 5 PM.

*GRAND OAKS OSTRICH RANCH
Hwy. 79, Vernon   535-2101

The Camps own this 96-acre ostrich ranch out in the sticks north of Panama City (see sidebar). They'll be happy to have you visit, personally show you around, offer some good investment advice and provide you with literature on the big birds to take home. To get to Vernon from Panama City, go north on Highway 77 to Highway 279 at Greenhead; turn left; Highway 279 dead-ends at Highway 79; turn right and go north 2 miles from the caution light. Look for the Grand Oaks Ranch sign, the huge house and the giant oaks that are more than 400 years old. There's no admission, but the Camps request that you please call ahead.

*BAY COUNTY JUNIOR MUSEUM
1731 Jenks Ave., Panama City   769-6128

Just a short drive from the beach is a place where kids can feel, hear, see and participate in science, art and nature. They'll have so much fun they'll never realize they're actually learning! Exhibits, puppet shows, classes and traveling displays are geared toward young scientists. Explore a life-size tepee or a hardwood swamp, or feed chickens and ducks in an authentic pioneer village. Admission is $4 for adults; $2.50 for children 2 through 12; children younger than 2 are free. The museum is open Tuesday through Friday from 9 AM to 4:30 PM and Saturdays from 10 AM to 4 PM.

*COCONUT CREEK
MINI-GOLF AND GRAN-MAZE
9807 Front Beach Rd.
Panama City Beach   234-2625

Although playing one of the two 18-hole mini-golf courses is great family fun, Coconut Creek's real lure is its giant-size human maze, the Gran-Maze, which spans the length of a football field to give you plenty of opportunities to lose yourself. Get a time card, then time yourself, stopping at four check points along the way to get your card stamped.

One round of golf for one person costs $6; it's $5 for a ticket to the bumper boats, $9 for the bumper boats and the maze; a combination of golf and bumper boats is $9; tickets for the maze and a game of golf are $10. Kids 5 and younger are free. Coconut Creek is open 9 AM to 11 PM every day.

Panama City Beach Area
Annual Events and Festivals

If you want to know where the action is in the Panama City Beach area, all you need to do is look at a map. There almost seems to be more water than land — water for boating, water for building a home near, water for surfing and swimming and, most of all, for fishing. There's the occasional festival or parade or fishing tournament, but mostly Panama City Beach is about recreation, doing your own thing for as long as you're here. The events listed below occur annually, but there are a number of other events, such as concerts in McKenzie Park, lectures on marine life at the community college and theatrical performances you might also enjoy. To find out more, call the Panama City Beach Convention & Visitors Bureau at 223-6503 or (800) PC BEACH.

March

SPRING BREAK
Panama City Beach   (800) PC BEACH

Maybe you don't think this should be listed as a special event, but we'll bet there are thousands of college students who would heartily disagree. They look forward to their week in the sun like no other — and Panama City Beach is the quickest Florida beach to get to from most points north. It's just sand, surf, sun and suds for

throngs that clog the hotels and T-shirt shops for about a month and a half each spring. MTV (Music Television) calls Panama City Beach "Spring Break Central," and shows up at various places around the beach to broadcast live. To be sure everybody has a safe and enjoyable time, you must be 21 to purchase or consume alcohol. Now get out there and have fun!

April

SPRING FESTIVAL OF THE ARTS
McKenzie Park, Panama City   747-0102

The Junior Women's Club sponsors this yearly spring fling, inviting artists in a variety of media to apply for a space in this juried show. The Spring Festival is primarily a fine arts festival, so you won't find the usual band of peddlers and home-made crafts. Look for watercolors, acrylics, ceramics, photography and many more original works on display and for sale. About $4,000 in prize money is awarded to artists in various categories. As many as 30,000 people come through to browse and buy during the two weekends of the show.

May

GULF COAST TRIATHLON
Various locations around Panama City Beach
234-6575

More than 800 professional and amateur athletes from the United States and several other countries compete for trophies, the Ironman World Championship qualification and way more than $30,000 in cold cash. Now before you sign up, here's what's expected of you: Begin with a 1.2-mile swim in the gulf (fortunately all warmed up by this time of year), a 56-mile bicycle course around St. Andrew and North bays and a 13.2-mile run around Panama City Beach. Still sound fun? Well, it certainly is fun to watch.

June

ANCHORAGE LADIES
BILLFISH TOURNAMENT

Bay Point Marina, 100 Delwood Beach Rd.
Panama City Beach   769-8321

Can female anglers be lured into competing in their own tournament without the temptation of big bucks? What if the top prize were a fishing trip for two — to Venezuela? That seems to do the trick, and more than 30 boats (with an average of four anglers each) are expected for the fifth annual tourney in 1995. Besides the big trip, second- and third-place winners receive exquisite pieces of jewelry or crystal. The contenders: blue marlin, white marlin, tuna, sailfish, dolphin and wahoo. Junior anglers have their own division with prizes too.

July

BAY POINT INVITATIONAL
BILLFISH TOURNAMENT

Bay Point Marina, 100 Delwood Beach Rd.
Panama City Beach   235-6911

The first 70 boats to enter the tournament at the stiff $5,000 entry fee vie for $300,000 in cash prizes. Not a bad deal. Nightly weigh-ins draw 10,000 spectators. For noncompetitors, there's plenty to do

on shore; barbecues and live entertainment take place Thursday through Sunday evenings.

TURTLE WATCH

St. Andrews State Recreation Area
Panama City Beach   233-5140

This watchdog volunteer group monitors nesting loggerhead sea turtles from July through August. The tiny newborns are subject to predators, vandals and a host of other dangers. Anyone spotting a nest or an egg-laying female is encouraged to report it to one of the park rangers immediately so protective measures can be taken.

SHARK TOURNAMENT

Half Hitch Tackle Co., 2206 Thomas Dr.
Panama City Beach   234-2621

You may possibly be aware that there are sharks in our beautiful gulf waters, and here's a safe way to see them up close! This individual tournament breaks shark catches into two divisions: pier fishing and boat fishing. Besides the daily prizes, there's a $3,000 savings bond for the person bringing in the largest shark overall, and a first-, second-, and third-place prize in each division. We're not talking Great White here. Five species are in the running, including tiger, bull, dusky, sandbar and those really strange looking hammerhead sharks. Between 100 and 125 anglers compete each year.

August

PANAMA CITY BEACH FISHING CLASSIC

Half Hitch Tackle Co., 2206 Thomas Dr.
Panama City Beach   769-2536

Local tackle shop owners, charter boat captains and restaurateurs are also savvy business people and sponsor this six-week event so they can sell more stuff. Great for them, great for anglers, great for you as a spectator. Competitors try their luck on private boats, on the jetties, in the surf and from the pier to snag a King mackerel, Spanish mackerel, barracuda, marlin, flounder or cobia (19 species in all) that will net them $10,000. And if that's not enough incentive, somebody could hook a mystery tagged fish and win — get this — $1 million! They've got plenty of time to try, since the tournament lasts for 47 days.

September

BEACH AND SHORE CLEAN-UP

St. Andrews State Recreation Area
Panama City Beach   233-5140

Dedicated volunteers arrive at various coastal locations throughout Northwest Florida to pick up trash and learn more about the preservation of our delicate coastal environment. It may not sound like much fun, but it really can be. The park rangers keep track of how many bags of trash are collected and from where, the most unusual items collected, etc. The media almost always show up to talk with volunteers and park rangers, and a very upbeat, positive atmosphere prevails. It's a great way for children to learn about ecology and how to preserve our most precious natural resource.

SHELL ISLAND STEAKS AT SUNSET

St. Andrews State Recreation Area
Panama City Beach   233-5140

What more fun and fascinating way to learn about natural Northwest Florida than a yacht cruise to a barrier island?! This is an annual fund-raiser the park staff and its volunteers put on each year. Board a private yacht at the park for the scenic half-hour trip over to Shell Island, where one of the park rangers fills you in

on a little history and area lore. Next is an outdoor cookout as you watch a colorful Florida sunset accompanied by live music. Space is limited, and reservations are necessary. Tickets are $27.50 per person.

TREASURE ISLAND KING

Mackerel Tournament
Treasure Island Marina, 3605 Thomas Dr.
Panama City Beach   234-6533

Always held the last full weekend in September, this tournament awards $10,000 in cash prizes. First place, for largest king mackerel overall, nets $4,000; second place, $2,000, and $1000 for third. The winnings are split between two divisions, both private and charter boats. Even with the $150 entry fee, the tourney usually gets about 100 boats participating. On Friday, join the captains and crews for a kickoff party at the marina. Sunday, there's a fish fry to cook up all of that good fresh fish caught by all of those boats! That's open to the public, as are the nightly public weigh-ins.

October

INDIAN SUMMER SEAFOOD FESTIVAL

Aaron Z. Bessant Park, across from the Dan
Russell City Pier   234-6575
Panama City Beach   (800) FAST-FLA

We're not sure the Gulf Coast ever really experiences an Indian summer like up north, but it's an absolutely perfect time of year to be here. Tourist traffic has thinned considerably (the kids are back in school), the days are warm and sunny, and the gulf — well, the gulf just couldn't be prettier or clearer. So bring along a few of your friends to munch on scrumptious delights such as grilled shark, broiled shrimp, Apalachicola oysters on the half-shell (yep, they're raw), seafood gumbo and fried mullet (a Southern favorite). Of course you need something else to keep you there besides just eating your way through the weekend. The festival coordinators comply in abundance with more than 100 arts and crafts booths, a sky diving exhibition, a parade, fireworks and great, continuous live entertainment. Advance three-day tickets are $13 ($15 at the gate); daily tickets are $5, with children younger than 12 admitted free.

BAY COUNTY FAIR

Bay County Fairgrounds, 15th St. at Sherman Ave. Panama City   769-2645

This six-day fair may be more like the fairs of your childhood than the star-studded, thrill-a-minute fairs now common in most larger cities. Several midway rides are set up to entertain kids and teens; there are lots of candy apples and popcorn and cotton candy, but the main attraction is still the exhibits, which are spread out in several buildings around the grounds. You guessed it — prize roses and pies, girl and boy scout displays, raffles for TVs and the big cattle show in the fair arena. Fairs are still big business — more than 40,000 folks attended in 1994.

"BLAST TO THE PAST" CLASSIC CAR SHOW

Holiday Inn Beach Resort/Shoppes at Edgewater Panama City Beach   234-6575

How old does your car have to be to be considered a classic? Some cars from the 1970s have snuck in here, but perhaps that has more to do with style than

age. More than 200 classic and antique cars will be on display from 9 AM until 5 PM at the two locations listed previously. Do you like those "muscle cars" from the '60s? Hot rods from the '50s? It's a festival of fins and flames (the painted-on kind), spoilers and sheepskin-covered steering wheels, mag wheels and fuzzy dice. On Saturday night, there's a benefit concert with some well-known "flashback" band at the Ramada Inn Beach Convention Center.

November

BOAT PARADE OF LIGHTS

St. Andrew Bay between Panama City and Panama City Beach   785-2554

It's the one time of the year to really let your lights shine — the lights on your boats, that is! The parade of gaily decorated fishing boats, yachts and charters winds its way along St. Andrew Bay with waving, cheering spectators on both the city and the beach shores. The parade is sponsored by local marinas.

December

CHRISTMAS PARADES

Panama City and Panama City Beach 234-3193

These parades are a wonderful complement to all of the Christmas festivities in town and on the beach, guaranteed to make you feel all warm and mushy inside. Sometimes it's hard to get

---

Want the latest on Panama City's restaurants, clubs and other hot spots? Tune in to Beach TV on cable channel 5 or 7 — it's Panama City's visitor information station.

Insiders' Tips

into the spirit when it's 70-plus degrees, there's no snow and you're wearing shorts. But most of the locals have been doing it for years, so the absence of bad weather doesn't concern them much. You'll see hordes of little ones lining the streets with shopping bags, knapsacks, and grocery bags, you may wonder why. It's to catch all of those great parade throws! It doesn't matter what is being thrown, the fun is in the acquiring. Watch out for strings of colorful beads, plastic cups and hard candy, especially when it hits you on the head! Prized possessions are Moon Pies — those foil-wrapped chocolate-coated food products with marshmallow middles. Get into the holiday spirit with marching bands, dance classes, Brownies, floats and, as the grand finale — Santa Claus!

Panama City Beach Area
Parks and Recreation

Perhaps no other area in Northwest Florida is as full of the party spirit as Panama City Beach, whose emphasis is on beach recreation. Fishing, volleyball, outdoor concerts and nature trails through the Florida wilderness accent the temperate climate, warm gulf waters and sun-filled, fun-filled days and nights.

Golf

BAY DUNES GOLF COURSE
5304 Majette Tower Blvd.
Panama City 872-1667
This golf course has operated under several names since its establishment eight years ago — including Majette and Phoenix Golf Course — but right now it's Bay Dunes Gold Course. This is a semiprivate city par 71 course featuring 18 holes, a lighted driving range and a putting green. It's a fairly open course, not too tight, and offers the perfect challenge for average players. Ask about the seasonal visitor rates.

BAY POINT YACHT & COUNTRY CLUB
100 Delwood Beach Rd.
Panama City Beach 234-3307
One of Bay Point's two courses was rated one of North America's top golf resorts by *Golf Illustrated* magazine in 1990 and remains scenic and challenging today. The two semiprivate 18-hole,

As these happy golfers can attest, sunbathing and swimming aren't the only activities available on Panama City Beach.

Photo: Panama City Beach Visitors Bureau

par 72 courses are aptly named Club Meadows and Lagoon Legend, which characterize the terrain. Club Meadows is a kinder, gentler course and an all-time Florida favorite. With a slope rating of 152 and water on 16 of 18 holes, Lagoon Legend received a USGA rating as the second most challenging course in America by *Golf Digest* magazine in 1990. Ask about special rates for visitors.

HOLIDAY GOLF & TENNIS CLUB
100 Fairway Blvd. on Back Beach Hwy. 98
Panama City 234-1800

The 18-hole, semiprivate course is one of the area's oldest (1964), but recent renovations keep it on par with many "just built" courses. You may find it to be one of the most enjoyable courses you've ever played, with its bunkers of pure white sand. Tee times up to five days in advance may be required. The par 72 course features a lighted driving range, clubhouse and pro shop.

HOMBRE GOLF CLUB
120 Coyote Pass
Panama City Beach 234-3673

With some of the best scenery Northwest Florida has to offer, this semiprivate, par 73 championship course is adorned with lakes, dogwoods and azaleas, with 15 of 18 holes bringing water into play. Besides its Florida-style clubhouse, Hombre has its own pro shop, lounge, driving range and golf instructors. Hole No. 2 will tend to stick with you; it's one tough Hombre.

SIGNAL HILL GOLF COURSE
9615 N. Thomas Dr.
Panama City Beach 234-3218

This 18-hole, par 72 course is open to the public, and that means it's first come, first served. Tee times are required. The golf shop rents clubs and offers a snack bar.

SUNNY HILLS GOLF COURSE
1150 Country Club Blvd.
Panama City 773-3619

Not much water, but the sand traps make up for it! Sunny Hills' 18 holes are open to the public. The course is located on Highway 77 between I-10 and Highway 20.

PELICAN POINT GOLF COURSE
On St. Andrew Bay at
Tyndall Air Force Base 283-2565

This is a semiprivate, 18-hole, par 72 course with mature trees and sweeping bay views all around. Pelican Point sponsors more than 30 tournaments each year.

Golf Shops

FLORIDA GOLF OUTLET
Hwy. 98 (Back Beach Rd.) across from
Holiday Golf Course
Panama City Beach 235-0391

Get 'em while they last — more than 1,000 pairs of golf shoes for men and women, custom clubs, 1,000 shirts and other sportswear, all at up to 60 percent off retail! There's one-day service on custom clubs and regripping service while you wait.

GOLF DISCOUNT CENTER
501 Hwy. 231, Panama City 769-4745

Let the Golf Discount Center put more than two decades of experience to work to improve your game. All types of equipment, top name brands, apparel and accessories will not only make you play better but look better too (and, after all, appearance is everything). If you need club repair, Steve offers prompt and professional service. You'll find them just 1 mile west of Panama City Mall.

BAY GOLF CLINIC
2521-A Thomas Dr.
Panama City Beach   *235-0927*

The doctor is in for sick and injured golf clubs. Regripping service is offered while you wait in addition to any type of club repair. Custom clubs can be made to fit your swing. Bay also offers new and used clubs for sale. The clinic is located at the entrance to Bay Point Country Club.

Watersport/Beach Rentals

SCOTTYBOAT RENTALS INC.
5611 W. Hwy. 98 at the foot of the Hathaway Bridge
Panama City Beach   *872-1714*

Do your own cruise, make your own fun with a pontoon boat (up to 15 people) or a small five-person runabout. The friendly staff will show you the ropes before you head out to fish, picnic, snorkel or dive. Call early to reserve your boat. Scottyboat Rentals is located behind the

Ashley Gorman Shell Island Cruise. Boat rental rates are $70 for three hours with 12 gallons' of fuel; four hours, $85; five hours, $99; and all day is $145. Fuel is included with the pontoon boat rental; you pay for the fuel you use with the runabout.

GREAT ADVENTURE WATER SPORTS
6426 W. Hwy. 98
Panama City Beach   *234-0830*

Great Adventure is your parasailing headquarters, if you're brave enough to try this sport. Parasailing combines the fun of waterskiing with the thrill of skydiving, where a boat actually pulls you along on water skis until you become aloft! Enjoy fabulous beach views only seen by airplane banner pilots! If you've had either water skiing or skydiving experience previously, then you'll most likely be a natural for parasailing. For newcomers, though, it can be a little tricky. Great Adventures also rents Waverunners and pontoon

Photo: Panama City Beach Visitors Bureau

The pristine white beaches of St. Andrews State Park are perfect for beachcombing, fishing and sunbathing.

boats. They're located beachside of the Hathaway Bridge, behind Hathaway's Landing Bar & Grill.

ISLAND WAVERUNNER
TOURS & LAGOON RENTALS

Next door to the Sea Screamer or behind Hamilton's on Thomas Dr.
Panama City Beach 234-SAIL

There isn't a sail in sight at this rental place, but maybe they just like the phone number. Rent a Waverunner (same as a jet ski, which is like a motorcycle on water) and take the 20-mile trip around Shell Island. The "tour" consists of a bunch of these machines going to the island en masse, then all stopping to play and comb the remote beaches for shells or to do whatever people do on a remote island. If it's your first time renting a Waverunner, maybe the calmer one-hour tour is in order, or just take the Waverunner anywhere you like around Grand Lagoon. The two-hour trip costs $69; bring an extra person for $10 more (Waverunners fit two people comfortably). One-hour trips are $49.

JIMBO'S BEACH SERVICE

145 Christopher Dr. just before City Hall
Panama City Beach 234-2122

Rent all your basic beach equipment here, like beach umbrellas and lounge chairs. Jimbo's also has Waverunners, torpedo tube rides, jet skis, sailboats and parasails, plus trips to Shell Island, dolphin feeding excursions and snorkeling and fishing trips.

Dive Shops

EMERALD COAST DIVER'S DEN

Panama City Marina on the water
Panama City 769-6621
On the east side at Tyndall Pkwy.
Parker 871-2876

Dive charters go out to many wreck sites in the bays. Emerald Coast Diver's Den also sells a full line of dive equipment. Air, rentals, service and instruction are offered.

PANAMA CITY DIVE CENTER

4823 Thomas Dr. on the curve
Panama City Beach 235-3390

Diving and snorkeling equipment is for sale or rent. This center also offers daily dive charters. Get your beginning instruction in one-week sessions. Even if you're not certified, you can take a half-day diving excursion with a certified diving instructor just to see if you like it or a snorkeling trip for which no particular skill is required (except maybe holding your breath!). For those who are already certified, PCDC offers daily dolphin excursions and four- and six-hour scuba trips.

HYDROSPACE DIVE SHOP

3605-A Thomas Dr. next to
the Treasure Ship 234-9463
6422 W. Hwy. 98
by the Hathaway Bridge 234-3063
Panama City Beach (800)874-3483

With a full range of diving and snorkeling equipment and services, Hydrospace is one of the Gulf Coast's largest dive operations. Especially for visitors, there's a half-day resort scuba course so you can experience what diving is like without having to go through certification. Daily snorkeling trips to the jetties are fun for everybody. Of course, the Hydrospace crew offers open water scuba classes and home study courses for those who want to experience the joy and excitement of diving.

CAPTAIN BLACK'S

Inside St. Andrews State Park
Panama City Beach 233-0504

This is a fairly new facility where

Photo: Panama City Beach Visitors Bureau

The Gulf waters off Panama City Beach offer some of the best saltwater fishing in the world.

divers and snorkelers can rent gear and take courses. The four-hour resort course is offered here, too, as well as more specialized courses for certification. Night dives are a specialty. Ask about Shell Island snorks trips, too.

Charter Fishing/ Sightseeing Cruises

CAPT. ANDERSON'S PIER
5550 N. Lagoon Dr.
Panama City   234-3435, (800) 874-2415

The Anderson fleet may be the originator of the charter fishing craze, but don't hold us to that. What we can say about them is that they've been in business a very long time and have the charter boat business down to a science. Start with charters for deep sea fishing, offering three trips on six vessels, accommodating up to 68 passengers. If you're a seasoned angler, you might opt for the 12-hour for $45 (manual reel). Riders are $20 and kids younger than 12 who want to fish are $12. Half-day trips are $27, with riders just $12. All boats are fully equipped with gear and bait, drinks

and restrooms. Not all trips are available all year, so please call to inquire about a particular trip.

Next, spend a night out on the *Capt. Anderson* dinnerboat. It's a three-hour inland cruise on St. Andrew Bay while you enjoy the scenery, the sunset, your choice of five dinner entrees and a three-piece band for dancing. The triple-decker boat provides plenty of room to move around if you want to bring the kids, but it may be your only opportunity for a little private romancing. Cruises run from $16.95 for kids during the week and $20 on Saturdays; adults are $18.95 during the week and $22.50 on Saturdays. All prices include taxes and tip. Call 234-5940 for reservations.

Take a cruise to undeveloped Shell Island, where you'll disembark for a brief time to wade in the clear water and look for shell souvenirs. Aboard the boat, your captain narrates a bit of history and humor about the area, while you keep a sharp eye out for dolphins, seabirds and marine life. Sandwiches and snacks are all available on board. Adult tickets are $9; children 6 to 11 are $5; ages 2 to 5 are $4. A separate Dolphin Feeding Cruise is $6 for adults and $4 for children.

BAY POINT'S ISLAND QUEEN
On the boardwalk at Marriott's Bay Point Resort
100 Delwood Beach Rd.
Panama City Beach   234-3307 ext. 1816

Take a calm and scenic Mississippi Riverboat ride out on St. Andrew Bay on this magnificent paddlewheeler. Shell Island Shuttles usually depart at 9 AM and 1 PM for a three-hour trip to this unique barrier island. Snacks, drinks and sandwiches are available to passengers, or you can bring your own picnic. Tickets are normally $10, $5 for kids 5 to 12 and $2 for children 4 and younger. Pick up a *See Panama City* booklet at most any convenience store for a 50 percent discount. A dinner cruise leaves the dock around 7:30 every evening for a Southern-style feast of Cajun seafood, fresh salads, pastas, cheeses and some kind of Old South dessert such as plantation coconut pecan cake, strawberry bread pudding with whiskey sauce or pecan pie. Cocktails are available throughout the cruise, as is live entertainment topside. Cost is $24.95 per passenger, which is all-inclusive, except for cocktails. Tickets are available at Teddy Tuckers Gift Shop behind the Marriott.

ADVENTURE SAILING CRUISES
Treasure Island Marina, 3605 Thomas Dr.
Panama City Beach   233-5499, 832-1454

Look at Slip No. 40 at the marina for *Glory Days*, a 51-foot ocean sailing yacht that will take you out into the gulf by the hour (there's a 2-hour minimum), half day, full day, weekend, week or more. The yacht is equipped with three private cabins, a 15-foot-wide main salon, seven feet of headroom, three TVs, a stereo and

VCR, an icemaker, a freezer, a fridge, two dinghies for exploring and a Coast Guard-licensed captain. Prices start at $20 per person plus tax for a two-hour cruise.

Parks

BAY MEMORIAL PARK
Garden Club Dr., Panama City

For those who like to keep in shape, this 13-acre nature park has a walking trail and 13 fitness stations.

FRANK NELSON, JR. PARK
23rd St. and Mound Ave., Panama City

Eleven acres of park feature a playground, a community building and three ball fields.

TRUESDELL PARK
10th St. and Chestnut Ave., Panama City

Truesdell is a small park with a small playground, two tennis courts and a community building for square dancing and community activities.

GLENWOOD RECREATION CENTER
14th Court and Palo Alto Ave., Panama City

The rec center has something for everybody with a playground area, basketball courts and a community building on two acres.

DAFFIN PARK
Everitt and Draft Aves. at Third St., Panama City

Ball fields, a playground, community building and tennis courts are just part of this 12-acre park.

BOB GEORGE PARK
East Ave. and First Plaza, Panama City

One of the city's neighborhood parks, this one sports a playground area and picnic shelters.

McKenzie Park

Oak Ave. and Park St., Panama City

This shady and scenic nature park in the heart of downtown features a succession of outdoor concerts during tourist season (March through October).

Oakland Terrace Park

11th St. and Flower Ave., Panama City

One of the largest city parks, Oakland Terrace has ball fields, a playground area, six tennis courts, a picnic area and a community building.

Joe Moody Harris Park

2300 E. Eighth Ct., Panama City

One of the most popular city parks, Joe Moody features a community building, picnic shelters, a large playground area and a nature trail.

Hathaway Bridge Park

Collegiate Dr. and Hwy. 98, Panama City

The one-acre park near the bridge on the water has good fishing and natural areas. Gulf Coast Community College and the Panama City Branch of Florida State University are adjacent.

Hentz Park

19th St. and Wilmont Ave., Panama City

Some parts of Hentz Park are left wild for your exploration; others provide playground equipment and picnic areas.

Lake Huntington Park

3504 W. 15th St., Panama City

This is a small park on three-quarters of an acre with a clubhouse fronting Lake Huntington.

Frank G. Brown Park

On Back Beach Rd., ¼ mile east of Hwy. 79, Panama City Beach

This extensive public beach park features a community center with an indoor gym, a picnic area and pavilion with grills and a fireplace, a softball complex, lighted tennis courts, a playground and a fitness trail.

Panama City Beach Area
Arts and Culture

Panama City is gaining a reputation as an artists' community, thanks in part to the Bay Arts Alliance, the city's umbrella arts agency, which incorporates visual arts, music, dance and theater groups. The Alliance is responsible for bringing in nationally known performing groups and arts events, opening up a world of experiences to locals without having to leave the area. Made up of more than 500 individual supporters, the Bay Arts Alliance serves to enhance the area's cultural upbringing by lending educational and financial support to talented area groups and individuals.

Literary

NORTHWEST REGIONAL LIBRARY SYSTEM HEADQUARTERS, BAY COUNTY PUBLIC LIBRARY
25 W. Government St.
Panama City   872-7500
The network of community libraries in the Bay County area works to promote community support through library materials and services. Other branches are on Panama City Beach, 110 S. Arnold Road, and in Springfield, 408 School Avenue.

THE PANHANDLE WRITERS' GUILD
231 Harrison Ave.
Panama City   763-2022
This group provides instruction and development of the writing craft. They publish an annual literary magazine, *Pelican Tracks*, and offer workshops and lectures on literature and writing to the community. The Guild meets at the address listed previously on the second and fourth Tuesdays of the month.

Music

BARBERSHOP HARMONY CHORUS
4630 Cato Rd.
Panama City   763-3200
Barbershop is one of the last vestiges of a cappella singing, and these gentlemen preserve it with a vengeance, performing anywhere they can and entering numerous competitions.

BAY ARTS STRING QUARTET
2508 Country Club Dr.
Lynn Haven   265-4937
The quartet, consisting of a violin, viola, cello and bass, performs at group functions, receptions and weddings.

BAY WIND BAND
1603 Maine Ave.
Lynn Haven   265-9028
This 50-piece community band plays at festivals, community events and as part of a performing arts series in the Panama City area. It is open to all comers and performs between six and eight concerts

"Desire"   30 x 40   Mary M. DeSieno
represented by

Lyn's Fine Art Gallery
(904) 785-6622
537 Harrison Avenue • Panama City, Florida 32401
Original Graphics, Watercolours & Oils; Posters & Prints
Featuring International, Regional & Local Artists
Pottery Artglass Gifts

Mon.-Fri. 11 a.m. - 5 p.m.   Sat. 10 a.m. - 2 p.m.

every year including a 4th of July concert at the Civic Arena, concerts at Tyndall Air Force Base and at the Automotive Extravaganza in McKenzie Park. The band rehearses at Mowat Middle School twice monthly on Thursdays.

HARMONY SHORES CHORUS OF SWEET ADELINES INTERNATIONAL
4035 Torino Way
Panama City   265-8402

This barbershop-type group exists solely to educate and entertain. The group performs publicly and will even do private parties or sing greetings for birthdays and anniversaries.

PANAMA BRASS QUINTET
343 N. Star Ave.
Panama City   871-1767

This rather loose-knit group, consist-

ing of two band directors, one FSU student musician, one mathematician and one firefighter, mostly plays for its own gratification. Jazz, ragtime, Bach and wedding music make up this group's repertoire.

PANAMA CITY YOUTH ORCHESTRA
329 Alexander Dr.
Lynn Haven   265-3834, 872-4570

Here's a chance for all budding violinists, violists, cellists and bass players to get sound experience. Classes and lessons are also offered through Community Education of Bay County Schools.

POLYTACTYL JAZZ COMBO
329 Alexander Dr.
Lynn Haven   265-3834

The five piece combo performs traditional and contemporary jazz styles and pieces, plus some that haven't even been invented yet. They do parties and school programs but particularly enjoy giving demonstrations on their various instruments and letting go during improvisational sessions.

Museums

JUNIOR MUSEUM OF BAY COUNTY
1731 Jenks Ave.
Panama City   769-6128

The Junior Museum provides a terrific "hands-on" educational experience for youngsters. Kids and teens learn about the arts and sciences in creative and interactive exhibits; guided tours are available. It's especially great for ages 2 and older, but all ages can benefit.

THE MUSEUM OF MAN IN THE SEA
17314 Back Beach Rd.
Panama City Beach   235-4101

Historical exhibits, artwork, photography and graphics tell the story of how people have lived, played and worked underwater for more than 5,000 years. The extensive collection of old diving equipment and an explanation of how it was used are fascinating, even to the layperson. Admission costs $4 for adults, $2 for children 6 to 16, and kids younger than 6 are free.

Theater

KALEIDOSCOPE THEATRE
207 E. 24th St.
Lynn Haven   265-3226, 769-2653

This theater, offering live stage drama, comedy and music, has been around now for more than two decades. Audiences are larger than ever with a succession of sure hits such as *God's Favorite*, *Romeo and Juliet* and *I Hate Hamlet*. Each Decem-

ber, *A Christmas Carol* is performed at the Martin Theatre on Harrison Avenue.

MARTIN THEATRE
409 Harrison Ave.   763-8080
Panama City   763-8900

Recently renovated by local artist/designer Paul Brent, the 1935 Martin Theatre started its life as the Ritz movie house, spent some time as the Martin Theatre in the 1950s, closed down during the '70s, then opened in the '80s as an indoor target range! Finally, in 1990, the Martin Theatre, restored to its original art deco glory, opened for live performances, children's shows, one-person traveling shows, concerts and Broadway plays.

Productions are staged by several local groups, including the School of Performing Arts, the Bay High School Drama Department, Mosley High School and the Kaleidoscope Theatre. The Greenroom, a separate annex for meetings and receptions, features art deco furnishings, lots of plants and a wall mural by local artist Charles Wilson. Tickets are available only at the Martin Theatre box office, open Monday through Friday from 9 AM to 4 PM. Season tickets are $60 and should be purchased in September. Write to the address listed previously to be put on the Martin Theatre's monthly newsletter mailing list.

Visual Arts

GALLERY IN GADSDEN
14 E. Washington St.
Quincy   875-ARTS

This gallery is an artists' cooperative of between 13 and 17 members featuring rotating displays of their own fine art as well as visual arts and crafts by other artists. Pottery, ceramics, watercolor, oils and works in other media can be purchased from the artists.

VISUAL ARTS CENTER
OF NORTHWEST FLORIDA

19 E. Fourth St.
Panama City   *769-4451*

Like the Pensacola Museum of Art, the Visual Arts Center also occupies the old City Hall and Jail. (Could it be a trend?) The Arts Center promotes local artists at the gallery as well as in the new arts "district" downtown and gets involved with the Gallery Night exhibition, a tour of downtown art shops and galleries held three times yearly (see the following entry). Admission is free to both the Arts Center and the gallery tour.

PANAMA CITY
DOWNTOWN ARTS DISTRICT

Downtown Panama City   *769-4451*

The district is a cooperative effort between the city and several downtown galleries to breathe new life into support for the arts. If you're a return visitor, you may have noticed some changes downtown — renovation of the Martin Theatre, awnings, tree plantings, carriage lamps and free concerts in McKenzie Park. The atmosphere is conducive to strolling, browsing and buying. Each of the galleries sports a bright magenta flag.

The Visual Arts Center of Northwest Florida
19 E. Fourth St.

State of the Art Gallery
537 Harrison Ave.

Under Glass Framery
28 W. Beach Dr.

Chip Lloyd's Photography
28 W. Beach Dr.

Bayou Gallery
125 E. Beach Dr.

Lyn's Fine Arts Gallery
214 Harrison Ave.

The Gallery of Art/Art Colony
36 W. Beach Dr.

Paul Brent Design Studio and Gallery
413 W. Fifth St.

BAY ARTS ALLIANCE/
MARINA CIVIC CENTER

8 Harrison Ave.   *769-1217*

Each year in April and November, these galleries team up for a gallery "tour," where they showcase their own gallery work and put on special exhibits and demonstrations for guests.

Panama City Beach Area
Retirement

Florida has long enjoyed a strong reputation as a retirement spot, and although the peninsula still attracts many retirees, people are discovering the charms of the Panhandle. Panama City's retirement rate has slowly risen over the years, and experts expect this trend to continue.

MARY ELLA VILLA RETIREMENT CENTER
526 N. Mary Ella Ave.
Calloway   *871-1611*

This facility began its life as a private, single-family dwelling, albeit a large and fancy one. Eighteen bedrooms have been added to the back of the house since Mary Ella Villa began serving the retiree population. Both private and semiprivate rooms are available (with shared baths), and all residents receive three full meals a day. Transportation for shopping and outside activities is part of the monthly fee, as is laundry service and medical supervision. One of the outstanding features of this newly remodeled facility is the private zoo featuring a llama, peacocks, turkeys, Shetland ponies, foxes, turkeys and deer. This wildlife refuge has attracted several exotic creatures over the years, and the residents love it.

Photo: Panama City Beach Visitors Bureau

More and more people are choosing Panama City as a retirement spot over other south Florida cities.

COVE MANOR RETIREMENT CENTER

521 E. Beach Dr.
Panama City   *763-3655, 784-1203*

Waterfront retirement living could be just a dream unless you're a resident of Cove Manor. Only five blocks from the Civic Center, McKenzie Park and the downtown area, Cove Manor offers a private view of St. Andrew Bay. Spacious units provide complete comfort in a cozy, relaxed setting. Residents enjoy delicious meals with each other, learn painting or pick up a new hobby with the many classes offered each month. The close proximity to the downtown area means that residents can enjoy more independence in planning their daily activities.

THE RETIREMENT CENTER OF PANAMA CITY

1313 E. 11th St.
Panama City   *785-1651*

The Retirement Center provides a more structured climate for those who may need a higher level of care. Staff members are always available for medical and personal supervision and assistance. Three balanced meals are served each day. Residents may choose from a spacious private room with its own bath or semiprivate lodging. Residents stroll the landscaped and fenced grounds, visit with friends and other residents in the living room, or catch up on their reading in the well-stocked library. The Retirement Center offers a free two-day "get acquainted" weekend for you and one guest. Call for reservations.

SUMMER'S LANDING

615 Florida Ave.
Lynn Haven   *265-9829*

This is a friendly retirement community where residents are free to come and go as they please. Independent living is the focus here, but there's always a friendly staff ready to assist you. Residents are encouraged to participate in a full range of recreational activities, and on-site visitors are most welcome. Summer's Landing offers a secure, maintenance-free environment and all the freedom needed to enjoy the golden years.

Senior Support Services

BAY COUNTY COUNCIL ON AGING

1116 Frankford Ave.
Panama City   *769-3468*

The Council on Aging provides a myriad of services for both elderly and low-income residents of Bay County. In-home services include assistance with housekeeping, assistance with hygiene, bathing and dressing and respite care to relieve caregivers. Other services include Meals on Wheels, transportation to medical appointments and socialization.

LIFE MANAGEMENT CENTER OF NORTHWEST FLORIDA, INC.

525 E. 15th St.
Panama City   *769-9481*

This center provides Senior Adult Specialization in a number of vital areas including counseling, mental health services and employee assistance. It also provides 24-hour emergency service.

Panama City Beach Area
Military

To the casual visitor, it may seem that the military keeps a low profile in Panama City. Residents know that's just not the case. Tyndall Air Force Base might not have a museum, but there are several units and squadrons assigned there. Just look to the skies, where you can see and hear pilots going about their business.

And while the Coastal Systems Station doesn't allow visitors at all, everyone who lives in Panama City knows that's because of the highly classified work conducted there.

The impact of these facilities on the local economy, however, is something everyone notices. Current estimates gauge that impact at more than half-billion dollars, a figure that's hard to ignore.

Tyndall Air Force Base

Tyndall Field, named after World War I aviator Lt. Francis B. Tyndall, was established by the Army just in time for America's entry into World War II. In fact, the first troops arrived at the newly completed Army facility on December 7, 1941, the day the Japanese attacked Pearl Harbor. Thousands of men were trained here as gunners, including actor Clark Gable.

After World War II, the Air Force became a separate branch of the armed forces, and the field's name was changed to Tyndall Air Force Base. It sits about 12 miles southeast of Panama City and currently occupies nearly 30,000 acres in Bay County. The base has an estimated annual economic impact of more than $280 million, employing more than 5,000 military personnel and nearly 2,000 civilians. More than 7,000 military retirees from all branches are also served by the base facilities.

Some of the units assigned here include the 325th Fighter Wing, whose history dates back to World War II, as well as the 325th Operation Group, the 325th Logistics Group and the 325th Support Group. Other units assigned to Tyndall Air Force Base include the 1st Air Force Headquarters, the Southeast Air Defense Sector, the North American Aerospace Defense Command System Support Facility, Detachment 1 of the 148th Fighter Group, the 475th Weapons Evaluation Group, the 84th Test Squadron and the 3625th Technical Training Squadron. Needless to say, these units and many others keep the skies around the base fairly busy.

Unlike Ft. Walton Beach's Eglin Air Force Base, Tyndall Air Force Base doesn't have a museum for the public to inspect. But there are several planes and jets parked along Highway 231 as you approach the base, and many drivers pull over to snap pictures and inspect the aircraft. There are public tours of Tyndall Air Force Base, and you can call 283-2983 for more information.

COASTAL SYSTEMS STATION

The Coastal Systems Station was established during World War II after the U.S. Navy field station in Solomons, Maryland, outgrew its Chesapeake Bay location. This field station was instrumental in mine and undersea countermeasure development, and Panama City's easy access to the Gulf of Mexico made it the most appealing candidate host for this station.

By the mid-1950s, the station's research and training mission had grown to include such naval weaponry as torpedo countermeasures, helicopter mine countermeasures and mine-hunting.

The station's mission and name have changed over the years, and currently the Coastal Systems Station conducts key research and training in fields such as surface and airborne mine countermeasures, Marine Corps systems development and support, naval special warfare, amphibious warfare and diving and salvage operations. These operations are carried out at the station's various facilities and state-of-the-art laboratories. More than 1,000 divers train here each year, and the station can confidently claim responsibility for much of the naval technology currently in the field.

The Coastal Systems Station employs more than 3,000 people, and fiscal year 1992 figures show that figure is split almost evenly among civilian and military personnel. The total economic impact of the station is estimated at more than $320 million.

Because most of the research and training conducted at the Coastal Systems Station is highly classified, no public tours are available. However, group tours for organizations closely related to the station's mission are granted. To see if your group or organization qualifies for such a tour, contact the station's public affairs office, 234-4803.

Panama City Beach Area
Community Information

Real Estate Companies

CENTURY 21 BEACH REALTY, INC.
11 Miracle Strip Loop   234-9865
Panama City Beach   (800) 225-4868

GRAND LAGOON COMPANY
2226 Thomas Dr.   234-3225
Panama City Beach   (800) 535-0887

GULF PROPERTIES OF PANAMA CITY
8101 Thomas Dr.
Panama City Beach   234-1122

RESORT WORLD REALTY
6104 Thomas Dr.
Panama City   234-1418, (800) 752-7111

KATHERINE RILEY REALTY, INC.
1838 Frankford Ave.
Panama City   769-1401

SAND DOLLAR
SURF 'N SAND PROPERTIES, INC.
9722 S. Thomas Dr.
Panama City Beach   235-2205

SEMINOLE REAL ESTATE SERVICES, INC.
7914 Lagoon Dr.   230-9445
Panama City Beach   (800) 230-9445

Health Care

Hospitals and Medical Centers

BAY MEDICAL CENTER
615 N. Bonita Ave.
Panama City   769-1511

HCA GULF COAST HOSPITAL
449 W. 23rd St.
Panama City   769-8341

Photo: Panama City Beach Visitors Bureau

The night comes alive with swirling neon colors along the
Miracle Strip in Panama City Beach.

Immediate Care Centers

BAY WALK-IN CLINIC
8811 Front Beach Rd.
Panama City Beach   234-8511
2306 Hwy. 77
Panama City   763-9744

SEAWIND MEDICAL CLINIC
4121 W. Hwy. 98
Panama City   872-9701

SPRINGFIELD MEDICAL CENTER
3308 E. Third St.
Panama City   785-9511

Physician Referral Services

REAL CONSUMER TIPS
747-3000

Substance Abuse/Mental Health/Geriatric Services

GULF COAST CONVALESCENT CENTER
1937 Jenks Ave.
Panama City   769-7686

MENTAL HEALTH ASSOCIATION OF BAY COUNTY
1137 Harrison Ave.
Panama City   769-5441

Higher Education

GULF COAST COMMUNITY COLLEGE
5230 W. Hwy. 98
Panama City   769-1551

FLORIDA STATE UNIVERSITY — PANAMA CITY CAMPUS
4750 Collegiate Dr.
Panama City   872-4750

HANEY VOCATIONAL-TECHNICAL CENTER
Hwy. 77
Panama City   769-2191

Photo: Apalachicola Bay Chamber of Commerce

The beaches of St. George Island are among the most beautiful in Florida and are regularly ranked among the nation's top-10 beach spots.

Inside
Florida's Forgotten Coast

Sometimes you look far and wide for something special, only to realize it's been right under your nose the whole time.

That's the story with Florida's Forgotten Coast, stretching nearly 50 miles east from Mexico Beach down to Apalachicola and on up to Carrabelle. It's unlike anywhere else in the state and sports what many call the most beautiful coastline in the nation. Miles and miles of unspoiled, pristine land beckon you, much of it carefully preserved, looking exactly as it must have appeared hundreds of years ago.

But why call something forgotten when so few have even known about it? Because despite the area's rich history and the growth seen in almost all other parts of Florida, the Forgotten Coast has remained just that: forgotten. This coastal region was once a very important shipping, transportation and political center. And though times have changed, the coast has steadily established a growing reputation as a quiet resort area, and it's paying off.

Led in no small way by the renovation of downtown Apalachicola, the Forgotten Coast now fills an important niche in Florida's booming tourist trade. To most, the words "south Florida" conjure images of sprawling parking lots, crowded theme parks and condos blocking the ocean view. The Forgotten Coast is a gentle reminder of a time when we lived in peaceful co-existence with Florida's vibrant landscape.

Following is an informational description of each town you'll encounter along this beautiful coastal region.

Apalachicola

Established during the early part of the 1800s, Apalachicola provided the cotton plantations and lumber yards of north Florida with a convenient port — at the time, the third-largest on the Gulf Coast.

Walk through the historic downtown district and you'll see plenty of evidence that cotton, lumber and seafood have been the backbone of this area. The majestic antebellum mansions in the old neighborhood also hint at the town's prosperous years before the Civil War. Just like so many other cities and towns throughout the panhandle, Apalachicola was hit hard by this war and its aftermath. A blockade by Union naval forces ensured that virtually nothing could get out of Apalachicola during the war, and the shipping industry suffered greatly.

Apalachicola slowly built up its other industries, and it wasn't long before it established a solid reputation as the seafood capital of Florida. It's something that residents are certainly proud of, and if you're in town during November, you can let them show you why. Read about the Florida Seafood Festival in the Annual Events and Festivals chapter.

PIED PIPER

LADIES BOUTIQUE

Beautiful clothes and accessories
for the discriminating lady.

We carry many top quality brand labels.

49 Market Street
Apalachicola, FL 32320
(904) 653-8196
Debra Stewart, Owner

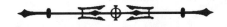

Even if you can't make this well-attended festival, Apalachicola on a quiet day is still a treat. The town has managed to preserve much of its historic architecture, which includes antebellum homes, large brick warehouses and other buildings of interest. The downtown district provides history buffs and sightseers with the chance to experience the port's past firsthand.

This 3-square-mile section features many important historic buildings and sites, some dating back more than 150 years. Take the walking tour — it's the perfect way to spend the day here. When you've walked your shoes off, relax at either of two waterfront parks, Lafayette and Battery parks.

Apalachicola sits just off Highway 98 between Port St. Joe and Eastpoint, across the bay from St. Vincent and St. George islands. It's approximately 70 miles east of Panama City and 85 miles southeast of Tallahassee.

Cape San Blas

We've got some of the best beaches in the nation along the coast of Northwest Florida, and most people agree that Cape San Blas is as good a place as any to enjoy sugar-white sand and sparkling blue water. Here you can enjoy sunbathing, swimming, shelling, snorkeling and one other important word that starts with the letter 's' — solitude.

A recent University of Maryland study named this and St. George Island as two of the nation's top-five beaches. There's plenty of sand for everyone, nearly 20 miles' worth. There are two parks on the cape, St. Joseph Peninsula State Park (see the Attractions chapter for more information) and Salinas Park, a new public park that features elevated boardwalks, picnic areas and a gazebo that lets you enjoy the coastal scenery.

You can also visit the site of the Old Confederate Saltworks — this facility was once a major saltworks plant until 1862 when it was destroyed by Union troops during the Civil War. And don't forget to check out the fascinating San Blas Lighthouse at the Coast Guard Station; this is one structure with a lot of history behind it. If you don't mind the 90-foot climb to the top, you can check out the light's

Fresnel lens — the cracks there were reportedly caused by Confederate musket balls fired during the Civil War.

You can reach Cape San Blas by taking County Road 30 from Highway 98, between Port St. Joe and Apalachicola. The Gulf County Chamber of Commerce has an excellent information package they'll gladly send you. Call them at 227-1223.

Carrabelle

Carrabelle, about 20 miles east of Apalachicola, is a port town of around 2,000 people. It's been dubbed the "Pearl of the Panhandle," and when you sample the seafood you'll know why: It's cause for a lot of celebration in these parts. Carrabelle hosts the Big Bend Saltwater Fishing Classic and the Carrabelle Waterfront Festival, both on Father's Day weekend, and these always manage to attract a few thousand people. The festival is a jam-packed day of fun, food and sunshine.

There are plenty of things to see and do here. Check out the historic Crooked River Lighthouse, just west of town and about a quarter-mile from St. George Sound. Carrabelle's Wayside Park can be found with a minimum of effort — it's just off Highway 98 (as is most everything else in Carrabelle) and is a perfect spot to picnic before heading on down to the beaches and islands farther west.

Don't blink as you pass through town or you'll miss the World's Smallest Police Station, a well-marked telephone booth that sits just off Highway 98 as it passes through town. It's a tourist attraction that many magazines, newspapers and TV shows across the country have featured, but it's also quite functional. Don't be at all surprised if you see a patrol car parked nearby with an alert officer waiting for that phone to ring.

Just east of Carrabelle is the community of Lanark Village, and beyond that is Alligator Point. Lanark Village was once the site of Camp Gordon, a former training ground during World War II. Since that time, it's been slowly and carefully developed into a tasteful resort and retirement area. Alligator Point doesn't really have any alligators — well, hardly any — but takes its name (say the locals) from its shape. Pull down the highway a bit to a quiet beach spot called St. Teresa and look out across Apalachee Bay to Alligator Point. We did and, with a bit of help from some friendly locals, were able to see, sure enough, the shape of a big grinning alligator.

Lanark Village and Alligator Point are low-key resort and retirement areas that cater to visitors who want to slow down to a panhandler's pace. Each offers waterfront camping and hotels as well as rental properties, and there are some fine places to eat too. We shouldn't have to tell you that fresh fish is the dish of choice here.

If this still isn't secluded enough for you, then we've got the answer. Superman has his Fortress of Solitude to retreat to when things get rough, and if he lived in Florida he'd surely rather be at Dog Island, which sits just off the coast of Carrabelle. It's the smallest of four islands off Franklin County's coastline and can be reached only by a ferry that runs

from Carrabelle. There are about 100 homes on the island and one hotel, the Pelican Inn. Most of Dog Island is a nature preserve, and in the fall and spring there are so many birds here you might not notice the beautiful water and sandy beaches. The island is known for its quiet, low-key residents and breathtaking landscape.

If you want more information on Carrabelle, just contact the Carrabelle Area Chamber of Commerce, 697-2585.

Mexico Beach

You won't hear much Spanish spoken here, but you might feel like you're in another country because of the strangely calm waters that rest like a comfy blue shroud just off the fine beaches. Mexico Beach is fronted by a peninsula that extends like a curled finger off Cape San Blas, and this natural barrier keeps the gulf waters quiet and steady. There's practically no undertow here at all, and that's one reason why it's

Photo: Apalachicola Bay Chamber of Commerce

Apalachicola preserves not only its natural resources but its architecture too. The Gulf State Bank is housed in the beautifully restored Flautauer House, which was built at the turn of the century.

such a popular family beach. The other reason is the beautiful white sand, another facet that might make you think of Mexico.

It's strange to think that less than 20 years ago, Mexico Beach didn't see a lot of action — people usually· passed through it on their way to somewhere else. Now that the Forgotten Coast has become more developed, few people take its relatively unspoiled beauty for granted anymore.

Wander out on the city-owned fishing pier, stroll through Canal Park or just rent a boat — you'll discover why so many people who live here are peaceful and easygoing. It's quite contagious.

Mexico Beach is a few miles west of Port St. Joe on Highway 98. Contact the Mexico Beach Chamber of Commerce, (800) 239-9553, for more information.

Port St. Joe

This is a very small town, and when you know its history you'll understand why. Though at one time, Port St. Joe — known initially as St. Joseph — was the site of Florida's first Constitutional Convention, and at one point in the early 1800s it was the sixth-largest city in the state. The reason? You guessed it: its proximity to the Gulf of Mexico. The 1835 construction of a railroad here allowed cotton from Georgia and Alabama to be easily shipped through here to Apalachicola.

No one expected St. Joseph to disappear completely, but that's exactly what happened. In the early 1840s, this growing boom town was blown away by the one-two punch of first a powerful hurricane and then a deadly yellow fever epidemic.

All that was a long time ago, and the town's recovery has been slow and steady.

Sea Dream to the Rescue

More than 50 years ago, World War II came to Florida's Forgotten Coast.

Troops were trained at nearby Tyndall Field (among them actor Clark Gable) and St. George Island, but until June 1942, the only action around here was on the firing range. That changed when a German submarine slid through the waters just off the Forgotten Coast in pursuit of a British tanker.

The 431-foot *Empire Mica*, laden with more than 11,000 tons of fuel, was on her maiden voyage. Two dozen miles offshore, the German U-boat caught up with the *Mica* and launched torpedoes, sinking her in 110 feet of water just 20 miles south of Cape San Blas.

An S.O.S. was transmitted, and among the ships that sped to the rescue was the *Sea Dream*, a U.S. Coast Guard patrol vessel built in 1932. Despite the rescue efforts, only 14 of the 47-member crew survived.

More than 50 years later, the *Empire Mica* is now a popular diving site in the gulf. The *Sea Dream*, battered and rotting, rests forlornly near the docks at Apalachicola, awaiting restoration by the Apalachicola Maritime Museum, the nonprofit group that engineered the restoration of the *Governor Stone* sailing vessel.

Contributions toward this worthy effort are tax deductible. For more information, and to find out more about Apalachicola's maritime history, visit the Apalachicola Maritime Institute, 77 Commerce Street.

Port St. Joe is now a deepwater port, but its shallow bay waters produce some of the best scallops in the gulf. They thrive here so well that, during certain summer months, visitors can wander out into the bay and harvest their own by the handful.

Port St. Joe is on Highway 98 between Mexico Beach and Apalachicola, just across the bay from Cape San Blas. For more information, contact the Port St. Joe Chamber of Commerce, 227-1223.

St. George Island

There are four barrier islands that sit just off Franklin County's coastline. St. George Island is the largest in the chain and the only one accessible by automobile. It sports several permanent and rental residences as well as the Dr. Julian

G. Bruce St. George Island State Park (for more information, see the Attractions chapter in this section), which features nearly 2,000 acres of sensitive, unspoiled beach landscape.

You'll see a lot of houses on the island as well as evidence that the growth here is carefully controlled and regulated. The residents have overall shown great consideration for the island's ecosystem and appearance, and it's something they love to share with visitors.

The state park is a lovely attraction. There's a free public beach visible as soon as you reach the island. You'll see beach-combers, sun worshippers and bird-watchers out here, but you'll probably be most impressed with the size of the beach; it's so large that people like to spread out

and claim their own little private chunk of sand. In fact, it's easy to feel like you're the only person on the entire island. Locals say that's why they live here, and visitors say it's why they return again and again.

To reach St. George Island, which sits across the bay from Apalachicola, take Highway 98 to Highway 300 S. This puts you on the causeway across Apalachicola Bay and lands you smack dab on the island.

For more information, contact the Apalachicola Bay Chamber of Commerce, 653-9419, or the St. George Island Business Owners Association, 653-9419.

Photo: Panama City Beach Convention & Visitors Bureau

Beautiful scenes like this bring many people to our coast.

Florida's Forgotten Coast
Accommodations

There are plenty of places to stay along Florida's Forgotten Coast, and because so many of them are rental properties, we've included listings for real estate companies here. You'll have to call them for their own prices, which vary widely. The key is for hotels and inns only.

For year-round, double-occupancy accommodations, per night:

$60 or less	$
$61 to $85	$$
$86 to $99	$$$
$100 or more	$$$$

Apalachicola

APALACHICOLA REALTY, INC.
18 Seventh St.   653-8990, (800)239-8990

Leon Bloodworth is a real estate broker with more than 20 years experience in the area. Currently he and his staff handle mostly commercial real estate properties on the mainland.

CENTURY 21 MARKS REALTY
61 Ave. E   653-8851, (800) 586-1408

If you're looking for a good selection of vacation rental properties, let sales agents Sheila Schoelles and Barbara Carlson help you discover the beauty and affordability of Florida's Forgotten Coast. This is the oldest operating real estate company in Apalachicola, and they consistently prove their worth by producing top sales for the area. Whether you want to stay in a beachfront palace or a no-frills hideaway, they can work within your budget and schedule to help you accomplish your goal: relaxation.

THE COOMBS HOUSE INN
80 Sixth St.   653-9199
$$

If you want a glimpse of turn-of-the-century Apalachicola life at its finest, you must stay at the Coombs House Inn. Built in 1905, this was home to James N. Coombs, one of Apalachicola's legendary lumber barons. Over the years it fell into disrepair and stood empty for a brief period before an international design team moved in to renovate and redecorate the place. Now the Coombs House is once again one of Apalachicola's prize possessions.

Innkeepers Marilyn and Charles Schubert run a tight and friendly ship. Formerly innkeepers in Vermont, they were brought out of their Florida retirement by the grandeur of this house and the great people in town. With their lovable golden retriever Sandy, they ensure that your stay here is one of refinement and relaxation.

There are 10 airy guest rooms, each with its own bath and cable TV. The rooms feature large windows, black cypress wood panelling, English antiques and fabrics and some gorgeous Oriental carpets. Each morning there's an English breakfast in the great dining room, and nearly everything in town is just a few minutes' walk away.

THE GIBSON INN

51 Ave. C   *653-2191*
$$

This turn-of-the-century house is in the heart of downtown Apalachicola, and rightly so. The Victorian house sports a stately wide veranda and is a striking reminder of Apalachicola's genteel past. It's one of the few inns on the Federal Register of Historic Places that still operates as a full-service facility. The renovation of this inn in the mid-1980s helped revitalize the town considerably. The 31-room hotel features beds made of either antique white iron or wooden fourposters, along with modern amenities such as full baths and television.

The lobby sports a comfortable bar, and the Gibson Inn's restaurant is worth the trip even if you're not staying overnight. The dishes include delectable seafood masterpieces such as shrimp, scallop and crab dijon, grouper papilliote (sauteed with shrimp in white wine) and oysters remick — and because the docks are just a stroll away, the seafood doesn't get any fresher than this. For land-lubbers, the steak chateau and chicken cordon bleu come highly recommended. Save room for the great desserts, including chocolate bourbon pecan pie and Mississippi mud pie, made fresh daily.

The Gibson also offers special weekend packages, including Murder Mystery Weekends, where you'll join other guests in solving an intricate crime. Special offers change seasonally, so call ahead. Reservations for dinner are recommended.

THE RAINBOW INN & MARINA

123 Water St.   *653-8139*
$$

If you get any closer to the water than this, you'll need a boat. The Rainbow Inn rests right on the Apalachicola River and offers a wide variety of room accommodations to fit your price range, everything from a no-frills basic sleepover to a spacious suite overlooking the river. This multifaceted facility offers not only a marina with transient dockage but also a complete restaurant, The Riverfront, which is as good a place as any to sample the local seafood. There's also a package store, a cocktail lounge and a raw bar with buckets of fresh oysters. Sit and sip something sweet while watching the fishing boats glide in for the evening, or take a stroll through the downtown historic district only a few blocks away. If you're looking to plan a fishing trip or sightseeing expedition to any of the nearby islands, the staff here can help you. The Rainbow Inn & Marina is something to savor.

THE RANCHO INN

240 U.S. Hwy. 98   *653-9435*
$

Unlike other Apalachicola hotels, the Rancho Inn isn't housed in a renovated turn-of-the-century manse, but it is a perfectly nice place to stay. The Rancho sits right off U.S. 98 — you'll know it by the Spanish-styled red roof tiling. Their 32 comfortable rooms offer telephones with free local calls and color TVs with HBO.

SPORTSMAN'S LODGE & MARINA

Hwy. 98, Eastpoint   *670-8423*

For years the Sportsman's Lodge & Marina has been a popular base camp for anglers, whether they're renting rooms or pulling in their own trailers. The lodge sits on the edge of Apalachicola Bay in the little fishing village of Eastpoint, about 5 miles east of Apalachicola. Bob and Edda Allen run the place, and they'll fix you up no matter what your plans are. Their comfortable, spacious rooms offer electric heat and air, kitchenettes and cable TV. Full hookups are available for trailers and RVs. Daily, weekly and monthly rates are available. You can grab a charter boat for bay or deep-sea fishing or moor your own craft at their marina. There's a bait and tackle shop on the premises too. The fishing's just great, and when you've fished yourself silly, you're just minutes from the beautiful beaches of St. George Island and the unique shops of Carrabelle and Apalachicola. It's easy to see why sportsfishers return to this spot year after year.

Cape San Blas

ANCHOR REALTY
Hwy. C-30   229-2777, (800) 824-0416

Anchor Realty is a top-seller in an area filled with aggressive Realtors, and they go all out to stay on top. With the lengthiest rental listing in the area, Olivier and Sandra Monod and their staff are prime players in the Forgotten Coast's recent land boom. They've recently developed a special branch, Anchor Vacation Properties, which is dedicated to transient rental property management.

Tell them what you want, when you want it and your price range, and they'll fix you up fast. From a bare-bones weekend rental to a summer vacation house, Anchor Realty will satisfy you. They publish a free information and rental guide to Cape San Blas and St. George Island, with photos and easy-to-understand charts detailing their various properties. Give them a call at the above phone numbers or write 212 Franklin Boulevard, St. George Island 32328.

CAPE SAN BLAS CAMPING RESORT
Hwy. C-30   229-6800
$

Not everyone can afford a weekly condo rental, and let's face it — not everybody wants that, either. Some people want to be as close to nature as possible, and amenities such as central air conditioning and cable TV just don't figure in the long run.

The Cape San Blas Camping Resort is secluded and idyllic, even when its 44 campsites and four cottages are filled to capacity. Sprawled across several acres on the cape, the resort has something for everyone. Park your RV in the nestled shade of tall pine trees or in full sunlight near the dunes. Full hookups and a dump station are available, and each site has a wooden picnic table. There's also a primitive campground for tent camping, and hot showers are available for all at no extra charge.

Don and Rhonda Thiel have been managing the campsite for more than a year, and they also run the camp store where you can rent canoes and buy ice, groceries and other supplies. Pets are most welcome, as Gulf County has no laws against leashed animals on public beaches.

The Cape San Blas Camping Resort offers private access to 2 miles of completely undeveloped beach; they sit adjacent to an Eglin Air Force Test Site; don't worry, this isn't where bombers practice strafing runs or anything. This year, two Patriot missiles were fired in a controlled test over the gulf and that was all. The rest of the year, things were perfectly peaceful at this resort, and that's why people return year after year.

PAN GULF REALTY

Hwy. C-30   229-8390

Richard Kaley and Ira Schoenberg run the Pan Gulf Realty office on Cape San Blas and spend most their time managing the Boardwalk, a recent upscale development just a mile or so down the cape. While there are some full-time residents in these beautiful platform houses, most of them are rental properties available to the public. No matter which rental property you get, the beach is only a few steps away.

Prices rise and fall according to the season — winter's usually a good time if you're on a budget. If you want anything between March and September, make

your plans many months ahead. The Boardwalk fills up quickly.

OLD SALTWORKS CABINS

C.R. 30   229-6097
$$-$$$

If you're looking for privacy and a great view, check out the Old Saltworks Cabins on Cape San Blas. These nine rustic cabins stand on the site of the old Confederate saltworks that was destroyed during the Civil War, and they offer great views of both the Gulf of Mexico and the bay. All the cabins are air-conditioned and offer ceiling fans, screened-in porches, decks and lounge chairs. If you're eating simple, or dining out, you can save a few bucks by renting what the managers call the "motel" cabins — no kitchen facilities. The other cabins come with stoves and fully equipped kitchens, for those who wish to keep their culinary skills sharpened while on vacation.

SKI BREEZE

Hwy. C-30   227-2136
$

The Ski Breeze is a great place for beachside RV camping. Technically, it's right on the beach, but since it's only minutes from Cape San Blas, folks will tell you to head for the latter when you're looking for it. Ski Breeze has several beautiful campsites as close as 50 feet to the water, so unless you hate sand and surf, this is your place. They offer full hookups, clean restrooms and showers and a dump station, and they welcome pets.

Daily rates for RVs are around $16, but Ski Breeze does offer special weekly, monthly and seasonal rates. So call ahead when planning your camping trip. Ski Breeze allows tent camping unless they're close to capacity, and then preference will be given to RVs.

TOM TODD REALTY

Hwy. C-30   227-1501

If you don't want to search through the endless property listings in search of the perfect rental property, let Tom Todd Realty handle the dirty work for you. Tom Todd's coverage area includes Cape San Blas, Mexico Beach and Port St. Joe, and he'll work to match your budget and schedule with the best available rental.

WHISPERING PINES

Hwy. C-30   227-7252
$

These cozy cottages offer visitors a very affordable way to enjoy the best of the Cape. Owned and operated by Susan and David Marley, Whispering Pines consists of only two rental cottages, but they're spacious enough to sleep six people comfortably. They come with fully equipped kitchens, including cookware and flatware, and each cottage has its own barbecue for outdoor cooking. The cottages are furnished with central heat and air and color televisions too. You probably won't need the latter because you're within easy walking distance of the beach.

The rates from September 16 to May 15 are $45 per night for two people; from May 16 to September 15 rates are $60 per night. There is an additional charge of $5 per day for each extra person.

Carrabelle

FLORIDA COASTAL PROPERTIES

Hwy. 98   697-2734

There's more to Carrabelle than meets the eye. The view from Highway 98 only scratches the surface. Sure, there are some fine waterfront vacation properties in the area, but if you're looking to really get away from it all, Carrabelle offers an assortment of hiding spots. Whether you want a luxury home or a simple lakeside fishing cabin, Florida Coastal Properties can help you find the perfect hideaway for your budget and schedule. They've also got offices in Shell Point and Crawfordville, so you know they've got a wide range of properties from which to choose.

GULF WATERS MOTEL & CAMPGROUND
Hwy. 98   697-2840
$$ (800) 633-2840

Just 4 miles east of Carrabelle in Lanark Beach lies this inviting hotel and campground. Owners Jack and Jean DePriest provide comfortable, reasonably priced rooms right on the Gulf of Mexico with stocked kitchenettes and cable TV. Their RV lots include full hookups as well, and there are plenty of picnic tables and barbecue grills for everyone. Bring your boat and launch it from their docks, or cast your line from their 250-foot private pier. They'll even arrange a charter fishing trip if you call ahead. Pets are welcome. Reservations are recommended.

Mexico Beach

EL GOVERNOR MOTEL & CAMPGROUND
Hwy. 98   hotel 648-5757
$$ campground 648-5432

Mexico Beach has a lot of rental properties to choose from, but if you're looking for a spacious, clean motel room or a shady campsite, the Governor is the place to be. The hotel sits right on the Gulf of Mexico, offering 120 rooms that overlook the beach. Each room has a private balcony, central heat and air, cable TV and

a full-size stove and refrigerator. There's also a gift shop and package store in the hotel.

Just across Highway 98 is El Governor Campground, where you can park the RV or pitch a tent. Full hookups, showers, picnic tables, laundry facilities and easy beach access make this an affordable way to spend your vacation.

St. George Island

ANCHOR REALTY AND MORTGAGE CO.
*212 Franklin Blvd.*927-2625, (800) 824-0416

Anchor maintains three fully staffed offices along the coast: two in Cape San Blas and one here on St. George Island. Olivier and Sandra Monod head up this successful company in the Forgotten Coast. With their friendly staff, they've proved that a first-class operation has to keep the customer in mind at all times. They've got a large rental property inventory in the area, and annual renters return to them again and again.

You can get a free copy of their magazine that features not only color photographs of several dozen rental properties but also a handy guide for comparing the features of each one.

CENTURY 21 COLLINS REALTY
60 E. Gulf Beach Dr.   927-3100

From shaded seclusion to bright beachfront, Century 21 Collins Realty has an impressive listing of rental properties from which to choose. The friendly staff will help you select a vacation rental home no matter what your budget or time frame. Owner Alice Collins and staff also stay busy handling the sales of homes, homesites, commercial property and condominiums on St. George Island.

LAND & CASTLE REALTY

33 W. Gulf Beach Dr.	*927-3557*
St. George Island	*(800) 927-3557*

This is one of St. George Island's newest real estate offices, but it's run by someone who knows the business well. Betty Jean Londono has been a Realtor for many years in this area, and her expert knowledge can be invaluable if you're looking for that perfect vacation rental. She provides a free sales brochure for the asking, and it details the various rental properties she handles.

LIGHTHOUSE REALTY

33 W. Gulf Beach Dr.	*927-2821*
$$$$	

St. George Island offers a wide variety of homes, and Lighthouse Realty's Marion Miley works with them all. Whether you desire a beachfront castle with plenty of neighbors or an isolated hideaway, she can help you plan your vacation. With more than a decade's experience in the area, she's a Realtor who understands the discriminating needs of the low-budget visitor.

SUNCOAST REALTY, INC.
H.C.R. 2   927-2282

One of the most active real estate companies on St. George Island, Suncoast Realty handles a wide variety of sales and vacation rental properties. Owner Walter Armistead oversees a friendly staff that includes Don and Marta Thompson, Larry Hale and Billy Grey. They'll work to help you get the most out of your schedule and budget.

Florida's Forgotten Coast
Restaurants

If you're looking for good seafood, you'll do just fine here. If you're not, you'll still do fine. The coastal cuisine is as diverse as the landscape here. Below are just some of the places that stand out along Florida's Forgotten Coast. The below key covers a dinner for two, minus any luxuries such as a bottle of wine or double-decker dessert. Unless otherwise noted, these restaurants accept all major credit cards.

For restaurants, dinner for two:

Less than $20	$
$21 to $35	$$
$36 to $50	$$$
$51 or more	$$$$

Apalachicola

CHEF EDDIE'S MAGNOLIA GRILL
133 Ave. E (U.S. Hwy. 98)   653-8000
$$ No credit cards

There are plenty of restaurants vying for your attention in this area, and this is one of the best. Over the years chef Ed Cass perfected his culinary skills in various other Florida restaurants. Lucky for you, he's set up shop right here in Apalachicola. The Magnolia Grill is one of the latest restaurants to open, and its ever-changing menu is practically unrivalled.

Start with seafood, fresh from the bay, and you can't go wrong. Chef Ed and his kitchen crew routinely offer up such dishes as Snapper Pontchartrain, cooked in a delicate pastry crust and topped with shrimp and artichoke sauce. Then there's the grilled tuna served with feta cheese, roasted red peppers and jalapeno hollandaise sauce. Steak and prime rib dinners are big attractions too. Do save room for the homemade desserts. They're every bit as mouthwatering as the entrees.

Chef Eddie's Magnolia Grill currently serves dinner only, Monday through Saturday. Reservations are recommended.

APALACHICOLA
SEAFOOD GRILL & STEAKHOUSE
100 Market St. (U.S Hwy. 98)   653-9510
$

This place has been around for more than a half-century, and it only gets better with each passing year. Smack dab in the middle of downtown Apalachicola, right next to the town's only traffic light, this unassuming restaurant never fails to please the palate and pamper the pocketbook. If you want a great sampling of local seafood, order the fried seafood platter, which features enough grouper, shrimp, scallops and Apalachicola Bay oysters to easily fill up two hungry diners. Other recommended menu items include blackened seabass with tomato basil butter and grilled triggerfish with hollandaise sauce.

You might expect to pay handsomely for such delicacies, but the Grill's dinner

prices are very affordable, and the lunch prices will make your jaw drop. Reservations are recommended, especially on the weekends.

DOLORES' SWEET SHOP

17 Ave. E   653-9081
$

Above the doorway to this charming, roomy place is a huge sign that says, quite simply, "EAT." If they pulled it down tomorrow, you could still find the Sweet Shop just by following your nose. Each morning Dolores Roux and her staff are up early baking some of the best bread, cakes, pies and cookies you've ever put in your mouth. Few people can withstand the delicious smells that come wafting through the big screen doors.

It's a great place for breakfast and a popular lunch spot. Make a meal of the soup and salad, or try one of the delicious subs: Served on wonderful homemade rolls, they come piled high with tasty meats, cheeses and fresh vegetables. And there's always something sweet for dessert — we wholeheartedly recommend the homemade ice cream.

Carrabelle

HARRY'S GEORGIAN RESTAURANT

Hwy. 98   697-3400
$$

The atmosphere is very casual at Harry's, but the food is first-rate. Harry Papadopoulos does brisk breakfast, lunch and dining business in Carrabelle, and the fare is highly praised by both tourists and locals. Specialties include the crab casserole (from an old family recipe), broiled shrimp and a tangy Greek salad.

Are oysters safe to eat? If your immune system is in good shape, you betcha. Apalachicola Bay oysters are as nutritious as they are tasty. Just six oysters provide more than 100 percent of the minimum recommended daily allowance of iron.

Insiders' Tips

We heartily recommend the combo seafood platter, which includes generous helpings of stuffed deviled crab, fried shrimp and oysters, mullet and scallops. Harry's serves up nice charbroiled steaks and hamburgers, but the seafood is hard to surpass when it's this fresh and prepared so well.

JULIA MAE'S SEAFOOD RESTAURANT

Hwy. 98   697-3791
$$

Resting at the foot of the Tillie Miller Bridge in Carrabelle, Julia Mae's is known throughout the panhandle for its delicious seafood. Ever had a scallop burger? You can find them right here, along with shrimp and oyster burgers too. Choose from more than a dozen seafood plates that come with crunchy brown hushpuppies, or try the house specialties, which include whole stuffed lobster, crab imperial and shrimp creole. If you want a definitive sampling of this area's seafood, try the popular seafood platter — bring a friend along, because you'll need help clearing the huge plate. For the best of both worlds, the steak and half-lobster dinner is also a good catch. If you don't have room for dessert, at least take home a slice from one of their excellent homemade pies. You'll thank us later, when you have room. Dinner reservations are recommended, especially on weekends.

Cape San Blas

SHEP'S CAPE CAFE

Hwy. C-30   229-8688
$$

Shep's Cape Cafe is an oasis of culinary delights in an area where eateries are scarce indeed. Less than a half-mile from the entrance to the St. Joseph Peninsula State Park, the Cape Cafe is a bright, clean and casual place that offers great salads, subs and pizzas for lunch. The dinner menu features delicious entries such as manicotti with basil pesto sauce and fresh shrimp served just about every way you can imagine. And if that's not enough to draw you in, the Cape Cafe recently opened for breakfast on Saturday and Sunday mornings, offering rise-and-shine treats such as Eggs Benedict with crabmeat and avocado slices.

Even those who come to Cape San Blas with the intentions of roughing it out at primitive campsites have been known to wander down to Shep's for a meal or two. It's that good. Dinner reservations are recommended.

Insiders' Tips

If your vacation brings you to Apalachicola, don't forget about the food. We're not talking about the area's great restaurants, but rather the eats and drinks you'll want to keep around your rental quarters. Whether you just want to build baloney sandwiches or serve up some of the bay's fresh seafood, Red Rabbit Foods, 130 U.S. 98, 653-8768, is a full-service grocery whose shelves are ready for you. The prices are reasonable, and the selection is great. They've got a deli with fresh foods prepared daily, and they also rent videos.

Sports Bar & Grill

English Darts	Pool League
Tournaments	Karaoke
Live Band	Burgers
Jam Session	Buffalo Wings
Sports TV	Daily Specials

A Friendly Place to Visit
3041 Highway 98, Mexico Beach

904-648-4464

TOUCAN's
Restaurant & Oyster Bar

Maine Lobsters	Steaks & Chicken
Pasta Dishes	Orleans Gumbo
Volley Ball	Baked Oysters
Fried Shrimp	Grouper Royale
Crawfish	Blackened Red Fish

Beach Fun - Casual Dress!
812 Highway 98, Mexico Beach

904-648-3010

Mexico Beach

JAM'S SPORTS BAR & GRILL
3401 Hwy. 98   *648-4464*
$

Jam's is a friendly little beach bar where locals mingle with tourists over cold beer and hot food. If there's a good game on TV, that's where everyone's attention will be, but it's an active place even if you're still mad and don't want to watch. There are weekly dart tournaments, pool matches (they've got six regulation-size tables), and even dance lessons for the country bands that take the stage on most weekends. The menu is your standard bar fare — burgers, steak sandwiches, buffalo wings, cheese sticks — but it certainly hits the spot.

TOUCAN'S
812 Hwy. 98   *648-3010*
$$

Overlooking the emerald green waters of the Gulf, Toucan's is a fine place to relax and enjoy some great food. Indoor seating is limited, but there's a great deck where, weather permitting, most people prefer to take their meals. Breakfast, lunch and dinner is served here, and plenty of good seafood comes pouring out of Toucan's kitchen. We're especially fond of the honey barbecue shrimp and the live Maine lobsters. Visitors might prefer to sample Capt. Mike's Platter, a healthy offering of gulf shrimp, grouper, scallops, oysters and clams. Try to save room for a slice of Key lime or peanut butter pie. If there's a volleyball game going on at the net below, you'll have a chance to work off some of what you just put on. If that's asking too much, then at least climb the stairs to Toucan's gift shop on the top level, where you'll find a wide assortment of souvenirs and gift items to choose from.

Port St. Joe

J. PATRICK'S RESTAURANT
412 Reid Ave.   *227-7400*
$

This casual, friendly restaurant was recently rated the most popular restaurant in Port St. Joe. For years, J. Patrick's has been serving up great seafood, and they've built a solid, steady local following. It doesn't take visitors long to figure out where everyone's headed for lunch, especially on Sunday, where a tasty and affordable seafood buffet often makes the place standing room only. Check out the daily lunch specials as well as the all-you-can-eat hot bar. J. Patrick's is open for dinner for parties of 10 or more with reservations.

St. George Island

OYSTER COVE SEAFOOD BAR & GRILL
E. Pine and E. Second sts.   927-2600
$$

Of all the restaurants on St. George Island, Oyster Cove arguably has the best view, with a dining room overlooking scenic Apalachicola Bay. Some say it's also got the best seafood, and with chefs Biff Newsham and Nathan Montgomery serving up succulent dishes such as oyster bordelaise and grilled lemon trigger, it certainly commands one's culinary attention. Several restaurants offer seafood platters designed to impress diners with the best of the bay, and Oyster Cove is no exception. Theirs comes piled high with oysters, conch fritters, shrimp, grouper fingers, deviled crab and your choice of baked potato, fries or red beans and rice, salad or cole slaw and a healthy mug of Cajun-style gumbo.

For a more casual atmosphere, check out the Cajun Cafe and Oyster Bar just below Oyster Cove. Many islanders make it their weekend watering hole. Pinball machines, dart boards and a big-screen TV make it a fun place, but many people think the best activity is to watch the sunset while sipping convivialities and tossing back a couple dozen oysters.

PARADISE CAFE
W. Gorrie Dr.   927-3300
$$

Open seven days a week, the Paradise Cafe is a great family restaurant with an elegant menu. Breakfast, lunch and dinner are served with fine flair. Some of the more popular menu items include shrimp orzo (sauteed to tangy perfection with fresh herbs, garlic and cherry tomatoes), fried stuffed flounder and some of the best crab cakes on the island. Seafood's not the only draw at the Paradise; steaks and burgers are grilled to perfection, and the chicken pesto dinner is divine. Daily chalkboard specials are always worth checking out. Owners Bill and Judy Blackburn also own BJ's Pizza & Subs on the island, where the atmosphere is more casual but the food is just as good.

THE ST. GEORGE INN
Franklin Blvd.   927-2903
$$$

Whether or not you stay overnight at the historic St. George Inn, you'll at least want to have dinner there. This Victorian-style building is elegant and surprising, as are the many specialties prepared in its kitchen. Highly recommended is the flounder stuffed with crabmeat, baked to flaky perfection and the Bulldozer homemade quiche — you might think you need a bulldozer to finish it. For dessert, we'd point you to the homemade chocolate mousse; along with any selection from the inn's fine wine list, you've got the makings of a perfect evening.

The St. George Inn also offers more than a dozen comfortable rooms, each with spacious beds and a balcony view of the water.

Florida's Forgotten Coast
Shopping

While the beaches here are the main attraction, there are also plenty of great shops along the Forgotten Coast. Yes, you've got your typical tourist joints selling bulk bags of seashells and alligator-shaped ashtrays — and those places are perfectly fine for what they are. But there are many special shops throughout the area that we think are well worth your attention. We've described a few of our favorites.

Apalachicola

APALACHICOLA SPORTS & STUFF
56 Market St.   653-2662

There's a lot to do outdoors, and Apalachicola Sports & Stuff can help you do it better than anyplace else. Owners Mike and Donna Parrish stock their store with an excellent variety of sporting goods. No matter what the season, it's time to play ball, and you'll find all your gear on these shelves, whether it's football, baseball, basketball or tennis. Sports & Stuff also rents bicycles — call ahead to ask for rates.

If you're here to hunt, you'll find everything you need in this one location. Their selection of guns, knives and bows is the place to start when planning deer, squirrel and duck hunting. They also carry a good line of fishing and camping supplies.

ARTEMIS GALLERY
67 Commerce St.   653-8304

Owner Hollis Wade opened ARTemis three years ago as primarily a fine arts gallery, featuring works by local and regional artists. She's since expanded her space into something of an artist's boutique, with art you can not only hang on your walls but wear as well. Alongside watercolors, paintings and pottery you'll find an intriguing selection of beauty and relaxation aids. She also carries a beautiful assortment of clothing and jewelry.

The ARTemis is in the old O.E. Cone Barber Shop building, built around 1900. Cone was one of the first blacks to own a business in Apalachicola, and from this wooden frame building he not only trimmed hair but ran a laundromat and lumber yard as well. Wade has extensively renovated and decorated the place, preserving its sense of history but also bringing it gracefully into the present day.

COAST LINE UNIQUES & ANTIQUES
Market St. and Ave. G   653-8668

One way to experience Apalachicola's history is to wander its streets and see the stories its buildings and landmarks tell. Another way is to duck inside an antique store and look at the variety of items its former residents once owned and held dear. Coast Line Uniques & Antiques lets you do both. This weathered, somewhat sagging structure was once the Candy Kitchen, and from the 1920s to the 1950s was the place for kids and grownups to get their sweets. Later it functioned as a juke joint called the Riverside Cafe, but closed down in the 1960s and stood empty for many years.

Enter Chuck and Virginia Spicer, two longtime Florida residents who moved to Apalachicola in 1991. They discovered that, despite its ramshackle appearance, the old wooden frame building was surprisingly sturdy. So they bought it and have spent their time filling both floors with artifacts and collectibles from another era. Browsing through several rooms filled to the ceiling with such stuff gives you an amazing, unspoken sense of the people who once lived here.

The Spicers also publish the monthly shopping guide *Coast Line*, which is available free just about everywhere along the Forgotten Coast. It's chock-full of area news, history and shopping information and always makes for a fascinating read.

CEDAR WOMAN GALLERY
94 Market St.   653-2797

If you're looking for a truly multicultural buying center, this is it. Located in a former mercantile store originally built in the mid-19th century, Cedar Woman Gallery offers a broad selection of gift and art items you probably won't find anywhere else along the coast. Owners Anne and Duke Epperson have been doing this sort of thing for years now, having owned similar stores in Colorado and New Mexico. This year they opened Cedar Woman, bringing to Apalachicola an ever-changing, always-fascinating assortment of Southwestern-themed artwork, including beautiful Navajo rugs and pottery. And although they've got a fond spot for that neck of the woods, you'll

find plenty of other items in stock here, such as Chinese porcelain and showpieces and seasonal art. Anne says they've based the flavor of the store on Pier 1 — not the current incarnation, but like the chain was back in the 1970s when it first opened and no two stores were alike. We guarantee you won't find another store like Cedar Woman Gallery anywhere along Florida's Forgotten Coast.

GALLERY 75
75 Commerce St.   653-2172, 653-8304

Here's a real find: a gallery that specializes in only two artists, letting you see through their work how they grow, think and create. Owner Charles Chapin has been painting for most of his adult life and has peddled his pictures in the streets of New York and other cities. Now he's retired to this comfy little cranny, a beautiful turn-of-the-century building that once housed the town's post office (check the sidewalk stones for proof). Here Chapin hangs his paintings, which contain abstract and surrealist elements. Also on display are sculptures by his son, Samuel, who works mostly in welded steel. Charles doesn't title his extraordinary paintings — if you buy one, call it whatever you like.

The gallery has no set hours; if you can't catch it open you can make an appointment. You can also drop by the ARTemis Gallery and talk to Hollis Wade, who shows the Chapins' work when they're closed.

GLEATON GALLERY
73 Market St.   653-2636

If you rent a condo or beach home during your stay in Florida's Forgotten Coast, there's a good chance it's been furnished by Lucia Ann and Jerry Gleaton. They've been specializing in superior

home furnishings for decades now, and Gleaton Gallery is a place where you can see the cream of the crop in home decorating and gift items. It's in the old Cook Building, which used to be a five-and-dime store. Now it's filled not only with striking furniture but also with gifts and accessories, including everything international artwork, birdhouses, decorative T-shirts, designer soaps imported from Munich and more. This is an extension of a similar store the Gleatons have in Arlington, Georgia; they also run Gleaton Vacation Properties on St. George Island.

HOOKED ON BOOKS
54 Market St.   *653-2420*

Whether you're hitting the beach by day or swinging in a hammock at night, you need a big fat book to keep you company. This is the place to find one. Hooked on Books carries the best and latest in fiction as well as children's books, books on tape and religious literature. They also specialize in Florida history books, if you want to catch up on the area. If they don't have what you're looking for, they'll cheerfully order it for you.

You can find them in the Gibson Inn Annex on Market Street.

LONG DREAM GALLERY
32 Ave. D   *653-2249*

Established in 1985, the Long Dream Gallery features an eye-catching, ever-changing assortment of paintings, stained glass, jewelry, textiles, photography, pottery and other items. Owner Kristin Anderson is a former Wisconsin resident who fell under Apalachicola's spell many years ago while traveling to an art fair. A professional gold and silversmith, her workshop occupies one corner of the gallery. Visitors can watch her practicing her craft as they browse the gallery's rotating selections, which include works by various contemporary American artists.

PALMYRA GALLERY
25 Ave. D   *653-9090*

Located in a wonderfully renovated downtown building, the Palmyra Gallery offers an eclectic assortment of bright and beautiful items created by local, regional and national artists. At any one time, the Palmyra features works from nearly 100

different artists. You can spend a lot of time perusing the gorgeous silk clothing or the fascinating handmade jewelry. Co-owner Carole Jayne, for example, produces Carole's Palmyra Stamp Jewelry, a popular series of pins designed around striking postage stamps from all over the world.

There's always a retro-modern assortment of refurbished furniture found here, and the enclosed back patio features a varied selection of wind chimes and other outdoor ornaments. Carole Jayne and Mike Athorn are always happy to show you the latest wares they've either discovered or designed themselves.

SUNFLOWER INTERIORS
12 Avenue D   *653-9144*

OK, you're buying gifts and souvenirs for everyone else back home ... what about your garden? We hope someone's taking care of it while you're on vacation, but we all know that plants are very sensitive and require extra attention to feel and look special. Betty Wirts' Sunflower Interiors offers a wide assortment of unique furnishings for the home garden, including beautiful sculptures, ornate bird baths, a variety of flower seeds, garden tools and elegant bird feeders. This place

is popular with locals and vacationers alike and well worth a stop to those with (or who want to have) green thumbs.

WONDERLAND HOME IMPROVEMENTS, INC.
115 Market St.   *653-2179*

Yes, we know you didn't bring your house with you on vacation, but if you're in an RV, listen up: Wonderland Home Improvements can attend to those minor RV repairs that always crop up when you're trying to enjoy yourself. After all, you're not here to work, are you? Of course not. Owners Gary and Jeanette McIntosh are probably better-known for their wide selection of carpet, vinyl, ceramic tile and wood floors, but they're more than willing to help out those tourists who need it. Besides, fixer-uppers might find a few bargains on materials while they're here. Don't miss Jeanette's display of musical figurines, a hobby she cheerfully shares with anyone who walks by the front window.

Carrabelle

DOWN UNDER DIVE CENTER
Timber Island Rd.   *697-3204*

The blue waters off Florida's Forgot-

Photo: Apalachicola Bay Chamber of Commerce

The historic Gibson Inn is the cornerstone of Apalachicola's downtown redevelopment as a tourist town.

ten Coast make for great diving — especially with all the artificial reefs. The Down Under Dive Center, owned and operated by Richard and June Saunders, is Carrabelle's one-stop shop for the best in diving equipment sales and rentals. It's more than just a dive store, however — Papa Pirate's Tiki Bar is on the premises, and it's a popular hangout, especially during happy hour (5 PM to 7 PM). You're right on the Carrabelle River, and there's plenty of good local oysters and shrimp to keep you feeling pleasant. Even famed treasure hunter Mel Fisher, who found the *Atocha*, has been known to drop by Papa Pirate's. The Down Under Dive Center is certainly a pleasure, and we're glad you don't have to look hard to find it.

LINDA'S TRADING POST

Hwy. 98   697-2547

If you visit Florida, you've got to take home a T-shirt or two. Linda's Trading Post has more than 1,000 designs to choose from. If you still can't find a shirt to your liking, they'll customize one any

way you want. Linda's also sells seashells, windchimes, jewelry, toys and beach floats. Be sure to check out the weekly and monthly specials on the chalkboard just inside the store. Linda's sits just across Highway 98 from the World's Smallest Police Station — and yes, you can have that on a T-shirt too.

TWO GULLS

54 B Market St., Apalachicola	653-2727
Hwy. 98, Carrabelle	697-3787
E. Pine St. Mini Mall	
St. George Island	927-2044

There are three Two Gulls shops (the one in Apalachicola is called Two Gulls Two), and none of them is alike. Owner Judy Taylor and her staff work hard to ensure that each store has its own distinctive offering of gifts, crafts, windsocks, handmade jewelry, trinkets, knick knacks and artwork. Their packed shelves are a browser's delight. Certain items are nautically themed, but there's always something to surprise you, no matter which store you stop at. Seemingly endless displays will keep you browsing.

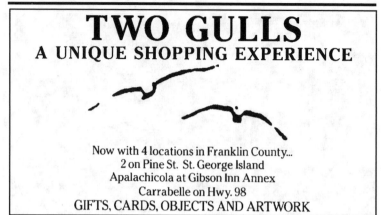
By the time you read this, St. George Island will have two Two Gulls — this one, and Two Gulls On The Beach, at Pine and First streets. We've no doubt that both will be worth visiting.

St. George Island

ISLAND EMPORIUM
Secnd and Pine St. 927-2622

Packing for vacation can be quite a chore, and when you're finally ready to relax the last thing you need is to worry about something you forgot. If you need it, the Island Emporium has it — sooner or later, people learn this when they arrive on St. George Island. Owners Bill and Mary Lou Short bill this as "the ultimate beach shop," offering everything from beachwear to souvenirs, gifts, kitchenware, games, and health and beauty aids.

TOTAL PHOTO
Pine St. Mini-Mall 927-3400

You remembered to bring your camera along, right? Let's hope so, because the Forgotten Coast is a visual delight at every turn. For your camera needs, you can rely on Total Photo, right next door to the Pine Street Mini-Mall. They've got a wide selection of film and will have your photos processed and back to you in as fast as one hour. And if you're having problems with your camera, don't fret: They've got a speedy repair shop that'll have you back on the beach snapping shots in a flash. Don't have time to drop by? If you're anywhere in Franklin County, they'll cheerfully provide pickup and delivery service.

Florida's Forgotten Coast
Attractions

There's plenty of natural beauty along Florida's Forgotten Coast, and we're not just talking about the sandy white beaches. Several state parks in the area highlight the landscape's diversity, from a lake filled with hundreds of bizarre dead trees to a former Civil War fort overlooking a wide and winding river. You can watch the autumn arrival of monarch butterflies heading south for the winter or fish the beautiful coastal waters for a seasonal assortment of fish.

CONSTITUTION
CONVENTION STATE MUSEUM
200 Allen Memorial Way
Port St. Joe   *229-8029*

St. Joseph coulda been a contender. It was one of the fastest-growing boomtowns in the mid-1800s and gave more than a few neighboring port towns a run for their money. At its peak, it served as the site for Florida's first State Constitution Convention. At its lowest point, the place was practically wiped off the map by a combination of poor business, yellow fever and a raging hurricane.

The Constitution Convention State Museum is a time capsule that holds the memories of a town long since gone. Oh, there's a town there now called Port St. Joe, and its relaxed beachfront lifestyle is something a lot of visitors find attractive. But as far as the original township goes, we're just fortunate to have found enough

material in the aftermath to fill this museum. To get to the Constitution Convention State Museum, take Allen Memorial Way off Highway 98 in Port St. Joe.

DEAD LAKES STATE PARK
Wewahitchka   *639-2702*

You could film a horror movie at Dead Lakes, and you could do it in broad daylight. Dead Lakes is full of dead trees, and they stand like the stark skeletons of fantastic creatures. Here's how it happened: Long ago the currents of the Apalachicola River created a sand bar that blocked the flow of the Chipola River. The water backed up and killed thousands of trees, and that's where the park gets its name.

You'd think that no one would have any use for a floodplain with a bunch of strange-looking dead trees, but think again. Tommie Godwin, a Gulf County deputy sheriff, has used a chainsaw to carve gigantic figures and foreboding faces into a few of the larger cypress stumps — they'll scare the heck out of you if you're not paying attention and are the subjects of several thousands tourist photographs and sketches. Even Ripley's Believe It Or Not! has featured Godwin's macabre artwork in newspapers around the world.

Some of the industries that made money off the park were quite innovative. There was a fish hatchery here at one time and later a turpentine factory

— you can still see markings that look like little cat faces where turpentine was drawn out of the trees. Even later, the place was one big moss factory — that's right, Spanish moss. People dried it out and used it for packing material and furniture stuffing back in the 1930s and 1940s.

And while most people think that tupelo honey comes from Tupelo, Mississippi, locals know that golden sweetness comes from none other than Wewahitchka. It's a century-old commercial industry most outsiders don't know about. If you see bees buzzing around, you'll know they're working hard to turn out that next batch of honey.

For 20 years now, the area has been a state park offering good fishing and some, well, interesting scenery. There are campgrounds with full-facility camping, boat ramps to the lakes and the Chipola River and a nature trail. The lakes as well as two ponds dug in 1936 offer plenty of bass, bream, crappie, gar and carp for the anglers. Don't forget the Florida freshwater fishing license. Dead Lakes State Park is in Wewahitchka, 25 miles north of Port St. Joe. Take State Road 71 from Highway 98 at Port St. Joe.

FORT GADSDEN STATE HISTORIC SITE
Sumatra   670-8988

Fort Gadsden is known to historians by another name: Negro Fort. During the War of 1812, this base was built by the British to recruit Indians and blacks in their efforts against the U.S. Territory some 50 miles to the north. The fort rested on Prospect Bluff above the Apalachicola River and was armed to the gills with guns, cannon and gunpowder.

The skirmishes between American and British forces continued, and this fort became a training ground and, after An-

drew Jackson took Pensacola, a refuge for blacks as well as Creek and Seminole Indians. In December 1814, records indicate that nearly 3,000 men, women and children were living on or near Prospect Bluff.

The British finally withdrew after signing the Treaty of Ghent in 1815, but when it became clear that Jackson had no intentions of honoring the treaty's provisions that protected the Indians from loss of their land, Maj. Edward Nicholls of the Royal Marines was careful to leave behind as much weaponry and ammunition as possible.

The fort offered a free and independent environment for the blacks, many of whom were escaped slaves. Because of its renegade nature, the fort also offered a haven for cattle rustlers, thieves and murderers. Jackson finally ordered the destruction of the fort, and the battle that ensued was probably about as brief as the order itself.

On July 27, 1816, a handful of gunboats and schooners approached the fort from the south while a unit of British and friendly Creek Indians moved in from the north. These ground troops were needed only for cleanup, however. The fifth shot from the gunboats landed squarely in the fort's magazine, detonating the stockpile of gunpowder.

When the smoke cleared, Negro Fort and 270 of its inhabitants were gone. The British troops discovered only 30 people who survived the blast.

Today, Fort Gadsden offers a visitors center that recounts the tragic history of the fort and contains a miniature replica of the fort as it must have appeared shortly before its destruction. There are picnic sites available, and a nature trail that wanders through the vibrant green landscape above the river.

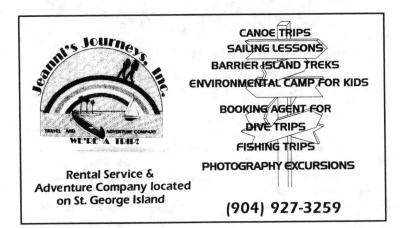
To get to Fort Gadsden State Historic Site, take State Road 65 for 20 miles from Highway 98 in Eastpoint.

St. George Island State Park
St. George Island   *927-2111*

St. George Island is one of a chain of barrier islands along the Gulf Coast, and although development is taking its toll on the natural beauty, the Julian G. Bruce St. George Island State Park is preserving a good-size chunk of it for everyone to enjoy. The 1,962-acre park is nearly 10 miles long and features some gently rolling dunes and salt marshes highlighted with oaks and pines.

The island has a rich history, and there's a marker at the western end where William Augustus Bowles was shipwrecked in 1799. Bowles was a renegade, self-styled leader of the Cherokee nation and a constant thorn in the side of the Spanish, who simply could not establish a military stronghold over their territory. Bowles had been captured once and sent to Spain, but he escaped and made his way back here aboard the schooner *Fox*, which ran aground on the island. Apparently unfazed by this incident, Bowles salvaged what supplies he could and set out for the Apalachicola River, leaving behind the ships' crew who were later rescued. In an attempt to secure an independent Indian nation under British protection, Bowles led a small army of Indians to the Spanish fort at St. Marks and overtook it.

It's illegal to bring your pets to Florida's panhandle beaches — unless you're in Cape San Blas, Mexico Beach or Port St. Joe. That's right: Gulf County has no law against animals on the beach, as long as they're on a leash. So if your morning jog or starlight stroll just isn't complete without a furry friend, snap your fingers, grab a leash and hit the sand.

Insiders' Tips

Fishing Florida's
Forgotten Coast

The Gulf of Mexico has some of the best fishing waters anywhere in the world. Seafood caught here is shipped around the world, and if you like fishing, you've come to the right place.

Some say the best fishing happens throughout the spring, when the waters warm up and several types of fish begin spawning, including mackerel, trout, flounder, cobia and tarpon. The summer months are just as good, though you're likely to find the best catch early or late in the day — and that's just as well from an angler's point of view, considering how hot it gets when the sun's up.

If you go it alone, just be sure you've got a valid license. Bait and tackle shops all along the coast sell them. Nonresidents can expect to pay around $5 for a three-day license and up to $30 for a year's license. Residents of Florida pay approximately double those rates. Of course, if you choose a charter fishing trip, chances are the boat has a commercial fishing license and you're covered by the cost of the charter.

Charters are recommended to newcomers for a number of reasons. For one thing, you're hiring an experienced charter captain who probably knows more about fishing these waters than you could hope to learn in a lifetime. They'll know exactly which fish are biting and the best places to find them. And unless you're pulling your own boat and have spent a few hundreds dollars on fishing gear, charters also afford you the use of their tried, tested and true equipment. And unless you're really into scaling and scooping, most charters will gladly arrange to have your catch cleaned afterward, sending you home with a broad smile and a cooler full of fish ready for the skillet or grill.

If the idea of jumping in the water and spearing your own fish strikes you as strange, you should know that the Gulf of Mexico is one of the most popular spearfishing spots in the world. The beautiful waters and abundant aquatic life make it a trip you won't soon forget. Sure, it can be a lot of fun to catch your Amberjack, Snapper or Grouper from the ship's deck. But those intrepid spearfishing souls who go it *mano a pescado* (hand to fish) say it's a thrilling and unique experience you'll remember for the rest of your life.

CAPT. BLACK'S DIVE CENTER

301 Monument Ave.
Port St. Joe   229-6330

The waters off Port St. Joe are great for fishing and diving — there are more than 20 dive sites off St. Joseph Peninsula alone. For years, Capt. Black's Marine has been helping residents and visitors have fun doing both. Whether you're buying or renting, you'll find everything you need in their fully stocked dive shop. Their helpful staff will even plan and lead a dive charter for you. Their Specialty Trips include the *Empire Mica* (see sidebar), Around the World (five sites in one day) and Night Diving (two sunken freighters from the early half of the century). There's a four-person minimum for each dive, but don't worry about a crowded boat. Capt. Black's Dive Center prefers uncrowded trips so you get the most out of each dive. If you've ever wanted to try snorkeling, scallop hunting or spearfishing, then Capt. Black's is the place to go in Port St. Joe.

CAPT. JOHN GRIMM
The Moorings, Hwy. 98
Carrabelle   971-5110

Grimm's charter boat is the *Solandri*, a 42-foot Hatteras sport fisherman, and it's one sleek vessel. Featuring the latest electronic fish-finding equipment, the Solandri is available for a variety of sport fishing charters. As with other charters, the rates vary with the length of the trip and number of people. Book your trip as far in advance as possible — during tourist season, the marinas along the Forgotten Coast are empty all day long, and you don't want to be the one left standing on the dock.

COOL CHANGE
H.C.R. Box 119
St. George Island   927-2604

Captains Larry Troy and Bill Corman offer great offshore fishing excursions in their 12-ton, 32-foot boat. If you're aiming to fill the boat with fish, you can just about do it in a day. Their family-oriented tours accommodate up to six people, and everything's furnished except lunch and beverages. Fishing trips are $600 per day, and you're advised to book your excursion as far in advance as possible. *Cool Change* stays very busy during tourist season.

JEANNI'S JOURNEYS
E. Pine St. Mini Mall   927-3259

True nature lovers won't just settle for a stroll along the beautiful beaches of St. George Island — they'll have to get out and do some real exploring. Outdoors enthusiast Jeannie McMillan can help you appreciate the natural wonders of the coast. She organizes special canoe and fishing trips throughout the area and even teaches a summer environmental workshop for kids. Guided tours, photography expeditions and dive trips are among her many specialties. She'll take you places you won't forget.

THE MOORINGS
Hwy. 98, Carrabelle   349-2112

Capt. Doug Kurtley of Deep Sea Charters offers day-long fishing charters for groups of up to 6, and he also specializes in deep-sea diving charters. If you're into spearfishing or you just want to hit some of the wonderful dive sites off the Forgotten Coast, this is for you. Among the many packages available is a dive charter for six people featuring up to three dives in one day — all for less $500. Other charter rates vary, and you're advised to make your plans as far in advance as possible.

RAINBOW MARINA

Apalachicola   670-8834

Whether you want fresh or saltwater fishing, Capt. David Giddens knows where the waters are best. He's been fishing these beautiful waters for quite a while and can help you plan the best fishing charter for your money. His 25-foot Robalo vessel has a tower and downriggers and comes completely outfitted.

This action embarrassed Spain greatly, because now it had no military fort between Pensacola and St. Augustine. Soon after, the British were not so interested in Bowles' welfare and he was again captured by the Spanish, spending the remaining years of his life in a Cuban prison. You'll agree that although Bowles met a tragic end, he couldn't have picked a better place to shipwreck.

Today there are several pavilions for picnics, two boat launches, hiking trails and full-facility as well as primitive camping areas.

If you're really adventurous you can hire a private boat to take you to Little St. George Island, also called Cape St. George, which sits just west of St. George Island. This island was once connected to St. George Island, but in the late 1950s the U.S. Army Corps of Engineers opened a pass for boaters between the two land masses. Little St. George Island features a lighthouse that was built in the mid-19th century — it's operational but not open to the public. There are places for camping, but you must notify the St. George Island State Park office if you want to camp there since the island is officially under their jurisdiction. To get to St. George Island, take State Road 300 S. from Highway 98 at Eastpoint.

ST. JOSEPH PENINSULA STATE PARK

Port St. Joe   227-1327

Every autumn there are two migrations to the St. Joseph Peninsula State Park on Cape San Blas. One brings nature and wildlife enthusiasts from near and far, and the other migration is what attracts them: the annual southern flight of the monarch butterfly.

The butterflies use this as a stopping point before heading to Mexico, and visitors have learned to take the time to observe the colorful spectacle. It's hard to think of something this remarkable park doesn't offer. It's got swimming and diving, some wonderfully white beaches, saltwater fishing (with license), boating and some leisurely hiking trails through the huge dunes that are home to thriving pine trees.

The 2,650-acre setting provides excellent viewing for bird-lovers, and it's one of the best places to observe the annual fall migration of hawks and other birds.

Nearby is Salinas Park, which offers surfside picnic areas and boardwalks that follow the dunes to an elevated gazebo providing a grand view. There's also the Cape San Blas Lighthouse, the sixth one to stand in that spot. Natural elements — everything from hurricanes to shifting sands — caused the collapse of the other five. This one's been standing for more than 100 years and should be with us for a long time to come.

The park offers furnished cabins and more than 100 full-facility campsites, and there's a special area for camping by organized, nonprofit youth groups. For handicapped visitors only, there's a special beach and recreational area just south of this park.

To get to the park from Highway 98, take County Road 30 between Apalachicola and Port St. Joe.

ST. VINCENT ISLAND
653-8808

The westernmost island in the barrier chain just off Franklin County's coastline, St. Vincent Island is a lush green wedge jutting out of Apalachicola Bay. It's home to the St. Vincent National Wildlife Refuge, and while this is a highly protected area, it doesn't mean visitors can't enjoy its beauty firsthand.

There are 14 miles of sandy white beach available for public use during the year. You have to hire your own boat to get out there, and visitors are welcome during daylight hours except during planned hunting or burning periods, which take place sporadically throughout the year. The interior of the island sports freshwater lakes and ponds as well as an abundance of wildlife. No camping is allowed on the island unless it's in conjunction with an overnight managed hunt approved by the refuge manager. The manager also grants permits to those who merely wish to explore the island's interior.

Don't fool with Mother Nature — the island features an abundance of wildlife such as wild pigs and snakes, and an encounter with either of these can certainly pose a bit of a problem with even the most hardened tourists. If you come out here, you'd best be prepared to rough it a bit. It's beautiful on the island, but its a beauty that demands great respect.

For more information, contact the St. Vincent National Wildlife Refuge office and tourist center in Apalachicola.

Florida's Forgotten Coast
Annual Events and Festivals

No matter what time of year you visit the Forgotten Coast, there's always something happening, even if it's just the rustle of waves along the beach. But there are three fantastic festivals you ought to know about so you can make your plans accordingly. St. George Island hosts the biggest regional chili cookoff in the nation, and Carrabelle is the site of the largest nonprofit fishing tournament in this part of the state. And Apalachicola devotes one full weekend each year to the reason so many people love the area: the delicious seafood.

Plan your vacation around any one of these great festivals, and we guarantee you'll be one happy camper.

March

THE ST. GEORGE ISLAND CHARITY CHILI COOKOFF AND AUCTION

St. George Island   653-9419

This fantastic food fest is held each year during the first weekend in March. It's the largest regional chili cookoff in the nation, and nearly 20,000 people from all over flock to the island to have a whole lot of fun. The public beach area just off Franklin Boulevard is filled with dueling chili chefs vying for the first-place title, and you can taste 'em all if you've got the room. There are plenty of other food booths, too, so don't pack a lunch or anything. Just bring your appetite.

Photo: Apalachicola Bay Chamber of Commerce

The crystal-blue waters of Florida's Forgotten Coast make this a swimmer's paradise.

There's also a lively antique and art auction and a 5-K run. Proceeds from these events go to the St. George Island Volunteer Fire Department, and over the years a lot of money has been raised for this worthy cause.

June

THE BIG BEND SALTWATER CLASSIC AND CARRABELLE WATERFRONT FESTIVAL
Carrabelle   697-2585

That's a big name for a big festival held each June on Father's Day weekend. This is the largest nonprofit saltwater fishing tournament in northern Florida, with proceeds going to a great cause: the Organization for Artificial Reefs. This group has provided several new artificial reefs just off Florida's Forgotten Coast, ensuring the richness and diversity of the fishing waters here. The fishing tournament awards prizes in four divisions: recreational, junior (anglers younger than 13), masters and fly rod. There are several prizes, and the lucky winner gets an all-expenses paid fishing vacation.

The Carrabelle Waterfront Festival is a lively arts and crafts show that features continuous entertainment, including a Seafood Gumbo Cookoff and live music. All this makes for a weekend that's jam-packed with people, good food and great fun.

November

THE FLORIDA SEAFOOD FESTIVAL
Apalachicola   653-8051

Sometime around the turn of the century, residents of Apalachicola began having seafood celebrations, and rightly so. The waters here provide some of the best seafood in the world, and these celebrations have given rise to the Florida Seafood Festival, which takes place each year in downtown Battery Park on the first Saturday and Sunday in November. The weather's cool and the fish are plentiful as more than 20,000 seafood-lovers turn out to show their support. You can sample the best of Apalachicola Bay, including oysters, shrimp, crab and fish. There's enough food to feed an army.

If you're really hungry, enter the festival's Oyster Eating Contest. You get 15 minutes to toss back all the bivalves you can hold. Contestants might want to skip meals for a couple of days prior to the event, because a recent winner consumed more than 300 oysters to take first prize. The competition is certainly stiff and, when the buzzer sounds, well-stuffed.

Need to work off some of that extra weight you're sure to gain during the festival? Try the Redfish Run, a 5K event that's open to people of all ages. Or you can just stroll through several maritime heritage exhibits that feature boat building and net making. There's also a popular arts and crafts show, and evening festivities usually include plenty of live music and dancing.

For more information, call the Florida Seafood Festival at the above-listed phone number or write them at P.O. Box 460, Apalachicola 32329.

Tallahassee
History

Exploration

Although there is evidence that people lived in Florida at least 12,000 years ago, the first written records of the land did not appear until the 16th century with the arrival of Spanish explorers. The first to reach the present-day Tallahassee area was Panfilo de Narvaez, whose expedition landed near Tampa Bay in 1528. Like Ponce de Leon and so many other explorers before him, de Narvaez was seeking gold, and when natives told him of a northern city called Apalachen — a city made of gold — he swore to find it.

Panfilo de Narvaez and his men made the long trek northward to the panhandle and then headed due west. They didn't find much gold but did encounter the Apalachee Indians, the earliest recorded inhabitants of the Tallahassee area. The Apalachee territory stretched as far west as Pensacola and was bounded to the east by the Aucilla River and the tribes of Timucuan Indians just beyond. An agricultural society first and foremost, the Apalachee Indians could also be fierce warriors when threatened. Unfortunately for de Narvaez, he and his men were perceived as a threat and faced constant attacks while exploring the area. The expedition finally decided to build seagoing vessels and head for Mexico.

Eleven years later, Hernando de Soto reached the Tallahassee area, also in search of gold. He and his men had to fight their way in but apparently fared much better than the earlier expedition. They spent the winter of 1539 here, marking the first known celebration of Christmas on the North American continent.

Settling

Hernando de Soto never returned to the area; he met his death the following year while exploring present-day Mississippi. In fact, for the next 100 years Spanish settlers generally ignored this area. They were busy establishing their Pensacola and St. Augustine missions, designed to import their religion and save the souls of the godless natives. It was only a matter of time before they trekked inland, and in 1633 two friars established the first mission in the red hills of present-day Tallahassee.

By 1647 there were eight churches in the area, and all but one was destroyed by an uprising of Apalachees who rejected the joint yoke of brutal Spanish rule and Christian faith forced upon them. Undaunted, the Spanish rebuilt the churches and in 1656 moved the main mission, San Luis, to a hill only a couple of miles west of the present-day capital. At its height, this mission became the centerpoint of activity in the Big Bend area, with a population of at least 1,400 people. In 1677, the Spanish also constructed a fort called San Marcos de Apalachee in St. Marks, effectively claiming the all-important coastal area.

Battling for Land

In spite of their strong foothold, however, the Spanish were eventually forced to abandon San Luis. By this time the English and Spanish settlers were grabbing madly for land, each side using the Native Americans as soldiers in their battles. In 1704, the San Luis Mission faced an impending attack by Governor James Moore of South Carolina. Moore had tried unsuccessfully to take the Spanish garrison at St. Augustine two years earlier, and he was so determined to make up for his failure that when the Legislature refused to fund his next attack, Moore financed it himself.

Moore's forces — 50 white men and more than 1,000 Creek Indians — plunged south to destroy the Spanish mission of Concepcion de Aubale, about 20 miles east of San Luis. As his unstoppable forces advanced westward, so did news of Moore's brutal methods. The Spanish decided to burn San Luis to the ground and abandon the area.

By the time it was all over, Moore's forces had tortured and killed hundreds of the Apalachee and were returning triumphantly to their home state with more than 3,000 Indian slaves in tow, most of them women and children. Moore's raid effectively depopulated the area, sending the remaining Indians either east to St. Augustine or west to Pensacola.

For many years Tallahassee was nothing more than a black slash on the quiet hills, a ravaged ghost town. This was only the first of many pivotal fires that would change the landscape and its inhabitants.

The Seminole Indians were originally Creek Indians whose homeland covered areas of Alabama, Georgia, Mississippi and other states. Their migration here is something of a mystery because it is known that the Creeks held the land of the dead sacred and considered it bad luck to live in places where people had been killed. Some historians believe these Indians simply had no choice, considering the expansionist example set by such men as Governor Moore of South Carolina. In the end, the Creek Indians might have concluded that bad luck was better than no luck at all.

Why were these Creeks suddenly called Seminoles? The first instance we have of the word comes from an Englishman, John Stuart, who served as an American Indian agent in the 18th century. Stuart believed the word meant "wild ones," but it's also quite close to the Spanish cimarron, which means "runaways" — too close, in fact, for the many Indians who disliked being called cowards simply because they'd broken off from their main tribe. Nevertheless, the name stuck and has become the accepted term over the centuries.

At the time the first Seminoles appeared, northern Florida wasn't entirely unpopulated. There was still a sizable Spanish presence around, often aided by a tribe called the Yammassee that moved into the area from other parts of the territory. After many battles with the fierce Seminoles, the Spanish were pushed back to the coastal areas and the Yammassees were virtually wiped out.

In 1763, after signing the Treaty of Paris that ended its war with Spain, England took control of Florida and, for safety's sake, sought to work more closely with the Indians. The British Empire offered better trading conditions and treated the Seminoles with respect, honoring nearly every treaty it signed with them. This was particularly fortunate during the Revolutionary War, because friendly relations with the Indians meant that retreating British Loyalists could be guaranteed a safe haven if they could make it this far south.

An Indian city appeared on maps of the area for the first time in 1778: Tallahassee Town, from an Indian word that translates aptly into old field or, more loosely, abandoned village. It was also known as Tonaby's Town, named after the powerful chief who founded it. Although Indians fared better under British rule, Chief Tonaby boldly declared his loyalty to the Spanish, who had employed him for two decades as a messenger.

Britain's defeat in the American Revolution ushered in the second era of Spanish occupation as Spain was rewarded the territory for its loyalty to Americans during the revolution. This time, however, Spain's grasp was even more tenuous as the Seminoles were by now used to the better trading conditions with the British. Friendly individuals like Chief Tonaby had disappeared from the scene, and Spain was forced to contract with a British trading firm to handle the commerce with the Seminoles.

By this time, the Southern states of the United States were producing cotton and other crops using the plantation system. This entire economy hinged upon the use of African slaves as a cheap labor force. Although some slaves were treated well, most were horribly oppressed. And if they wanted to escape, the safest places to seek refuge were the relatively unexplored west, or down south to the Florida Territory.

The Indians were generally receptive to escaped slaves and often helped them establish their own towns and villages. Sometimes lone escapees would be captured by the Seminoles and forced into labor, although this form of slavery was far different from that of the white plantation owners to the north. The Indians

not only allowed these blacks to marry into their tribes and live among them, but children from those unions were born into freedom and not extended generational slavery. Before long, the racial mix was diverse for such a small area, with English, Spanish, Indians and Africans often in daily contact with each other.

Quelling Resistance

In Alabama there arose a violent Indian faction whose aim was to divide the races. These Creek Indians called themselves Red Sticks, and they followed the teachings of Tecumseh, a Shawnee chief who preached that the white man must be driven from the land by any means necessary. In 1813, the Red Sticks slaughtered more than 250 people at Fort Mims in Alabama.

Enter Andrew Jackson, general of the U.S. Army, diehard expansionist and something of a hero for his role in the Battle of New Orleans in 1814. Not long after the Fort Mims massacre, he and his troops, which included many Cherokee Indians, killed 800 Creeks in the Battle of Horseshoe Bend while suffering only a handful of losses themselves. The defeated Creeks signed the Treaty of 1814, giving up more than 20 million acres of land in Georgia and Alabama. It was only a matter of time before other Indian territories would be claimed.

Some of the Red Sticks escaped Jackson's wrath and disappeared into the swamps and forests of Florida. Many of them continued their attacks and raids against white settlers, though often it was necessary to make deals with the British and Spanish to get the supplies they needed.

In 1818, Jackson single-handedly came close to starting a war with Britain. He captured and executed two British agents who had been charged with instigating Seminole hostility. While the arrests were probably justified, the resulting trial was questionable, and many historians agree that such punishment was probably illegal. To temper England's wrath over the incident, the U.S. House of Representatives passed a resolution condemning Jackson's actions.

Undaunted, Jackson moved to quell Indian resistance. In March of 1818, Jackson's advancing army reached Tallahassee, not long after the forewarned Indians there had abandoned it. He ordered all buildings burnt to the ground, and once again Tallahassee was reduced to smoldering ruin.

The First Seminole War flared from 1818 to 1819, and Jackson's raids during the conflict eventually forced the Spanish to sell its territory to the United States. Jackson was rewarded for his efforts by being named the Governor of the Florida Territory in 1821, and he in turn rewarded his many friends with comfortable jobs and insider advice on investing in the territory's economy.

But Jackson did not care for Florida. The area was not exactly a hotbed of activity, and he felt that he'd been given this post by influential enemies who wanted to keep him out of national politics. After only a few months he and his wife returned to their home in Tennessee. Florida, however, would feel the man's influence for years to come.

A New Capital

One of Tallahassee's most prized assets is its location. History reveals, however, that this site was chosen not because of its north-south boundaries, but because of what lay directly east and west of it.

In 1821, when Florida became a Territory of the United States, the land was divided into two areas. During the 20 years of British rule, two capitals had been established. On the Atlantic coast was the historic settlement of St. Augustine, and nearly 400 miles away on the Gulf of Mexico was the equally historic settlement of Pensacola. Both functioned well as centers of trade and legislation for their respective regions, but when the time came to coordinate the eventual consolidation of the area, the 400 miles of undeveloped swamp and piney forests between the two capitals proved to be a daunting barrier.

After much discussion, the two capitals decided to find a midpoint on the panhandle that would accommodate a yearly meeting of both lawmakers. By anyone's map, Tallahassee was the logical choice.

In 1824 the first white settlers moved into the red hills area and began cutting down trees for the first capitol building, which was a log cabin.

For many years, Tallahassee was little more than a tiny town of log cabins and dirt roads. William DuVal was named Jackson's successor, and they were similar in their general and frank dislike for the territory. At one point, the secretary of state had to order DuVal to return to his duties after the governor went to Kentucky for an extended stay.

Tallahassee was little more than a frontier town at this point, although several rich families had moved here. Among them was Prince Achille Murat, the nephew of Napoleon Bonaparte and exiled crown prince of Naples, who married the great-grand niece of George Washington. Francis Eppes, the grandson of Thomas Jefferson, also relocated to the area to run a plantation.

Tallahassee was growing. Streets had been planned, plantations built and routes of commerce established with the nearby

Gulf Coast as well as other cities and towns. There was a genteel aristocracy in place, one that delighted itself with ring tournaments straight out of the legends of King Arthur, complete with chivalrous silk-clad knights on horseback, crowned ladies and splendid balls. Several long-lived celebrations were held by the citizens, including the Fourth of July, the anniversary of the Battle of New Orleans and the May Day Festival.

In spite of all this transplanted aristocracy, Tallahassee was still a rather primitive settlement and not a very nice one at that. In 1827, writer Ralph Waldo Emerson visited the area and later described Tallahassee as "a grotesque place, selected three years since as a suitable spot for the capital, and since that day rapidly settled by public officers, land speculators, and desperadoes."

Duelling and drunken brawls killed plenty of people, and the yellow fever plague of 1841 didn't help the town's reputation. The toll from the plague was so great that a new graveyard — Old City Cemetery — was quickly established.

Two years after the plague came another catastrophe, one that would again change the face of this young town: the fire of 1843. It started in the kitchen of a hotel called Washington Hall and raged for only three hours one hot May evening. Most of the town's closely packed buildings were wooden, and Tallahassee was almost wiped off the map for the third time in its history. It was decreed, and smartly so, that all future buildings must be constructed of masonry.

Through all of these tragedies, one aspect of life in Tallahassee became increasingly clear: Whites and Indians could not live together. The settlers eagerly wanted as much land as possible, and the Indians bitterly felt they had already given

too much. Numerous meetings were held, promises and treaties were made and broken and the antagonism between the two sides inevitably led to the Second Seminole War.

This conflict lasted from 1835 to 1842 and was much more costly than the first. Led by famous warriors such as Osceola, the Seminoles inflicted heavy losses on the U.S. Army forces that moved in to quell uprisings. By retreating into the swamps, the Indians easily evaded the clumsy, ill-trained troops pursuing them. As Americans slowly realized the extent to which these Native Indians were dedicated to their land and freedom, the war began to seem useless and cruel. An army surgeon, Jacob Rhett Motte, would echo this sentiment years later in *Journey Into Wilderness*, an account of his experiences during the war, "Why not in the name of common sense let them keep it [the swamp]? Every day served but to convince us of their inflexible determination to fight or die in the land of their fathers." Historians such as Gene Burnett have even likened the unpopular conflict to Vietnam.

In the end, the Seminoles were defeated because of their limited resources and dwindling manpower. Almost all of them were shipped off to reservations, and all the escaped slaves captured with them were returned to slavery.

Although there weren't any Indian attacks closer than within 10 miles Tallahassee, the Second Seminole War had been on everyone's mind. Citizens had watched as thousands of soldiers from Tennessee and Georgia marched southward, sometimes camping just outside of town. Now that the conflict was over, Tallahasseans could finally breathe a sigh of relief and return their attention to the landscape unfolding around them.

Northern Florida had become a dynamic agrarian economy, producing cotton as well as other crops such as tobacco. The latter was introduced to the area by Governor DuVal.

The first real Capitol building was completed in 1845, the year Florida became a state and William D. Moseley its first elected governor.

But not long after the end of the Second Seminole War, another racial problem loomed on the horizon: the abolitionist movement. In the 1860 presidential election, Abraham Lincoln received no votes at all from the state of Florida, and that's because his name was not even allowed on the ballot. The Southern states reverberated with speeches and literature demanding secession from the Union.

The Civil War

In 1861, South Carolina was the first state to break away from the Union. Mississippi was second and Florida was third. Of all the Confederate states east of the Mississippi, Florida was the only one whose capital did not fall to Union forces.

Though most Floridians supported the decision to secede, there were a few bold citizens who made public their stand against it. Richard Keith Call, a former governor, is remembered by his daughter as declaring to a group of secession-happy people, "You have opened the gates of hell, from which shall flow the curses of the damned."

The First Infantry Regiment of Florida Volunteers was pooled mostly from Leon County and its neighbors, Gadsden, Jackson, Jefferson and Madison counties. Col. James Patton Anderson, a Jefferson County planter, was in command. They first marched to Pensacola and helped fend off attacks from Union forces at Fort Pickens. Later the First Florida fought in Tennessee at Shiloh, one of the most tragic battles of the war. They also saw action at the Battle of Perryville in Kentucky and Murfreesboro, Tennessee.

John Milton, a planter from Marianna, was elected governor during the Civil War, and his ideas concerning states' rights were even more radical than those who supported secession. Let the states stand entirely alone, he reasoned, dismissing the need even for a Confederacy — although he was more than willing to let them direct the war effort.

Milton didn't like it when Florida's First and other regiments were pulled out of the state to fight elsewhere, and his paranoia was well founded. Not long after their departure, Federal troops seized Pensacola and St. Augustine, as well as several other port towns.

By 1863, the general attitude in Tallahassee and other parts of the state was similar to national reaction during the Second Seminole War. Confederate troops were deserting their posts in great numbers and hiding out in woods and swamps, where Union forces gave them food and shelter as they waited for the war to end.

It was an understandable reaction from the lower-class soldiers conscripted into battle. If you had an extra few thousand dollars in your pocket, you could simply buy your way out of service, hire someone else to do the dirty work for you. The poorer folk could only hide and hope they wouldn't be captured and executed for desertion.

The lack of soldiers in the Tallahassee area makes the Battle of Natural Bridge all the more incredible. Union forces — including many black soldiers — landed south of Tallahassee at St. Marks in March of 1865. They planned to proceed northward and take the capital city by surprise.

Tallahassee got word of the impending invasion, however, and mustered up as many able-bodied men as possible. Old men and young boys took up arms along with the remaining Confederate troops, and together they hurried the 15 miles south to Natural Bridge, a spot on the St. Marks River where the river disappears underground for 100 feet. When the Union forces attempted to cross here, they were repelled and forced to retreat back to their ships. This was a small victory for the Confederacy, but to Tallahassee it felt as if the war had been won. The soldiers received heroes' welcomes when they returned.

This joy was short-lived, however, as news of countless Southern defeats and Union advances reached the city. "Death would be preferable to reunion," Governor Milton told the Legislature and then proceeded to prove the point. On April 1, 1865, eight days before Gen. Lee surrendered at Appomattox, Florida Governor John Milton shot himself dead.

Restoration

People struggled to survive in the aftermath of the Civil War. No matter who you were, things had changed drastically. Tallahassee was now the capital city of a confused and defeated state that had to drastically restructure and rebuild itself.

Some of the area plantations offered to pay their former slaves to resume their jobs, but it was a tough sell. Many of the blacks felt they had to shed every aspect of their old lives in order to truly be free, and this sometimes included moving away and changing one's name, even leaving one's family. The Freedmen's Bureau was established to help the blacks assimilate themselves into society, but because of the lifelong hardships they had

endured, many blacks simply preferred to "drop out" and enjoy their freedom 24 hours a day. By 1866, though, most blacks were working again on plantations under a contract system that was sometimes not much different than slavery.

Old habits die hard, but they do indeed die. Many whites felt as if all they had known was crumbling around them. Agriculture quickly dwindled to a small fraction of what it had once been, and the cotton industry all but disappeared from the area.

Other industries sprang up: Old plantations were turned into hunting preserves, while peanuts and tobacco replaced cotton as major crops. Still, the sense of dislocation was numbing to many, and it's no surprise that Federal troops occupied Florida for more than a decade after the end of the war.

There was happiness to be found on a small scale. The poet Sidney Lanier visited Tallahassee not long after the war and wrote in his 1875 book *Florida: Its Scenery, Climate and History*, ". . . no one has starved, and albeit the people are poor and the dwellings need paint and ready money is slow of circulation . . . it must be confessed that the bountiful tables looked like anything but famine, that signs of energy cropped out here and there in many places, and that the whole situation was but a reasonable one for a people who ten years ago had to begin life anew from the very bottom. . . ."

Into the 20th Century

The first two decades of this century were boom years for Florida, and it all boiled down to one word: land.

After the Panama Canal project proved that swamp land could be drained and filled in, Florida suddenly found itself abuzz with investors and developers.

Once the railroads and highways connecting southern Florida were in place, big money moved in. Two of the state's largest industries — citrus and tourism — were established during this period.

Tallahassee itself was also modernized to a large extent. At the turn of the century there had been a fruitless attempt to relocate the capital to either Jacksonville, St. Augustine or Ocala. There were several powerful factions who felt that Tallahassee was too distant from the rest of the state, especially the burgeoning southern peninsula. This move never took place, of course, but the threat was something of a wake-up call to the citizens. The lawmakers soon approved funding to improve the existing Capitol, and the city decided to update its services and utilities. An electric power plant and sewer system were constructed to support the city's increasing population.

This boom period, which lasted from the turn of the century to the 1920s, helped revitalize the state's stricken economy. But all booms must bust. The Depression made things tough all over, and Florida felt the blow as much as any state.

People were desperate for money, and that included lawmakers. After the Stock Market Crash of 1929, more than 150 cities and towns in Florida were in default on their debts, and the state government was burdened with a huge deficit its constitution wouldn't allow.

Governor Doyle Carlton (1929-1933) couldn't have picked a lousier time to head the state government, but he buckled down and got to work anyway. His feuds with lawmakers are legendary, and while they did pass a controversial gambling bill that reportedly had the backing of some big-time underworld figures, Carlton fought them to the end. He also campaigned heavily for Franklin D.

Roosevelt during his run for president and was a presidential advisor for many years.

To make things worse, there was a Mediterranean fruit fly invasion the same year as the stock market crash, and that year's bountiful citrus crop was more than halved.

During World War II, Florida's vast coastline and friendly climate made it a prime spot to train soldiers, and this boosted the state's economy considerably. Governor Spessard Holland was instrumental in attracting the military to the state, and Tallahassee's Dale Mabry Airport, now the Tallahassee Regional Airport, became an important air base.

When the war was over, the resulting boom had a great impact on Florida. More people began to visit and relocate here than ever before. In fact, many of these people had been stationed here during the war and were returning for the state's climate and landscape.

But by the mid-1950s, Tallahassee seemed out-of-step with the rest of the state. Public transportation, health care and segregation were issues that needed to be addressed, and LeRoy Collins, elected as the state's 33rd governor, was instrumental in bringing about many needed changes in Florida.

All was not peaceful in paradise, however. Beneath the Formica veneer of the 1950s lurked renewed racial tension. Governor Collins was an important player during this era, and so were the students at Florida A&M University.

In 1956 there was a massive bus boycott in Tallahassee. Blacks refused to ride the city bus line because they were forced to sit in the back. Their unified actions brought about a permanent change in policy.

In 1960, FAMU students staged a sit-in at Woolworth's lunch counter in protest of segregated dining facilities. Three years later, blacks cleverly protested at the Florida Theatre, which admitted whites only. They formed a huge line to purchase tickets, and as each one was turned away they'd return again to the end of the line.

Photo: Tallahassee Area Convention & Visitors Bureau

The Union Bank is the oldest surviving bank building in the state.

This was a turbulent decade for the nation and Tallahassee, which was quite resistant to change. The race issue was so controversial that when President John F. Kennedy was assassinated, many opponents of his civil rights policies could be heard openly laughing and joking throughout the city. And many agree that Collins lost his 1968 bid for re-election because of his work on the civil rights issue. His opponents simply handed out photos of the governor standing beside Martin Luther King Jr. in Selma, Alabama.

One of the most violent and tragic racial episodes happened in April of 1968, after the assassination of King. Riots erupted on the FAMU campus, and the entire area was cordoned off by police following mob attacks on motorists. FAMU was closed down for more than a week to allow tensions to subside. In the midst of it all, there was a peaceful march past the State Capitol to mark King's funeral.

This decade also saw the national space program take root in Florida, and it has remained a vital industry and tourist attraction. The first of Florida's many theme parks also began construction, and corporations continued their relocation here to take advantage of Florida's business-friendly environment and growing work force.

Florida has grown and changed considerably in the last quarter-century, and the Capital City has remained at the center of it all. Its citizens take pride in the fact that this old town on a hill still serves as the focal point for state politics. Tallahassee today is more diverse than it ever was, and yet there's also a sense of unity among its residents. It has passed from a rural agricultural center to a growing urban city, and since 1980 its population has almost doubled to more than 200,000.

Often in the city's past, its residents have been afraid of the uncertain future. But they learned that the best way to overcome their fear was to remain in touch with their colorful, violent and often inspiring past.

Inside
Tallahassee

What's a city like Tallahassee doing in a state like Florida? That's the big question a lot of visitors ask themselves after paying us a visit, and it just goes to show that you can't always trust a preconceived notion.

When most people think of Florida, they usually picture what the peninsula has to offer from Orlando on down: wide sunny beaches, crowded theme parks and a sense of hustle-and-bustle that is notably absent from life in the northwest part of the state.

The capital city of Tallahassee is found at the thinnest point of Northwest Florida — 15 miles to its north lies the Georgia state line, and 25 miles due south is the Gulf of Mexico. This geographic midpoint affords its inhabitants the best of both worlds, from tropical beaches normally associated with south Florida to the hilly pine forests one might encounter in the Deep South.

When people spend time in Tallahassee, they are struck by how Southern the city seems. Unlike the more populous parts of the state, Tallahassee is a place where time seems to slow down a bit. People are more easygoing here than in, say, Miami or Tampa. There's an almost genteel sensibility in the air, one that captures the best aspects of Southern tradition.

Another facet that sets Tallahassee apart from the rest of the state is the landscape, rippled with hills and winding rivers. In south Florida, the only hills you'll encounter are the on-ramps and off-ramps of interstate highways. There are palm trees all over Florida, but here they grow side-by-side with forests of pine and oak.

While life is certainly paced leisurely in these parts, residents never forget that Tallahassee is the focal point of state politics, and the decisions made here affect every county, town, city and person in Florida. For all its small-town charm, you can't deny the fact that the buildings of the Capitol Complex are what give the city its skyline.

Tallahassee is a city that looks and feels young. Leon County is home to more than 200,000 people, and the biggest chunk of them are between their late 20s and early 40s. Not surprisingly, the largest local employer is the government, whose state and local jobs employ around 40 percent of the civilian labor force. And nearly 25 percent of the residents work in the service industry that in no small part supports the government.

Economically, the area is fairly stable. The median family income is around $37,000 annually, and the unemployment rate is consistently less than 5 percent.

Tallahassee's hilly, green landscape is dominated by the New Capitol and, at its base, the Old Capitol.

The cost of living is not much less than in other areas of the state, but keep in mind that the relaxed lifestyle is a big plus to most people.

A good portion of Leon County residents have been here a long time and can trace their roots back for generations. But most people you meet are from elsewhere. People from south Florida move here to get away from the hectic and harried pace of things, and residents of neighboring states like it here because the city has many of the features found in other Southern cities.

Tallahassee is a good place to raise children. Most parents feel that the city offers a good, safe environment, and the school system generally gets high marks. Part of that might have to do with the fact that, on the average, there is one teacher for every 20 students, and this lessens the chance of a child being overlooked in class. And nearly 65 percent of the high school graduates continue their education at either college or technical schools.

With the exception of screaming football, basketball and hockey fans, the biggest noisemaker in town is the state government. The Legislature can sometimes get things cranking in late fall if there's a special session. Then in spring the lawmakers come to full session, and Tallahassee's downtown sidewalks are filled at lunchtime not only with elected officials but also small armies of lobbyists and journalists. For a few weeks it seems like all eyes of the state are on us, and we don't mind it one bit.

That could be because summertime is near, and that's when life here slows almost to a halt. The heat and humidity rise considerably. The oppressive air just doesn't move, and if you're not headed for a nearby lake or the Gulf of Mexico, then you really don't want to stray too far from the air conditioner.

Tallahassee is a big college town, too, and every summer two-thirds of the city's nonpermanent student population of 48,000 depart for vacation. The downtown strip of student-oriented businesses is so empty that you could fire a cannon right down the middle and not hit a soul.

Then, when it feels like everyone is

going to melt like the Wicked Witch from *The Wizard of Oz*, the first cool snap of fall gives residents reason to hold out. Toward the end of September the temperatures cool quite a bit, especially at night, and the city comes to life again.

Driving through the remote areas of Tallahassee, you can see beautiful land that was probably once part of an old plantation being developed into housing tracts and subdivisions. The city must perform a tricky balancing act so its steady growth does not get out of hand.

There are plenty of leisure-time activities to do here, and people love to be outdoors enjoying the natural beauty around them. But even if you get bored, there's a major city only a few hours away in any direction. To the north, Birmingham and Atlanta are each about a 5-hour drive away. Jacksonville is about 3 hours to the east, and Pensacola is about 3 hours west, the halfway-point if you're heading for New Orleans' French Quarter. Head south for 5 hours and you're in the Orlando/Tampa area.

For most folks, there's no real need to travel that far. From the hilly pine forests on down to the warm waters of the Gulf of Mexico, Tallahassee has just about everything you could need.

It's a growing city, but thank goodness it still feels like a small town.

Visitor Information

TALLAHASSEE CHAMBER OF COMMERCE
100 N. Duval St.   224-8116

TALLAHASSEE CONVENTION & VISITORS BUREAU
200 W. College Ave.   413-9200

TALLAHASSEE VISITOR INFORMATION CENTER
The Capitol
Monroe St.and   413-9200
Apalachee Pkwy.   (800) 628-2866

Tallahassee

Tallahassee
Getting Around

Tallahassee rests gently in what is known as Florida's Big Bend or East Panhandle. It's easy to get to, and once you're here it's relatively simple to find your way around.

If you're driving, you'll probably be arriving by one of four major routes — I-10, U.S. 27, U.S. 90 or U.S. 319.

Commercial transportation is a growing business in town. Tallahassee Regional Airport features daily service from several national and regional airlines, and Greyhound-Trailways Bus Lines offers service from its downtown terminal. And after a long hiatus, the Amtrak *Sunset Limited* recently resumed passenger service through Tallahassee.

The city itself is bisected quite neatly from north to south by Monroe Street and from east to west by Tennessee and Mahan streets. This more or less splits the city into four easily navigable areas. An old truck route, Capital Circle, encircles the city and has been upgraded to handle much of the traffic around Tallahassee's perimeter.

The city's bus line, TalTran, provides service throughout the city, and the Dial-A-Ride service provides transportation for the elderly and disabled.

The Old Town Trolley offers free trolley rides and historical tours throughout the downtown area.

Photo: Tallahassee Area & Convention Visitors Bureau

The Old Town Trolley is a commuter servive that zips around the downtown area — it's the best free ride in town.

If you're traveling by train, Amtrak's Sunset Limited will be your ticket into and out of Tallahassee.

Airports

TALLAHASSEE REGIONAL AIRPORT

Capital Cir.   891-7800

The Tallahassee Regional Airport currently offers air service through six national and regional carriers. The airport is located just 6 miles south of the city on Capital Circle and also hosts several car rental agencies. Need a taxi or limo instead? Just check the listings later in this chapter, as all of them offer service to and from the airport.

Airlines

AirSouth	(800) 247-7688
American	(800) 433-7300
Atlantic Southeast	(800) 282-3424
Comair	(800) 354-9822
Continental	(800) 525-0280
Delta	(800) 221-1212
USAir	(800) 428-4322

Airport Automobile Rentals

Alamo	(800) 327-9633
Avis	(800) 831-2847
Budget	(800) 527-0700
Dollar	(800) 800-4000
Hertz	(800) 654-3131
National	(800) 227-7368

TALLAHASSEE COMMERCIAL AIRPORT

Hwy. 27   562-1945

This is the only private airport in Leon County, and it sits 1 mile north of Old Bainbridge Road on U.S. 27 (N. Monroe Street).

General Automobile Rentals

Tallahassee's population fluctuates wildly during the year. You've got lawmakers, lobbyists and news media in town during the legislative session, not to mention the 50,000 or so college students who come and go during the year. Needless to say, not everyone brings their own car, so car rental agencies are fairly numerous around here.

Agency	576-0196
Alamo	(800) 327-9633
Avis	(800) 831-2847
Budget	(800) 527-0700
Dollar	(800) 800-4000
Enterprise	(800) 325-8007
Hertz	(800) 654-3131

Honey-Bee	575-9175
Lucky's	575-0632
National	(800)227-7368
Sears Rental	575-8238
Snappy	575-8808
Ugly Duckling	575-7631

Bus Service

For those who love riding the bus, take heed: You can not only ride the bus into town, but once here you can ride TalTran, the city bus line, all over town. The Greyhound-Trailways bus station is open 24 hours, seven days a week.

Riding the TalTran bus line will get you most anywhere you want to go within Tallahassee city limits, and it's generally 75¢ a ride. The TalTran bus routes begin around 7 AM and run until 10 PM, but you should know that the hours do vary for each route. TalTran buses are not 100 percent handicapped accessible, but some do have special wheelchair lifts. Contact the TalTran office ahead of time for more information.

The Old Town Trolley isn't really a trolley at all; it's a bus that looks a heckuva lot like a trolley. It's a fancy little commuter service that zips through the downtown area, and best of all, it's free. The trolley runs from 7 AM to 6 PM Monday through Friday, and no matter which of the dozen or so stops you're at downtown, the trolley will usually come chugging along every 15 minutes or so.

Greyhound-Trailways Bus Lines	222-4240
Old Town Trolley	891-5200
TalTran Bus Line	891-5200

Train Service

Amtrak offers service through Tallahassee, including stops in the nearby towns of Chipley and Crestview. There's a newly refurbished train station at 918½ Railroad Avenue, near the downtown Civic Center. Schedules are always changing, so contact Amtrak yourself concerning actual dates and times for train service.

Amtrak	(800) 872-7245
Tallahassee Amtrak Station	224-2779

Taxi and Limousine Service

Ambassador Limousines	942-2200
Capital Limousine	574-4350
City Taxi	893-4111
Elite Street Limousine Service	222-7006
Yellow Cab	222-3070

Tallahassee
Restaurants and Nightlife

If you think that most Florida cuisine is based on seafood, you're not too far off the mark. Residents will readily admit it'd be foolish not to take advantage of the excellent fishing waters that surround most of the state.

But Floridians are also risk-takers. How else can you explain the fact that so many of us have chosen to live in a geographic region frequented by hurricanes? We like challenges and diversity, and that's definitely reflected in the culinary heritage of the state's melting-pot population.

If you love seafood, you've come to the right place. If you're looking for other kinds of cuisine, you won't be disappointed. Tallahassee is home to a wide variety of fine restaurants whose offerings range from the strictly Southern down-home cookin' to more exotic and adventurous international dishes.

There are plenty of restaurants in Tallahassee, and new ones open each year. Keep in mind that the following is only a partial listing. We don't include the many national chain restaurants you'll find in most any town, because you already know what to expect from these places. Rest assured that Tallahassee is well-served by these popular establishments.

As far as nightlife goes, we've got a few things to teach you there, as well. Believe it or not, Tallahassee has an active nightlife that goes back more than 100 years.

During the antebellum years, as Tallahassee grew from a frontier village to a small town, recreation and relaxation became something of a fine art. This was mostly due to Southern aristocracy's penchant for dignified and extravagant spectacles. Local history books are filled with accounts of genteel garden parties, gallant ring tournaments in the tradition of English royalty as well as brash and sometimes deadly duels.

You can of course still find an abundance of lawn parties and modern-day chivalry. As far as duelling goes, the city forefathers were wise enough to outlaw gun duels in 1840, thereby helping Tallahassee's image in no small manner.

Today, Tallahassee caters to a large and sometimes fluctuating population of fun-seekers and party-lovers. During the fall, students back from summer break eagerly fill the warehouses, bars and dives that cater to the younger set by offering cheap beer and loud bands. This continues into winter, which leads to spring, when the more upscale places are filled with lobbyists and lawmakers in town for the legislative session, either making complex deals or taking breathers from such hotbed activity.

Summer offers a brief and welcome respite for locals, as students and politicians retreat for a few months. The sun is sweltering, and nobody moves very much. Depending on the time of day, summer visitors might think they've stepped into a ghost town, but all they have to do is find where everyone is cooling down. If it's not at a lake or the beach, then it just might be at one of the following places.

Usually, there's a core cross-section of bars and nightlife spots that operates year round. Things may slow down a bit at times, but they never come to a complete stop. And when things are moving, you'd best be assured that they can move mighty fast.

Restaurants

The following list contains information on credit cards and pricing. The price guidelines are, of course, subject to change but are based on a basic dinner for two (without all the fancy extras such as wine or double-decker desserts). Be sure to check out the chalkboard as you enter a restaurant; often the nightly specials will match or even beat regular menu items in both price and palatability.

Less than $20	$
$21 to $35	$$
$36 to $50	$$$
More than $51	$$$$

ANDREW'S
228 S. Adams St.   222-3446
$$

Tallahassee's skyline might not impress city slickers — and they'll forgive us if we're more proud of the landscape than the buildings. But if you feel the urge to look at architecture while you dine, Andrew's has the best view of downtown Tallahassee and some of the best food as well. This two-story restaurant offers something different at every level. The downstairs restaurant offers mostly contemporary American fare, and the best bets are any of the pasta, chicken or seafood dishes. There's a popular jazz lounge upstairs (called, naturally, Andrew's Upstairs) where music aficionados can usually be found sampling the cold buffet, salad bar and appetizers. Diners can opt for the outdoor dining courtyard during warm summery nights (this is Florida, and we get a lot of 'em around here).

ANTHONY'S
Betton Pl., 1950 Thomasville Rd.   224-1447
$$

No offense to Anthony, but we think this place should really be called Eddies — plural because chefs Eddie Davis and Eddie Hogan are mostly responsible for the fine, traditional Italian fare served here. From the Eggplant Parmesan to the elegant veal dishes, you'll truly think you've taken a trip to rural Italy. Anthony's also serves up some other fine dishes, such as steaks — especially the New York strip — and seafood (our favorite's the grouper).

BAHN THAI RESTAURANT
1319 S. Monroe St.   224-4765
$$

There are only two Thai restaurants in Tallahassee, and both are so popular it's a wonder there aren't three or four of them — perhaps there will be by the time you read this. Bahn Thai sits less than a half-mile south of the Capitol Building. One bite of the food and you're in another world. The chefs here create some of the spiciest fare in town. Even the most devoted heat-seekers usually settle for "medium" when specifying how hot they prefer a dish because they know it'll come out scorching. Recently the dining room was renovated and now sports an Eastern decor that perfectly complements the food.

BARNACLE BILL'S SEAFOOD EMPORIUM
1830 N. Monroe St.   385-8734
$

The atmosphere here is casual, but the seafood is dressed to kill. Barnacle Bill's trucks it in fresh daily and serves it up steamed, smoked or grilled. We recommend you stick around long enough to try it all three ways. Sit at the oyster bar and you'll find a fourth way: raw. Seafood's not the only reason to come here — the menu also sports hamburgers, chicken wings, pasta and vegetables — but it's the best reason. The place can get pretty packed on football weekends, but if standing room only is your bag, by all means do attend.

CAFE DI LORENZO
1002 N. Monroe St.   681-3622
$$

This exciting Italian restaurant recently moved to a new location but wisely kept the core of its mouthwatering menu. There are more than a dozen thoughtfully prepared pasta dishes to choose from, as well as veal and seafood favorites. Owner Lorenzo Amato has a flair for decorating as well, and the rich surroundings here are almost as enjoyable as the food. There's a good wine selection to choose from too.

CHEZ PIERRE
115 N. Adams St.   222-0936
$$

This charming and affordable bistro has been serving excellent French cuisine for nearly two decades now, and it's only getting better with age. Quiche and crepes dominate the lunch menu, while dinners are usually fish or fowl. There are some tantalizing desserts and pastries (of course) and a wine and espresso bar. To top off the French cafe motif, the owners are currently displaying the work of local artists on the walls. You'd have to travel someplace very, very far away to get French fare this authentic. We'll give you one guess.

CHINA GOURMET
2580 N. Monroe St.   385-1124
$$

China Gourmet continues to receive high ratings from residents as well as the local restaurant critic. These folks must know something, right? Eat a meal here and you too can be "in the know." The China Gourmet stands above many other Chinese restaurants because they go that extra mile to ensure that a dish is extra-flavorful and cooked to perfection. Their not-to-be-missed buffet line is designed to feed the masses while still assuring the items are prepared with individual attention.

EASTSIDE MARIO'S
2756 N. Monroe St.   385-1774
$$

This American-Italian eatery is one of Tallahassee's latest culinary additions but has already established quite a reputation based on its pizza alone. The flavorful pie is baked New York-style in a wood-burning brick oven, and if you've never tried it this way, it *does* make a difference. Other zesty pasta, seafood and meat dishes fill out the impressive menu. The atmosphere is fun and casual, even though you'd normally expect formal wear to accompany cuisine this superb.

FOOD GLORIOUS FOOD
1950 Thomasville Rd.
Betton Place   224-9974
$

If there's one restaurant in town whose name perfectly embodies the concept of "truth in advertising," then this is the place. Residents call it "FGF" for short, and its rotating menu is tantalizing and surprising. Fresh salads and gourmet entrees are the specialty here, along with sandwiches and croissants. Be sure to save room for the homemade desserts, which seem to quickly disappear with the lunch crowd. Seating can sometimes be at a premium, but they don't take reservations. Outdoor seating was added last year to great acclaim, and it offers some much-needed space. Your best bet is to take an early or late lunch. Even if you show up with the crowd, you're sure to agree that it's worth the wait.

GOLDEN EAST

2696 N. Monroe St.   422-2881
$$

This is a very popular Chinese restaurant, and you need look no farther than its impressive lunch and dinner buffets to understand why. There are always at least 12 main courses offered on the line as well as several appetizers and delicious soups. The specialty here is the Mongolian barbecue — it's heavenly. Choose from these and many other items on the menu; it's darned near impossible to go wrong. Just head east and you'll do fine.

KITCHO

Market Square
1415 Timberlane Rd.   893-7686
$$

The master chefs here serve up a variety of traditional Japanese dishes and adventurous specials. Kitcho also sports one of the Tallahassee's few sushi bars, giving those in the north end of town a convenient place to toss back raw delicacies. The place fills up quickly on weekend evenings, so call ahead or hit it on a weeknight. The lunchtime sushi roll buffet usually packs them in too.

LA FIESTA

911 Apalachee Pkwy.   656-3392
$

This is one of the most authentic Mexican restaurants in town, and that's because the fare is good, cheap and plentiful. If you've ever been down to Mexico, you'll know what we're talking about here. Tacos, enchiladas, burritos and other specialties keep the masses satisfied. You can wash it all down with a good selection of Mexican beer and tequila. It's just off a major parkway through the city, and it's no wonder that traffic here is sometimes pretty heavy.

THE LIEUTENANT GOVERNOR'S

Public House and Grill
1215 Thomasville Rd.   222-4547
$$$

OK, this is a little joke that may need explaining. This new and elegant restaurant takes its name as a jibe to a private club in the downtown district. That one is called — you guessed it — the Governors Club. The Lieutenant Governor's Public House and Grill has quickly surpassed the amusing novelty of its name and established a reputation for some truly innovative American cuisine. Chef Bryant Withers assembles a new handwritten menu daily, featuring a wide range of seafood and steak meals. He also serves several crepe dishes that will literally melt in your mouth. If you can, save room for the delicious desserts. This place may not be a private club, but they sure treat you special anyway.

LUCY HO'S BAMBOO GARDEN

2814 Apalachee Pkwy.   878-3366
$$

Lucy Ho's gives us the best of two worlds: Japanese and Chinese. Their menu offers great selections from both cuisines. There's a popular dinner buffet as well as an elegant sushi bar. For the purist, you can even shed your shoes and dine in the tatami room. There's usually weekend entertainment in the adjoining lounge, which also boasts a karaoke machine.

THE MELTING POT

1832 N. Monroe St.   386-7440
$$

This Swiss fondue restaurant keeps 'em dipping around here. There's a wide range of tableside fondues to choose from, as well as what to dip: chicken, seafood and meat. You should know that this kind of food can be quite rich and filling, so plan to go on an empty stomach. Trust us, you'll have no trouble reversing the trend. Reservations are recommended, especially on weekends.

THE MILL BAKERY AND EATERY

2136 N. Monroe St.   386-2867
2329 Apalachee Pkwy.   656-2867
$

With two locations, the Mill has Tallahassee well covered when it comes to thick sandwiches, gourmet pizzas (especially the pesto chicken), vegetarian chili and some of the biggest fresh-baked muffins you've ever seen. The Mill is a small Southeastern chain that also brews its own beer. There are four kinds of ale, each highly recommended. Weekends can get a little crowded, as students pile in for live music and drink specials. So if you can, plan dinner a bit on the early side of the evening.

THE MUSTARD TREE

Market Square
1415 Timberlane Rd.   893-8733
$$

Formerly the Mustard Seed, this place changed its name to reflect its popularity — and growth. The Mustard Tree serves exceptional American cuisine with a flair for the Cajun. The menu features standard fare as well as more adventurous seafood dishes — if you like spicy adventures, any of the blackened offerings should please you. The Mustard Tree recently reopened for lunch service with outdoor terrace dining.

NINO'S

6497 Apalachee Pkwy.   878-8141
$$

It's a few miles outside town, but Nino's is a Tallahassee favorite — a friendly Italian restaurant whose fine food is something you'd easily pay twice as much for in a big city. Here, it's cheap and plentiful and prepared with a gourmet touch. You can come as casual or as dressy as you like; as long as you're ready for some good food, you'll fit right in. Note that Nino's serves dinner only and is not open for lunch.

THE OLD TOWN CAFE

1415 Timberlane Rd.   893-5741
$$

The Old Town prides itself on knowing how to cook prime rib and baby back rib, but they're pretty good at seafood and burgers too. This may sound fairly standard but it's the special flourishes that count here — Caribbean and Cajun, in particular. They also make excellent salads that are meals unto themselves. The walls are muted pastels, but the food is colorful and distinctive. Be sure to save room for the homemade desserts.

THE PARADISE GRILL & BAR

1406 Meridian Rd.   224-2742
$

If good food and a friendly crowd is

your idea of paradise, then look no further. The Paradise Grill & Bar's active social setting should serve as an indicator of the quality of food here. On weekends and during football season, the place can be standing room only. If you don't want to rub elbows, however, pick most any night during the week and sample the delicious Cajun-style seafood and Jamaican jerk chicken. If your palate is more conservative, there are some sizzling hamburgers and hot dogs that come highly recommended. The Paradise has a glassed-in porch and open-air deck. There's plenty of room here, and it's easy to see why they need it.

SAMRAT INDIAN RESTAURANT
2529 Apalachee Pkwy.   942-1993
$

One of the newest and most exotic restaurants to appear on Tallahassee's culinary landscape, Samrat offers fine Indian dining — something this area has been lacking for years. The atmosphere may leave a little to be desired, but the expert cooks make up for that many times over with their flavorful, authentic Indian dishes. Start out with an appetizer such as Vegetable Samosa, a fried turnover filled with spicy potatoes and peas, or have the sampler plate, which is a meal unto itself. Main courses include delicious Tandoori Chicken, Lamb Vindaloo in a very spicy sauce, a mouthwatering Shrimp Curry and Malai Kofta, balls of vegetables and spices lightly fried and covered with cream sauce. There are so many great dishes that we recommend you go with a crowd; that way everyone can sample as many entries as possible. If you can't make it for dinner, there's a weekday lunch buffet well worth catching.

THE SHELL OYSTER BAR
114-A E. Oakland St.   224-9919
$

These people do raw oysters and that's about it. For years this tiny oyster bar just south of the capitol was housed in a former gas station, and all it offered was a bench, a bar, Apalachicola oysters and sliced lemons. You brought your own drinks. The amiable no-frills atmosphere made it an instant classic with residents and visitors alike. It's moved back half a block to slightly larger digs, and the owners smartly haven't messed too much with the menu. This is about as casual as you can get.

THE SILVER SLIPPER
531 Scotty Ln.   386-9366
$$$

The Slipper has been around for half a century, and it's still going strong. The reason? The thick and juicy Angus steaks, not to mention the appetizing seafood and Greek dishes. There's an adjoining lounge with weekend entertainment, and private dining rooms are available. During the legislative session, those private rooms are usually filled with lawmakers and lobbyists. But no matter what time of year, you shouldn't take any chances on this venue, folks: Make reservations.

THE WHITE SWAN CAFE
The Verandas, 1355 Market St.   668-2812
$$$

Master Chef Tim Waingraw has served his delectable dishes to U.S. Presidents and foreign heads of state, and most Tallahasseans feel lucky he moved here after leaving Washington, D.C. The White Swan has quickly established a reputation of offering classic American cuisine at very affordable prices. The Steak Alexander and Beef Wellington are hard to pass up, and the roast duck and Salmon Mousseline also come highly recommended. The lunchtime crowd moves steadily enough to accommodate most everyone, but reservations for dinner are almost mandatory here.

Nightlife

THE ABBEY

2425 Spoonwood Dr.   *386-3000*

What sets The Abbey apart from other nightclubs is the fact that it's a nonalcoholic party place. They offer more than 100 different drinks, and people still manage to look like they're having a great time. There's food and dancing and a spacious outdoor deck. Mostly The Abbey is reserved for the use of church and civic organizations, but Friday nights find the place open to a receptive public.

THE CAB STAND

1019 N. Monroe St.   *224-0322*

One of the rockingest bars in town, The Cab Stand has quickly established itself as great place to enjoy live music and lively people. The crowd varies widely from the marginal to the very upscale, especially on weekends. There's live music during much of the week, mostly jazz or blues. When the patrons stop chatting long enough to take a sip of something cold, they seem to enjoy the tunes.

CLYDE'S & COSTELLO'S

210 S. Adams St.   *224-2173*

This is a cool, casual place where college students rub elbows with professionals, good cheap drinks are hoisted and, if there's not a live band playing raucous rock, the DJ is spinning something that's best left in the background. Clyde's & Costello's sounds like two places, but it's only one — unless you're seeing double

(in which case, take a taxi home, please). It's a cut above most places in Tallahassee, but it doesn't have any pretensions. It's a popular downtown spot where you come to relax and enjoy yourself.

DOOLEY'S DOWNUNDER

2900 N. Monroe St.   *386-1027*

This Australian-themed bar is tucked away inside a Ramada Inn. Dooley's is a tasteful little nightspot that has made a name for itself by offering some of the best stand-up comedy and live jazz music in town. Comedy Zone nights sometimes bring nationally known stand-up comedians. Jazz nights get very hot, especially when featuring national recording artist Marcus Roberts, a hometown talent who plays a few shows here each year. Other artists of note to appear here are Lynee Arriale and Travis Shook. It's a long list, one that grows each year. Check it out — no joke.

FAT TUESDAY

101 S. Adams St.   *224-5000*

One of the newest bars in town, Fat Tuesday bills itself as a taste of New Orleans in The Sheraton in downtown Tallahassee. They've certainly got the exotic drinks to prove it, from a heady concoction called Swampwater to another life-threatening conviviality known as the Triple-Bypass. It's loud and bright, and weekends usually find it full of laughing, dancing people.

THE WATERWORKS

104 S. Monroe St.   *224-1887*

There's not a lot of room at this downtown Tallahassee gathering spot, but some say it's the intimacy that makes it cool. Although the scene caters mostly to the college crowd, it's upscale and smart enough to feature live jazz music at least one night each weekend. Monday nights usually see an "open mike" night where aspiring poets and singer/songwriters can be heard. Depending on your frame of mind, the slick pastels and neon lighting just might prove to be the perfect backdrop for some loud music and people-watching.

Tallahassee
Accommodations

Tallahassee plays host to thousands of visitors each year, and it knows how to take care of them. Whether they're in town for a Seminole game, the legislative session or any of the other events that take place here, people find that Tallahassee has plenty of accommodations for everyone.

The city's 56 hotels and motels provide more than 5,000 rooms for the city's visitors, and during peak periods — championship sports events or the legislative session, for example — things can get very crowded in these parts. Most of the time, however, visitors can be assured of finding a place to stay with minimal difficulty. Any and all tastes can be met, whether you're looking for quaint bed and breakfast inns, no-frills economy lodging or upper-crust corporate hotels.

The following is a random sampling of some of the accommodations Tallahassee has to offer. Note that rates are subject to change, and when making reservations always remember to ask if there are any special rates available. Sometimes you'll find prices so low you'll be tempted to extend your trip for a couple of days. The codes below are for a one-night stay for two adults. All establishments accept major credit cards unless otherwise noted.

$60 or less	$
$61 to $85	$$
$86 to $99	$$$
$100 or more	$$$$

Bed and Breakfast Inns

Tallahassee only has one bed and breakfast inn. This is amazing, especially when you realize how many historic downtown homes would make perfect spots for such a venture. Thankfully, the nearby communities of Quincy, Havana, Monticello and Thomasville provide more than a dozen additions to the city's short list, and we've given these nearby inns complete coverage in our Tallahassee Daytrips chapter. If Tallahassee's Riedel House is full, you can try any of the others and rest assured that, for the cost of a short drive, you can have that homey, personalized atmosphere bed and breakfast inns are known for.

THE RIEDEL HOUSE
1412 Fairway Dr.   222-8569
$$

Built in 1937, the stately Riedel House sits on an acre of land in the Myers Park area of town, only a few blocks down the hill from the Capitol. Owner Carolyn Riedel opened it up as a bed and breakfast less than a decade ago and never seems to have much trouble keeping its two guest rooms and one suite filled. There are private baths and, of course, breakfast. Many weekends find the downstairs part of the house rented out for parties and wedding receptions.

Hotels and Motels

GOVERNORS INN

209 S. Adams St.	681-6855
$$$$	(800) 342-7717

This is the downtown place to stay for the upscale movers and shakers and power players — and those who want to rub elbows with them. Only a five-minute walk from the Capitol complex, Governors Inn is elegant and extravagant without going overboard; there's a sense of refinement in the air. There are 40 tasteful, friendly rooms and eight suites, and these fill up quickly when the politicians flock to town. The inn features a fitness facility, continental breakfast, in-room refrigerators, dry cleaning service, morning newspaper and copier and fax facilities. There's also a complimentary airport shuttle that runs whenever you need it.

RAMADA INN TALLAHASSEE

2900 N. Monroe St.	386-1027
$$	(800) 228-2828

Less than 4 miles from the Capitol on N. Monroe Street, the Ramada Inn Tallahassee is the second-largest motel in the area, sporting nearly 200 rooms and half-dozen suites. Like any Ramada Inn, it's great value for the cost and features a fitness facility and walking trail, an on-site restaurant, swimming pool, cable TV and computer, copier and fax services. Their lounge, Dooley's Downunder, is a popular nightspot for many Tallahasseans (for more information see our Tallahassee Restaurants and Nightlife chapter). Two other Ramada Inn locations are the Ramada Limited, 1308 W. Brevard Street, 224-7116, near FSU, and the Ramada Inn Capitol View, 1355 Apalachee Parkway, 877-3171.

HOLIDAY INN CAPITOL PLAZA

101 S. Adams St.	224-5000
$-$$$$	(800) 325-3535

The Holiday Inn Capitol Plaza is the area's largest motel, with nearly 250 rooms and half-dozen suites available. As you can see from its price rating, the hotel can accommodate any and all travelers, no matter how large or small their budgets. The Holiday Inn sits downtown only a couple of blocks from the Capitol and features indoor parking, in-room refrigerators, microwaves, dry cleaning and fax

and copier services. There's an on-site restaurant and lounge too.

RADISSON HOTEL
415 N. Monroe St.　　　　224-6000
$$-$$$$　　　　(800) 333-3333

The Radisson's spacious rooms, reasonable rates and close proximity to the heart of town are big attractions for people with business in downtown Tallahassee — the walk to the Capitol is only a half-mile and carries you through the historic downtown district and past the Park Avenue chain of parks. The Radisson's 116 rooms and eight suites are usually jam-packed during the legislative session and football season (two sporting events that draw tons of people around here), and it effortlessly hosts those seeking business as well as pleasure. There's a restaurant and lounge in the lobby, not to mention a fitness facility, whirlpool and sauna. Copier and fax services are well-used by lobbyists and business people.

HOLIDAY INN UNIVERSITY CENTER
316 W. Tennessee St.　　　　222-8000
$-$$$$　　　　(800) 465-4329

You can always trust a Holiday Inn to deliver spacious, clean rooms in a conve-

nient setting. There are three Holiday Inns in Tallahassee, but we choose this one because of its close proximity to the Capitol — about a half-mile. If you're driving, by all means check out the other two — there's the Holiday Inn Parkway on the Apalachee Parkway about a mile from the Capitol, and the Holiday Inn Northwest about 5 miles from downtown. Their rooms top out a bit cheaper too. But if you're walking — and this is a walking town — this is the place to be. There are 174 rooms to choose from, with a restaurant and lounge on the premises. You'll also enjoy a swimming pool, fitness facility, dry cleaning, copier and fax services.

CABOT LODGE NORTH
2735 N. Monroe St.　　　　386-8880
$-$$　　　　(800) 223-1964

There are two Cabot Lodges in Tallahassee, and both are popular because they offer more of a relaxed and secluded setting than is found in most roadside motels. Their sign claims they're a bed and breakfast, but don't expect an inn. This is simple, spacious and clean lodging with several pleasant extras. The

Cabot Lodge East, 1653 Raymond Diehl Road, 386-7500, with its Executive Floor offering many business-oriented amenities, is more suited for visiting professionals. The Cabot Lodge North is the larger of the two — 60 rooms — but both are equidistant from the Capitol (about 4 miles) and the airport (around 9 miles). There are several restaurants within walking distance, and Tallahassee Mall is only a few blocks away. The Cabot Lodge North offers dry cleaning, fax and copier services as well.

COURTYARD BY MARRIOTT

1018 Apalachee Pkwy.   222-8822
$$-$$$$ (800) 321-2211

Visitors who commute by car are likely to be found at the Courtyard by Marriott, which meets the high standards set by the nationwide chain. It sits on the Parkway about a mile from the Capitol, but unfortunately it's not a place for people who prefer to walk to their destination. Still, its 154 rooms and 13 spacious suites attract their fair share of visitors. You'll probably enjoy the quiet seclusion, and the on-site restaurant, lounge and fitness and swimming facilities should please you.

DAYS INN

722 Apalachee Pkwy.   224-2181
2800 N. Monroe St.   385-0136
3100 Apalachee Pkwy.   877-6121
$ (800) 325-2525

With three locations in the Tallahassee area, Days Inn provides nearly 300 rooms for people looking to make the most of their travel dollars. They're priced for tight budgets, but they offer many of the same amenities as other hotels charging twice as much, including swimming pools, cable TV, free local calls and copier and fax services. The Days Inn Downtown, on Apalachee Parkway, sits only a half-mile from the Capitol, while the Days Inn North, on N. Monroe Street, is about 3 miles from the Capitol and close to I-10. The Days Inn South is the largest of the three and offers additional amenities such as complimentary morning newspapers, in-room coffee makers, refrigerators and microwave ovens.

LA QUINTA

2905 N. Monroe St.   878-5099
2850 Apalachee Pkwy.   877-4437
$ (800) 531-5900

For the cost-conscious, La Quinta offers deals that can't be beat. Its two fine locations in Tallahassee are equidistant from the Capitol — about 3 miles — and offer nearly 300 spacious rooms, including suites. Both also have swimming pools, breakfast and cocktail service, cable TV and free local telephone calls. Business travelers will want to note their dry cleaning, fax and copier services too. If you're traveling with pets, you know how hard it can be to find hotels that will accommodate them — La Quinta is one of them. The location on Monroe Street is close to I-10, while the other one sits right on U.S. 27.

EXECUTIVE SUITE MOTOR INN

522 Scotty's Ln.   386-2121
$ *(800) 342-0090*

Those seeking a great place to stay for a no-frills price should look no farther. The Executive Suite Motor Inn sits about a mile south of I-10, conveniently near Tallahassee Mall and several restaurants. The Capitol is only 2 miles away, with the airport about 5 miles beyond that. The 115 rooms are spacious and clean, and the hotel sports a swimming pool, fitness facility, cable TV, VCR, movie rentals and copier and fax services. Every morning you'll awaken to a complimentary breakfast and newspaper, not to mention a dirt-cheap bill.

Tallahassee
Shopping

Tallahassee is truly a shopper's paradise. It boasts two large malls, several shopping centers and enough eclectic boutiques, crafts and antique shops to whet anyone's appetite.

And even if you just can't find that special item here, try the neighboring towns of Quincy, Havana, Monticello or Thomasville. All are less than an hour's drive from Tallahassee.

Please note that this list doesn't include many of the standard stores you'll find across the nation. What you'll find here are some of the individual stores that make Tallahassee a unique and exciting place to go shopping. If, after all that shopping, you'd like to kick back and read, B. Dalton, Waldenbooks and Books-A-Million, one of the fastest growing bookstore chains, should have just what you're looking for in books and magazines.

Malls and Shopping Centers

GOVERNOR'S SQUARE MALL
1500 Apalachee Pkwy.   *671-4636*

In addition to anchor stores such as Burdines, Dillard's, JCPenney and Sears, Governor's Square mall offers more than 150 specialty stores such as Suncoast Motion Picture Company. Suncoast Motion Picture Company, with videos and laserdiscs; The Disney Store; African Safari, with clothes and gifts; Barnie's Coffee & Tea; Family Bookstore; Sunglass Hut; and Living Planet, with nature-related gifts. For those who like to shop till they drop, the central food court, which seats 500, offers a great place to relax and recharge.

TALLAHASSEE MALL
2415 N. Monroe St.   *385-7145*

The recently remodeled and expanded Tallahassee Mall features three main anchor stores — Parisian, Gayfers and Montgomery Ward as well as a new food court, a two-screen movie theater and dozens of specialty stores such as Gloria Jean's Coffee Beans, Piercing Pagoda, Shoe Works, Victoria's Secret, Bourbon Street Candy and Champs Sports.

CARRIAGE GATE SHOPPING CENTER
3425 Thomasville Rd.

This shopping center has a whole lot for everyone, no matter what your age or interest. Kids really flip over the new Discovery Zone, a gigantic indoor playground with enough tunnels, obstacle courses and games to keep them busy for hours. Adults, on the other hand, will probably want to slow down and browse the fine clothing at such stores as Tails & Tweeds and Jason's & Jason's Petites. Everyone can enjoy the great food at Georgio's & Filks.

THE PAVILIONS
1410 Market St.

There are plenty of ways to look and feel good at the Pavilions. This shopping plaza lets you choose from Chelsea Hairsmith Salon, Career Woman Fashions, Arthur Murray Dance Studio, Narcissus Swimwear and Lingerie, Peggy's Fine Arts, Wallpaper It Now, the Mandarin Chinese Restaurant and Nu-Life, a ladies-only fitness center.

THE VERANDAS
1355 Market St.

Talbots is the anchor store at this north Tallahassee shopping plaza, but you can also say that the gourmet dining at the White Swan Restaurant is another big draw. These two establishments rub elbows with such shopping attractions as Oldfield Interiors; Someone's In the Kitchen, a kitchen shop; The Mole Hole, a unique gift shop; and many others.

PARKWAY SHOPPING CENTER
Apalachee Pkwy. and Magnolia

This popular shopping plaza is almost 30 years old but you wouldn't know it from looking. It sports a wonderful bookstore, Books-A-Million, a browser's delight; Spec's Music, offering the latest and greatest in music and movies; and several clothing stores. If you're hungry, try the Italian fare at the Olive Garden, the fine Mexican offerings from Cabo's Tacos or some healthy and delicious food from the New Leaf Cafe.

BETTON PLACE
1950 Thomasville Rd.

This plaza bills itself as "a delightful shopping place," and we can't argue. Nestled within this small but spacious plaza are nearly a dozen excellent shops and boutiques, such as A Stitch In Time; the Museum Shop, featuring assorted history- and nature-themed gifts; Ivy Rose Garden and Gifts; Strauss Gallery; and Planned Furnishings, an elegant home

furniture store. Food Glorious Food offers elegant and inexpensive dining on the lower level.

VILLAGE COMMONS
1400 Village Square Blvd.

At first glance, this is just another strip shopping center with Wal-Mart and Stein Mart clearly visible. But look closer and you'll find an exciting collection of most uncommon shops such as the Wildlife Gallery, featuring nature-themed gifts; My Favorite Things, a charming gift shop; Lissie Petites, a clothing store; Eleni's Coffee & Tea Company; and restaurants including Applebee's.

MARKET SQUARE SHOPPING CENTER
1415 Timberlane Rd.   893-8627

This spacious shopping plaza features more than two dozen specialty shops and restaurants as well as an open square that houses a farmer's market each weekend. After seeing the wares at gift stores such as Festivity Factory, Designs & More, Art House and Lamb's & Ivy, you can catch your breath at eateries such as Kitcho, Au Piche Mignon French Pastry Shop and the Phyrst Grill.

PEDLERS ANTIQUE MALL
660 Capital Cir. N.E.   877-4674

There are plenty of places to hunt for antiques, and this is one of the most popular ones. Not only does this mall feature a great assortment of antiques and collectibles, but Pedlers is also known for its gifts, quality wood furniture and accessories.

FLEA MARKET TALLAHASSEE
200 S.W. Capital Cir.   877-3811

This is one of the largest flea markets in northwest Florida, covering more than 22 acres and featuring more than 500 covered booths. You can find just about anything here: antiques, collectibles, clothes, furniture, fresh vegetables and more. Admission and parking are free.

Specialty Stores

RUBYFRUIT BOOKS
666-4 W. Tennessee St.   222-2627

This eclectic bookstore has a wide range of new, used and out-of-print books, and they're well-known for catering to the smaller presses. They also sport a fine assortment of magazines, cards, jewelry, music and children's books.

TRAIL & SKI
2020 W. Pensacola St.   576-6225

This store can outfit you for the outdoors no matter what you want to do. They've got a great selection of camping gear, athletic shoes, sportswear and many other items. Chances are if they don't have it, you really don't need it.

NICE TWICE
931 N. Monroe St.   224-5435

This popular consignment shop is aimed at women, and many say it hits the mark. Nice Twice has been around for more than a dozen years, so you can bet that their inventory and selection have gotten pretty good over that time. They usually rotate their merchandise for the winter and spring seasons accordingly. Some of their clothes look brand new. If you don't tell, no one will know — but finding a great bargain is something worth shouting about.

BLACK CAT NEWS EXCHANGE
115 S. Monroe St.   222-1920

Two laid-back black cats — Smudge and Soot — lord over this popular downtown bookshop. You might have to search a while to find them — they sometimes kick back behind stacks of books or newspapers, but they're there. The Black Cat News Exchange has a good selection of fiction and nonfiction including the latest releases and discounted hardcover and softcover titles. They also carry daily newspapers from around the state — in any capital city, that's always a popular draw. The huge magazine rack is also well-stocked, with surprising attention paid to the smaller presses. Check out the sale shelf they wheel out in front of the store each morning, which usually offers some great buys.

MOON'S
536 N. Monroe St.   224-9000

If you're looking for jewelry, this is the place. Moon's has been a rather opulent fixture in Tallahassee for many, many years now. Their reputation rests solely on the beauty, selection and affordability of their jewelry. They've got a great staff that can help you pick out the perfect gift no matter what the occasion.

INDIAN NOTIONS
4176 Apalachee Pkwy.   942-0582

Looking for some authentic Indian arts and crafts? This is the place. Indian Notions carries a great assortment of handmade drums, pipes, rugs and other crafts, and they freshen up their shelves with new inventory each month.

AGYEIWA'S AFRICAN BOUTIQUE
211 Wallis St.   656-2700

Plenty of African arts and crafts await you at this boutique, including beautiful handcrafted wooden carvings. The bright and cheerful clothing is another attraction, and there's plenty of uncut fabric for those who wish to sew their own creations.

THE COTTAGES ON LAKE ELLA
1600 Block of N. Monroe St.

Several cottages line Monroe Street on Lake Ella, and they've been turned into a delightful assortment of specialty shops. Among them are tantalizing names such as The Quarter Moon Import Shop, featuring unique jewelry, clothing and gift items; Tabanelli & Lee, featuring jewelry and watchmaking; the Blind Pig Antique Shop; and Cornhusk & Creations, an arts and crafts store.

HEPBURN'S
119 S. Monroe St.   222-2234

The antiques and gifts alone are good reasons for browsing at Hepburn's. When you throw in the wonderful and sometimes startling antique furniture the owners manage to procure, Hepburn's proves itself to be a must-see on the list of any antique hound. For a quick cup of coffee or light lunch, have a seat at Too Chez, a small counter along one wall that's operated by Chez Pierre restaurant a few blocks away.

AMEN-RA'S BOOKSHOP
1326 S. Adams St.   681-6228

The shelves of this bookshop are lined with great works of literature by and about African-Americans. There's also a fine selection of cards, poster and photographs to choose from.

CARE PACKAGES
112 E. College Ave.   224-8727

If you're buying gifts for those hard-to-buy-for people, let Care Packages solve all your problems. They've got an incredible collection of items to spur your instincts, including handmade chocolates, stained-glass ornaments and delicate wind chimes.

Tallahassee
Kidstuff

What's a kid got to do in Tallahassee? Plenty.

Here's a short list of things that should please even the most stubborn and hard-to-please kids visiting or living in the Tallahassee area.

The following items have been thoroughly tried, tested and found true by the various children of friends and relatives. These kids are highly trained professionals in the art of having fun and staving off boredom, and their following recommendations are guaranteed to satisfy kids of all ages.

• Go to the top of the Capitol — it's a great view, and most kids just love heights. Thunderstorms and lightning look great from way up here.

• Hit the Tallahassee Museum of History and Natural Science — where else can you see panthers, alligators and bald eagles?

• Get out that frisbee and head to any of the city's beautiful parks — there's a complete listing in the Parks and Recreation chapter of this book.

• If it's a weekend, head on down to the Flea Market Tallahassee, where there's always plenty of booths that offer comics, toys and other things kids can't live without. See our Shopping chapter for more information.

• Got a computer and modem? Dial up Tallahassee FreeNet, 488-6313, a public computer bulletin board that features a special forum where kids can exchange ideas about everything from the newest Nintendo game to more serious issues such as peer pressure and summer school.

• Go to the Museum of Florida History in the R.A. Gray Building — we've yet to see a kid who wasn't wowed by the standing skeleton of Herman, the resident mammoth.

• Head out to the popular Discovery Zone at the Carriage Gate Shopping Center, 3425 Thomasville Road. Discovery Zone is a pretty awesome indoor playground that features giant tubes and tunnels, an obstacle course, snack bar and enough games to keep you busy for hours! The rules say you have to bring a grown-up along, but that doesn't mean you can't have gobs of fun anyway.

• Sharpen your shooting at Laser Storm in Sugar Creek Center, 2810 Sharer Road, a gigantic laser tag arena whose floor designs are rearranged on a regular basis. Kids as well as adults have a blast hunting each other down in this fun-filled environment. After your match, enjoy more shootin' in the nearby arcade room.

• Take the boat tour at Wakulla Springs State Park a few miles south of Tallahassee — one look at the thick forest and huge alligators and you'll see why they filmed the classic horror movie *Creature From the Black Lagoon* here!

• Take an hour's drive west to the

Florida State Caverns where you can walk hundreds of feet below the earth and see some pretty amazing — not to mention creepy — rock formations.

• Head for the beach! The Gulf Coast is only 30 minutes away and makes for a perfect daytrip.

Tallahassee
Historic Sites and Attractions

The major difference between Tallahassee and almost every other vacation spot in Northwest Florida is the beach. Granted, the capital city is only 30 miles from the nearest stretch of sand, so it's really no big deal. But when people think about Tallahassee's major attractions, they usually think of what the city means in terms of politics and history.

Tallahassee's history is special, and some of the best attractions around not only entertain you but tell a story as well.

The Florida Vietnam Veterans Memorial stands solemnly across the street from the New and Old Capitol buildings.

Photo: Tallahassee Area & Convention Visitors Bureau

There's plenty of history beneath the stained-glass cupola of the Old Capitol building, which rests at the foot of the New Capitol.

We're not talking freeze-dried exhibits here; there are plenty of attractions, such as the Tallahassee Museum of History and Natural Science, that bring history to life and make you a part of it.

Ask around and you'll discover that Tallahasseans are pretty proud of their city's heritage. To residents, the word history doesn't mean anything passive. We know that this area's rich history is alive all around us — noted by inclusions not only in this chapter's listings but in others, such as the Arts and Parks and Recreation sections, as well.

This isn't the beach, and it's certainly no tourist trap. The attractions here offer exciting experiences that cannot be mass-produced and sold in stores. And that's what makes them special.

Like they say, the best way to know history is to experience it firsthand. So, here are a few special time machines offering you fun-filled trips that rival those of any theme park.

BLACK ARCHIVES RESEARCH CENTER AND MUSEUM

Florida A&M University   599-3020

This is just one of many national treasures Tallahassee can boast as its own. The Black Archives Research Center and Museum documents vital chapters in the history of African Americans with a series of exhibits and an exhaustive library of rare books and maps as well as artifacts such as slave irons. It's located in the recently refurbished Carnegie Library, which is the oldest building on the FAMU campus. The Museum is open Monday through Friday from 9 AM to 4 PM. Guided tours should be scheduled in advance. Admission is free.

BROKAW-McDOUGALL HOUSE

329 N. Meridian St.   488-3901

This handsome house is a magnificent example of Classic Revival architecture. Built in the 1850s, it's now used as a conference center and as home to the Historic Preservation Board. And these people know how to take care of it. The house is open Monday through Friday from 9 AM to 5 PM. Admission is free.

THE COLUMNS

100 N. Duval St.   224-8116

Built in 1830 by banker William "Money" Williams (who's also responsible for the Union Bank building listed below), this is the oldest surviving building in the city. The house gets its name from the thick Greek-style pillars featured prominently on its porch. Over the years it's been a bank, a boarding house, a doctor's office and a restaurant. The house was almost demolished in 1971 to make way for newer buildings, but many citizens rallied behind the Tallahassee Chamber of Commerce and managed to move the stately manor across the street, where it now rests. It currently serves as the Chamber's headquarters and was recently renovated and restored to its original splendor.

The Columns is open Monday through Friday from 9 AM to 4:30 PM. Admission is free.

FIRST PRESBYTERIAN CHURCH
110 N. Adams St.   222-4504

This is the oldest church building in Tallahassee. Built in 1838, it is noted as one of the few churches that allowed slaves to become members, even without the consent of their masters. Inside you can still see the narrow balconies where blacks were allowed to sit. Today the church has more than 500 members and is a registered historic site.

The church is open Monday through Friday from 9 AM to 4:30 PM. Admission is free.

FLORIDA VIETNAM VETERANS MEMORIAL
S. Monroe St. and Apalachee Pkwy.   487-1533

Twin granite slabs face each other like giant soldiers standing at attention. Between them hangs a massive, 40-foot American flag. The Vietnam Veterans Memorial is stark and simple and powerfully moving. Carved into the base of each slab are the names of the Florida soldiers who died or are still missing in Vietnam.

Standing at the Memorial, you can look across the street at the Old Capitol and see a small black flag flying beneath the stars and stripes on the cupola there. That's the official emblem for those soldiers listed as missing in action, and it's a symbol that the state hasn't forgotten about them.

GOVERNOR'S MANSION
700 N. Adams St.   488-4661

Florida's first family lives less than a mile away from the Capitol. This Geor-

Canopy Roads

Just what and where are these? Canopy roads are lined with live oak trees so huge and thick that they create a lush green canopy. The five canopy roads — Centerville, Meridian, Miccosukee, Old Bainbridge and Old St. Augustine — were once major transport routes for cotton and others crops. Once the crops were harvested from area plantations, they were sent to the center of town and prepared for transport down to the gulf for shipping. These beautiful moss-draped trees make travels along the roads cool and pleasant even in the hottest part of summer. Now they're specially protected parts of the environment.

gian-style mansion has a portico similar to that of the Hermitage, Andrew Jackson's heavily columned manse. Inside it's just as resplendent, with several rooms featuring antique furniture and gifts from around the world.

Tours are available Monday through Friday from 9 AM to 4:30 PM. The Governor's Mansion is closed to the public during the summer months. Admission is free.

KNOTT HOUSE MUSEUM
301 E. Park Ave.   922-2459

This grand old house was designed and constructed in 1843 by George Proctor, a free black man who built a half-dozen homes in the area. It's a fitting irony that this particular house was built by a black man because of the historic events that would later unfold in the shade of its porch.

In May of 1865, the Civil War came

This mastodon skeleton — affectionately named Herman by the museum staff — proudly greets visitors to the Museum of Florida History.

to a close. Union Gen. Edward McCook took possession of Tallahassee and set up his headquarters in the house. On May 20 of that year, all enslaved blacks were freed as the *Emancipation Proclamation* was read aloud from the front steps of the Knott House.

Sometime after the Civil War, the house fell into the hands of Tallahassee physician Dr. George Betton, whose buggy driver was a black man named William Gunn. In time, Betton realized that his driver had higher dreams and aspirations and paid to put him through medical school. Although he was born into slavery, William Gunn later became Florida's first black physician.

Currently the Knott House is frozen at a specific moment in the 1930s. That's when State Treasure William V. Knott and his family were in residence there and the house was at the height of its splendor. His wife, Luella Pugh Knott, wrote poems for nearly every piece of furniture in the house and tied them all to their respective subjects with bits of ribbon. When you hear people refer to this

as "the house that rhymes," you'll know what they mean.

Out back there's a daylily garden that blooms frequently during the year, and during the holiday season you can enjoy special evening candlelight tours of the house, which is decked out for a very Victorian Christmas.

The Knott House Museum is open Wednesday through Friday from 1 PM to 4 PM and on Saturday from 10 AM to 4 PM. It is closed during the month of August. Admission is $3 for adults, $1.50 for children. There's a special Family Rate of $7.

MUSEUM OF FLORIDA HISTORY
R.A. Gray Building
500 S. Bronough St.   *488-1484*

Say hello to Herman, the skeleton of a prehistoric mastodon that was dredged out of nearby Wakulla Springs in the 1930s. He currently serves as the official mascot of the Museum of Florida History. You'll find a lot of fascinating history here, including treasure recovered from a sunken Spanish galleon, a reconstructed steamboat, a homemade Depres-

The Florida Black Heritage Trail

Tallahassee has several prominent stops along the Florida Black Heritage Trail, which was created by the Department of State to highlight the contributions of African Americans to the state's history. There are more than 140 sites along this trail, which stretches from Pensacola to Key West. Here's what you'll find in Tallahassee.

• Florida A&M University on S. Adams Street, the oldest historically black university in the state

• FAMU's Black Archives Research Center and Museum in the university's Carnegie Library Building, whose collection of early African-American artifacts is among the most comprehensive in the nation

• First Presbyterian Church at 102 N. Adams Street, a church built in the 1830s that allowed slaves to become members of the congregation, although they were required to sit in the north gallery

• The Gibbs Cottage on S. Adams Street, home of lawmaker Thomas Van Renssalaer Gibbs who worked to establish the Florida State Normal and Industrial School for Negroes, which later became FAMU

• The Knott House at 301 E. Park Avenue, from whose steps Union Gen. Edward M. McCook read aloud Abraham Lincoln's *Emancipation Proclamation* at the end of the Civil War in 1865

• The John Gilmore Riley House at 419 W. Jefferson Street, home to Riley, a noted educator and civic leader who became the first principal of Tallahassee's first high school for blacks, the Lincoln Academy

• St. James A.M.E. Church at 104 N. Bronough Street, the oldest black church structure still standing in Tallahassee

• The C.K. Steele Memorial at 111 W. Tennessee Street, honoring Steele, a civil rights activist who organized a bus boycott in Tallahassee that helped to end segregated public transportation

• The Union Bank Building at the corner of the Apalachee Parkway and Calhoun Street, which housed the National Freedman's Bank for newly freed slaves after the Civil War

sion-era mobile home and a four-foot armadillo who was probably good friends with old Herman.

Guided tours are available, and the museum gallery also hosts several traveling exhibits during the year. There's a great gift shop and special programs for kids.

The Museum is open Monday through Friday from 9 AM to 4:30 PM, on Saturday from 10 AM to 4:30 PM and on Sunday from noon to 4:30 PM. Admission is free.

OLD CITY CEMETERY
Park Ave. and Martin Luther King Blvd.599-8712

The oldest public cemetery in Tallahassee is downtown just west of the Park

Avenue Chain of Parks. Established in 1829, this was the only public cemetery for decades, and its markers, gravestones and monuments relate Tallahassee history in a unique way. It seems sooner or later everyone comes here, so you have governors and slaves, Union and Confederate troops, old people and infants all buried within a stone's throw of each other.

Here you can see the final resting places of several movers and shakers, including Dr. William J. Gunn, Florida's first black physician, and Thomas Vann Gibbs, founder of the Florida State Normal Industrial School, now FAMU. You'll also notice a number of markers for citizens who died during the yellow fever epidemic of 1841.

The years haven't been kind to the Old City Cemetery. A new restoration project has corrected some of the damage done by vandals and the weather, but because of the markers' delicate condition, visitors are not allowed to make stone rubbings of them. The cemetery is open daily from sunrise to sunset.

ST. JOHN'S CEMETERY

Call St. and
Martin Luther King Blvd.   222-2636

Across the street from Old City Cemetery is St. John's Cemetery, which was established in 1840 for the church's congregation. Some of the graves you'll find there are those of Prince Achille Murat, nephew of Napoleon Bonaparte, and the Prince's wife, Madame Catherine Murat, the great-grandniece of George Washington. Governor William D. Bloxham is also buried there.

The cemetery is open daily from sunrise to sunset.

SAN LUIS ARCHAEOLOGICAL AND HISTORIC SITE

2020 W. Mission Rd.   487-3711

Long before the Spanish erected their mission here in the mid-15th century, the Tallahassee area was populated by tribes of Apalachee Indians. When the Spanish arrived and decided to build a mission and fort here, there were some Indians who chose to live with them, and they erected a massive council house and plaza. In 1704, however, the Spanish and many of the Indians abandoned San Luis rather than face the threat of advancing British soldiers and Creek Indians. The fort and village were burned to the ground.

In 1983, the state bought the land containing the buried ruins of San Luis and began excavations. For four months each spring, archaeologists descend on the site and spend the rest of the year studying the artifacts and structures they've dug up. This means that each year something new could be uncovered at the site, making this one museum that really changes its exhibits on a regular basis.

The San Luis Archaeological and Historic Site offers guided tours on weekdays at noon, on Saturday at 11 AM and 3 PM and on Sunday at 2 PM. Tours for large groups should be arranged prior to visiting. The site is open Monday through Friday from 9 AM to 4:30 PM, on Saturday from 10 AM to 4:30 PM and on Sunday from noon to 4:30 PM. Admission is free.

TALLAHASSEE MUSEUM OF HISTORY & NATURAL SCIENCE

3945 Museum Dr.   576-1636

This used to be called the Tallahassee Junior Museum, but that name really didn't do this place justice. Everyone agreed that by calling the museum "junior," visitors might think the facility was meant only for children.

Well, kids love it but so do the adults. It's hard not to feel young at heart when you visit the Tallahassee Museum of History and Natural Science because the best parts of this 52-acre museum are outdoors. You can wander a raised wooden walkway and see red wolves, alligators, Florida panthers and bald eagles roaming in their natural habitat.

The museum's aim is to present an accurate depiction of early life in Florida, and needless to say, those beautiful animals, many of them endangered, do the trick. There's also the Big Bend Farm, an authentic 19th-century farm where visitors can get an up-close look at how early settlers lived.

Also on the museum grounds is the Bellevue Plantation House, which was the home of Madame Catherine Murat, wife of Prince Achille Murat and great-grandniece of George Washington. The Bellevue House was her home after the Prince died and has been restored to its original beauty.

The museum is open Monday through Saturday from 9 AM to 5 PM and on Sunday from 12:30 PM to 5 PM. Admission is $5 for adults, $4 for seniors, $3 for children 4 to 15 years; children younger than 4 years get in free.

UNION BANK BUILDING
Apalachee Pkwy.   *487-3903*

This small blue stone structure sits across from the Capitol next to the Florida Vietnam Veterans Memorial and is the oldest bank building in the state. It was constructed in 1840 by William "Money" Williams, who also built the Columns (see earlier entry). Over the years the bank has probably seen more bad luck than good, and its history gives us rare glimpses into Tallahassee's past. The bank was forced to close just three years after its opening due to the rotten financial climate brought about in no small part by the Second Seminole War. After the Civil War, the bank housed the National Freedman's Bank and was later used as a shoe factory, beauty shop and bail-bond office.

The building originally sat next to the Columns on Adams Street, and in 1971 both structures faced demolition to make room for new construction. Fortunately the Columns was lifted and moved across the street, while the Union Bank Building found safe berth here.

The Union Bank Building has no active staff, but you can call the above number to schedule a tour at your convenience.

WALKER LIBRARY
209 E. Park Ave.   *224-5012*

This charming building housed Tallahassee's first public library. Now it serves as the headquarters for Springtime Tallahassee, but you wouldn't know it from looking. The well-preserved interior sports fine woodwork as well as a collection of rare books and historical items. It's open to the public from September through May every year Monday through Friday from 8:30 AM to 1 PM. Admission is free.

Tallahassee
Annual Events and Festivals

The year-round good weather in these parts means that people who like to enjoy the outdoors will seize upon almost any chance to do so. Tallahassee has got a long history of sponsoring well-attended events and celebrations, one that stretches all the way back to the old May Day Festivals, which were the oldest annual events in the state.

Whether you're looking for high-brow culture or down-home fun, there are happenings for all age groups. Some of them are just plain dumb fun, while others may be associated with a cause or charity.

Tallahassee is known for its friendly and fun-loving people, and the only way to meet them is to go where they go. And right here is a good listing of when and where to find them.

January

RATTLESNAKE ROUNDUP
Whigham, Ga. (912) 762-4215

Needless to say, if you don't like snakes, don't come here. This annual festival usually attracts a lot of attention. Where else can you see a bunch of people who like to hunt snakes? Prizes are awarded for the biggest and longest snake, and over the years this roundup has produced some whoppers. There's also an arts and crafts show, animal rides for the kiddies and lots of good food. And yes,

you can even eat snake if you want to. This cultural gem is found 40 miles north of Tallahassee on U.S. 84.

February

HARAMBEE ARTS AND CULTURAL HERITAGE FESTIVAL
Tallahassee/Leon County
Civic Center 656-8388

This black culture and arts festival is always fun, lively and well-attended. You can browse the arts and crafts booths for African-American jewelry and wares, or just listen to some of the good and diverse musical offerings.

TALLAHASSEE KENNEL CLUB DOG SHOW
North Florida Fairgrounds 877-6795

Sanctioned by the American Kennel Club, this show brings out the beast in everyone. Actually, you'll be amazed at the beautiful and well-trained dogs that come here to compete for prizes and titles. Here's where you can see some of the best dogs in town.

BIG BEND CARES
Annual Aids Walk
St. Pauls Methodist Church 656-2437

This walk benefits Big Bend CARES, an agency that provides services to people with HIV and AIDS in the Big Bend area. We hope one day walks like this won't be needed; until then, Tallahassee has proven that it can get out there and offer its support in large numbers.

March

NATURAL BRIDGE BATTLEFIELD HISTORIC SITE
Natural Bridge Rd.
Woodville   922-6007

This re-enactment of the famous Civil War battle gets bigger and better each year. Come and see the decisive victory that made Tallahassee the only Confederate capital east of the Mississippi that did not fall to Federal troops. Authentic uniforms and weapons are used.

WALKAMERICA
Downtown   422-3152

Held at a park across from the Department of Transportation downtown, this national event benefits the March of Dimes Birth Defects Foundation.

ANTIQUE SHOW AND SALE
Tallahassee Museum of
History and Natural Science   576-1636

Tallahasseans love their antiques, so this annual event is always a big draw. The proceeds from the event go to the Tallahassee Museum of History and Natural Science. Call for each year's exact location.

SPRINGTIME TALLAHASSEE
Downtown and vicinity   224-1373

This is a biggie. Spring is one of the most beautiful seasons in Tallahassee, and this festival gives everyone a chance to get out there and soak up some sunshine among the blooming flowers. Some of the many events include the Andrew Jackson Breakfast in the Park, the Springtacular Children's Parade, the Annual Arts and Crafts Jubilee and the

American Indian Cultural Society's Annual Pow-wow.

JAZZ & BLUES FESTIVAL
Tallahassee Museum of
History & Natural Science   576-1636

Come hear some soulful music in a comfortable woodsy environment. This festival features lots of musical acts throughout the day as well as good food and fun for the kids.

April

FLORIDA STATE UNIVERSITY FLYING HIGH CIRCUS
Jack Haskin Circus Complex
W. Pensacola and Chieftain Way 644-4874

And you thought all students cared about was football. These students will have you thinking otherwise as they fly, flip, tumble and swing from the trapeze and perform other amazing airborne feats. Kids love it, and so do the adults who bring them.

SPRING FARM DAYS
Tallahassee Museum of
History and Natural Science   576-1636

So you think your mornings are hectic, hard and fast-paced? Well, come and see what early Tallahassee settlers had to do each morning. You'll see a demonstration of spring farm chores at the restored, turn-of-the-century farm buildings on the museum grounds. And you'll be so exhausted from just watching that you'll need to stay around for the pioneer breakfast they offer.

EASTER EGG HUNT
Wakulla Springs Park, 14 miles south of
Tallahassee on S.R. 267   224-5950

Open to the public, this Easter egg hunt is as much fun for the parents as it is the children. Sit back and watch the little

Each September theTallahassee Museum of Science and Natural History hosts the Native American Heritage Festival, featuring authentic arts and crafts.

ones search through the park's beautiful greenery for hidden eggs and treats.

CITY-WIDE EASTER EGG HUNT
Myers Park Dr., Myers Park   891-3866

If you can't get down to Wakulla then head for Myers Park, only a few blocks from downtown. Toddlers and older children through the age of 10 have five different areas in which to hunt for eggs. There are games and prizes and more, all courtesy of the Easter Bunny.

THOMASVILLE ROSE FESTIVAL
Broad St.
Thomasville, Ga.   (912) 225-5222

A rose by any other name would still get its own festival, according to our friends in nearby Thomasville. They grow some of the prettiest roses around, and they love to show them off. Some of the festivities include a parade, county fair, juried rose show as well as golf and soc-

cer tournaments. Thomasville is 40 miles north of Tallahassee on Highway 319.

STEPHEN C. SMITH MEMORIAL REGATTA
Shell Point Beach   921-3816

The Steven C. Smith Memorial Regatta is one of the largest sailing events in the region. Catamarans, rowing shells and sailboards (and their occupants) show up in this benefit for the American Cancer Society to memorialize Steven C. Smith, a local sailor who died of a rare form of leukemia. Take Highway 363 S. from Tallahassee to Highway 98, go west and take County Road 365 S., which eventually branches off onto County Road 367.

May

BLUE CRAB FESTIVAL
Wooley Park, Panacea   681-9200

There's plenty of good crabbin' in these parts, and this is the time of year when resident fisherfolk and chefs like to show you why. This well-attended festival also has a parade, music, entertainment, an arts and crafts show, a road race and, of course, plenty of great food. Skip breakfast and head down there. Panacea is 42 miles south of Tallahassee on Highway 319.

DANCE FOR SPRING
Ruby Diamond Auditorium, FSU   222-1287

Want to see another way to think about Tallahassee's favorite season? Come watch the agile and fluid dancers of the Tallahassee Ballet Company.

FLORIDA FOLK FESTIVAL
White Springs
Stephen Foster State Folk
Culture Center   397-2192

About 1.5 hours east is one of the biggest folk festivals in the Southeast. People from all over come to hear the dozens of musical artists who perform. There's also dancing, storytelling and down-home-style food.

June

PLANET PARTY

Tallahassee Museum of
History and Natural Science   576-1636

Other people call it Earth Day, but here it's known as Planet Party, and it's a festive occasion indeed. There are plenty of environment-related activities for kids and adults, and there's no better place to appreciate the Earth's beauty than here at the museum's wonderfully wooded site.

July

FOURTH OF JULY CELEBRATION

Eastwood Dr.
Tom Brown Park   891-3866

This celebration is one of the city's largest, and rightly so. Thousands of people sprawl out across the park to enjoy music, theater productions, a road race, arts and crafts booths and what are definitely the most spectacular fireworks around.

SUMMER SWAMP STOMP

Tallahassee Museum of History and Natural
Science, 3945 Museum Dr.   576-1636

Local and regional artists highlight this popular folk and bluegrass festival.

August

"TELL" AHASSEE TALE-TELLIN' TIME

Tallahassee Museum of History and Natural
Science, 3945 Museum Dr.   576-1636

Oral history is Southern tradition, and leave it to Floridians to throw in some tall tales for good measure. This festival features several well-honed story-tellers who never fail to captivate and entertain.

September

NATIVE AMERICAN HERITAGE FESTIVAL

Tallahassee Museum of History and Natural
Science, 3945 Museum Dr.   576-1636

For a taste of Tallahassee before settlers arrived, come to this festival. There are numerous American Indian exhibits, crafts, tribal dances and authentic period music.

"AN EVENING OF MUSIC AND DANCE"

Opperman Music Hall, FSU   222-1287

They've been practicing all summer, and now you can see why. This dance showcases members of the Tallahassee Ballet Company and is always a popular event.

October

QUINCYFEST

Courthouse Square, Quincy   627-2346

This is a down-home family festival that features good music, a fine arts and crafts show, several international food booths and a special children's section for the little ones. Quincy is 15 miles northwest of Tallahassee on Highway 90.

OLD TIME/BLUE GRASS FESTIVAL

Tallahassee Museum of History and Natural
Science, 3945 Museum Dr.   576-1636

The museum continues its tradition of mixing music and the outdoors in this fun, foot-stompin' fest. The old-time country music you'll hear is some of the best around and really takes you back to another era.

NORTH FLORIDA FAIR

Hwy. 319
North Florida Fairgrounds 671-8400

This large agricultural fair features many exhibits from nearly two dozen North Florida counties. There are livestock shows, rides for the kids and entertainment nightly.

GREEK FOOD FESTIVAL

Holy Mother of God Greek Orthodox Church,
1645 Phillips Rd. 878-0747

Southern food is mighty fine around here, but if you're looking for a change of pace, try this festival. It offers an amazing and tasty assortment of traditional Greek dishes.

SAN LUIS HERITAGE FESTIVAL

San Luis Archaeological and Historic Site, 2020
W. Mission Rd. 487-3711

This festival commemorates the Spanish settlers who came here in the 17th century. You can see how they lived back then as well as examples of their crafts, music and food.

November

BRADLEY'S OLD FASHIONED FUN DAY

Bradley's Country Store
Centerville Rd. 893-1647

Take a trip back in time as this popular country store pulls out all the stops to show you how country folk used to have fun. This all-day celebration includes a cane grinding (they even use a friendly old mule to pull the grinding wheel), syrup cooking, free wagon rides, free Model-A Ford rides, a country band, arts and crafts and plenty of smiling faces. Thousands of people wait all year long for the chance to ride this time machine. One visit and you'll see why.

MULE DAYS

Calvery, Georgia (912) 377-6853

This mule show and beauty contest (yes, they're separate events) takes place about 20 miles northwest of Tallahassee on Georgia State Road 111, just beyond Havana, Florida on Highway 27. It also offers an arts and crafts show and a big parade.

MARKET DAYS

Hwy. 319
North Florida Fairgrounds 576-1636

Sponsored by the Tallahassee Museum of History and Natural Science, this easygoing fair has plenty of food booths, arts and crafts displays, handmade toys and ceramics.

SWINE TIMES

Climax, Georgia (912) 246-0910

Oink! This hog-heaven festival is full of backwoods fun. There's a contest for the best-dressed pigs, and the highlight is probably the greased pig contest. Yes, they still do that around here. There's also an arts and crafts show and parade. It's about 40 miles north of Tallahassee; take Highway 27 to State Road 263.

December

A CHRISTMAS CAROL "ON THE AIR"

Location announced each year 847-3479

The Charles Dickens classic is presented by the Nucleus Group, and it's staged as an old-time radio show complete with music, sound effects and audience participation. The old story of Scrooge really comes to life under the direction of this talented and innovative group.

WINTER FESTIVAL: CELEBRATION OF LIGHTS

Downtown 891-3866

This is by far the biggest fall festival. Winter Festival signals the beginning of the holiday season. More than 100,000 people fill the downtown area to see the Park Avenue Chain of Parks set ablaze with miles of twinkling lights. Kids love the parade and the giant animated toys and candy-makers. Ice skating is big on the list for both kids and adults (isn't it wild to think of that cold-weather sport in Florida?!). You'll enjoy plenty of good food and music too. And don't miss the Jingle Bell Run, either — participants each get a red cap with a bell on it, and there's probably nothing more surreal than seeing and hearing thousands of joggers clad in Santa hats running through the downtown streets.

DECEMBER ON THE FARM

Tallahassee Museum of
History and Natural Science 576-1636

We only think that getting up on cold winter mornings and cranking up the heater is a pain! You should come and see what early settlers and pioneers had to go through. Several farm chores are demonstrated here, and afterward everyone gets to sidle up to the breakfast table for a country breakfast.

QUINCY'S VICTORIAN CHRISTMAS STROLL

Quincy 627-2346

This very popular holiday extravaganza features old-time carriage and hay rides, Santa's Secret Shop, strolling carollers and plenty of great holiday goodies.

THOMASVILLE'S VICTORIAN CHRISTMAS

Broad St.
Thomasville, Georgia

Though we mention this event featuring a live nativity and walking tours in the Thomasville section of our Tallahassee Daytrips chapter, we want to make sure you don't miss it, so here's another reminder.

NUTCRACKER BALLET

Ruby Diamond Auditorium, FSU 222-1287

This timeless favorite is staged by the Tallahassee Ballet Company in association with the Tallahassee Symphony Orchestra.

HOLY COMFORTER EPISCOPAL SCHOOL ANNUAL TOUR OF HOMES & HOLIDAY CRAFT SHOW

1500 Miecosukee Rd. 877-2126

And if you think the name of this festival is a mouthful, just wait until you see the sights. This open house tour through four of Tallahassee's historic homes, all of them beautifully decorated for Christmas, can really put you in the spirit. There's also a craft show at the Dorothy Oven Park.

Photo: Tallahassee Area Convention & Visitors Bureau

Built in the 1930s as a hunting resort, Wakulla Springs Lodge and Conference Center offers fine dining and overnight accommodations.

Tallahassee
Parks and Recreation

When most people think of Florida, they usually picture white sandy beaches — with a condo or theme park always lurking in the background.

Florida's climate and landscape presented great challenges to early settlers and pioneers, but progress prevailed and the state is one of the fastest-growing in the nation. Unfortunately, such progress also threatens much of the remaining unspoiled landscape.

While things might be getting a little crowded down on the peninsula, Florida's northwest sports many undeveloped areas, and several key places are fortunately preserved as parks. There are more than 100 state parks throughout Florida, and some of the best are in the Tallahassee area, which also boasts many fine city parks as well.

With all that beautiful scenery and warm weather out there, why are you sitting there reading this book? Pick a park, put the book down and just get out there.

National Parks

APALACHICOLA NATIONAL FOREST
942-9300
Florida has three national forests, and Tallahasseans tend to think that we've got the best one right here. If you fly into Tallahassee, you'll get a bird's-eye view of this forest because Tallahassee Municipal Airport sits right on the northeastern edge of the Apalachicola National Forest.

The forest is huge, made up of more than 600,000 acres of pristine woodland covering several counties. Needless to say, there's a lot to see and do out there.

The wildlife, for example, is incredibly diverse. Black bear, deer, wild pigs and more make their home in the forest.

The recreation area nearest to Tallahassee is Silver Lake, a few miles outside of town on Highway 20 W. This beautiful lake offers swimming, camping and hiking and is pretty popular during spring and summer.

Another hot spot is Camel Lake on the northwestern edge of the forest. This beautiful lake has a campground, swimming beach and picnic area and is popular with boaters and anglers. From Tallahassee there are two routes. Take Highway 20 W. to Hosford, where you drop south for a few miles on State Road 647 to State Road 12. Or just take Interstate 10 W. about 25 miles to the State Road 12 Exit, and drop south. It's a bit of a drive, but well worth it.

The Ochlockonee River snakes along two lake areas, Whitehead Lake and Hitchcock Lake. Both of these parks offer primitive camping areas and are greatly enjoyed by boaters and anglers. To reach them, take Highway 319 S. out of Tallahassee to Crawfordville, where you'll go west on State Road 12. This

Looking for 20 miles of safe, fun and historic bicycling? Look no further than the Tallahassee-St. Marks Historic State Trail.

quiet and lovely drive will take you out through the middle of the huge forest. You'll cross the Ochlockonee River after about 25 miles, and just beyond it you'll head south on State Road 67. Whitehead Lake is only a couple of miles down the road, and Hitchcock Lake just a few miles beyond that.

About 20 miles south of the above-mentioned Camel Lake is Cotton Landing, which also offers primitive camping, fishing and boating along Kennedy Creek. And just southeast of Cotton Landing are Wright Lake and Hickory Landing, either of which would make a great sidetrip while visiting Fort Gadsden State Historic Site (see following).

One of the more impressive geological features is **Leon Sinks**, a chain of sinkholes that were formed when the underlying limestone was dissolved by rainwater made acidic by carbon dioxide and decaying vegetation. There are three walking trails through the Leon Sinks area. To get there, take Highway 319 S. out of Tallahassee. The sinks are about 5

miles past Capital Circle. Though these sinks are often filled with water, swimming is not allowed.

ST. MARKS
NATIONAL WILDLIFE REFUGE

St. Marks   925-6121
$4 per vehicle

Along with the Apalachicola National Forest, the St. Marks Wildlife Refuge preserves two important facets of Florida history: wildlife and landscape. This 63,000-acre refuge was established in 1931 and was one of the first such refuges created. It's about a half-hour's drive from Tallahassee down Highway 363 to Highway 98. Head east for a few miles and you'll reach the entrance to this sight-filled preserve.

You'll want to stop by the visitors center to orient yourself to the wildlife refuge. It's got several educational displays about what you can expect when you enter the area. There's also the Plum Orchard Pond Trail behind the center, which offers a third-of-a-mile trail with interpretive markers that highlight some of the local plants and trees found in the refuge.

If you don't want to hike either of the walking trails (one's 7 miles and the other is about 13), then stick to your wheels. The main road through the refuge is County Road 59, a 7-mile stretch that curves through the wilderness and stops at the St. Mark Lighthouse. There are several places where you can pull off and do some wildlife watching. There's a picnic area about 5 miles into the refuge, and you'll also pass several dikes that allow you to get off the beaten path a bit.

Keep your eyes open, because you never can tell what might cross your path. Deer, foxes, raccoons and armadillos can sometimes appear out of nowhere, and if you're a bird-watcher, be sure to pick up the free guide to birds in the refuge visitors center.

You can't camp at St. Marks Wildlife Refuge, but just across from the entrance is the Newport Recreation Area, which has camping facilities. On the other end of the park is the Ochlockonee River State Park (see following explanation), which also has campgrounds.

There's good fishing in these parts. Cast a line and find out why it's still a booming industry around here. Boats can be launched from the lighthouse but aren't permitted in the refuge pools except from March 15 to October 15, and leave the big outboard at home because boat motors can't be more than 10 horsepower. Canoeing remains a popular way to see the sights from the water.

There's good crabbing too, but the refuge warns you to watch out for alligators that may try to steal your bait. And they know what they're talking about.

Hunting is allowed on a select basis in fall and spring. You should contact the refuge for dates, regulations and permits.

State Parks

Not only can you spend days wandering through the wonderfully varied landscape in the local state parks, but they also present plenty of activities. There's a free Florida State Parks Guide available for residents and visitors. All you have to do is ask for one. Write the Florida Department of Environmental Protection, Division of Recreation and Parks, 3900 Commonwealth Boulevard, Mail Stop 525, Tallahassee 32399. Or call 488-9872.

All Florida State Parks are open from 8 AM until sundown, 365 days a year. State museums are open from 9 AM to noon and again from 1 PM to 5 PM. Many museums and historic sites are

If you want to check out Wakulla Springs State Park from the comfort of your living room, go rent the monster movie classic *The Creature From the Black Lagoon*, the kitschy *Airport '77* or *Joe Panther*, a great 1976 family film about a Seminole Indian boy struggling to maintain his heritage in the modern world. Or you can check out several of the old Tarzan movies from the 1930s featuring Johnny Weissmuller. These were all filmed in the park's lush, jungle-like setting.

Insiders' Tips

closed two days each week, so be sure to contact the park before you visit.

Enjoy these parks, but also treat them with respect. The natural resources within state parks are protected, and rightly so. Any hunting, livestock grazing or timber removal could severely damage the ecosystems. You'll probably see some amazing wildlife, but don't feed the animals. And don't drink — alcoholic beverages are a no-no. The same goes for firearms.

Pets aren't allowed in camping areas, bathing beaches or concession areas but are generally welcome anywhere else. Leashes are required. Guide dogs for the deaf and blind are, of course, welcome in all park areas.

Handicapped persons should note that not all state parks are readily accessible — it's something the park system is certainly working toward, but it's not there yet. Accommodations can be made, however, in parks where access is not permanently available. For more information, just call the individual park office at least 10 days before your visit.

Campers have a lot of sites to choose from. Some parks offer modern facilities, while others are strictly for primitive camping.

Many state parks offer some great fishing, so pack your rod and reel. Note that saltwater and freshwater fishing licenses are required for those 16 and older. Licenses are available for a fee at county tax collector offices and at most bait and tackle shops. Keep in mind that some parks do have size and species limits. For a free copy of the pamphlets *Know Your Limits* and *Go Fish . . . But First Get A License*, in either English or Spanish, write the Department of Environmental Protection, Office of Fisheries Management & Assistance Services, Mail Station No. 240, 3900 Commonwealth Boulevard, Tallahassee 32399, or call 922-4340.

Unless otherwise stated, here's the fee structure for Florida state parks:

Per vehicle (8 passengers maximum)	$3.25
Pedestrians, Bicyclists, Extra Passengers	$1
Museum/Visitor Center Fee	$1

Camping fees vary from park to park. It's a good idea to call ahead prior to any park visit to check the fees.

Tallahassee

LAKE JACKSON MOUNDS STATE ARCHAEOLOGICAL SITE
1022 DeSoto Park Dr.   922-6007

This park is just a few miles north of I-10, just off U.S. 27 and down Indian Mound Road. From 1200 A.D. to 1500 A.D., this area near Lake Jackson was a major trading, religious and social center for early Indians in the area. Archaeologists and historians generally agree that these Indians were part of a complex Indian society knows as the "Southeastern Ceremonial Complex," or "Southern Cult." Among the many artifacts and re-

Insiders' Tips

If you're wandering the trails and levees of St. Mark's National Wildlife Refuge, keep your eyes open for wide, shallow depressions covered with grass and sticks. Alligators are known to lay their eggs in such places, and you don't want to crush or disturb them — especially if Mama Gator is around.

mains unearthed here was evidence that these Indians had extensive contact with tribes all over the Southeast.

There are six earthen mounds here, but only three are accessible to visitors. There's a large picnic area bisected by a small stream that feeds into the nearby lake. A nature trail through the woods displays an abundance of plant life.

Each October the mounds are alive with the sound of music during Sounds of the Mounds, a free outdoor concert designed to promote environmental awareness of the area. The actual date changes each year, so if you want to attend, call the park office for the schedule.

LAKE TALQUIN
STATE RECREATION AREA
1022 Desoto Park Dr.   *922-6007*

About 15 miles west of the city on Vause Road, just off State Road 20, lies the Lake Talquin Recreation Area.

Unlike Lake Jackson, Lake Talquin hasn't been around very long. In 1927 the Jackson Bluff Dam was built on the Ochlockonee River, and the lake was formed then. Of course, you wouldn't know this was a relatively new lake from the fishing — the plentiful largemouth bass, shellcracker and speckled perch will have you thinking this must have been a favorite fishing hole for hundreds of years.

Even if you don't fish, it's a good spot for boating and canoeing. But it's strictly BYOB (Bring Your Own Boat) because the park doesn't rent them.

Lake Talquin's friendly campsite offers cabins and spots for recreational vehicles and tents too.

Nearby Whippoorwill Sportsman's Lodge rents boats and also provides a nice campground.

Even if you don't want to overnight it, Lake Talquin is still a great spot to spend the day. There's a great picnic area at the River Bluff Picnic Site that has one of the best views in town. After you've eaten your fill you can walk it off on one of the nature trails. Walk quietly and you might catch a glimpse of some of the wildlife peeking back at you from the pines and hardwoods — wild turkey, deer and bald eagles frequent the place almost as much as people do.

MACLAY STATE GARDENS
3540 Thomasville Rd.   *487-4556*

New York financier Alfred B. Maclay loved flowers, and he'd probably be proud his name is connected with one of the most beautiful sculpted gardens in the South. When his estate was donated to Florida in the early 1950s, it quickly became a notable tourist attraction that even the locals can't get enough of.

Just a mile north of I-10 on Thomasville Road, Maclay State Gardens is home to hundreds of varieties and species of plants. There are more than 100 varieties of camellias alone, and each week from January until summer a different variety reaches full bloom. Along with the other plants this creates a never-ending festival of color that many residents return to witness each year.

The Maclay house sits atop gently rolling hills that feature great pine and live oak trees. The house appears as it was furnished when the Maclays lived there and is well worth a tour for its preserved history.

Down the hill rests Lake Hall, which is home to fish, turtles and alligators. Along its banks can be seen many birds and, if you're lucky, an occasional bobcat or fox. The surrounding area is accessible by way of the Big Pine Nature Trail and makes for a brisk walk. There are spots for picnics, including a large pavilion that's available for rental, and the lake is open for swimming and boating — no motors are allowed, however. Bring your own sailboat or canoe, or just rent a canoe from the park. Also note that the opposing shoreline of the lake is private property and the last thing its owners want are boatloads of visitors coming ashore.

The fishing is excellent. Local anglers report great success in catching largemouth bass, bream and bluegill. Just don't forget your Florida freshwater fishing license.

Each December Camellia Christmas is a hot ticket in town. The lanes through the park are lit for special nighttime tours and the air is filled with Christmas carols. This usually takes place the first weekend in December as part of the city's Winter Festival, so call ahead to check the actual date.

The gardens are free except during the peak bloom season that officially runs from January 1 through April 30. Then the gardens admission fee is $3 for adults, $1.50 for children. Guided garden tours are usually offered in mid-March, and special tours may be booked with a three-week advance notice.

The Maclay Home is open only during those same peak bloom months, from January until April.

If you've got a green thumb, you might want to note that a special seminar on ornamental plant care is offered on the first Saturday of each month and is taught by the Maclay State Gardens landscape gardener.

NATURAL BRIDGE
BATTLEFIELD STATE HISTORIC SITE
Natural Bridge Rd., Woodville 922-6007
Free admission

During the Civil War, Tallahassee was the only Confederate state capital east of the Mississippi that did not fall to Union forces. The reason for this can be found in a tiny town called Woodville that sits 9 miles south of the city on State Road 363 (South Monroe Street). Six miles east of Woodville is Natural Bridge, an area along the St. Marks River where the water flows through an underground cavern for a brief stretch, creating a natural crossing.

In early March 1865, a joint Union Army and Navy force sailed into Apalachee Bay some 25 miles south of the capital. Their mission was to land and take the St. Marks lighthouse. After that, they planned to move north and destroy unsuspecting Confederate forces in a sneak attack that would culminate with the taking of Tallahassee.

The Confederate forces got wind of the invading troops and tried to halt the Union forces at Newport. They could not gain a foothold, however, and were forced to retreat. The Confederate troops were at least able to channel the Union forces towards Natural Bridge, the only safe crossing at the St. Marks River. Because the Confederate ranks were thin, young boys, old men and even wounded soldiers from the area found themselves pressed into service, and they all waited for the Union troops to begin their assault.

At 4 AM on March 6, 1865, the attack began. The Union forces — reportedly made up of many black soldiers — were swift and strong, but the Confederates were braced for the attack. After repelling three powerful charges over a 10-hour period, the Confederates themselves advanced and eventually forced the Union troops back down the river to St. Marks, where they took to their ships and departed. The Union dead numbered 21, and the Confederates lost three.

Today the pivotal battle site is marked by a huge obelisk monument to the troops who fought and died there. Each year this historic battle is re-enacted by volunteers sporting authentic uniforms and firearms. The re-enactment takes place on a weekend close to the actual date of the battle. Call the park for the actual date each year.

Picnic tables are available, and park admission is free.

Tallahassee - St. Marks Historic Railroad State Trail

S.R. 363 and Capital Cir.   922-6007
Free admission

In the early 1800s, Tallahassee planters and merchants needed a railroad to ship their wares down to ports at St. Marks and then bring supplies and passengers back. It took a long time and a lot of hard work, but the Tallahassee-St. Marks Railroad was completed in 1837. Of course this was a great convenience at the time, but one must remember that passengers and freight rode in open wooden box cars. And it's not like there was a good breeze to cool things down, because the first few trains were pulled slowly by oxen, and it took them nearly half a day to make the 16-mile journey.

Even after the addition of a nice new engine, things were only moderately better. Writer Bradford Torrey, in his 1894 book *Florida Sketchbook*, rode the train and wrote, "I could never have imagined the possibility of running trains over so crazy a track."

These days that crazy track has been replaced by a smoothly paved track, and you can make the journey at your own speed, whether it's by foot, skates, bicycle or horseback. In 1987 the Florida Rails-to-Trails Program was established and this, its first completed project, runs from just south of Tallahassee all the way down to St. Marks.

When it ceased operating in 1984, the railroad was the oldest one in the state. Fortunately, now it can enjoy many more years as a unique and historic nature trail.

Water fountains are dotted along this piney path, and there are several places to stop and picnic, so we suggest you pack a meal. If you're bold and want some good seafood, however, you can take the entire trail down to St. Marks, where it empties out practically at the doorstep of several good restaurants. If you eat or drink your fill, you've got a 16-mile bike ride back to Tallahassee that'll help you work it all off.

Also nearby is San Marcos de Apalachee State Historic Site, if you want to do some sight-seeing. It's only about a mile from the end of the trail.

If you want to take your horse along the trail, there's a separate path that runs parallel to the paved trail. If you're accompanying persons on foot or bike, you're asked to keep your horse on the shoulder to protect the pavement. Note that proof of a recent negative Coggins test for sleeping sickness is required of all horses that enter the trail.

Bike and skate rentals are available at the beginning of the trail.

As the Tallahassee-St. Marks Trail crosses over several streets and state roads, you should always be alert for cross-traffic. The crossings are well-marked for drivers, but play it safe and treat it like any other crossing. It shouldn't break your stride too often.

Edward Ball Wakulla Springs State Park

Wakulla Springs   922-3633

This is probably the busiest, hardest-working park in the region, possibly even the state, and one look tells you why: It's got one of the largest and deepest freshwater springs in the world. This beautiful spring is the centerpiece of an unspoiled natural habitat that sprawls for nearly 3,000 acres.

Boat tours take you out over the spring and down the river a bit, where you can observe wildlife such as alligators, anhinga birds, wild turkeys and turtles. And though the springs have a depth of 185 feet, the waters are so clear that most of the underwater plant and animal life is easily visible.

We know that the Apalachee Indians greatly valued this area as a hunting ground and fresh water source, but its history goes even farther back than that. Several pre-Ice Age bones and fossils have been discovered by dive teams in the underwater cave from which the spring flows. In fact, a mastodon skeleton retrieved from this very spring in 1930 now stands in the Museum of Florida History.

The Wakulla Springs Lodge and Conference Center was built in 1937 as a private hunting lodge. It has overnight accommodations, a restaurant, snack bar and gift shop. Conference rooms are also available, and you might see several attendees ducking out of busy meetings for a quiet stroll along the river.

There are spots for picnics and several nature and hiking trails through the park. Swimming is allowed only within the designated area near the spring.

There are so many monthly activities at the park that to list them all would probably take another book or two, but note that there are regular tours, hikes and lectures as well as seasonal activities such as night cruises and sunrise boat tours. Call ahead for a current schedule.

To get to Wakulla Springs State Park and Lodge, take State Road 267 south for 14 miles.

Other Area State Parks

FALLING WATERS
STATE RECREATION AREA
Chipley   638-6130

Whoever names the Florida state parks usually gets them right, and this park is no exception. Yes, there is a waterfall here, a 70-footer that falls into a deep sink, or cylindrical pit in the limestone aquifer upon which Florida sits.

There's camping here, nature trails and spots for picnics. It's about 90 miles west of Tallahassee. Take I-10 west to State Road 77A and drop south about 3 miles.

FLORIDA CAVERNS STATE PARK
Marianna   482-9598

For many years, people knew about the caves in Marianna. Indians were living in them when the first settlers arrived, and many early explorers also used them for shelter. Historians believe that many Indians hid in these caves during Andrew Jackson's brutal raids in the early 1800s.

But in the early part of this century, a hurricane swept across the Panhandle and uprooted a huge tree near the caves. Beneath its exposed root structure was a huge dark cavern, one the Indians hadn't discovered because until the hurricane there had been no opening.

The current irony here is that this latter cave is the only one you can visit. The other caves have been closed to the public due to misuse and abuse. Park officials still grumble justly about the graffiti that constantly appeared on those ancient walls.

While that important bit of history is now lost to visitors, the good news is that these more recently discovered caverns are open to the public. What's more, they offer some fascinating and beautiful rock formations. Tours take about 30 minutes (after you sit through a sleep-inducing short video about the history of the park, or something) and the park guides are knowledgeable enough to explain the difference between stalactites and stalagmites, which everyone seems to forget as soon as they hear it.

The formations are caused by carbonic acid in the rainwater washing over the limestone hollows, which are usually filled with water. This residue is called calcite, and it builds up slowly over the years. The resulting formations, which bear exotic and apt names such as rimstone, flowstone and draperies, are thousands, even millions of years old and a truly amazing sight to behold.

Those who suffer from claustrophobia probably wouldn't go inside a cave in the first place, but here's an official warning anyway: Some parts of the cave are really tight. You wander 65 feet below the surface and are asked to navigate passages with names like Fat Man's Squeeze, where the ceiling hangs at about four feet.

Even if you can't do that, the 1,280-acre park still has a lot to offer. There are plenty of full-facility campsites for those who wish to explore the swimming, canoeing, fishing and hiking. There are also horse trails and stables. Be sure to check out the natural bridge where the Chipola River dips underground for a few hundred feet.

PONCE DE LEON SPRINGS STATE RECREATION AREA

Chipley   *836-4281*

There's a sardonic joke about Ponce de Leon that sums up a lot of attitudes about Florida. If the famous Spanish explorer had actually found his Fountain of Youth and achieved immortality, then one look at today's endangered Florida environment would have the old-timer desperately seeking the services of one Dr. Jack Kevorkian.

OK, maybe it's not as bad as all that, but it's often useful and refreshing to retreat to a state park to see some unspoiled natural landscape. This park is one good place to do just that. The park is named after Ponce de Leon because its several crystal-clear springs probably attracted his attention during his exploration of the panhandle. Maybe he didn't acquire much longevity from drinking their waters, but then again, a good cold drink on a hot day can certainly make you feel born again.

The park offers swimming in the year-round 68-degree springs, picnic areas, hiking trails and fishing. Due to state restrictions on empty promises, however, the park management cannot guarantee immortality to those who drink from the springs.

Ponce de Leon Springs State Recreation Area is about 100 miles west of Tallahassee on Interstate 10.

OCHLOCKONEE RIVER STATE PARK

Sopchoppy   *962-2771*

There's plenty of camping and hiking do to in this 400-acre park, but the real reason to come is the 50-mile Ochlockonee River, which winds through the nearby Apalachicola National Forest. It's great for swimming and just perfect for boating and canoeing.

In fact, the water probably provides the best view of the surrounding forest, which is home to abundant wildlife such as deer, bobcats and foxes. The birdwatching is excellent, so don't forget your binoculars and field guide.

To get to the park from Tallahassee, take Highway 319 S. for 22 miles. The park is 4 miles south of Sopchoppy.

SAN MARCOS DE APALACHE STATE HISTORIC SITE

St. Marks   922-6007

For nearly 500 years, this historic site has been the setting for some of the most pivotal, dramatic and tragic events in the history of Florida. The Spanish explorer Panfilo de Narvaez arrived here in 1528, having walked his expedition up the peninsula from present-day Tampa. Narvaez should have stayed around to enjoy life a bit more, but he insisted on building wooden boats and sailing to Mexico. He and his 300 men were lost at sea not long after.

Originally a wooden fort stood on this wedge of land where the Wakulla River joins the St. Marks River as they flow southward. Erected by Spanish explorers, this structure was destroyed in a hurricane in 1758. The following year a masonry fort was built, and ownership passed from the Spanish to the local Indians and to the Spanish again.

The fort was briefly held by William Augustus Bowles, an Indian sympathizer who wished to establish an independent Indian nation. He held it for less than a month at the turn of the 19th century before Spanish forces drove him away.

Gen. Andrew Jackson claimed the Spanish fort in 1819, and the fort became an army outpost from which Jackson dealt severe blows to the Indians. When Jackson caught two British citizens among the Indians, he tried and executed them on the spot. To soften the outcry from Britain, the U.S. Congress passed a resolution condemning Jackson's misguided actions.

Jackson withdrew, and the fort returned to Spanish rule for two years. Then Florida was ceded to the United States. In 1830, the nearby town of St. Marks was created and became a bustling port town. The fort was again pressed into military service during the Civil War and called Fort Ward. Its formidable presence discouraged forces from the ever-present Union blockade from landing.

The museum, which stands on the foundations of a pre-Civil War hospital for yellow fever victims, has a fascinating exhibit about the history of the fort. There are self-guided walking tours through the site featuring the remains of Confederate earthworks, bastion walls, Spanish moats and other features. There is also a picnic area available.

Each May the park plays host to HuManatee, a small but heartfelt festival that welcomes the manatees back to the immediate area.

To get to the San Marcos de Apalache State Historic Site from Tallahassee, take State Road 363 south for 16 miles.

THREE RIVERS STATE PARK

Sneads   482-9006

Two's company and three's a crowd, as the old saying goes. Whoever coined that phrase obviously never visited Three

---

Insiders' Tips

The Tallahassee-St. Marks Historic Railroad State Trail was the first of several rails-to-trails projects to be established in Florida. Construction on other trails is continuing at a rapid pace. When completed, bikers, runners, walkers and skaters will be able to enjoy hundreds of miles' worth of Florida's natural beauty.

Rivers State Park, where the Apalachicola, Chattahoochee and Flint Rivers meet near Lake Seminole.

Needless to say, activities here are geared for maximum use of the available water resources. There's excellent swimming, fishing, canoeing and boating to be done here.

But don't ignore the surrounding terrain. The hilly pine forests and hardwood hummocks are great for hiking and camping.

From Tallahassee, take Interstate 10 W. to State Road 271, about 45 miles. Head north for 10 miles and there you are.

TORREYA STATE PARK

Bristol   *643-2674*

Torreya State Park might take its name from a tree, but the park is perhaps best known for its magnificent 150-foot bluffs overlooking the Apalachicola River, which is too bad, considering that the rare Torreya trees might be on the verge of extinction. In the 1960s, a disease practically wiped out the species, and the few remaining ones in this park may not survive.

There are several other rare species of plants and animals in the park as well as quite a bit of history. Indians once lived along the banks of this river. Later it was an important waterway for settlers and early industry.

Along one of the bluff's hiking trails you can see the huge pit where a six-cannon battery once stood, which was designed to keep Union ships from passing during the Civil War.

The park also sports the Gregory House, a mid-19th-century plantation house. The house was built by Jason Gregory, a cotton farmer, and is furnished with articles from that time period. The Gregory House is open for tours on week-

days at 10 AM and on weekends and state holidays at 10 AM, 2 PM and 4 PM. A fee of $1 per adult and 50¢ per child younger than 13.

There are several nature trails, including a 7-mile hiking trail that displays most of the park's features. There are also picnic areas in addition to a full-facility and primitive campsites.

To get to Torreya State Park from Tallahassee, take Interstate 10 W. for about 45 miles, and take the State Road 12 Exit.

Tallahassee City Parks

The city park system is an active one, and there's a special hotline for events and programs. Call 891-3866 for more information.

A.J. HENRY PARK

Just south of Killearn Estates in the northern part of town. There's a place for picnics, a playground and walking trails through this 70-acre park.

CAMPBELL POND

Just south of Four Points, this park features a 24-acre lake, picnic pavilions and a playground.

CAPITAL PAR

Down Old Tram Road, this park features a youth baseball field, a picnic area and playground.

CARTER-HOWELL-STRONG PARK

In Frenchtown, bordered by Georgia, Copeland, Deqey and Virginia Streets, this is one of the city's newest parks.

CHAPMAN POND (SYLVAN LAKE)

Located on Circle Drive, this park features a large pond and benches. Fishing is allowed for children 14 and younger.

You can see hundreds of different varieties of flowers in bloom at Maclay State Gardens.

COUNTRY CLUB PARK

There are three softball fields at this park, which is found at the intersection of Magnolia Avenue and Golf Terrace Drive.

DOROTHY B. OVEN PARK

Impressive flower gardens and a classic manor-style home are the two main reasons to visit this park on Thomasville Road.

INDIANHEAD ACRE PARK

Indianhead Drive is home to this 30-acre park that offers walking and open grounds.

JOHN G. RILEY PARK

Just off Indiana Street, this park offers five acres of passive park land.

KOUCKY PARK

This three-acre park has a playground and a picnic area and is found on Chowkeebenee Drive.

LAKE ELLA

This midtown lake just off N. Monroe Street is a popular walking spot.

LEVY PARK

At Tharpe Street and Gibbs Drive, this park has a swimming pool, baseball fields and a picnic area.

MYERS PARK

Forty acres of hilly wooded land makes for good brisk hikes through this park, which also features a playground, youth baseball field, tennis courts and a year-round swimming pool.

OLD FORT PARK

Just a few blocks from Myers Park on Old Fort Road is this one-acre Civil War site, which features a historic earthen fort.

OPTIMIST PARK

Just off E. Indianhead Drive, this park has a picnic area, playground, softball field, basketball court and volleyball field.

PARK AVENUE CHAIN OF PARKS

As a safeguard against Indian attacks and wild animals, early settlers in Tallahassee cleared out a northern buffer zone known as 200-Foot Street. As the township grew, it eventually extended beyond this swath, which exists today as a downtown chain of seven parks along Park Avenue. Cherokee Park, E. Peck Green Park, McCarty Park, Ponce de Leon Park, Bloxham Park, Lewis Park and Genevieve Randolph Park all offer downtowners the chance to relax and enjoy the sunshine among live oaks, thick grass and several historic markers.

In Lewis Park, for example, you can visit the gigantic stump where Tallahassee's May Oak once stood. For more than 100 years, this great tree was

Recreation Centers

Looking to improve your volleyball technique while in town? Would you be interested in a karate lesson or two? Perhaps you just want to sign your children up for gymnastic lessons during your visit here.

Whatever recreational activity or sport you're looking for, Tallahassee has six recreation centers throughout town, and these are busy and fun places with plenty to offer. There's so much, in fact, that we can't list it all here. Each community and recreation center has its own lengthy schedule, and if you ask, they'll gladly provide a detailed program listing with fees and schedules. There's a wide range of programs to choose from. If you want to get physical about it, the ever-busy Athletic Division offers such sports as tackle and flag football, baseball, softball, soccer, gymnastics and aquatic sports. Arts and crafts programs include quarterly workshops and courses in drawing, water-color, shirt decorating, sewing and pottery classes.

These centers are open Monday through Saturday from 9 AM to 5 PM, and many offer evening classes too.

DADE STREET COMMUNITY CENTER
1115 Dade St.   891-3910

FOURTH AVENUE RECREATION CENTER
Fourth Ave. and Macomb St.   891-3930

JAKE GAITHER COMMUNITY CENTER
801 Tanner Dr.   891-3940

LAFAYETTE PARK COMMUNITY CENTER
403 Ingleside Dr.   891-3946

PALMER MUNROE COMMUNITY CENTER
1900 Jackson Bluff Rd.   891-3958

WALKER FORD COMMUNITY CENTER
2301 Pasco St.   891-3970

the site of the May Day Festival, one of the oldest annual celebrations in Florida. The aging tree collapsed in the mid-1980s, but its huge flat stump is a historic marker in its own right.

A few blocks west, in McCarty Park, you can see the camellias bloom from December on into summer at the Will-iam Lanier "Red" Barber Memorial Garden. The flowers were favorites of the legendary sports broadcaster, and he spoke of them often during his heartwarming, wise and popular commentaries on National Public Radio. Locals like to think that Red is looking down on his flowers and smiling broadly.

Some of the historic structures you'll see on a stroll through the parks are the Knott House (open for tours), Tallahassee's first library (now headquarters for Springtime Tallahassee — duck inside for a look at its magnificent woodwork), the Lewis Home (main offices for the Florida Council for Community Mental Health, Inc.), the Murphy House (shops and offices), the Columns (Tallahassee Chamber of Commerce), the U.S District Courthouse and the First Presbyterian Church, the oldest public building in Tallahassee.

Springtime Tallahassee and the Winter Festival are just two of the many events that make use of this beautiful stretch of greenery. We encourage you to explore all of the parks — heading from east to west lands you are at the old City Cemetery, which is also a fascinating place to spend a couple of hours.

SAN LUIS MISSION PARK

On San Luis Road, this 70-acre park has picnic pavilions, walking trails and a boardwalk around Lake Esther.

SOUTHSIDE PARK

Enjoy this 50-acre park on Paul Russell Road with basketball, tennis and volleyball courts and a picnic area.

SWEETBAY SWAMP

This five-acre field is found at the intersection of Yaupon Street and Redbud Avenue.

TOM BROWN PARK

On Easterwood Drive just off Capital Circle, this sprawling park has picnic pavilions, playgrounds, baseball, soccer and softball fields, tennis and racquetball courts, bike tracks, walking trails and even a track for remote-control toy vehicles.

WAVERLY POND PARK

This seven-acre park on Waverly Road has a pond and picnic area.

WINTHROP PARK

This park, at the intersection of Betton Road and Mitchell Avenue, offers a picnic area, playground and softball field.

Tallahassee
Golf and Hunting

Let's face it, golf and hunting aren't for everybody.

Avid fans often lapse into Zen-like trances when speaking of the pleasures found in either sport. The rest of us just sit there nodding calmly, waiting for the whole episode to pass.

Golfers say that there are some mighty fine holes to be played in these parts. And hunters claim that there's nowhere to go but Myrtlewood Plantation up the road in Thomasville, Georgia.

Here's where you'll find the people who take such endeavors very, very seriously.

Golf

There are plenty of private golf clubs in Tallahassee and its environs, but we list only the ones that will allow members of the public to play without being accompanied by a member.

Don't let the silly stigma of playing a public course affect you. Tallahassee golfers we know and trust say that some of the courses are every bit as well-maintained and challenging as the private courses.

HILAMAN PARK
MUNICIPAL GOLF COURSE
2737 Blairstone Rd.   *891-3850*

This par 72 course offers a driving range and putting green. It's open from 7 AM until sunset all week long. Green fees

with cart are $22.38 weekdays, $27.82 weekends.

JAKE GAITHER GOLF COURSE
801 Tanner Dr.   *891-3942*

This nine-hole municipal golf course is open from 7:30 AM until sunset every day of the week. Green fees with cart are $11.70 for nine holes, $14.98 for 18 holes.

PLAYERS CLUB AT SUMMERBROOKE
7505 Preservation Rd.   *894-4653*

One of Tallahassee's newest golf clubs, Summerbrooke is a semiprivate club that welcomes the public. It's open from dawn to dusk all week long. Green fees with cart are $30 weekdays, $35 weekends.

SEMINOLE GOLF COURSE
AND COUNTRY CLUB
2550 Pottsdamer St.   *644-2582*

This public course allows walking anytime after 4 PM. It's open from 7:30 AM until dark every day each week. Green fees with cart are $25 weekdays, $29.96 weekends.

KILLEARN COUNTRY CLUB AND INN
100 Tyron Cir.   *893-2186, (800) 476-4101*

The Killearn Country Club and Inn is a private club, but there's something you should know: If you stay at the inn then you can play the 27-hole golf course. The inn itself is worth the trip — and don't miss the wonderful food in the Oak

View Dining Room. An overnight stay gets you access to the swimming pool and tennis courts too. You'll see plenty of out-of-towners here, as well as a healthy smattering of residents hiding out for the weekend. The par 72 course is open from 7 AM to 6:30 PM all week long. Green fees with cart are $41 weekdays, $46 weekends. Cart rentals are required on weekends.

Hunting

MYRTLEWOOD PLANTATION
Campbell Rd.
Thomasville, Ga.   *(912) 228-6232*

Thomasville has always been known for its fine quail hunting, and Myrtlewood Plantation is where some of the finest happens.

The beautiful house that lords over these 3,300 acres of prime forest was built in 1887 by John Masury of New York. Masury was among the many wealthy Northerners who spent winters in rustic Thomasville because of its climate and scenery.

Masury built a popular hotel that was later torn down, but his lasting achievement was this impression mansion, which was acquired by R.C. Balfour Jr. in the 1930s. Balfour was an avid hunter and wildlife enthusiast who turned Myrtlewood into the hunting preserve you see today.

This is truly a hunter's paradise. It's not cheap, but those who come here seem very satisfied with what their money buys them.

Fall season brings deer and quail hunting, and there's plenty of good blue gill bream and largemouth bass fishing from March through October of each year.

Whether you want a full-blown classical quail hunt or just a little practice time shooting the sporting clays, Myrtlewood has a national reputation that's sure to please even the most discriminate hunter.

Myrtlewood Plantation is in Thomasville, Georgia, just 3.5 miles off Highway 319.

Tallahassee
Spectator Sports

If you're looking for year-round spectator sports, you need look no farther than Tallahassee. With two state universities and one large community college in the area, residents and visitors have quite a lineup to choose from.

Now there's another big player on the scene, and it's got nothing to do with collegiate sport. The Tallahassee Tiger Sharks, the latest franchise in the East Coast Hockey League, began their feeding frenzy in late 1994.

Tallahassee's great climate means that plenty of people like to get outdoors and soak up some action with their sunshine. Be warned that some sporting events are so popular that tickets are often impossible to find. Then again, if you're a die-hard Seminole or Rattler fan, you're not gonna listen anyway.

THE TALLAHASSEE TIGER SHARKS
Tallahassee/Leon County Civic Center
505 W. Pensacola St.   224-0400
Ste. I   (800)322-3602

The Tiger Sharks had a great inaugural season in Tallahassee, with impressive showings against teams from Birmingham, Nashville and South Carolina. They didn't always win, but they played with a lot of spirit and drive and even managed the most impressive feat of making it to the East Coast Hockey League's semifinals to cap off their first season. This is the town's only professional sports team, and Tallahassee fans turned out in droves to show their support. With Jacksonville's upcoming National Football League franchise, you can bet that people won't just think "south Florida" when it comes to sports anymore.

FLORIDA A&M UNIVERSITY
Sports Information   599-3200

Everyone knows that rattlesnakes are things to be avoided. That's the image that the FAMU Rattlers like to convey, and most of the time they live up to it. The Rattlers and the Rattlerettes have broken several impressive sports records over the years and show no signs of slowing down.

Neither do the fans. Excited residents crowd the bleachers alongside screaming students and alumni, and sometimes you'll leave a game with your ears literally ringing from the roar.

Take earplugs. The next scream you hear might be your own.

FLORIDA STATE UNIVERSITY
P.O. Box 2195
Tallahassee 32316   644-1403

Just say Seminoles.

It's a magic word in these parts, and most of the time it works wonders. If you haven't heard about the recent achievements of the Seminole football team, you've obviously had your head under a rock and probably aren't reading this chapter anyway. It's a popular team right now, and some folks get downright rabid about it.

But residents are careful not to forget the other fine Seminole athletes, although hysteria over football can sometimes get a little out of hand. Doak Campbell Stadium is always packed for home games, but you'll also be impressed by the energetic, supportive fans who crowd into the Tallahassee/Leon County Civic Center for basketball and Dick Howser Stadium for baseball.

It's all just a matter of how you get your kicks. Some people retreat to sports bars and sit in air-conditioned comfort. Others paint their faces garnet and gold and spend hours screaming their throats raw and doing the tomahawk chop. When it comes right down to it, it's the game that matters most. And the FSU Seminoles play a lot of good games. If you're in town, you might want to catch one.

TALLAHASSEE COMMUNITY COLLEGE

444 Appleyard Dr.

Baseball	*922-0230*
Basketball	*922-8201*
Softball	*922-8200*

OK, these aren't the biggest games in town. With FSU and FAMU taking up most of the athletic horizon, it's only expected that TCC sports might not generate the excitement and crowd base they deserve.

But it's understood that many excellent athletes often start their collegiate careers at community colleges, and TCC has certainly been a helpful stepping stone for many of them. There are a number of reasons why the college has been able to build and maintain a steady support base among Tallahassee residents.

One big plus at TCC is the addition of women's sports, specifically baseball, softball and basketball. Another big attraction is the new EagleDome, a modern sports arena recently constructed on the campus.

Tallahassee
Arts and Culture

Tallahassee's vibrant cultural scene is just as diversified as its surrounding landscape, and you'll see that reflected in the fine arts and attractions offered here.

Recently there's been a lot of public discourse on the arts and its role in Tallahassee's future. Residents last year voted down a tax that would have funded a new arts center in the downtown district. The debate was active and lively, reflecting the community's strong interest in its economic and cultural future. It's still a hot issue, and if it doesn't lead to another referendum, it may at least stoke some fires under various arts group in the area.

The presences of Florida State University, Florida A&M University and Tallahassee Community College contribute greatly to Tallahassee's arts scene. You'll find listings for their many programs and galleries as well as in this book's Inside Tallahassee Colleges and Universities chapter.

One big problem is how to keep up with everything. There have been a variety of arts-oriented publications over the years, but the place where most people

Photo: Tallahassee Area Convention & Visitors Bureau

The Tallahassee-Leon County Civic Center stages several major concerts and events every year.

turn is the city's major daily newspaper, the *Tallahassee Democrat*, which does a fine job of keeping its readers abreast of current cultural happenings. The arts listings in the newspaper's "Limelight," a weekend pullout section, are highly recommended for residents and visitors alike.

Dance

FLORIDA STATE UNIVERSITY SCHOOL OF DANCE
404 Montgomery Gym
Landis St.   *644-6500*

The renowned FSU School of Dance is one of the nation's most respected programs. Its faculty and students offer several performances during the year. Each November the school presents the popular "Twelve Days of Dance" program, with all works choreographed and danced by students, faculty and guest artists. Most performances are held in the Dance Theater of the Montgomery Gym, which faces Landis Street in the center of the FSU Campus.

TALLAHASSEE BALLET COMPANY
444 Appleyard Dr.
Tallahassee Community College   *222-1287*

The city's own regional ballet company, led by artistic director Joyce Straub, serves as the official "Dance Company in Residence" at Tallahassee Community

College. The Tallahassee Ballet Company presents several programs each year, as well as its annual major performances of *The Nutcracker* (with the Tallahassee Symphony Orchestra) and Dance for Spring.

Exhibits and Galleries

THE NEW CAPITOL
Monroe St. and Apalachee Pkwy.   *488-6167*

There's a rotating exhibit of work by Florida artists in the Capitol Gallery, 22nd Floor observation deck. The New Capitol is open Monday through Friday from 8 AM to 5 PM and on weekends and holidays from 8:30 AM to 4:30 PM (with access from the West Plaza entrance only). Weekend visitors must be accompanied to the observation deck by a tour guide. Admission is free.

FLORIDA STATE UNIVERSITY GALLERY AND MUSEUM
Tennessee and Copeland Sts.   *644-6836*

The works of local and national artists are displayed here in a two-story gallery and museum. FSU has several permanent works that it keeps in rotation while simultaneously offering student artists a space to exhibit their work. Many traveling national and regional exhibits are also displayed here.

Want to know just how large a blip Tallahassee makes on the cultural arts scene? Several well-known artists make their homes in Tallahassee, including internationally renowned pianist Helene Grimaud, filmmaker Victor Nunez and performance artist Terry Galloway, who performs regularly in New York City and various other cities. Jazz virtuoso Marcus Roberts also makes his home here, as do fiction writers such as Bob Shacochis and Janet Burroway.

Insiders' Tips

FOSTER TANNER FINE ARTS GALLERY

Martin Luther King Dr.
Florida A&M University Campus   *599-3161*

This impressive gallery features both permanent and rotating works of regional and national artists. FAMU art students also present shows and programs here throughout the year.

LEMOYNE ART FOUNDATION

125 N. Gadsden St.   *222-8800*

This is Tallahassee's premier visual arts gallery, located in the historic George Meginniss House that was constructed in 1853. The center offers several well-attended exhibitions, educational programs and special events each year. You'll also find a gift shop and a beautifully sculpted garden. This year (1995) marks the center's 31st anniversary. The Gallery is usually closed during the last two weeks of July.

LEROY COLLINS LEON COUNTY PUBLIC LIBRARY

200 W. Park Ave.   *487-2665*

There are several places in the library where the works of local artists are featured. Downstairs in the children's section you can see artwork from area schools. The three-story building can at any time feature dozens of diverse exhibits. Call ahead or just take a stroll and see for yourself.

THE MUSEUM OF FLORIDA HISTORY

R. A. Gray Building
500 S. Bronough St.   *488-1673*

The Museum of Florida History's main gallery offers several rotating exhibits each year, all of them pertaining to some element of the state's history. There's an annual Quilt Show that displays modern and antique quilts, and one recent exhibit consisted of early photographs of Seminole and Miccosukee Indians. There's also a great permanent exhibit of items and artifacts from the state's history (see our Tallahassee Historic Sites and Attractions chapter for more details).

NOMADS

508 W. Gaines St.   *681-3222*

Nomads bills itself as an "eclectic emporium," and we'd agree with that label. This little gallery midway between Florida A&M and FSU just celebrated its first anniversary. It features rotating exhibits by local artists but also specializes in art you can wear. They have a unique display of jewelry fashioned by area artists.

OLD ARMORY GALLERY

1400 N. Monroe St.   *891-6800*

The Old Armory Gallery features a changing exhibit of work by members of the Tallahassee Senior Center. Admission is free.

THE OLD CAPITOL

Monroe St. and Apalachee Pkwy.   *487-1902*

The lower level rotunda of the Old Capitol features occasional exhibits from Florida artists across the state. The Old Capitol is open Monday through Friday from 9 AM to 4:30 PM, Saturday from 10 AM to 4:30 PM, and on Sundays and holidays from noon to 4:30 PM. Admission is free.

621 GALLERY

Railroad Square Industrial Park
621 Industrial Dr.   *224-6163*

Railroad Square is quickly becoming a hotbed for local artists. This collection of renovated warehouses and buildings serves as work space and gallery space for a number of visual artists in the area. The 621 Gallery is a good place to sample some of the latest contemporary and often experimental efforts.

TOWNE GALLERY

410 E. Sixth Ave.   *222-8565*

This traditional gallery usually displays a strong exhibit of watercolors and prints, as well as pottery, sculpture and handmade toys. Admission is free.

Music

There's plenty of music to be heard in Tallahassee, and up front we thought we'd clue you in to a couple of the larger-sized venues the city sports.

The Tallahassee-Leon County Civic Center is the granddaddy of them all, with an arena that can seat 14,000 people. It hosts sporting events and conventions during the year, as well as several major musical events. Hot stars of all sorts have packed the arena: Janet Jackson, Garth Brooks, Metallica and Nirvana are but a few of the diverse stars who have found enthusiastic receptions at the civic center. It sits at 505 W. Pensacola Street, and the box office can be reached at 222-0400.

Another, somewhat smaller venue is The Moon, an entertainment facility at 1105 E. Lafayette Street. The Moon has been around for nearly a decade, and in that time its stage has been graced with musicians as diverse as Bonnie Raitt, the Neville Brothers, B.B. King, Los Lobos, Leo Kottke and the Buddy Guy. It holds about 1,500 people and also hosts several other public and private events during the year. Friday nights are usually given over to live country music, while Saturday evenings feature dance music. The box office can be reached at 878-6900.

FLORIDA STATE UNIVERSITY SCHOOL OF MUSIC

Ruby Diamond Auditorium
Westcott Building
Opperman Music Hall, Kuersteiner
Music Building   *644-6500*

The FSU School of Music is a large

and well-respected program that has been turning out topnotch musicians for almost a century. They don't show any signs of slowing down, either. Each year they present approximately 350 concerts and recitals, most of which are free to the public. During any given season, you'll hear symphonies, jazz, opera and other styles of music. The annual fall Prism concert series, which features dozens of FSU performers playing a wide and often unexpected range of material, is just one of the school's major events. They also sponsor a Summer Music Camp Program, where FSU faculty offers instruction to young musicians between the ages of 12 and 18.

TALLAHASSEE BACH PARLEY, INC.

1127 Victory Garden Dr.   *386-3812*

This group is dedicated to the preservation and public performance of music from the Baroque period. They usually produce four concerts a year — three with local musicians and one featuring a special guest from out of town. Often these concerts are performed with actual period instruments, and some shows also feature guest lectures about Baroque music.

The organ-based compositions and performances are held at the First Presbyterian Church, 110 N. Adams Street, because it has a wonderful handmade Taylor and Boody organ. Other instrumental works are usually performed at the Epiphany Lutheran Church, 3208 Thomasville Road.

TALLAHASSEE COMMUNITY CHORUS

c/o Dr. Andre J. Thomas
FSU School of Music 32306   *539-8959*

In the first year of the Tallahassee Community Chorus' existence, it had only 35 members. The following year there were more than 200. The chorus is now in its seventh year, and it just keeps on growing. They perform a handful of concerts each year, including a Spring Pops Concert every April. They also perform classical and larger choral works with the Tallahassee Symphony Orchestra.

TALLAHASSEE MUSIC GUILD
2311 Ellicott Dr.   *877-2878*

Since 1958 this guild has been promoting the appreciation of music through its FSU School of Music scholarships. Their major fund-raiser for this worthy effort is the annual sing-along *Messiah* held the first Tuesday in December at Faith Presbyterian Church at N. Meridian Street and John Knox Road. Here voices and musicians from all over the community gather for a spirited performance of Handel's holiday classic. They welcome any and all voices and appreciate listeners, as well.

TALLAHASSEE SYMPHONY ORCHESTRA
203 N. Gadsden St.   *224-0461*

The city's symphony orchestra presents seasonal concerts throughout the year. Every December the orchestra teams up with the Tallahassee Ballet for a spirited and graceful performance of the perennial favorite, Tchaikovsky's *The Nutcracker.* Music director and conductor David Hoose fills out the rest of the concert season with a fine roster of guest musicians and conductors. Concerts are held in FSU's Ruby Diamond Auditorium at the corner of College and Copeland streets.

Theater

FAMU ESSENTIAL THEATRE
Charles Winter Wood Theatre   561-2524

The FAMU Theatre Department gives black playwrights and actors their due through the Essential Theatre. Several times a year they showcase the works of new playwrights such as Judy Ann Mason (who scripted the PBS drama *I'll Fly Away*) as well as the classics — a recent all-black production of Shakespeare's *Hamlet* drew large, enthusiastic crowds of all colors. Recent graduates of the FAMU Theatre Department include Meshach Taylor, who has appeared on several sitcoms including *Designing Women*, and T'keyah Keymah, who was a regular on the now-defunct comedy show *In Living Color*. If you're looking for innovative, exciting and often ground-breaking theater, check out the Essential Theatre. Tickets are available on a per-show basis.

FSU SCHOOL OF THEATER
Fine Arts Building
Call and Copeland Sts.   *644-6500*

The School of Theater at FSU has a long tradition of excellence. Several of its former students have gone on to great success in the performing arts. The university's Mainstage program always features a strong offering of classic and contemporary plays and musicals. It pays to check out a show because you never know who will be the next big star from FSU

TALLAHASSEE COMMUNITY COLLEGE WEST END PLAYERS
444 Appleyard Dr.   *488-9200*

The TCC West End Players serve up an annual offering of dramas, comedies and musicals. These energetic and well-honed student productions always draw crowds, so it's advisable to get your tickets early if you plan to attend.

THE TALLAHASSEE-LEON COUNTY CIVIC CENTER BROADWAY SERIES
505 W. Pensacola St.   *222-0400*

This popular series trucks in some of the most extravagant Broadway road shows that tour the Southeast. Everything from the recent revival of the musical *Grand Hotel* to Neil Simon's recent comedy *Lost in Yonkers* has been staged here. Each season brings half a dozen impressive and professional Broadway shows to the civic center stage.

TALLAHASSEE LITTLE THEATRE

Thomasville and Betton Rds.   224-8474

This active community theater has been staging solid shows for nearly 50 years. They display a penchant for including modern Broadway fare, such as Alfred Uhry's *Driving Miss Daisy,* with traditional dramas such as *The Little Foxes* by Lillian Hellman. They usually stage five or six shows per season; the season runs from September to May.

QUINCY MUSIC THEATER

118 E. Washington St., Quincy   875-9444

Established in 1983, this group makes its home in downtown Quincy in the refurbished Leaf Theatre, a charming 1940s-era moviehouse. Each year this theater stages a handful of dramas and musicals, and the rest of the season the stage is given over to various local music and choral ensembles.

THE NUCLEUS GROUP

P.O. Box 15391, 32301   847-3479

The Nucleus Group is a versatile company that breaks from traditional theater and puts on entertainment of a different sort. Their most popular offering is *A Christmas Carol on the Air*, where audiences get to watch — and participate in — an old-fashioned radio drama version of Charles Dickens' classic holiday story. The Nucleus Group also stages murder mystery dramas and comedy shows.

YOUNG ACTORS THEATRE

609 Glenview Dr.   386-6602

This active troupe usually performs around five shows per season, all of them featuring local performers from kindergarten to high school. This may not be the most sophisticated theater fare in town, but give them a chance and these youngsters will certainly surprise and entertain you when they hit the stage.

Other Activities

FSU DISTINGUISHED LECTURE SERIES

Leon County Civic Center
505 W. Pensacola St.   644-3801

Sponsored by the Florida State University Center for Professional Development and Public Services, this annual lecture series brings acclaimed writers, artists, scientists and others to Tallahassee. Past speakers include Dr. Carl Sagan, columnist William Raspberry, filmmaker Spike Lee and writer Joyce Carol Oates. The lectures are held at Leon County Civic Center, and the season runs from September to April.

Tallahassee
Higher Education

One reason Tallahassee's median age is so low is because of the large number of students in the area. There are two universities and one community college in town, with the total student population approaching the 50,000 mark and rising. And these are remarkably good schools. They rank nationally in dozens of areas, and their alumni are often as distinguished as the faculty and administrators that graduate them. Surprisingly, there's not much real competition or rivalry. Certainly there's a little healthy friction from time to time, but overall each has managed to carve out its own specialty niches while at the same time providing a solid core curriculum.

Needless to say, there aren't nearly as many students in Tallahassee during the summer. They make quite an impact on the local economy, and while the town doesn't exactly roll up the sidewalks during the warmest months of the year, things do slow down a bit, particularly with the restaurants, bars and shops that cater almost exclusively to the student population. But some of these merchants actually welcome the slow pace because during the regular school year the business is brisk and hectic. Summer is a

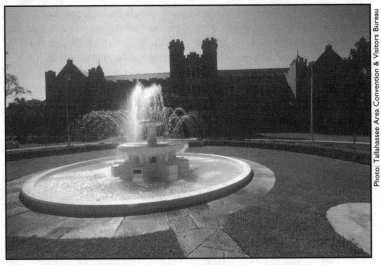

Photo: Tallahassee Area Convention & Visitors Bureau

The campus of Florida State University sits just west of the Capitol.

chance for everyone to reenergize and prepare for fall.

FLORIDA A&M UNIVERSITY
Visitor Center/Public Affairs
103 Lee Hall   *599-3000*

Florida Agricultural & Mechanical University, FAMU, is one of the nation's premier historically black colleges, boasting fine programs in pharmacy, journalism, engineering and business, among others. Established by the Florida Legislature in 1887 as the Florida State Normal and Industrial School for Negroes, the university now boasts a student population of more than 9,000 and has seen steady increases in enrollment over the past several years.

The stately campus sits just south of the Capitol. While its faculty and student makeup are multiracial, FAMU still plays an important role in minority issues. One recent study, for example, found that the university's College of Education produces nearly half of Florida's minority teachers. As FAMU is one of 28 Florida institutions of higher education with teacher education programs, that's an impressive and important figure.

There are guided tours of the campus, and the Black Archives Research Center and Museum is one of the high points. Pivotal chapters in African-American history are recorded in the museum's voluminous collection of books, photographs and artifacts. The Research Center and Museum is located in the Carnegie Library Building and is open from 9 AM to 4 PM.

Then there are the FAMU Rattlers, whose records in football, baseball, basketball, track and other sports have gained them a loyal legion of fans. The popularity of men's and women's sports here is matched only by that of the FAMU Marching "100" Band, whose electric halftime shows and parade appearances always bring crowds to their feet.

FAMU has a lot to offer visitors. Guided tours are available upon request. The campus is open to the public from 8 AM to 5 PM weekly.

FLORIDA STATE UNIVERSITY
Visitor Information Center
100 S. Woodward Ave.   *644-2525*

Established in 1857 as the Seminary West of the Suwannee (how's that for a site-specific name?), Florida State University, FSU, is the second-oldest institution of higher learning in the state. Its name was changed in 1905 to the Florida State College for Women, and it remained as such until 1947 when it went co-ed as FSU.

The handsome campus sits on several hills just west of the Capitol, and for the better part of each year it's filled with nearly 30,000 students. They make a sizable impact on the city's social, cultural and economic scene.

FSU has more than a dozen schools and colleges, including arts and sciences, business, education, law and social sciences. Its School of Theatre is ranked among the top 10 in the nation. The university is also a big player in the field of research. After a white-hot contest with other universities, including the Massachusetts Institute of Technology, FSU was named as the site of the ultra-high-tech National High Magnetic Field Laboratory. The lab, operated by a consortium composed of FSU, the University of Florida and Los Alamos National Laboratory, will usher in the coming age of high field magnetics, an area that many forecasters say will be every bit as important and earth-changing as electricity was at the turn of the century. This facility hosts the world's fastest supercomputer and has already attracted a great deal of attention and funding.

But not everything here is bookish and scholarly. Needless to say, men's and women's sports also feature prominently on FSU's landscape. During football season, things can get positively insane as the 1993 national-champion Seminole football team takes to Doak Campbell Stadium. Basketball, baseball, track and other events also draw crowds and awards. See our Tallahassee Spectator Sports chapter for more information.

The FSU campus welcomes visitors Monday through Friday from 8 AM to 5 PM and Saturday from 9 AM to 1 PM. There's a free one-hour guided tour available three times a day during the week at 11 AM, 1 PM and 3 PM. From September through April, this tour is also available on Saturdays at 10 AM only. For more information, contact the Visitor Information Bureau at 644-3246.

TALLAHASSEE COMMUNITY COLLEGE
444 Appleyard Dr.   *488-9200*

Sometimes community colleges can seem invisible, especially in a city like Tallahassee, which is not only the state capital but also home to the above-mentioned high-profile universities.

So credit is due to the students, faculty and administration at Tallahassee Community College, TCC, for not disappearing into the background. With an enrollment of just less than 10,000 students and a newly refurbished campus, TCC manages to make its presence known on an almost daily basis.

Established in 1966, this is primarily a transfer institution and serves as a primary feeder school for FSU. Although its core student base comes from Leon, Gadsden and Wakulla counties, students from all over the state are enrolled here.

TCC's major programs include two-year degrees in nursing, criminal justice technology, computer programming, business administration, emergency medical services technology and legal assisting.

The athletic program has expanded rapidly over the last few years. Initially, men's basketball and baseball were the major sports here, but recently women's teams were added. There's lots of action in the college's modern EagleDome arena, with the men's basketball team ranking among the top 10 in the state and the women's softball team taking the Panhandle conference title in its first year of existence.

There are also several arts groups and organizations, including the West End Players, who stage theater productions during the year.

The TCC campus welcomes visitors and is open to the public from 8 AM to 5 PM. Guided tours can be arranged by contacting the Counseling Department, 922-8128.

The Old and New Capitol buildings stand at the center of downtown Tallahassee.

Tallahassee
State Government

Tallahassee is the center of palm tree politics.

If you are a political junkie, this is the place to watch governmental power-shifting. The regular 60-day legislative session gets under way in March and lasts until May, and extensions and special sessions are always a possibility. During this time Tallahassee is filled with legions of lawmakers and lobbyists, armies of activists and aides. The media arrives en masse as well, armed with cameras, tape recorders and laptop computers.

It's quite a transition. Tallahassee awakens from its seasonal slumber, and suddenly the downtown sidewalks are crowded, the local eateries are standing-room only during lunchtime and the city literally buzzes with a nervous and somewhat contagious energy.

And each session is different in its own way, the issues and policies shaped by a constantly rotating cast of people and events across the state. Recently, the high crime rate has been the subject of several bills, with legislators regularly delivering tough sound-bites over the airwaves. Environmental issues always loom large on the state's political horizon as Florida struggles to encourage growth while maintaining and preserving its valuable and irreplaceable natural resources.

Needless to say, it's an exciting place to be. If you want an up-close look at how state government operates, then the legislative and special sessions offer invaluable lessons. If you just want to take advantage of the visitor sites that some buildings host, then sit out the session and dodge the crowds. There's plenty of parking spaces if you know where to look. If the streetside metered parking spaces are all filled, be sure to check out the various parking decks in the vicinity, as many of them have metered spaces that aren't visible from the outside.

Not every building in the capitol complex is really worth the attention of visitors. Most simply serve as office space for the various state agencies. The ones listed below offer special attractions for visitors.

For more information about any of the state agencies, call 488-1234.

THE OLD CAPITOL
Monroe St. and Apalachee Pkwy.   487-1902

Constructed between the years 1839 to 1845, this proud and impressive building has seen several additions and renovations over the years. There's plenty of history here beneath the stained-glass cupola and candy-striped awnings, so it's no surprise that the building is now a museum. There are self-guided tours available, so at your own pace you can wander through the old Senate and House chambers and inspect intriguing displays of political memorabilia. The original capitol building was a log cabin; fortunately, this one was built soon thereafter to stand the test of time. There's a gift shop downstairs and exhibits detailing the history of Florida politics. It's the sensible starting point on any tour of the capitol complex.

The Old Capitol is open Monday through Friday from 9 AM to 4:30 PM, Saturday from 10 AM to 4:30 PM and Sunday and holidays from noon to 4:30 PM. Admission is free.

THE NEW CAPITOL
Monroe St. and Apalachee Pkwy.   413-9200

If you approach the capitol from the Apalachee Parkway, the towering New Capitol seems to sprout majestically out of the Old Capitol that sits at its base. Constructed in the 1970s, the 22-story building is the center of political action (or inaction, depending on the issue). The setting is at once user-friendly and highly functional. On the first floor, or plaza level, you'll find the *Tallahassee Area Visitor Information Center*, where you can pick up information about the area or sign up for a free guided tour of the building.

The fifth floor sports special viewing galleries of the House and Senate chambers, and these are open during the legislative and special sessions. Many visitors find it fascinating to sit in for a bit and see how state government operates. Often you'll see kids on field trips from state and local schools getting a close-up civics lesson. Free copies of House and Senate agendas are available from the information desk at the fourth floor rotunda. If you really want to match lawmakers' names with their faces, you can order a copy of the annual *Pocket Guide to Florida's Government*, which is published by the Florida Chamber of Commerce. They can be reached at (800) 204-6002. The price of the guide is around $8, and it's money well spent if you need a comprehensive listing of who's who in the Florida Legislature.

Continue upward in the elevator until you reach the 22nd-floor observation deck, which offers a spectacular 360-degree bird's-eye view of the city and its surrounding environs, especially the nearby campuses of Florida State and Florida A&M universities. There are plenty of seats here, and not one of them has a bad view. Be sure to turn your view away from the windows long enough to check out the art gallery on the observation deck, which features rotating exhibits from Florida artists across the state.

Back down the elevator to the lower-level plaza and you'll find the capitol cafeteria, which offers a good cheap lunch, as well as a gift and snack shop. If you don't stop to gawk at the lawmakers for too long, you can get through the New Capitol in an hour or so.

The New Capitol is open Monday through Friday from 8 AM to 5 PM, and on weekends and holidays from 8:30 AM to 4:30 PM (with access from the West Plaza entrance only). Admission is free.

THE RALPH D. TURLINGTON FLORIDA EDUCATION CENTER
325 W. Gaines St.   487-1785

Although the New Capitol houses the education commissioner's office, this sleek, modern structure a few blocks south houses much of the agency's administrative staff. Visitors are encouraged to visit the first-floor lobby where the visual artwork of students from across the state is often displayed. On the 17th floor of the Turlington Center there's an observation deck that offers a stunning view of the capitol complex. It also sports a gallery with rotating exhibits as well as sculpture.

The Turlington Building is open Monday through Friday from 8 AM to 5 PM; it's closed weekends. Admission is free.

STATE SUPREME COURT

500 S. Duval St.   *488-8845*

Sitting just behind the New Capitol, the State Supreme Court building is an impressive sight. Its thick marbled columns and great doors hint at the sophisticated proceedings that go on inside its chambers. The Supreme Court was originally located in the south wing of the Old Capitol. This building was completed in 1949, and extensive renovations were done in 1991.

This is primarily an appeals court for cases across the state. Oral arguments are usually held during the first week of each month, and the public is welcome to attend. Sometimes you can catch students from local schools holding mock trials in its hallowed chambers; these trials are often more interesting than the actual cases presented here.

Tours are available, and group tours should be scheduled in advance. The State Supreme Court is open Monday through Friday from 8 AM to 5 PM. Admission is free.

Tallahassee
Retirement

Tallahassee's social makeup reflects much about Florida in that a sizable number of its residents have relocated here from other parts of the country. But it differs from the rest of Florida in one important aspect: Its long-term residents are overwhelmingly young and mobile.

Not too many people retire to Tallahassee. A recent Quality of Life Report from the Tallahassee Chamber of Commerce reveals that Leon County has the second-youngest median age of any county in the state. Only 7.7 percent of the city's population is older than 65 years, while the rate for the entire state is 17.6 percent.

We can look at the area's two largest employers to find reasons for this. The state government and educational systems provide employment for much of the area's white-collar workers, and working life in the city can be quite active and hustle-bustle. Chances are that when a worker retires, the last thing they want to do is remain in a relatively fast-paced environment with a high turnover rate.

Nonetheless, there are indeed some people who retire to this area. Some have family here, while others just prefer its dual blend of city life in a country setting. Those retirees who still love Tallahassee but want to back off a bit are finding calm havens in nearby Quincy, Monticello and Thomasville.

There are 10 adult retirement communities in Tallahassee, and along with seven nursing homes they easily provide quality living for the area's senior citizens.

Retirement Communities

CASA CALDERON APARTMENTS
800 W. Virginia St. 222-4026

Established in 1981, this 111-room apartment complex houses persons 62 years and older who are capable of independent living. The carpeted, unfurnished apartments afford elderly citizens the luxury of private living with round-the-clock security.

GEORGIA BELL DICKINSON
301 E. Carolina St. 224-8021

This is a federally subsidized, independent living unit for persons 62 or older. There are 49 one-bedroom units and 101 efficiency units. The complex offers plenty of activities, and Elder Care provides lunch on weekdays.

LAKE ELLA MANOR
1433 N. Adams St. 224-1341

This HUD-subsidized apartment complex is for low-income and mobility impaired senior citizens. The 72-unit complex was established a decade ago and sits conveniently next door to the Senior Citizens' Center.

MABRY VILLAGE APARTMENTS
315B Mabry St.   *576-1188*

Mabry Village isn't really a retirement community — most of its units are open to the public — but it does have a special block of apartments for elderly and handicapped independent living.

THE MEADOWS OF TALLAHASSEE
1978 Village Green   *385-4533*

The Meadows of Tallahassee is a private, assisted-living complex. It was established six years ago, and its private and semiprivate rooms have a capacity of 120 residents.

MICCOSUKEE HILLS
3201 Miccosukee Rd.   *878-5844*

Miccosukee Hills, a subsidized retirement community established in 1979, rests on several acres of wooded landscape. Its 106 units accommodate independently living senior citizens.

OAK RIDGE TOWNHOUSES
4704 Warehouse Rd.   *878-5612*

This 17-year-old apartment complex offers independent living for the elderly. Its 60 units afford ambulatory senior citizens the privacy and comfort of full-fledged one- and two-bedroom apartments.

WESTMINSTER OAKS
4449 Meandering Way   *878-1136*

Westminster Oaks sits on 96 heavily wooded acres of land, and this vibrant setting provides the backdrop for its apartments, duplexes and single-family dwellings. This continuing-care facility host around 350 residents and offers independent and assisted living as well as a health center.

WOODMONT RETIREMENT COMMUNITY
3207 N. Monroe St.   *562-4123*

This adult congregate living facility was established almost a decade ago. Its 102 units exist in a homey atmosphere that features a community courtyard. Two full-time activities directors ensure that the residents always have something to do.

Nursing Homes

CAPITAL HEALTH CARE CENTER
3333 Capital Medical Blvd.   *877-4115*

Established 16 years ago, this is the

second-oldest nursing home facility in Tallahassee. This skilled-nursing facility provides 24-hour care, and its rehabilitation team offers several therapy programs for the 156-bed center. It has received a Superior Rating from the state several years in a row.

CENTERVILLE CARE CENTER
2255 Centerville Rd.   *386-4054*

The 8-year-old Centerville Care Center is a skilled-nursing facility with 120 beds and 24-hour care. Its rehabilitation team provides many services, including subacute care.

HERITAGE HEALTH CARE CENTER
1815 Glonger Dr.   *877-2177*

Heritage Health Care Center is a skilled-nursing facility with rehabilitation programs in physical, speech, occupational and respiratory therapy, among others. Established 12 years ago, it currently has 120 beds.

TALLAHASSEE CONVALESCENT HOME
2510 Miccosukee Rd.   *877-3131*

This is the oldest nursing home in Tallahassee, having been established in 1966. It's a skilled-nursing facility offering 72 beds and a full range of rehabilitation programs.

TALLAHASSEE MEMORIAL REGIONAL MEDICAL CENTER LONG-TERM NURSING
1609 Medical Dr.   *681-5440*

This skilled-nursing care facility is affiliated with Tallahassee Memorial Regional Medical Center, whose resources it can tap whenever needed.

MIRACLE HILL
1329 Abraham   *224-8486*

Established 27 years ago, this skilled-nursing facility is owned by the Florida Primitive Baptist Association. It offers 24-hour nursing care, rehabilitation programs and has received a Superior Rating from the state for the last five years.

Tallahassee
Daytrips

Tallahassee offers plenty of things to see and do. But one of its best facets is its close proximity to Monticello and the Georgia towns of Havana and Thomasville.

Pick a direction. Any one will do. From Tallahassee, you can drive north 15 minutes and spend the day in a thriving community of spectacular antique shops. Or go east for 20 minutes and enjoy a concert in a magnificent turn-of-the-century opera house.

We use two codes in the listings below to approximate costs. The price guidelines are, of course, subject to change. Prices for accommodations are based on per-night stays, and prices for restaurants are based on a basic dinner for two (excluding extras such as wine or double-decker desserts).

For accommodations, per night:

$60 or less	$
$61 to $85	$$
$86 to 99	$$$
$100 or more	$$$$

For restaurants, dinner for two:

Less than $20	$
$21 to $35	$$
$36 to $50	$$$
$51 or more	$$$$

Unless otherwise noted, these restaurants accept all major credit cards.

Havana

Twenty miles north of Tallahassee, Havana is a phoenix that has risen from the ashes twice in its lifetime (to show how local you are, pronounce it HAY-vah-nah). The town has grown from a tobacco boomtown to a popular antique district in fewer than 100 years.

Established at the turn of the century, Havana and its sister town, nearby Quincy, were prime places to grow tobacco. Quincy had already risen to prominence once as a tobacco producer, but after the Civil War the town fell on hard times. Havana was established thanks to a "second wind" that had to do with a unique new method of tobacco farming.

Growers discovered that tobacco grown in the shade had a texture and flavor vastly different from that of normal tobacco. At the same time farmers were realizing this, the national rail systems were slowly extending into north Florida, providing the perfect pipeline into the lucrative cigar market.

Quincy recovered to some extent, and Havana literally exploded. Huge brick warehouses were constructed to cure and store all that tobacco. Farmers became rich and built amazing houses in fields where shacks once stood. A lot of money came into this area, and when tobacco farming eventually moved to climates far-

Havana's recent growth is attributed to its ever-expanding cluster of antique and gift shops.

ther south, a lot of money abruptly left this area. For many years, downtown Havana was practically deserted, its once-grand brick buildings suddenly empty and shuttered.

In the mid-1980s, however, Havana began its comeback, thanks to a small but dedicated group of artists and merchants who realized that the buildings would be perfect as studios, galleries and gift shops.

Now you'll wonder how these buildings could ever have stood empty. During the week these new shops and galleries don't see much traffic, but art and antique lovers throughout the Southeast make a point to visit Havana on weekends.

To get to Havana from Tallahassee, take Monroe Street (Highway 27) north out of the city for about 15 miles. The highway cuts right through downtown Havana.

For more information, contact the Gadsden County Committee of 100 at 627-9231.

Accommodations

GAVER'S BED AND BREAKFAST
301 E. Sixth Ave.   539-5611
$$

This well-preserved 1907 house was remodeled in the mid-1980s and is a great place to stay, whether you're visiting Tallahassee, only 12 miles down Highway 27, or just shopping for antiques in any of downtown Havana's numerous stores. It sports private baths, pine walls and restored antique furniture. Innkeepers Bruce and Shirley Gaver provide a continental breakfast and airport service. The back porch swing is always rocking gently with visitors who know when to slow down and appreciate the finer things in life.

Restaurants

LENORA CHARLES COURTYARD CAFE
211 First St.   539-0073
$

Shopping for antiques can be exhausting, especially in a place like Havana, where nearly every building harbors hundreds of intriguing items. If you need a place to have a cup of coffee or a full lunch, the Lenora Charles Courtyard Cafe is the place to be. It's in the middle of the downtown antique district and you find savory lunch specials here. Their well-portioned salads are always popular, and they serve a variety of gourmet

sandwiches and croissants. Their chalkboard menu changes daily. You can eat in the sunny courtyard or in the cool comfort of the indoor dining room.

THE NICHOLSON FARMHOUSE
S. R. 12   539-5931
$$$

Just a few miles from Havana down State Road 12, the Nicholson Farmhouse serves some of the best steaks in Northwest Florida. Owner Paul Nicholson's great-great grandfather built this handsome house in 1828, and it's been beautifully restored. The dining area spills out into three other houses on the property, one of which was the farm's original smokehouse. All have been renovated and offer a unique rustic country setting. Although they serve fine fish and fowl, the seasoned and aged steaks are the prime dishes here. An evening at the Nicholson Farmhouse is a fascinating and gastronomically pleasing trip back in time.

Shopping

H & H ANTIQUES
302 N. Main St.   539-6886

Featuring one of the largest selections of antique furniture around, H & H Antiques was one of the first such businesses to take root in Havana. Owners Lee Hotchkiss and Keith Henderson stay busy seeking out great old furniture from auctions and estate sales, and when they find something worthy, they truck it back here where any necessary restoration or refinishing is done. They carry bedroom sets, dining room tables and shelving, as well as oddities such as a vintage 1930s gasoline pump and, on one wall, a mounted moose head. Most items in the store are for sale, but special one-of-a-kind pieces are displayed for your enjoyment only.

HAVANA'S CANNERY ANTIQUE AND GIFT MARKETPLACE

115 E. Eighth Ave.   *539-3800*

If you need proof that Havana is a boomtown for antique and gift dealers, take a look at this: a restored 1940s all-brick canning factory, recently renovated and packed with more than 80 antique and gift dealers.

The Cannery is an antique and gift lover's dream, offering more than 25,000 square feet of shopping. Several stores in Havana have set up stalls here so browsers can get a sampling of what they'll find at their main locations. Strolling through the Cannery, you not only understand present-day Havana, but the town's past as well.

In the 1920s, a Havana schoolteacher named Eulalia Stephens began canning preserves from her kitchen and turned such a profit that she soon quit teaching altogether. One of the first women in Florida to successfully own and operate an internationally renowned business, Stephens built the cannery in 1943. At its peak, the plant was earning more than $1 million annually, and although products were shipped around the globe, Stephens never forgot to treat her neighbors with kindness. Even at the height of production, locals could take their preserves to Stephens and have them canned for a dime. After 1961, the building was owned and operated by Cal T. Albritton, who turned out jars of world-famous Cal's Tupelo Honey as late as 1994.

You can find Cal's Tupelo Honey at a stall inside the cannery — it's produced off-premises now. You can also find a stunning array of antique, collectible jewelry and gift dealers here. Several gourmet food shops have taken seed here, most notably Melissa's, owned and operated by the same people who run a fine restaurant of the same name in nearby Thomasville, Georgia. There's also the Java Stop if you need a place to sit and refuel with gourmet coffee and pastries.

As renovation efforts continue, the second floor of the warehouse will also be filled with merchants and vendors. Only one year old, the Cannery has already established itself as a cornerstone in Havana's popular antique market.

THE HAVANA DEPOT

First St. N.W.   *539-7711*

Before 1995, not too many shoppers paid attention to this old brick train station and warehouse on the west side of town, and with good reason. Unlike the rest of Havana, this place was empty. But recently a group of town merchants purchased and renovated the old depot, and inside you'll find an assortment of popular stores such as Wanderings, an ethnic gallery featuring handmade crafts, jewelry, gifts, furniture and clothing from around the world; the Nice Picture Company, a gallery featuring artwork by local and regional artists and photographers; and the Nature Company, a store featuring environmentally oriented gifts, handcrafts, games and much more.

THE HISTORICAL BOOKSHELF, LTD.

104 E. Seventh Ave.   *539-5040*

Several Havana shops offer a few shelves of books for your perusal, but die-hard book buffs will want to visit the Historical Bookshelf, Ltd. Owned by Jim and Pat Wilkinson, its shelves are stacked to the ceiling with rare first editions, international selections and fine prints. The store's specialties include military and political history, but there are several aisles devoted to fiction and general nonfiction as well. Some antiquarian booksellers will arbitrarily slap prices on old volumes without much regard to condition or desirability, but the Wilkinsons consult several pricing guides before determining their always reasonable prices. That's called doing business by the book.

Monticello

Monticello is in nearby Jefferson County, the only Florida county that touches the Georgia state line to the north and the Gulf of Mexico to the south. It's oddly shaped: When you drive to Monticello from Tallahassee along Highway 90, you'll hit a stretch just below Lake Miccosukee where you weave in and out of both Jefferson and Leon counties.

It's a beautiful drive, and the trip was once even more spectacular, especially if you were a Northerner heading south. In the late 1800s, many vacationers spent the winter in nearby Thomasville, Georgia, and often stopped off in Monticello on their way south to the gulf. The county had been named in honor of Thomas Jefferson in 1827, and the county seat was suitably named for his famous residence. For a while, Monticello was frequented by a large number of tourists who readily appreciated and supported the local economy.

After the turn of the century more and more railroads began extending from the northern part of Georgia, and soon Monticello was no longer a critical stop for tourists. The area suffered greatly because of this disruption, but today its many residents believe that if Monticello had kept on growing, it certainly wouldn't be the picturesque town we see today.

As you approach Monticello from Tallahassee along Highway 90, your first sight of the town will be of the county courthouse, a stately turn-of-the-century structure at the end of a broad, tree-lined avenue. While other counties feature extravagant homes that were built on cotton and tobacco money, many of Monticello's regal homes were constructed by northern businessmen who wintered here. The town's tree-laden skyline is highlighted by dozens of such houses, many of which are open for tours. At the least, Monticello is worth driving through just to sample the amazingly varied architectural styles.

One shining example of Monticello's history that will impress anyone is the Monticello Opera House, W. Washington Street, 997-4242. Built in 1890 by local merchant John H. Perkins, the building was designed to house businesses on the lower levels while the upper level contained an ornate and acoustically perfect opera house. Perkins' daughter wanted to be a singer, and Perkins himself hoped that the stream of tourist traffic through town would readily support his venture. Unfortunately this was not the case, and later attempts at transforming the opera house into a movie theater were quashed by residents who feared the advent of such newfangled technology. While the first floor played host to several business ventures over the years (including the town post office and the original furniture shop of well-known woodworker Homer Formby), the upstairs opera house stood empty for several decades, and vandalism took its toll. Fortunately, the opera house has been rescued and restored by a dedicated band of residents, and if you're in town you may want to see if they're putting on a show. So far they've showcased everything including popular jazz, country and classical music; everyone agrees that the Perkins Building, which sits across from the courthouse, is a vital cornerstone in the downtown district.

To get to Monticello from Tallahassee, take Tennessee Street (Highway 90) east out of the city for 25 miles until you reach Monticello.

For more information, call the Monticello-Jefferson County Chamber of Commerce, 997-5552.

Accommodations

THE CLARKE HOUSE
500 W. Washington Ave.   *997-1348*
$$

One of Monticello's newest inns, the Clarke House is owned and operated by Lou and Muriel Waldmann. Former Miami residents, the Waldmanns are among many south Floridians who've fallen in love with north Florida's rural and easygoing lifestyle.

Built around 1890 by Monticello lawyer Thomas Clarke, the inn is a beautiful example of the "Old South" Victorian style of architecture and has been restored to its original beauty. The inn's two bedrooms each come with a fireplace, plush bedding and ornate windows. The house is filled with an assortment of antique furniture. An overnight stay also gets you a full English breakfast in the dining room.

The Waldmanns also run a little antique and book store in one wing of the house, and Muriel displays and sells some of her impressive Miami photographs. The Clarke House is a short walk from downtown Monticello and is the perfect place to stay whether you're in town for business or pleasure.

PALMER PLACE BED & BREAKFAST
625 W. Palmer Mill Rd.   *997-5519*
$$$

This home is not only listed on the National Historic Register but recently received a Meritorious Award from the Florida Trust's Historic Preservation Board — when you see it you'll know why. This beautiful, heavily columned Southern-style manse rests among the shade of several gigantic live oak trees near downtown Monticello and was built in 1830 by Martin Palmer, a cotton plantation owner and prominent businessman from South Carolina.

Lovingly restored by present-day owners and innkeepers Eleanor and Don Hawkins, the Palmer House has five big guest rooms and offers a full-service breakfast each morning. Its large sunporch out back is perfect for relaxing and is available for private parties and receptions.

SOMEWHERE ELSE
625 E. Washington St.   *997-1376*
$$

Built in 1888, this renovated house is owned by Alex and Sharon DiMuro — Alex, who is also a certified public accountant, offers special "Tax Break" weekend specials for those who need to hole up somewhere peaceful and fill out those IRS forms. Even if you've already done your taxes, however, this is still a great place to stay. The house, which boasts an impressive assortment of antique music boxes, sits on an acre of land that features fig, peach, pear and walnut trees. There are four guestrooms that share a common bath and extensive balconies on both floors.

TWELVE OAKS BED & BREAKFAST
CR-149   *997-1408*

Open to the public just a few short years ago, Twelve Oaks is a magnificent house that rests atop gently rolling hills just outside of Monticello. This three-story structure was built from the top down, with the top two floors constructed in 1880 as part of a farm house. Nearly 30 years later, H.K. Miller moved in, jacked up the house and added an expansive ground floor.

Recently renovated and restored by owners/innkeepers John and Audrey Durst, Twelve Oaks features antique furniture at least a century old, including the comfortable four-poster French-style beds. Five of the eight guest rooms have their own baths, and the fenced-in backyard features a tennis court and large swimming pool. There's a full breakfast each morning, and if you stay more than one day the Dursts promise you'll never eat the same one twice.

Restaurants

THE COURTYARD CAFE

110 E. Dogwood   *997-1990*
$$

In the heart of downtown Monticello, the Courtyard Cafe is always busy for breakfast, lunch and dinner. Good service and a great menu selection are the reasons why. Start the day off with buttermilk pancakes that melt in your mouth, or large three-egg omelettes filled with vegetables and meats of your choice. The lunch crowd files in a few hours later for burgers, sandwiches and salads, and the tantalizing evening menu includes fresh catfish, shrimp in Creole sauce, prime rib and fiesta chicken. Daily specials spice up the offerings, and on Sundays there's an all-you-can-eat buffet that packs 'em in.

The Courtyard Cafe is in an old turn-of-the-century livery stable, which explains the very large doorways (the patrons also make good use of these). It's been extensively refurbished but still retains a timeless charm that perfectly complements a wonderful dining experience.

ROBERTS FAMILY RESTAURANT

175 N. Railroad St.   *997-2443*
$

If you've come to Monticello to find some down-home Southern cooking, this is the place for you. Owners Frank and Clarice Roberts know how it's done: They've got country-fried steak and chicken, the freshest vegetables right off the farm and plenty of pies and such to cap it all off. Folks eat here all the time, but it really gets hopping each weekend at the all-you-can-eat barbecue buffet. The atmosphere is very casual and friendly.

Shopping

COURT HOUSE ANTIQUES

205 E. Washington St.   *997-8008*

No, this store is not in the courthouse — it's across the street in a former Masonic Lodge and movie theater. If you're looking for a wide range of antiques, from upscale large furniture to inexpensive trinkets, you'll find a good selection here. Owners Bill and Dee Counts have been in the business for a number of years, and their finds are your treasures. Their services include refinishing and appraisals, and on the upper floors of this old building they publish the *Cotton & Quail Antique Trail*, a comprehensive monthly shopper covering antique dealers and shows throughout the Southeast. It's the largest publication of its kind in the region and at only a buck and a half, it's a steal for antique hounds.

"ME TOO" HOUSE OF TREASURES

340 S. Jefferson St.   *997-1090*

Most children get bored with antique stores, but this one features an entire room with antique toys and dolls, as well as modern-day collectibles. The other four rooms of the house are filled with a variety of furniture, clothing, handmade crafts and gifts. Owners Earl and Joan Black add to their stock on a regular basis, so it's always worth a look to see what's new.

NICE STUFF

185 E. Walnut St.   *997-4707*

We think it's fitting that you can find some of the oldest antiques in Monticello in one of its oldest houses. Built around 1830, this is one of the oldest wooden structures still standing — you'll know it by its tin roof. Nice Stuff owner Ruby Stalvey has filled its rooms with a careful assortment of antiques, furniture, collectibles and gifts. She shares space in the house with Peggy Hutto, who runs a fabric and sewing store called Peg's Alterations.

Special Events

THE JEFFERSON COUNTY WATERMELON FESTIVAL

The annual Jefferson County Watermelon Festival is a big event for Monticello and area residents, one that dates back almost 50 years. The festival is held each year during the last week in June, and events include a lively parade and a heated golf tournament, as well as a street dance, rodeo, softball tournament and the crowning of the Watermelon Queen. Pets also get in on the action. There's a children's pet show, sponsored by the Jefferson County Humane Society, and a new event called the Melon Mutt Mile, where you and your best friend can run for the record.

Needless to say, there are also about a million melons to help you keep cool. If you're of the mind, you can even compete in the watermelon seed-spitting contest, but you'd best be warned that there are some real professional puckerers who turn out for this age-old event.

For more information on the Jefferson County Watermelon Festival, contact the Monticello-Jefferson County Chamber of Commerce, 997-5552

Quincy

Quincy was named in 1825 after then-president John Quincy Adams. The town was the seat of a county that featured many successful cotton and tobacco plantations. To say that this area flourished would be an understatement. At one point just before the Civil War, Quincy was the second-largest city in Florida in terms of population.

The Civil War cut deep and wide into the area's prosperity. These plantations were forced to abandon their more lucrative crops in order to grow food needed by Confederate troops. After the war ended, a raging fire blazed through the downtown district, and most of the wooden buildings were destroyed. Along with the poor postwar economic situation, this signalled the beginning of a recession that was to last until the turn of the century, when tobacco — grown under shade trees this time — again proved to be a popular crop.

As Quincy slowly recovered its economic power base, the nearby community called Havana sprang up, and the industry was strong enough to support both places. Just after the turn of the century, Quincy State Bank president Mark W. "Pat" Monroe talked several residents into purchasing stock in the fledgling Coca-Cola Company. When this company took off just before World War II, two dozen Quincy residents suddenly found themselves to be millionaires, and the town was briefly the wealthiest town per capita in the nation.

Quincy was once again a boomtown, and much of its growth from this period has been preserved in the historic downtown district. At its center is the Gadsden County Courthouse, built in 1913, and it proudly presides over the 36-block downtown area that has been designated as an official Nationally Registered Historic District.

There's a great little booklet available from the Gadsden County Chamber of Commerce that details more than 50 historic buildings and houses in downtown Quincy.

To reach Quincy from Tallahassee, the easiest route is to take Tennessee Street (Highway 90) west for 20 miles; this takes you right into the downtown area. Or you can take Monroe Street (Highway 27) north to I-10, then take I-10 west eight miles to the Highway 90 Exit. Go west for 10 miles until you reach Quincy.

Contact the Gadsden County Committee of 100, 627-9231, for more information.

Accommodations

THE ALLISON HOUSE
215 N. Madison St.   875-2511
$$

This is truly a house with two stories — the first floor was built in 1925, the second in 1843. Here's how it happened: The second floor was originally a one-story house on brick pilings. When it was moved from an adjacent lot in the 1920s,

it was decided another floor should be added, and it was simply easier to build up than down. As was common practice in those days, they lifted the first floor and built a new level underneath. Originally that old one-story house was the home of Governor A.K. Allison, who served as Florida's governor after John Milton killed himself at the end of the Civil War in 1865.

Innkeepers Clay and Kate Ingram tend to the many travelers who stay in the Allison House. Its Greek Revival-style architecture and charming antique furnishings make it a special place to stay, and it's only 20 miles from downtown Tallahassee.

Restaurants

CARRIAGE FACTORY
RESTAURANT AND ANTIQUES
104 E. Washington St.   875-4660
$$

For more than three years, the Carriage Factory has been wowing diners from all over with its elegant European-styled menu. In case you're wondering, the turn-of-the-century brick structure did at one time serve as a carriage factory, not to mention a tobacco warehouse. Chefs Dutch Swart and Bryan Minear create delightful dishes such as shrimp scampi, fettuccine Alfredo with scallops and duck nivernaise, a boneless roasted half-duck topped with delicious ginger plum sauce. The filet mignon is also superb.

Country music sensation Billy Dean is one of Quincy's most profitable and popular exports.

Insiders' Tips

LUTEN'S

1214 W. Jefferson St.　　　　627-6069
$

This is Quincy's oldest family restaurant, serving breakfast, lunch and dinner since 1927, and that makes it something of a fixture in these parts. This diner-style cafe is very casual and has a diehard core crowd of local patrons who swear by it. Out-of-towners will be pleased by its traditional Southern-style menu, from burgers to fried chicken and fish. You'll also like its old-style prices.

Special Events

QUINCYFEST

If you visit the area in September you may have the pleasure of attending Quincyfest, a huge festival that features art, food, music and fun. This event sometimes attracts more than 10,000 people, and it's a sure bet that those numbers will climb as more people find out about this not-so-secret secret. For more information, call the Gadsden County Committee of 100, 627-9231.

Thomasville, Georgia

Northwest Florida offers so much to see and do that you really don't need to leave the state at all — but it'd be a mistake not to include a visit to Thomasville, Georgia, just beyond the state line to the north.

Thomasville was established in the 1820s and, like other area communities, much of its initial success was founded in farming. Unlike much of Northwest Florida, however, Thomasville sits on higher ground and is therefore a bit cooler and drier. This was something to consider if you were a Northerner vacationing in the 1800s, as yellow fever and malaria epidemics routinely claimed hundreds, even thousands, of lives.

From the end of the Civil War to just after the turn of the century, Thomasville became a booming resort town known for its appealing countryside and clean air. Many wealthy families built winter homes there, but some moved there permanently. Most of the opulent and elegant houses built during this period still stand, and they form the core of the town's historic district.

What ruined Thomasville's reputation as a resort town? Believe it or not, it was the Panama Canal, whose construction proved that swamp drainage over large areas was feasible and effective. As a result South Florida, once shunned by those fearing death by germ-carrying insects, was suddenly flooded with wealthy

Insiders' Tips

When you're in town, be sure to stop by and say hello to Thomasville's oldest living resident: Big Oak. This oak tree is estimated to be more than 300 years old and has a limbspan of more than 160 feet with a height of almost 70 feet. On a plot of land at the corner of N. Crawford and E. Monroe streets, this giant tree looms over Thomasville like a trusty and steadfast soldier — albeit an elderly one, as evidenced by the support cables and struts that help stabilize the oak against high winds.

Plantation Homes Offer Fascinating Glimpse into Florida's Past

America's largest concentration of plantation homes — more than 70 of them — lies in the 28-mile stretch between Tallahassee and Thomasville.

Although more than 70 of these plantation homes still exist, the public really had no idea what they were like on the inside until 1984. That was the year that Pebble Hill Plantation opened for public tours. This huge Georgian and Greek Revival-style mansion was built years before the town was even

Photo: Tallahassee Area & CVB

established, and its unique exhibits and meticulously kept grounds afford us a crystal-clear view of Thomasville's amazingly ornate past. Pebble Hill was originally a working plantation but over the years was transformed into a classy hunting and sporting lodge. One-hour tours are avail-

A tour of stately Peeble Hill Plantation affords a rare glimpse of Thomasville's plantation homes.

able (and highly recommended), or you can just spend time wandering the grounds. Pebble Hill Plantation, (912) 226-2344, sits just off Highway 84 about 5 miles east of Thomasville.

Another fascinating house is the Lapham-Patterson House, 626 N. Dawson Street, 225-4004, whose history is as odd as its design. Charles Lapham was a shoe manufacturer from Chicago who just barely survived that city's great fire of 1871. His lungs were severely damaged from smoke inhalation and he chose Thomasville as a fresh-air winter resort for his health. Lapham decided to build a house here, and from its design we can surmise that the fire must have instilled a deep fear in his mind. His three-story house has the distinction of having 19 rooms, 45 doors — and absolutely no right angles. Poor old Lapham was so deathly afraid of being trapped in a burning building again that he built his house with as many escapes and safeguards as possible. All the windows slide up into the wall, for example, becoming instant doors in case of emergency. All doors were also designed to allow smoke to rise and exit the house so no one would be trapped in a smoke-filled room. Lapham's concerns were understandably well-founded. Thomasville is fortunate that fire never threatened the man again. This incredible house, open for tours, is one of the town's major attractions.

vacationers, and towns like Thomasville and nearby Monticello, Florida, lost their seasonal residents.

There's so much history here that a visit to the Thomas County Historical Museum is doubly recommended. The strange and colorful history of Thomasville is presented here through several exhibits and photographs, and it certainly helps new visitors get a handle on some of the amazing sights that await them.

Thomasville is about 40 miles north of Tallahassee. Take Thomasville Road (Highway 319) north out of town. Depending on traffic, the drive can take about an hour. Note that northbound traffic on Thomasville Road is usually jam-packed during rush hour, and there's a bottleneck just past I-10 north of town that can often bring traffic to a standstill. If you can't leave before 4:30 PM on a weekday, consider waiting until after 6 PM before you depart.

If you need more information on Thomasville, you can get a free Visitor's Guide from the Destination Thomasville Tourism Authority, (912) 225-5222.

Accommodations

1884 PAXTON HOUSE
445 Remington Ave.   *(912) 226-5197*
$$-$$$$ *(800) 278-0138*

This Victorian Gothic house is a wonder to look at, with a circular staircase, a dozen fireplaces, rich pine floors and a neoclassical porch. You can bet it's also pretty pleasant to stay here too. There are several suites and rooms to choose from, and basic amenities include a gourmet breakfast, private baths, bedside chocolates or fruit and turndown service. In the heart of downtown Thomasville's historic district, the 1884 Paxton House is a grand place to spend your time.

DEER CREEK BED & BREAKFAST
1304 Old Monticello Rd.   *(912) 226-7294*
$$

Deer Creek Bed & Breakfast operates two houses, the one listed here and another on S. Dawson Street. Both houses have been beautifully restored and feature huge windows with impressive views of trees and the surrounding landscape. If you're a gourmet chef, they'll even let you cook your own breakfast (though theirs is pretty good and shouldn't be passed up so easily).

THE EVANS HOUSE
725 S. Hansell St.   *(912) 226-1343*
$$

The Evans House is lucky to be here. Ten years after its construction in 1898, the house suffered a fire that caused extensive damage. Fortunately, the local fire department wasted no time in saving this Victorian-style home. Innkeeper Lee Puskar says the inn offers four guest rooms with private baths, all furnished with turn-of-the-century antiques. The Evans House offers visitors a full continental breakfast and bicycles for those

Insiders' Tips

Academy Award-winning actress Joanne Woodward was raised in Thomasville, Georgia, and started her acting career on the stage of the East Side School Center, now the Thomasville Cultural Center who wish to tour the nearby 27-acre Paradise Park or, just a few blocks farther, downtown Thomasville. Commercial and long-stay rates are available upon request.

THE GRAND VICTORIA INN

817 S. Hansell St.   *(912) 226-7460*
$$

Built in 1893, this Victorian house offers a quartet of large guest rooms and is conveniently located across from Paradise Park and just a few blocks from downtown Thomasville. Innkeeper Anne Dodge not only serves up a full breakfast but provides an afternoon tea as well. The antique furniture is complemented by plenty of books and fresh flowers. The backyard offers a pond and rock garden for strolling and relaxation.

OUR COTTAGE ON THE PARK

801 S. Hansell St.   *(912) 227-0404*
$$

Almost every bed and breakfast inn here in Thomasville has a wide, spacious porch with rockers or swings, and this quaintly named inn is no exception. The house was built by George Cox in 1893, when a big porch ensured shade and air circulation during the hottest months of the year. Proprietor Constance Clineman also runs the Cottage Shoppe out of the Cox House; this is one gift shop you'll want to visit even if you're not staying overnight.

SERENDIPITY COTTAGE

309 E. Jefferson St.   *(912) 226-8111*
$$

What some people call a cottage, others would call a very large house. That's the case with this beautiful home, which was built in 1906. Innkeepers Kathy and Ed Middleton offer an irresistible full-course breakfast that features their delicious homemade jams, jellies and breads. Each room has a private bath, and, if you desire, you might get a visit from any of the resident cats and dogs. The library not only offers books for relaxation but a selection of movies as well.

SUSINA PLANTATION INN

Hwy. 155   *(912) 377-9644*
$$$$

As inns go, the Susina Plantation is the cream of the crop. Twelve miles south of Thomasville and 18 miles north of Tallahassee, this magnificent antebellum mansion was built in 1841 by noted architect John Wind. It rests on 8,000 acres of rolling green countryside, an area roughly half the plantation's original size. The eight rooms are breathtaking, with four-poster beds and private baths that feature claw-footed tubs. Completing the plantation atmosphere are tennis courts, a swimming pool, walking trails, ponds and a croquet court. Even if the Susina weren't an inn, the gourmet food that comes out of its kitchen would certainly ensure its continued popularity. Lunch is served for groups of 10 or more.

Restaurants

THE GRAND OLD HOUSE

502 S. Broad St.   *(912) 227-0108*
$$$

One of the finest restaurants around, the Grand Old House is in the turn-of-the-century Neel House, a beautiful example of neoclassic architecture. Its renovated, stately interior is the perfect setting for the culinary creations of Chef Alberto Ughetto, who specializes in French and American cuisine served with his own special touches. The menu changes continually, but if you're a seafood lover, you can almost always count on excellent salmon and grouper dinners and lobster if you're lucky. The sirloin steaks and beef tenderloin are also popular entrees. Don't skip the appetizers, which include wonderful crab cakes or escargot, unless you're trying to save room for the homemade desserts. The Grand Old House also has a sophisticated wine list.

MELISSA'S

134 S. Madison St.   *(912) 228-9844*

Situated in what was once a steam laundry warehouse, Melissa's offers innovative cuisine at unbelievable prices. Owner Melissa Summitt has slowly and steadily built a strong reputation for her restaurant, which features classic American cuisine and surprising specialties. The lunch menu features thick sandwiches such as the Monkey (a healthy offering of crunchy peanut butter, honey, raisins and bananas on whole wheat bread) and the Virginia Ham (ham and boursin cheese with mango chutney on pumpernickel). Dinner brings out daring appetizers such as black bean cakes, which can lead you to Chicken Taos (a spicy Mexican-flavored dish), zesty ratatouille (served over pasta with Parmesan) or the grilled chicken, spinach and apple salad. Homemade desserts only add to the quandary you face when deciding how to treat yourself. But as they say, we'd rather have too many choices than too few.

Also in Melissa's, you'll have the opportunity to inspect wares from several area antique stores and merchants. They provide several shopping stalls for browsing either before or after your meal. It's a great way to see the town in a nutshell and decide where you want to go. Again, you've got some choices to make here, but with selections like these, it's impossible to go wrong.

Shopping

ANTIQUE EMPORIUM & AUCTION CO.

111 S. Broad St.   *(912) 228-1889*

Michael Booth's downtown emporium specializes in one-of-a-kind, high-end antiques. Even if your pocketbook can't handle the price tags here, you need to drop by just for the spectacle of it all. Imported furniture, beautiful Oriental rugs, ornate sculptures, carvings and artwork of every sort awaits your ever-widening eyes. Bloom and his staff spend a lot of time attending antique auctions and estate sales, so their stock is continually changing. In fact, once a month the Antique Emporium holds a special auction just to thin out their store and make room for new items. You can call for their monthly schedule.

GENERATIONS

127 N. Broad St.   *(912) 227-9100*

If you like woodwork, you'll love Generations. Formerly The Wood World, it's now under the ownership and management of Joe and Alacia Herring, a young couple who know how to keep a good thing going. Whether you're in the market for an old-fashioned pine bed frame or just some tiny scented wooden apples, Generations has the finest woodcraft selection around.

THE GIFT SHOP

103 S. Broad St.   *(912) 226-5232*

This stylish gift shop offers an eye-catching assortment of glassware, china, handmade jewelry, trinkets, figurines, leather handbags and other items. They're downtown in the old Inman's Drugstore building, which was constructed around 1885. Its striking second-floor bay window may remind you of another famous Thomasville home — the

Lapham-Patterson house, mentioned in the earlier introduction. The houses were designed by the same architect. Compare the windows as well as the Moroccan archways and you'll get a sense of Thomasville's history that many people see but few stop to consider.

THOMASVILLE ANTIQUE MALL
117 W. Jefferson St.   *(912) 225-9231*

Nearly a dozen different dealers have their prize finds displayed in this spacious old warehouse, and you'll spend a lot of time picking through it all. We're always impressed with the changing selection of artwork, lamps, furniture, trinkets and collectibles such as vintage children's toys and figurines. Owners Kathryn and Leverne Smith are longtime players in the city's antique scene.

Special Events

HOLIDAY HOMECOMING

This annual celebration, held during the first week in December, features candlelight tours of Pebble Hill Plantation, a live nativity scene, a Victorian reader's theater and a historic walk through Thomasville during the Downtown Victorian Christmas. Wrap a scarf around your neck, pocket that shopping list and get in the spirit.

THE ROSE FESTIVAL

One of the city's biggest annual attractions is the Rose Festival, held each April. Thomasville is known as the rose capital of the world, and this festival, dating back to 1921, justifies that reputation splendidly. Don't keep your nose buried in the flowers for too long, however, or you'll miss all the other events, such as the various sports tournaments,

animal shows, parades, balls, dances and fairs. In other words, this is a huge week-long celebration you don't want to miss.

Wakulla County

Crawfordville is the seat of Wakulla County, which also is home to the towns of St. Marks, Panacea and Sopchoppy. The towns are so small and the county so big that when you talk about any one of the towns, you may as well be talking about all them. So here we'll take the opportunity to tell you not only about Crawfordville, but about all of Wakulla County as well.

There's a lot of history in this rich landscape that sits just a few miles south of Tallahassee. It is believed that when Ponce de Leon first ventured into the area in 1521, he walked ashore at nearby St. Marks in the southern part of the county. In the early part of the 1600s, the Spanish erected San Marcos de Apalache, a fort that has been restored and preserved as a state park (see the Tallahassee Parks and Recreation chapter for details).

As American settlers moved into north Florida, they came to rely heavily on access to the Gulf of Mexico to import supplies and export their valuable cotton. In 1836, railroad tracks were laid down from St. Marks to Tallahassee, thus allowing a greater supply of goods and visitors through the Wakulla County area. This track has since been paved over and serves as the Tallahassee-St. Marks Historic Railroad State Trail (see the Tallahassee Parks and Recreation chapter).

Crawfordville became the county seat shortly after the Civil War, when resident Noah Posey deeded some land to the county on the condition that the courthouse be moved to Crawfordville, which is named after Dr. John Crawford, Florida's Secretary of State from 1881 to 1902. The original courthouse burned down and was rebuilt at the turn of the century. Currently the stately white building serves as the Wakulla County Library.

Crawfordville is a little town, and the piney woods and vibrant landscape that attracted its early inhabitants are still easy to find. People come to Wakulla County when they want to get back to nature. Here you not only have the St. Marks Wildlife Refuge (detailed in Parks and Recreation) but also the Gulf Specimen Marine Lab in Panacea, Rock Landing Road and Clark Drive, 984-5297, whose 30,000-gallon aquarium is filled with hundreds of species of marine life, including starfish, octopuses, sea horses, eels and more. Crawfordville's Lost Creek Stables, off Arran Road, 926-3033, offer horseback riding through the Apalachicola National Forest, while St. Marks' TNT Hideaway, Highway 267, 925-6412, rents canoes for unforgettable trips up and down the Wakulla River, which teems with a wonderful assortment of wildlife. The county's three other rivers — St. Marks, Sopchoppy and Ochlockonee — are also popular waters for rowers and boaters. Be advised that the wildlife here requires and demands mucho amounts of respect. It's not dangerous if you're careful and sensible. But if you feel uneasy seeing alligators and snakes up close, let the tour guides of the Edward Ball Wakulla Springs State Park, Lodge & Conference Center (see Parks and Recreation) introduce you to such reptiles from a safer distance.

For more information, contact the Wakulla County Chamber of Commerce, 926-1848.

Accommodations

ALLIGATOR POINT CAMPGROUND
Hwy. 370, Alligator Point   349-2525

You're right on the gulf at Alligator Point Campground, a full-service camping area that provides full hookups, cable TV and laundry facilities. Experience some of the last unspoiled beaches on the coast. Daily, weekly and monthly rates are available.

FLORIDA COASTAL PROPERTIES
Hwy. 319, Crawfordville   926-7811

Wakulla offers an assortment of hiding spots, from a fancy luxury home to a simple lakeside fishing cabin. Florida Coastal Properties can help you find the perfect hideaway for your budget and schedule. They've also got offices in Shell Point and Carrabelle, so you know you'll find a wide range of properties from which to choose.

SHELL POINT RESORT
Hwy. 367   926-7163

Everything you need to enjoy the gulf coast is right here. Shell Point Resort has a motel, apartments and RV hookups, with daily, weekly and monthly rates. There's also a marina and camp store with all the supplies you'll need and a fine restaurant. Tallahassee's only 30 miles north, but it feels like it's a world away.

Restaurants

ANGELO'S
Hwy. 98, Panacea   984-5168
$$

Angelo Petrandis' seafood restaurant is one of the best in the biz. There are few restaurants that attract so many Tallahasseans over such a distance, but this is one of them. Jump-start your appetite with openers such as fried squid or a cup of grouper chowder, perhaps even some golden-fried hushpuppies or cheese grits. Then move on to house specialties such as South of the Border (broiled grouper with salsa), stuffed snapper (filled with Angelo's famous deviled crab stuffing) or charbroiled mullet and amberjack. And this doesn't even scratch the surface of a menu with the tiniest print in the Panhandle. The steaks and burgers are cooked to perfection here, but even die-hard landlubbers may find it hard to resist the mouthwatering aromas in the air. Angelo's also sells bottles of his house dressing and cups of their whipped garlic butter for you to take home. And if you're too stuffed for dessert, grab a slice of homemade pie to go.

MYRA JEAN'S
Hwy. 319, Crawfordville   926-7530
$

This old-fashioned sandwich shop takes you back to the good old days.

Cheap home-style breakfasts with free coffee refills, the wonderful smells of homemade bread and pastries in the air, thick sandwiches piled high with anything you want and sweet ice cream for dessert — Myra Jean's is one very special, very casual place. If you're headed south out of Tallahassee or north up from the coast, plan to make a pit-stop here.

POSEY'S OYSTER BAR
St. Marks   925-6172
$

This modest seafood shack is known for its smoked mullet and fresh raw oysters. The weekend lunch and dinner crowds can be intimidating, and Sunday nights are usually the busiest as Tallahassee residents flock down for an evening of food and karaoke before the work week starts up again. It's in St. Marks about 15 miles south of Tallahassee; just take Monroe Street south out of town. It turns into Highway 363, which dead ends at Posey's.

What's In Our Name?
Community.
For 15 Years.
And Many More.

Tallahassee
Community Information

Real Estate Companies

ARMOR REALTY
1519 Killearn Center Blvd.   893-2525

BESTSELLERS REALTY, INC.
2121 Killarney Way   893-5000

BLUE CHIP REALTY OF TALLAHASSEE
2840 Remington Green Cir.   385-6613

BOUTIN BROWN & BUTLER
REAL ESTATE SERVICES
822 N. Monroe St.   681-6332

CENTURY 21 ADVANCED REALTY
1924 Welby Way   385-9889

CENTURY 21 TOWNE REALTY, INC.
2882 Remington Green Cr.   385-1162

COMMUNITY REALTORS OF KILLEARN, INC.
2707 Killearney Way   893-2115

COMMUNITY REALTY GROUP
1300 Metropolitan Blvd.   385-1300

COLDWELL BANKER
HARTUNG & ASSOCIATES, INC.
3303 Thomasville Rd.   386-6160

CONNIE MORGAN
2810 Remington Green Cir.   386-4663

ELLIOT & CHAVERS
2910 Kerry Forest Pkwy.   668-2008

FEZLER & RUSSELL REAL ESTATE, INC.
3360 NE Capital Cr.   385-4646

INVESTORS REALTY OF TALLAHASSEE, INC.
3531 Thomasville Rd.   224-6900

MONTGOMERY & ASSOCIATES, INC.
3370 NE Capital Cr.   386-5244

NOBLIN MILLARD REALTY, INC.
1300 Metropolitan Blvd.   385-1400

RE/MAX REALTY
2804 Remington Green Cr.   385-6936

TURNER HERITAGE HOMES, INC.
508 S.E. Capital Cir.   656-4663

Health Care

Hospitals/Medical Centers

TALLAHASSEE COMMUNITY HOSPITAL
2626 Capital Medical Blvd.   656-5000

TALLAHASSEE MEMORIAL
REGIONAL MEDICAL CENTER
Magnolia Dr. and Miccosukee Rd. 681-1155

Immediate Care Centers

SHERMAN WALK-IN CENTER
AND SKIN CLINIC
3721 N. Monroe St.   562-1128

MAHAN MEDICAL WALK-IN

1705 E. Mahan Dr.   877-7164

PATIENTS FIRST MEDICAL CENTERS

2907 Kerry Forest Pkwy.   668-3380
3258 N. Monroe St.   562-2010
1160 Apalachee Pkwy.   878-8843

PHYSICIAN CARE

1690 N. Monroe St.   385-2222
3401 NE Capital Cr.   386-2266
3721 N. Monroe St.   562-1128

TALLAHASSEE WALK-IN MEDICAL CENTER

2451 Centerville Rd.   386-6000

Support Services

EASTSIDE PSYCHIATRIC HOSPITAL

2634 Capital Cr. N.E.   487-0300

HEALTHSOUTH REHABILITATION HOSPITAL OF TALLAHASSEE

1675 Riggins Rd.   656-4800

Physician Referral Services

Capital Medical Society   877-9018
Tallahassee Community Hospital   656-3627
Tallahassee Memorial Regional
Medical Center   681-5063
Telephone Counseling Referral   224-6333

Treatment Centers

RIVENDELL OF TALLAHASSEE

220 John Knox Rd.   386-7111

Index of Advertisers

Index

ORDER FORM
Fast and Simple!

Mail to:
Insiders Guides®, Inc.
P.O. Drawer 2057
Manteo, NC 27954

Or:
for VISA or
Mastercard orders call
1-800-765-BOOK

Name _____

Address _____

City/State/Zip _____

Qty.	Title/Price	Shipping	Amount
	Insiders' Guide to Richmond/$14.95	$3.00	
	Insiders' Guide to Williamsburg/$12.95	$3.00	
	Insiders' Guide to Virginia's Blue Ridge/$14.95	$3.00	
	Insiders' Guide to Virginia's Chesapeake Bay/$14.95	$3.00	
	Insiders' Guide to Washington, DC/$14.95	$3.00	
	Insiders' Guide to North Carolina's Outer Banks/$14.95	$3.00	
	Insiders' Guide to Wilmington, NC/$14.95	$3.00	
	Insiders' Guide to North Carolina's Crystal Coast/$12.95	$3.00	
	Insiders' Guide to Charleston, SC/$12.95	$3.00	
	Insiders' Guide to Myrtle Beach/$14.95	$3.00	
	Insiders' Guide to Mississippi/$14.95	$3.00	
	Insiders' Guide to Boca Raton & the Palm Beaches/$14.95 (8/95)	$3.00	
	Insiders' Guide to Sarasota/Bradenton/$12.95	$3.00	
	Insiders' Guide to Northwest Florida/$14.95	$3.00	
	Insiders' Guide to Lexington, KY/$12.95	$3.00	
	Insiders' Guide to Louisville/$12.95	$3.00	
	Insiders' Guide to the Twin Cities/$12.95	$3.00	
	Insiders' Guide to Boulder/$12.95	$3.00	
	Insiders' Guide to Denver/$12.95	$3.00	
	Insiders' Guide to The Civil War (Eastern Theater)/$14.95	$3.00	
	Insiders' Guide to North Carolina's Mountains/$14.95	$3.00	
	Insiders' Guide to Atlanta/$14.95	$3.00	
	Insiders' Guide to Branson/$14.95 (12/95)	$3.00	
	Insiders' Guide to Cincinnati/$14.95 (9/95)	$3.00	
	Insiders' Guide to Tampa/St. Petersburg/$14.95 (12/95)	$3.00	

Payment in full (check or money order) must
accompany this order form.
Please allow 2 weeks for delivery.

N.C. residents add 6% sales tax _____

Total _____